W9-BKS-743

DISCARD

ALSO BY CHRISTOPHER MATTHEWS

Hardball: How Politics Is Played—
Told by One Who Knows the Game

CHRISTOPHER MATTHEWS

Kennedy & Nixon

The Rivalry
That Shaped
Postwar America

A Touchstone Book
Published by Simon & Schuster

TOUCHSTONE
Rockefeller Center
1230 Avenue of the Americas
New York, NY 10020

Copyright © 1996 by Christopher Matthews
Afterword copyright © 1997 by Christopher Matthews
All rights reserved,
including the right of reproduction
in whole or in part in any form.

TOUCHSTONE and colophon are registered trademarks
of Simon & Schuster Inc.

Designed by Karolina Harris

Manufactured in the United States of America

5   7   9   10   8   6

Library of Congress Cataloging-in-Publication Data is available.

ISBN 0-684-81030-1
0-684-83246-1 (pbk)

For Mom and Dad

ACKNOWLEDGMENTS

The list of those who made this book possible begins and ends with research director Barbara Daniel. It was her persistence, more than any other factor, that brought a great American story onto these pages.

I want to acknowledge, too, the help of those who knew the two antagonists of this saga as friends, bosses, politicians. Billy Sutton joined the first Kennedy campaign just hours after his return from World War II. He retains his wondrous gift for mimicry, his wistful memories of sharing that Georgetown town house that the young congressman made a "Hollywood hotel." Ted Reardon, who served Kennedy from that first day in Congress to the day he set off for Texas, kept his proud leather-bound collection of "Lodge's Dodges" high in his apartment closet till the day he died. Ted Sorensen, the brilliant counsel Jack Kennedy called his "intellectual bloodbank," remains the standard to which all top political lieutenants aspire.

John Kennedy's pals gave me another glance into the rivalry that marked his stunning emergence into history. Chuck Spalding exudes the genuine humility of a fellow who "just happened to be friends" with the most charismatic figure of the time. Red Fay is grateful, even today, for the fun, high times, and grand occasions he shared with the navy pal who met him in the South Pacific, then kept him aboard for the entire voyage. Charles Bartlett, who introduced Jack to future wife, Jacqueline, recalls his lost pal with tear-filled eyes a full three decades after his passing. Ben Bradlee, another reporter pal, is a storyteller with the same salty language and stylish irreverence as the Washington neighbor who became a president. George Smathers, who remembers Kennedy as the "most charming man he ever met," evokes his and Jack's don't-give-a-damn times better than all the written-down legends together.

Thomas P. "Tip" O'Neill, Jr., my boss for six years, shared a rich perspective on both of this book's antagonists through many a languid session in the Speaker's backroom office.

On the Richard Nixon side of the rivalry, I owe much to the late Pat Hillings, who took Richard Nixon's seat in Congress and shared so many of his crises. From the moment I discovered Pat waiting patiently for me in a Palm Springs hotel lobby, he was a friend and correspondent of great cheer and helpfulness. Bob Haldeman, who died just a month after our long interview, could not have been more generous. His diaries provide the best possible record of this saga's final chapters. I want to thank John Ehrlichman for shedding light on the darker period of the Kennedy-Nixon story. John asked Richard Nixon at an anguished moment how he could explain the tragedy of Watergate to his children. I'd like to believe that this book performs that service. Thanks to Richard Nixon's friend and speechwriter Ray Price, I am able to exploit an insider's narrative of the forces that drove this troubled White House in its final days. Thanks to Alexander Haig, I could plumb the political calculation that guided Richard Nixon until those last steps toward the helicopter.

I would also like to thank those who allowed me to interview them on the events and personalities in this book: Clark Clifford, Charles Colson, Prof. Archibald Cox, Mark Dalton, Fred and Nancy Dutton, Bob Finch, James Flug, President Gerald Ford, Joan Gardner, Leonard Garment, Bill Gavin, Vic Gold, Bob Griffin, Louis Harris, Richard Helms, Stephen Hess, Don Hewitt, John F. Kennedy, Jr., Herb Klein, Tom Korologos, G. Gordon Liddy, Evelyn Lincoln, Sen. Eugene McCarthy, Pete McCloskey, Charles McWhorter, Rod MacLeish, Earl Mazo, Sen. Frank Moss, Sen. Daniel Patrick Moynihan, Martin Nolan, Esther Peterson, David Powers, George Reedy, Pierre Salinger, Rex Scouten, John Sears, Sargent Shriver, George Tames, Helen Thomas, Ron Walker, and Speaker Jim Wright.

There are two historians to whom I owe the most: Herbert Parmet's *Jack: The Struggles of John F. Kennedy* is the best book I have ever read on this fascinating man. Stephen Ambrose's three-volume biography of Richard Nixon was the scaffold on which I have worked these past years. Three other books were indispensable: *Nixon Agonistes* by Garry Wills, *JFK Reckless Youth* by Nigel Hamilton, and *President Kennedy* by Richard Reeves.

I want to thank my researchers Christopher O'Sullivan, Christopher L. Matthews, Joseph Walsh, and Jason Kibbey; Thomas Whalen and Allan Goodrich at the John F. Kennedy Library; and John Taylor and Susan Naulty at the Richard M. Nixon Library and Birthplace. Others who helped in this project include Mark Johnson, Margaret Carlson, Turner and Elizabeth Kibbey, Robert Schiffer, Hendrik Hertzberg, Evan Thomas, Michael Gillette, Sven Holmes, Lois Romano, Gail Thorin, Steven Katze, Nancy Morrissey, and the Honorable Edward Markey.

I want to thank my literary representative, Raphael Sagalyn, who proved his faith and loyalty long ago. I want to thank, more than I can put in words, Michele Slung, for her masterful editorial work on this volume. The hours she dedicated to detonating paragraphs and challenging sentences have transformed a long and turbulent narrative into a coherent and dramatic saga.

I want to especially thank my editor, Dominick Anfuso, who shared my excitement with this historic rivalry from the outset. It was he who recognized the classic tale that lay beneath the history and urged me to tell it.

Finally, as before, I thank my loving wife, Kathleen, and our God-given children for sharing with me a world that any writer would envy.

Contents

DRAMATIS PERSONAE

Charles Bartlett, columnist, *Chattanooga Times;* personal friend of Jack Kennedy's.

Benjamin Bradlee, Washington bureau chief, *Newsweek,* 1961–65; executive editor, *Washington Post;* personal friend of Jack Kennedy's.

Paul Corbin, Robert Kennedy operative, 1960–68.

Paul "Red" Fay, PT boat friend of Kennedy's in World War II; U.S. undersecretary of the navy, 1961–64.

James Flug, chief counsel, Sen. Edward Kennedy's Subcommittee on Administrative Practices.

Lawrence O'Brien, campaign aide, Kennedy for Senate, 1952; field director, Kennedy for President, 1959–60; presidential aide, 1961–63; chairman, Democratic National Committee, 1969–72.

Kenneth O'Donnell, Kennedy political strategist, 1952–63.

Dave Powers, campaign aide, 1952–60; presidential aide, 1946–60.

Timothy "Ted" Reardon, administrative assistant to John F. Kennedy, 1947–61; presidential aide, 1961–63.

George Smathers, U.S. House of Representatives from Florida, 1947–51; U.S. senator, 1951–69.

Theodore "Ted" Sorensen, legislative assistant to Senator Kennedy, 1953–61; special counsel to the president, 1961–63.

Charles "Chuck" Spalding, personal friend of Jack Kennedy's, 1940–63.

William "Billy" Sutton, staff aide, Kennedy for Congress campaign, 1946; congressional aide, U.S. congressman John F. Kennedy of Massachusetts, 1947–50.

Richard "Dick" Tuck, campaign volunteer, Douglas for Senate, 1950; Brown for Governor, 1962; Robert Kennedy campaign aide, 1968.

Patrick J. Buchanan, political aide to Richard Nixon, 1966–68; presidential speechwriter, 1969–74.

Murray Chotiner, political adviser to Richard Nixon, 1946–74.

Charles Colson, administrative assistant to U.S. senator Leverett Saltonstall of Massachusetts; presidential aide, 1970–73.

Thomas E. Dewey, governor of New York, 1943–55; strategist, Eisenhower for President, 1952.

John Ehrlichman, advance man, Nixon for President, 1960; campaign aide, Nixon for President, 1968; assistant to President Nixon for domestic affairs, 1969–73.

Dwight D. Eisenhower, Supreme Commander, Allied Expeditionary Force, 1943–45; chief of staff, U.S. Army, 1945–48; president, Columbia University, 1948–52; Supreme Commander, 1950–52; president of the United States, 1953–61.

Robert Finch, administrative assistant to Vice President Nixon, 1958–60; campaign manager, Nixon for President, 1960; lieutenant governor of California, 1967–69; secretary of health, education and welfare, 1969; counselor to the president, 1970–72.

H. R. "Bob" Haldeman, advance man, Nixon for President, 1960; campaign manager, Nixon for Governor, 1962; head of advance, Nixon for President, 1968; chief of staff to President Nixon, 1969–73.

Christian Herter, U.S. congressman from Massachusetts, 1943–52; chaired the Herter Committee to promote the Marshall Plan; governor of Massachusetts, 1953–57; secretary of state, 1959–61.

J. Patrick Hillings, U.S. congressman from California, 1951–59; campaign adviser, Nixon for Vice President, 1952, and Nixon for President, 1960.

Herbert Hoover, president of the United States, 1929–33.

E. Howard Hunt, Central Intelligence Agency; presidential aide, 1971–72.

Herb Klein, *Alhambra Post Advocate,* 1940–50; press secretary to Vice President Nixon; communications manager, Nixon for President, 1968; director of communications, President Nixon, 1969–73.

Henry Cabot Lodge, U.S. senator from Massachusetts, 1937–44, 1947–53; strategist, Eisenhower for President; U.S. ambassador to the United Nations, 1953–60; Republican candidate for vice president, 1960; U.S. ambassador to South Vietnam, 1963–64, 1965–67.

INTRODUCTION

This is the story of a rivalry. It's how two men's pursuit of the same prize changed them and their country.

When Americans think of John F. Kennedy and Richard Nixon, they recall their close, bitter 1960 fight for the presidency. They picture them in their "Great Debate," the debonair Kennedy outshining an awkward Nixon. But behind this snapshot lurks a darker, more enduring saga that began with their election to Congress in the months just after World War II, then crept for fourteen years along those old Capitol corridors where politicians, even rivals, share the same small space. It would survive even the assassin's bullets, climaxing a decade later with a haunted president trying to defend himself against the imagined onslaught of his rival's brother.

During the early years, Nixon was the man to beat. He was the best politician of his time, articulating more ably than anyone else the nervous mood of post–World War II America. By the age of forty-three, he had been elected to the House, the Senate, and twice to the vice presidency of the United States. Even the respected liberal columnist Murray Kempton called the 1950s the "Nixon decade." Kennedy was the late bloomer.

The relationship between the two men was complex. As a freshman congressman, Jack Kennedy had pointed out Nixon to friends as someone to watch. Even with the 1960 election looming, Kennedy retained a measure of respect for the Republican vice president. If the Democrats didn't nominate him, he said wistfully over dinner New Year's Eve before the 1960 election, he would vote for Nixon. His tycoon father said much the same to Nixon's face. "Dick, if my boy can't make it," a congressman heard him tell the vice president, "I'm for you."

Dick Nixon, the socially ill at ease Californian who had grown up in his parents' grocery store, had been flattered from the outset by Kennedy's early attention. "I have always cherished the fact that Jack and I were friends when we first came to Congress," he wrote Jacqueline that grim night in 1963.

His rapid, early rise from House to Senate to the vice presidency had made Nixon an electoral role model for Jack Kennedy —but also a rival. No one from the World War II generation had traveled so fast or so far. To succeed the beloved commander in chief, Dwight D. Eisenhower, Jack Kennedy would have to defeat him. "From the beginning," JFK aide Ted Sorensen recalled of Nixon's chances for the 1960 Republican presidential nomination, "we knew it was his to lose."

As early as 1952, the Kennedys found Nixon a useful target. Sargent Shriver prompted Adlai Stevenson to say it was brother-in-law Jack, "not Richard Nixon," who moved the first perjury charge against a Communist. In 1956, Kennedy ran for the Democratic nomination for vice president, Nixon's job. "One takes the high road, and one takes the low," he said—a direct shot at Eisenhower's running mate.

Even Kennedy's assassination did not end the rivalry waged so fiercely in 1960. As he began his Lazarus-like revival, Nixon was left to face not only Jack's brothers Bob and Ted but the specter of "Camelot." But one who knew him well saw the unquenched fire. "I know how you feel—so long on the path—so closely missing the greatest prize," Kennedy's widow wrote, responding to Nixon's letter of condolence, "and now for you, the question comes up again, and you must commit all your and your family's hopes and efforts again."

Having won the prize in 1968, Nixon would still feel shadowed by the Kennedys. Despite his dramatic opening to Communist China, he worried that some last-minute maneuver would make Ted Kennedy his 1972 rival and deny him a second term. "It was like we were running against the ghost of Jack Kennedy," Nixon aide Charles Colson recalled. Ambushed by Jack in 1960, and nearly again by Robert in 1968, Nixon and his men now saw yet another Kennedy approaching. The dread led to Watergate.

It started with a friendship. In April 1947, the two freshman U.S. congressmen briskly debated national politics before a rambunctious crowd in McKeesport, Pennsylvania. The Californian showed a fighter's edge, challenging his gaunt, genteel opponent at every point. The rival refused to take his bait; instead, he spoke directly to the audience, charming the steel-town crowd with his smooth delivery and quaint Massachusetts accent. Both men were impressive. "It was hard to tell who had come from the wealthy family and which had worked his way up," the debate's moderator told his wife later that night. What struck him most was the genuine friendliness of the two young politicians as they chomped hamburgers and talked sports at a local diner before catching the midnight *Capital Limited* back to Washington.

Both antagonists had won election to the House of Representatives in that first postwar Congress. Kennedy had run as a "fighting conservative," a phrase he chose himself; Nixon, on a commitment to "practical liberalism." Both were anxious for higher office. Though one was a Democrat and the other a Republican, the rivalry over who in the class of 1946 would move up first was a cordial one. When Nixon did, running for the Senate in 1950, Democrat Kennedy showed up at the Republican's office with a large financial contribution from his father. When Dwight Eisenhower picked the Californian as his vice-presidential running mate two years later, Kennedy cheered. "I was always convinced that you would move ahead to the top," he wrote in a longhand letter. "But I never thought it would come this quickly."

Within months, the two were thrown back together. Nixon and Kennedy spent the 1950s across the hall from each other, the vice president in room 362 of the Senate Office Building, the new senator from Massachusetts in 361. When Kennedy went into the hospital for dangerous back surgery in 1954, Nixon regularly stopped by his colleague's office after-hours to check how "Jack" was doing. When the vice president sent word that, as presiding officer of the Senate, he would not allow the Democrat's absence to give the Republicans control of the Senate, Kennedy's twenty-five-year-old wife was touched. "There is no one my husband admires more," Jacqueline wrote. With reports that Kennedy lay near death, a Secret Service agent riding with Nixon in the car saw him cry. "Poor brave Jack is going to die. Oh, God, don't let him die." Back then Nixon was as charmed by his handsome, joke-loving hall mate as anyone. He liked Kennedy, wanted to be like him, and very much wanted Kennedy to like him.

In September 1960, presidential candidate Richard Nixon was readying to leave his Chicago hotel for his nationally televised debate with John F. Kennedy when he received an urgent phone call. "Erase the assassin image," his running mate Henry Cabot Lodge warned. Nixon needed to go easy on his rival lest he stir the public's sympathy for the boyish challenger.

Bad advice. In the Great Debate, it was Nixon who would elicit sympathy. The sickly senator who teetered on the edge of death six years before now beamed with vitality. The playboy from across the hall conducted himself like a statesman. The familiar face was suddenly a stranger—the easygoing colleague, a predator; the old friend, the new enemy. Before the evening's contest had been joined, Richard Nixon was visibly deflated by this cold apparition with whom he now shared the stage. Before the ON-AIR light had flashed, the ambush was complete.

But the Nixon versus Kennedy struggle was not quelled with the 1960 election. Even after Nixon lost a race for governor of California, he had emerged by the following autumn as a live prospect to challenge Kennedy for reelection.

In November 1963, a gleaming President Kennedy campaigned through Texas. Former vice president Nixon, who left Dallas the morning of Kennedy's arrival, had spread his mischief. "Nixon Predicts JFK May Drop Johnson," the *Dallas Morning News* reported that Friday, November 22.

Riding by cab back to his New York office that day, Nixon saw a man yelling from a Queens curbside. The president had been shot! Stricken by the macabre turn of fate, Nixon brandished his quote in the Dallas newspaper urging "a courteous reception" for the visiting president.

In February 1968, half a decade later, Nixon watched from a Portland hotel as Robert Kennedy announced for the Democratic presidential nomination. After the televised picture of the glamorous Irish-American clan had faded from the screen, the Republican front-runner stared grimly at the black TV screen. "We've just seen some terrible forces unleashed," he said.

When the second Kennedy was assassinated four months later, the hopes of the divided Democrats passed to the youngest brother, Ted, who refused to run. On his second try for the presidency, Richard Nixon succeeded.

In July 1969, the new American leader presided over the successful *Apollo 11* moon landing, the mission launched by Jack Kennedy. Amid the national excitement, word came that Ted Kennedy, the reelection rival Nixon now feared most, had been in a car accident that cost the life of a young woman. The president was fascinated by the news. "Strange!" he muttered to an aide.

From early in his presidency, Nixon was haunted by the fear of a Kennedy "restoration." After the death at Chappaquiddick, Nixon sent detectives to the area in search of evidence that would finish Ted Kennedy's presidential prospects once and for all. To besmirch the family legacy, aides faked a Washington-to-Saigon cable tying the late president's own hand to the assassination of South Vietnam leader Ngo Dinh Diem. Unable to shake his fear of a Kennedy restoration, Nixon instigated a covert campaign to gather intelligence on the Democrats, starting with veteran Kennedy strategist Lawrence O'Brien.

June 23, 1972: To cover up the White House role in the break-in of Democratic headquarters by a band composed largely of Cuban exiles, and believing in the party's plan to nominate Ted Kennedy "at the last minute," Nixon ordered his aides to say that pursuing the Watergate break-in would expose what he believed to be Kennedy's secret bungling and betrayal of the 1961 Bay of Pigs invasion. "They play it tough," he reminded his aides of past tactics used by his political enemies. "We need to play it the same way." Within minutes, he had fashioned the "smoking gun" of impeachment.

In August 1974, Richard Nixon became the first American president to resign. Surrounded by loyalists within the White House and by his enemies without, he confessed the terrible price of his obsession. "Always remember, others may hate you, but those who hate you don't win unless you hate them back, and then you destroy yourself."

It was a stark pairing. John F. Kennedy was handsome, debonair, witty, wealthy, and a decorated war hero to boot. He was by any measure the most beloved president of modern times. Three decades after his death he remains the standard by which we measure our country's leader. What he possessed was an innate ability to be *liked*, to have people want him as a friend, lover, son, brother, leader. Men and women both wanted to follow him. Millions voted for him with no questions asked, then liked him even more after the Bay of Pigs blunder. Before his dazzling success in the Great Debate, we didn't know the Greek word *charisma*. After his early, ghastly departure, the name "Jack Kennedy" evoked it. He had the gift.

Richard Nixon won four national elections and, in 1960, quite nearly a fifth. Between 1952 and 1972, he was a Republican candidate for national office in every election but one. He appeared on the cover of *Time* magazine fifty-six times and was a central figure in American life from 1948 until his death in 1994 —a span of half a century. Yet he could not best John F. Kennedy, not the one time that mattered: their 1960 encounter before a spellbound nation.

Nixon used not only his talents but also his deficiencies to propel himself in the contest. Lacking a distinctive charm, he made a virtue of his *regularness*, offering himself as champion of the squares. Bereft of spontaneity, he drafted and rehearsed speeches for hours. Ill at ease with strangers, he briefed himself before even the most casual of meetings. Starting with small stakes, he made himself a gambler. Resentful of fortune, he made resentment his fortune. If Americans viewed John F. Kennedy as their shining hero, they also recognized the five o'clock shadow of Richard Nixon in the fluorescent light of their bathroom mirror.

"There was something mysterious and inexplicable" in the Nixon relationship with Jack Kennedy, his aide H. R. Haldeman said the month before he died. Here is the strange saga of what went on between the two: one man favored by fortune, the other relying on craft, a Mozart against a Salieri, two antagonists with the same ambition—to be the great young leader of post–World War II America. More than either man, it was the rivalry itself that marked and drove the era.

STUDENTS

As a seventeen-year-old senior at the exclusive Choate School, John Kennedy organized the "Muckers Club." Both the idea and the name came from a sermon given at chapel one afternoon by the prep school's starch-collared headmaster. George St. John had railed that day against those troublemaking students who he said lacked the proper Choate spirit. He called them "Muckers," slang for the local Irish-American ditchdiggers who were a familiar sight around campus. To show his contempt, young Kennedy recruited a dozen friends to meet every evening just after chapel. They would have a single purpose: concoct pranks aimed at wreaking havoc on the proper Choate order. The chance to plot mischief with young Kennedy's Muckers proved so popular that admission was limited, by the founder's decree, to those too rich for the school to expel.

What sealed the Kennedy gang's doom was a bold scheme to disrupt a major social event by dumping cattle manure onto the school's dance floor, with the Muckers arriving, shovels in hand, to save the day. Tipped off to the escapade, headmaster St. John angrily summoned Joseph Kennedy, Sr., from Washington, where he was chairing Franklin Roosevelt's Securities and Exchange Commission (SEC). Beneath a mien of solemn indignation, the arriving paterfamilias secretly cheered his son's spit-in-the-eye bravado. When the headmaster left the room, he said that his only qualm was the choice of name. "If that crazy Muckers Club had been mine," the tycoon conspired with his vastly relieved son, "you can be sure it wouldn't have started with an M."

Jack Kennedy went on to defeat the chairman of the student council in a contest for the Choate senior "most likely to succeed." Even St. John was finally seduced. "His smile was . . . well, in any school he would have gotten away with things just on his smile. He was . . . very lovable."

From his first run for Congress, Jack Kennedy's grown-up politics would bear the Muckers imprint. No group or institution was spared: the street-corner factions of Massachusetts politics, the labor unions, the Democratic party's liberal establishment, big business, or the eminences of Capitol Hill. From the early canvasses of Cambridge's working-class neighborhoods to that last motorcade in Dallas, his only allegiance was to the "Kennedy party" and its triumph. Driving the enterprise was its ringleader's delightful gift for getting other men to follow him into battle.

ARRIVING at California's Whittier College, the Quaker school not far from his Southern California home, Dick Nixon didn't like what he found. Unable to accept a scholarship to Harvard because his family lacked the necessary money for travel and board, he now found himself a victim of class distinction in his own backyard. The entire life of the Whittier campus revolved around a social elite known as the Franklins. The rest of the student body seemed resigned to its exclusion, its *nerd*-dom.

Nixon, just seventeen, rejected the yoke. He organized a rival social club of precisely those rejected by the Franklins: the poor students who had to work their way through school, the football linemen, and others judged too awkward or unattractive for the elite fraternity. To celebrate its resentment, the new club employed parody. The Franklins wore black ties for their yearbook photo; the contrarians wore shirts with open collars. The Franklins held formal dinners; the new crowd got together over beans and hot dogs. As one of Nixon's club mates put it, the Franklins were the "tuxedo boys . . . the aristocrats on campus." The Nixon crew constituted "the bourgeois . . . the bean boys."

Even Nixon's name for the new club, the Orthogonians, poked fun at the social caste system the Franklins had imposed. Denied admission to the Franklins for lacking the requisite sophistication, his band took defiant pride in being the "straight shooters." Within weeks, its ranks outnumbered those of the established club, and Dick Nixon went on to defeat a Franklin to become

Whittier's student-body president. While having no interest in it himself, Nixon based his winning campaign on a promise to have dancing permitted on campus.

Nixon would employ the same Orthogonian politics in his adult career. From his first run for Congress, he pointed to the elite holding power, then raised an army of the excluded against it. In 1946, he spoke for the small businessmen angry at the liberal New Dealers still clinging to office in Washington. In 1952, he and wife, Pat, embodied the young "cloth coat" Republican couple indignant at the mink-warmed Democratic elite. As president, his constituency became the "silent majority" angry at the long-haired children of privilege who protested their country's war in Southeast Asia. Each time, the Nixonian rage derived its strength from the same Orthogonian resentment.

When Kennedy and Nixon took their seats in Congress just after World War II, the Mucker and the Orthogonian could unite against a common enemy: the old New Deal establishment trailing, like a retreating army, behind the funeral cortege of Franklin D. Roosevelt. Toward this crowd, the George St. Johns of Democratic liberalism, Jack Kennedy would feel a Mucker's contempt; Dick Nixon, an Orthogonian's resentment. One had watched his wealthy father manipulate this crowd; the other knew the painful sting of being born among those millions excluded by it. The odd bond would for many years make them friends.

CHAPTER ONE

World War II Was Their Greatest Campaign Manager

I N April 1945, as Adolf Hitler and mistress Eva Braun spent their last days in a Berlin bunker, the celebrating in San Francisco had already begun. From Washington, London, and Moscow, the Allies converged for the first great pageant of victory. Artie Shaw had taught his band every national anthem, even scoring one for Saudi Arabia, whose strict Muslim royalty saw the composition as blasphemy. Pianist Arthur Rubinstein and New York Metropolitan Opera star Ezio Pinza were at the San Francisco Opera House, where Secretary-General Alger Hiss was preparing for the inaugural session of the new United Nations. Hotel lobbies bustled with the arrival of the men World War II had made celebrities. Up on Nob Hill, the American secretary of state, Edward Stettinius, held court at the Fairmont penthouse. Several floors down, aide Adlai Stevenson leaked so much news his room was christened "Operation Titanic." At the St. Francis, young assistant secretary Nelson Rockefeller hosted an around-the-clock reception for Latin American delegates. Up on the tenth floor, the conference's most mysterious delegation, the Soviet mission, headed by Vyacheslav M. Molotov, had rifle-toting guards posted from one end of the hall to the other.

Everyone guessed at Moscow's intentions. Would America's "great Russian allies" cooperate in the new postwar order or resort to their pre-1941 truculence? At a Palace Hotel suite, Kremlin expert Charles "Chip" Bohlen gave a briefing one evening on the situation he had just left behind in Moscow. The prestigious group included top British envoy Anthony Eden and U.S. Ambassador to the Soviet Union Averell Harriman. At one point in Bohlen's talk, Harriman went out on the balcony with a young woman. "I give him about two more minutes, and then he's going to hang himself," Jack Kennedy, the twenty-seven-year-old host of the gathering, whispered to his navy pal Paul "Red" Fay. "What do you mean?" Fay asked, thinking that Kennedy was talking about the briefing they were getting from the Soviet expert. "I'm not talking about Bohlen," Kennedy corrected him. "I'm talking about *Harriman.*"

"That's pretty much the way it was," agreed Chuck Spalding, another Kennedy pal along for the fun. "Jack's attitude, as it was in so many other crises, made you feel you were at a *fair* or something." Kennedy, a stringer for the *Chicago Herald American*, was something of a celebrity himself due to his wealthy father's controversial tenure as U.S. ambassador to Great Britain in the prewar years and his own publicized exploit in the South Pacific, saving his crew after his PT boat was rammed in half by a Japanese destroyer.

Like other returned servicemen, Kennedy worried that an ailing President Roosevelt, dead just two weeks, had conceded too much to Joseph Stalin during the recent Allied meeting at Yalta. The stone-faced Soviet delegation attending the UN conference only added to the sense of postwar menace. "Americans can now see that we have a long way to go before Russia will entrust her safety to any organization other than the Red Army," Kennedy wrote after covering a Molotov press conference. "The Russians may have forgiven, but they haven't forgotten."

The Hearst reporter had his own postwar agenda: politics. His older brother, Joseph Kennedy, Jr., had been killed in a bombing mission the year before, leaving the hopes of Joseph Kennedy, Sr., riding on his second oldest. The job covering the UN conference, a plum assignment won through his father's friendship with William Randolph Hearst himself, was a warm-up for what Jack called his dad's scheme to "parlay a lost PT boat and a bad back into a political advantage." His weeks covering the UN conference would teach Kennedy the superiority of his father's plan to his own notion of becoming a full-time journalist. He learned the hard way that the statesmen passing through the hotel lobbies of San Francisco carried far more prestige than those milling around trying to snag interviews. Red Fay, who had convinced his navy superiors to let him accompany his mustered-out pal to San Francisco, recalled a telling incident from those days and nights in San Francisco. "He had this attractive gal, and—I will never forget—somebody came in and ran his hand through Jack's hair and was very condescending. I've never seen Jack so mad." Kennedy was learning firsthand the lack of respect shown to lowly reporters, even well-connected ones. When word came that his father had persuaded, with the help of a huge financial gift, the legendary James Michael Curley to give up his seat in the U.S. Congress and run again for mayor of Boston, young Kennedy was ready for the leap. "I've made up my mind," Kennedy told Spalding not long after. "I'm going into politics."

JOSEPH Kennedy prepared the way for his son's electoral debut in 1946 much as the U.S. Navy had prepared an enemy-held island for an invasion by the marines. To replant his family's roots in a state deserted years earlier for New York, Kennedy drenched the Commonwealth of Massachusetts in philanthropy. The archdiocese of Boston got a check for $600,000; the Guild of Appolonia, the association of Catholic dentists, got $10,000. With each gift came a sole proviso: Son Jack got his picture in the newspaper handing over the check.

To make young Kennedy a recognized figure in the area, his father retained a public relations firm to book his son at every local club that needed a free speaker. Lieutenant Kennedy used the occasions to share with his less-traveled audiences his firsthand impressions of postwar Europe. Like most Americans of the day, he missed the drama taking place on the other side of the globe in the Indo-Chinese capital of Hanoi, whose streets and docks were crowded that September with a million people celebrating the Japanese evacuation and what they thought was their nation's independence. But what young Kennedy lacked in oratorical skill—and knowledge of Indochina—he supplied in charm, especially the winsome smile he flashed after each stumble over the text.

To offset the resistance of the local political organizations, the Kennedys built one of their own. Sgt. Billy Sutton was the first aboard, hired by the younger Kennedy for seventy-five dollars a week just hours after arriving home from the war. To establish a voting residence, Kennedy used the Bellevue, a hotel and political hangout across from the Boston State House. But while he busied himself trudging through the working-class neighborhoods of the Eleventh Congressional District, Kennedy overlooked an impressive detail: He had missed the deadline for filing his petitions. The papers that should have been presented to the election board by close of business April 23 were instead sitting in a filing cabinet at the candidate's headquarters. It was 6:30 P.M. The statehouse closed at 5:00 P.M.

Joseph P. Kennedy's son refused to accept catastrophe. Some frantic phone calls located a well-placed accomplice. Entering the statehouse that night, Kennedy found his way to the appropriate office and deposited the all-important documents in their proper place. Though unaware of the after-hours entry, his rivals were outraged already by Kennedy's blatant carpetbagging into an area where he had neither lived nor paid taxes, much less served politically. Boston city councilman Joseph Russo, another candidate for the Eleventh District seat, expressed the street-corner attitude in a newspaper ad:

Congress Seat for Sale.
No Experience Necessary.
Applicant Must Live in New York or Florida.
Only Millionaires Need Apply.

Instead of becoming angry at Russo, the Kennedys got even. They got a twenty-eight-year-old custodian named Joseph Russo to agree, for a modest payment, to put his name on the ballot, thereby splitting the *Joseph Russo* vote in two. Front runner Mike Neville faced even tougher treatment. The Kennedys tried bribing him out of the race. "Joe Kennedy called my dad, who was a lawyer," his son Robert recalls. "They wanted him to get out of the fight. They offered him a job with the Kennedy Foundation. Twenty-five thousand dollars a year . . . for life." When the proud Neville refused, Kennedy senior called once again on his friendship with William Randolph Hearst. For the last sixty days before the election, the Hearst-owned *Boston American* did not run a single Neville ad, print a single Neville photo, or so much as mention the man's name. "The Kennedy strategy was to buy you out or blast you out," Neville would ruefully recall of a family that possessed ample clout for either method.

Assemblyman Tom O'Neill, a Neville backer known on the street corner as "Tip," was not all that impressed by the Kennedy operation, not at first. To O'Neill, comfortable at the neighborhood clubhouse, the rules were basic. A fellow worked for the party and was rewarded, perhaps with a snow button that meant you would be a regular on the city road crew come winter. If you wanted to run for office, you waited your turn, something young John Kennedy apparently knew nothing about. "I couldn't believe this skinny, pasty-faced kid was a candidate for anything!" he thought after being introduced to the young interloper one Sunday in front of the Bellevue Hotel.

Kennedy looked better than he actually was. His war injuries masked more serious health problems. His bad back, aggravated in the PT boat incident, was congenital. His yellowish skin, a condition the Kennedy campaign blamed on malaria, was actually a symptom of Addison's disease, which produced jaundice, stark changes of appearance, and deathly bouts of illness. "He wasn't looking healthy then," Billy Sutton recalled. Another aide, Mark Dalton, remembered his candidate as "a skeleton."

But Kennedy's sickliness seemed only to add to his appeal. As with other young veterans, he had come home to run for office wearing a badge of courage. As Sutton would declare again and again in the years ahead, "World War II was their greatest campaign manager." And in Jack Kennedy's case, the power of his father's money magnified his back-from-the-front appeal. Tip O'Neill soon noticed an extraordinary sight on his North Cambridge street: a caterer's truck. Even his own block was being infiltrated by the Kennedy campaign. "If you agreed to invite a few friends to your house to meet Jack, they brought in a case of mixed booze, hired a caterer, and gave you a hundred dollars, which was supposed to pay for a cleaning woman to come to your house both before and after the party." For the ready host, that hundred dollars was money in the bank. In those days, working-class families of North Cambridge didn't employ cleaning women. They raised them.

As the election neared, the pace of vote buying escalated. "A few weeks before the primary, the Kennedys approached a number of large families and promised them fifty dollars in cash to help out at the polls," O'Neill recalled. "They didn't care if these people showed up to work. They were simply buying votes, a few at a time, and fifty bucks was a lot of money." Opposition campaign workers took to pinning twenty-dollar bills to their lapels. They called them "Kennedy buttons."

To Joe Kennedy, twenty dollars was small change. Thanks to his Hollywood connections, local movie theaters began running newsreel features on young Jack Kennedy's campaign for Congress. One hundred thousand bootleg reprints of a *Reader's Digest* account of Lieutenant Kennedy's PT-109 exploits were mailed first-class to voters.

Jack Kennedy lived up to the Hollywood image his father was promoting. He had become a local celebrity, especially among the young women of the area. Despite his gaunt features, the bobby-socks crowd looked upon the rich, young Irish American as the political equivalent of that other skinny star Frank Sinatra. His prospects zooming, Kennedy turned on the charm. After hearing one rival after another use a joint appearance with him to describe his hard-knocks upbringing, the target of these Uriah Heepish performances took the wry road. "I do seem to be the only one here," he deadpanned to the delight of the working stiffs, "who did not come up the hard way."

As the primary approached, Jack would be reminded that his new career in politics was a hand-me-down from a brother lost in war. With Joe Kennedy's polls showing his second son with a solid lead, members of the family sat around the dinner table in Hyannis Port, each taking a turn to toast the candidate's twenty-ninth birthday. Finally, the senior Kennedy called on thirteen-year-old Teddy. "I would like to drink a toast to the brother who isn't here," he said.

It took several minutes for the room to recover.

Try as he did, trudging dutifully up the stairs of one second- and third-story family dwelling after another, Jack Kennedy could not ignore his own mortality. The day before balloting, the front-running candidate marched in the Bunker Hill parade, then fell ill before the finish. Yet in the June 18 primary, tantamount to election in that Democratic stronghold, Jack Kennedy won 22,183 votes, Neville 11,341, Cotter 6,677, the real Russo 5,661, Kennedy's Russo 799.

GEN. Dwight D. Eisenhower, Supreme Commander of Allied Forces in Europe, accepted the Nazi surrender documents at Rheims on May 7, 1945. Days later, he was driven through the canyons of Wall Street, ticker tape flying down from the highest windows as the general stood in the back of his car, both hands held high with the V sign, a gesture he and the world had learned from Britain's Winston Churchill. Twenty floors above, a thirty-two-year-old navy lieutenant beheld the sight. It was the closest he had ever come to so great a man.

For Dick Nixon, World War II was not yet over. As an aviation ground officer in the Solomons, he had earned the nickname "Nick" and learned enough poker to bring home a nest egg of $10,000. He was spending the rest of the war back East, terminating defense contracts. On V-J Day he celebrated with others in New York's Times Square, only to realize a pickpocket had gotten to his wallet. Weeks later, back in his apartment in Baltimore, where the Californian was still on active service, he experienced a different stroke of luck. It came in a surprise from home.

October 3, 1945

Dear Dick,

   I am writing you this short note to ask if you would
like to be a candidate for Congress on the Republican ticket
in 1946.

   Jerry Voorhis expects to run—registration is about
50–50. The Republicans are gaining.

   Please airmail me your reply if you are interested.

                                                    H. L. Perry

   P.S. Are you a registered voter in California?

Herman Perry, a prominent banker and longtime friend of the
Nixon family, had played a role in an early Nixon political success. He was the Whittier College board member who backed the
young student leader's call for legalized dancing on the Quaker
campus. Calling Perry in California, Nixon discovered that Perry
was head-hunting on behalf of a local business group, the Committee of 100, which hoped to unseat Democrat Voorhis, the
ten-year incumbent seeking reelection. Nixon told him he was
"honored" and "excited" at the chance being offered to appear
before the group. He would run, he promised Perry in a letter sent
the next day, "an aggressive, vigorous campaign" on a platform of
"practical liberalism."

   Within the month, Nixon was back in Los Angeles, telling
eight wealthy leaders of the Committee of 100 what its members
wanted very much to hear. "There were two ways of looking at
America's economic future," the young man in his navy officer's
uniform said. "One, advocated by the New Deal, is government
control in regulating our lives. The other calls for individual
freedom and all that initiative can produce. I subscribe to the
second view. I believe the returning veterans, and I have talked
to many of them in the foxholes, will not be satisfied with a dole
or a government handout."

   The earnest young man was giving voice to the Committee of
100's implicit credo. Yet one point still concerned him. Nixon
asked the Committee of 100's leaders if they were ready to foot
the bill for a serious campaign. Assured there would be adequate
financing, he made his position clear. "Well, I'm in your hands. If

you say for me to run, I'll run." Facing its general membership that night at Whittier's William Penn Hotel, Nixon found the same seething resentment he had felt so keenly among the squares at Whittier College. Here again he sensed the passion of the angry, striving middle class against the social and cultural elite, represented, in this case, by Jerry Voorhis, well-born, well-spoken graduate of Yale, the ultimate *Franklin*. Nixon was last to be heard of six candidates, several of them lured by a newspaper advertisement. His well-composed lines did the trick, putting the group's pro-business ideology in sharp relief from that of the despised New Dealers. Dick Nixon had done his homework.

Three weeks later, Roy Day, Committee of 100 leader, phoned the Nixon apartment at two o'clock in the morning and shouted the news. "Dick, the nomination's yours!" The vote had been unanimous. Too excited to go back to sleep, Pat Nixon was to remember, she and her husband talked until dawn.

That same morning, Nixon launched his campaign, soliciting negative information on Jerry Voorhis, calling up anyone in Washington who might help him get the goods. "His conservative reputation must be blasted," Nixon wrote enthusiastically to one Committee of 100 leader of the liberal Democrat who had been a socialist in his younger years. "I'm really hopped up over this deal!" Yet one problem remained: the Nixon family finances. His entire personal kitty consisted of the $10,000 he'd brought home from the South Pacific. He was willing to spend it, though, for a seat in Congress.

His first investment was hiring a $500-a-month Beverly Hills public relations man, Murray Chotiner. The overweight, sallow-faced Chotiner had two working precepts. The first held that voting was a negative act: People don't vote for someone; they vote against someone. Chotiner's second rule was that voters possessed the mental capacity for grasping just two or three issues at one sitting. The goal of every campaign was therefore to limit the number of issues to two or three, all of them tied to the opponent, all of them negative. "I say to you in all sincerity that if you do not define the opposition candidate before the campaign gets started," Chotiner taught his disciples, "you are doomed to defeat."

For Nixon, defeat loomed as a real possibility. At the campaign's outset, Chotiner told him to exploit his veteran's status to the hilt. "Just stand there in your uniform, keep your mouth shut, and I'll get you elected to Congress!" Since his candidate had no civilian suits, it seemed an unremarkable set of orders. But within a matter of weeks the Nixons learned the harsh realities of political life. A break-in at party headquarters cost the campaign its entire stock of pamphlets that Pat Nixon had financed with the $3,000 she realized by selling a piece of land. "No one cared when it happened to us!" she was to recall decades later in the aftermath of a more celebrated burglary. A worse calamity concerned the campaign itself. Nixon's tales of the South Pacific, and his self-portrait of the young returning vet building a family, were not stirring up the voters. He had failed to ignite enough anger toward the well-turned-out Voorhis to wrest his seat from him. By early April, Chotiner was starting to get nervous. "We don't have enough meat!" he complained to his candidate. If they didn't turn up something on Jerry Voorhis, the Nixon campaign would go nowhere.

Thanks to Chotiner, the meat was soon in Nixon's refrigerator. It arrived on April 23, the same day Jack Kennedy delivered those nocturnal nominating petitions to the Massachusetts secretary of state's office. Nixon had found his issue: Jerry Voorhis's backing by the giant Congress of Industrial Relations. Freed from wartime "no strike" pledges, the country's great labor unions, led by the CIO, were demanding catch-up wages. In January 1946, the electrical, machine, and auto workers had struck. Next to go out were the mine workers, who forced President Truman's hand. Dick Nixon would now charge Cong. Jerry Voorhis with being in the hip pocket of labor's political action committee, the CIO PAC.

The Committee of 100 delivered the anti-Voorhis blow: "Now that the Political Action Committee has endorsed the candidacy of Jerry Voorhis for Congress, one of the real issues of the campaign is out in the open. There can be no mistake. The choice now is: Shall it be the people represented by Nixon or the PAC by Voorhis?"

There was only one problem with the charge: It was false. The CIO executive board in California had voted on April 1 to endorse every Democratic congressman except Voorhis. He had been passed over for criticizing the many postwar strikes. He had committed the further offense in the eyes of the CIO PAC of condemning the Soviet Union's grab of Eastern Europe. "I believe the Communists are in substantial control of CIO," Voorhis had written a friend afterward, "and between you and me I think that is why I didn't get the endorsement."

Nixon found such details unimpressive. A liberal, anti-Communist faction in the Southern California branch of National Citizen (NC) PAC, an auxiliary group organized by CIO PAC leaders, had pushed through a local endorsement of Voorhis. Thanks to an informant, Murray Chotiner had this sugarplum of opposition research in hand a full month before Voorhis even knew of the local NC PAC's action. The Nixon team had all the evidence it needed.

Congressman Voorhis had been attacked for his CIO PAC endorsements in the previous election campaigns to little effect. But Nixon's use of the "PAC" charge in 1946 came amid a sea change in voter attitudes. A Gallup poll in July showed that six out of ten Americans saw Russia's actions in Eastern Europe as a first step toward world rule. "Foreign policy and relations with Russia" had become the number-one voter concern. The CIO PAC had become a popular target of this concern. In Detroit, rank-and-file workers charged it with being Communist, refusing to contribute to it. "There are no strings attached to me," Nixon told a Whittier audience that August. "I have no support from any special-interest or pressure group. I welcome the opposition of the PAC with its Communist principles and its huge slush fund."

But victory still seemed elusive. In the June primary, Nixon and Voorhis took advantage of California law permitting them to cross-file for the other party's nomination as well as their own. When both Democratic and Republican ballots were counted, Voorhis won a total of seven thousand more votes than Nixon, a dim portent for November. Another obstacle rose up in the form of Republican governor Earl Warren, who refused either to endorse Nixon or to withdraw a letter of commendation Voorhis had received from him and was using as a bragging point in his campaign. It was an impolitic gesture by Warren that Nixon would never forget.

It was still Jerry Voorhis's campaign to lose. In mid-September,

the congressman met face-to-face with Nixon in a South Pasadena high school gym. The challenger had prepped fanatically,
even sneaking in to listen to Voorhis's speeches, studying him as
an aide scribbled down everything the incumbent said. For three
days prior to the debate, Nixon skipped everything else to study
and rehearse.

Jerry Voorhis took the platform first that night, speaking for
fifteen minutes on postwar planning, full employment, and foreign
policy. It was earnest, good-government stuff, and dull. Nixon,
arriving late, waited backstage. Storming onto the stage just as
Voorhis was winding down, he grabbed his rival's hand and shook
it briskly. Then, after rousing the pro-Republican crowd with his
usual anti–New Deal barn burner, Dick Nixon waited patiently
for the question-and-answer period.

It was worth the wait. A Voorhis ringer in the audience demanded that Nixon recant his "false charges" that the Democratic
congressman had gotten the endorsement of the CIO PAC. Hearing this, Nixon pulled a piece of paper from his pocket. It was an
in-house bulletin from the Los Angeles chapter of NC PAC reporting the local group's support for Voorhis. Nixon had been
saving this five-month-old product of Murray Chotiner's opposition research for just this opportunity.

Exploiting the moment for maximum indignation, Nixon
walked toward Voorhis, holding the paper high over his head. He
asked that his rival read what was in his hand. Stunned by this
unaccustomed theater, the congressman started toward his predator. It was too late. Reading the document Nixon had presented
him, the five-term veteran now made a fatal error. Instead of
dismissing the document as an internal, local recommendation
ignored at the state and national level, Voorhis quibbled. He said
the document was not from CIO PAC but from NC PAC, its
associate organization. Nixon had him. To the hoots of the crowd,
the challenger read aloud the names of board members, then the
same names on the board of the CIO PAC. Instead of calling
Nixon a liar for claiming erroneously that he had the national
labor group's endorsement, Voorhis had only struggled deeper into
the quicksand. "How did it go?" Voorhis asked a fellow congressman afterward.

"Jerry," the colleague answered, "he cut you to pieces."

When Voorhis, answering a question at a subsequent debate, called him "Commander Nixon," the young vet let loose with a stinging riposte. "If Mr. Voorhis had been in the navy, he would know that the correct way of addressing someone of my rank was 'Mister.' " It was a masterful eye gouge at the older man, who had spent the war in Washington while Dick Nixon was in steamy Bougainville.

In the next weeks, Nixon turned to mockery. "Out of a mass of 132 bills introduced by my opponent in the last four years," an October newspaper claimed, "only one has become law, and that was one that transferred the activities affecting domestic rabbits from one federal department to another." You have to be "a rabbit," he told the audience in the candidates' last joint appearance, to get any representation from Jerry Voorhis.

The attacks grew nastier. The *Alhambra Post Advocate*, edited by Nixon booster Herb Klein, compared Voorhis's voting record with that of New York congressman Vito Marcantonio, a reflexive leftist and Communist apologist. "How Jerry and Vito Voted" screamed the headlines. "Notorious Fellow Traveller." The Los Angeles newspapers carried front-page boxes exhorting:

Vote Against New Deal Communism.
Vote Republican. Vote American.

The smearing of Democrats as un-American Communists was hardly a Southern California monopoly. On election eve, House Republican leader Joseph Martin of Massachusetts voiced equally strong language. "The people will vote tomorrow between chaos, confusion, bankruptcy, state socialism or communism, and the preservation of our American life." To further stoke the Communist issue, unidentified phone calls began arriving in Twelfth District homes. "This is a friend of yours, but I can't tell you my name," one of the nine-dollar-a-day hired callers would recite into the receiver. "I just wanted you to know that Jerry Voorhis is a Communist." Many would forever attribute those calls to Nixon personally.

* * *

A billboard in Boston aptly defined the nation's appetite for change that fall of 1946: "Had Enough? Vote Republican!"

Jack Kennedy, running in a deeply Democratic district, had no reason to fear the national trend. Calling himself a "fighting conservative," he harbored private contempt for the social and economic policies of the New Deal. "Mr. Roosevelt has contributed to the end of capitalism in our own country," he wrote in his diary the summer before, "although he would probably argue the point at some length. He has done this, not through the laws which he sponsored or were passed during his presidency, but rather through the emphasis he put on rights rather than responsibilities."

Kennedy had formed a close tie that summer in Hyannis Port with a Catholic priest, Edward Duffy, a student of Soviet communism. Having watched events in Europe since the Yalta agreement of February 1945, Kennedy now spoke as someone alarmed by Moscow's belligerence and scornful of those in America who failed to see it. He told an October radio audience how he had stood down a left-wing meeting of Young Democrats in New York. "I told them that the people of the United States have been far too gullible with respect to the publicity being disseminated throughout the world by the clever and brilliant Moscow propagandists. I told the group that I felt that Soviet Russia today is run by a small clique of ruthless, powerful, and selfish men who have established a government which denies the Russian people personal freedom and economic security. I told them that Soviet Russia is a slave state of the worst sort. I knew that my remarks would alienate the entire group, and I did alienate them."

Kennedy now raged at those in the Democratic party, led by Secretary of Commerce Henry Wallace, who chose to ignore the Soviet Union's expansionism in Eastern Europe. What angered Kennedy most was Wallace's words at a Madison Square Garden rally of NC PAC, the organization that Dick Nixon was attacking that fall: "We have no more business in the political affairs of Eastern Europe than Russia has in the political affairs of the United States," the man FDR had dropped from his 1944 ticket said. "If we can overcome the imperialistic urge in the Western world, I'm convinced there'll be no war." Wallace was blaming America for Soviet belligerence.

B Y the end of their campaigns, Kennedy and Nixon were both combatants in a global war that had not yet been given a name. For the next decade, their shared antipathy toward the Soviet Union would make them oddly compatible, their common foe being not just the Communist threat but those in the country who turned a blind eye to that threat. That first campaign sealed another, less attractive bond. Long before election day, each had lost his political virginity. While Kennedy had shown himself a worthy student of his new profession, a master at how this or that group voted, an old friend noticed that he now selected his companions on the same basis: who could help him get ahead. A Whittier classmate told Nixon biographer Stephen Ambrose of the disturbing change he noticed in the local political newcomer: He'd become ruthless. "Dick knew that a lot of us who are liberal are not Communists; in fact, we are anti-Communists."

On November 5, John F. Kennedy won with 73 percent of the vote. Across the continent, that same night, Richard Nixon pulled a major political upset, defeating a well-known, respected Democrat with 56 percent of the vote. Nixon was euphoric. "Pat and I were happier on November 6, 1946, than we were ever in our political career," he would recall years later. But as he looked at the morning-after newspaper that victorious day in November 1946, a new challenge had already arisen. The *Los Angeles Times* carried its account of Nixon's local victory on page 2, while on the front page was an item reporting a more distant result. From three thousand miles away, across the full breadth of this nation, came the message: "Son of Kennedy Congress Winner."

It had begun.

A week after the election, *Time* showcased some "new faces" to watch in the next Congress:

Richard Milhous Nixon, dark, lank Quaker attorney who turned a California grass-roots campaign (dubbed "hopeless" by wheelhorse

Republicans) into a triumph over high-powered, high-minded Democratic incumbent Jerry Voorhis. To beat Voorhis, ex-Navy Lieut. Commander Nixon, 33, passed around 25,000 white plastic thimbles labeled: "Elect Nixon and needle the P.A.C." He plugged hard for veterans' housing, end of controls, a bipartisan foreign policy; politely avoided attacks on his opponent.

John F. Kennedy, 29, boyish, raw-boned, Harvard-bred son of ex–U.S. Ambassador Joseph P. Kennedy. To win the Democratic primary in Massachusetts' 11th District, which has rarely sent a Republican to Congress, ex–PT boat commander Kennedy made 450 speeches, plumped first for international issues, then switched to such local matters as the restoration of Boston's port and the encouragement of New England industries. One of his biggest jobs: to convince 37 nationalities in some of Boston's grimmest slums that he was no Fauntleroy.

CHAPTER TWO

Strangers on a Train

Two freshman congressmen could not have come to Washington in more wildly different style that turbulent January of 1947. Richard Nixon arrived in the nation's capital resembling more an economic itinerant than a political conqueror. He and Pat drove cross-country with their family possessions strapped to the roof of their new 1946 Ford like an Okie family headed the wrong way. A side trip to Mexico produced an added indignity when a U.S. border guard insisted that the pair unload the entire car for inspection. In Washington, more trouble: The young California family could find no place to live, at least not on the $12,500 that a member of Congress drew a year. He, Pat, and daughter Tricia would spend three months living out of suitcases at the Mayflower Hotel. Nixon would admit to having the "same lost feeling" he had experienced upon entering the navy.

Jack Kennedy's entrance into the postwar capital was a study in nonchalance. In late November the *Boston Post* pictured the new lawmaker looking through the real estate ads. But this was just a human-interest ploy for the voters back in Cambridge and Charlestown. Joe Kennedy's son was hardly the typical young vet scavenging for housing. Soon a comfortable Georgetown town house was leased, and the congressman-elect was vacationing in Palm Beach.

Billy Sutton, who had driven down from Massachusetts a few days earlier, greeted Kennedy when the twenty-nine-year-old arrived in the nation's capital to take the oath of office. Kennedy walked into the Statler Hilton gleaming with his Florida tan, hair tousled, carrying a black cashmere overcoat and wearing a gray suit and a pair of brogues elegantly stretched by shoe trees.

"Billy, is Ted with you?" Kennedy asked, wondering about the whereabouts of his new congressional secretary.

"He's in having some coffee," Sutton told him, leaning his head in the direction of the Statler's drugstore. But Kennedy, he warned, would not have time for such amenities. John W. McCormack, the majority leader and unquestioned head of the Massachusetts delegation, had been calling all morning. "You should be in a hurry. You have a caucus meeting!" To soften the admonition, Sutton delivered some good news. "You've got two pretty good committees: Education and Labor and District of Columbia." Kennedy was undeterred. "Well, I'd like a couple of eggs."

With that, the young congressman took a seat alongside Ted Reardon at the drugstore counter and ordered two soft-boiled eggs and tea. Sutton continued to hover. "We've got to get up there! Mr. McCormack is anxious that you get there!" The most powerful Democrat in Massachusetts and, next to Sam Rayburn, in Washington as well was up there waiting for the freshman!

"How long would you say Mr. McCormack has been here?" Kennedy asked.

"Twenty-six years," the detail-minded Sutton answered after an instant's calculation.

"Well," the veteran Mucker answered, still eating his eggs, "don't you think Mr. McCormack wouldn't mind waiting another ten minutes?"

Just off the plane, Kennedy was exhibiting the same politics of contempt he had displayed at Choate and in his campaign. His inherited disdain for the John McCormacks of the world would free him from the entangling alliances that brought down men like Jerry Voorhis. This young politician had no use for badges of party loyalty like those Tip O'Neill's father passed out in Cambridge. Jack Kennedy didn't need a snow button. He was born with one.

After the noon swearing-in ceremony, the first and only session the tradition-bound House would allow to be televised until the late 1970s, Kennedy and his two aides headed back downtown to the National Press Club, where a reception was being held for new congressmen who had served in the war. Walking into the crowded press club's ballroom, Sutton noticed that "there was this fellow over in the corner, a young fellow, very dapper-dressed, who seemed to be the star of the show." When Sutton introduced him to his boss, Kennedy, "who had been sort of taking things easy," suddenly perked up.

"So you're the guy who beat Jerry Voorhis!" he said, moving toward his new classmate. "That's like beating McCormack up in Massachusetts! How's it feel?"

"I suppose I'm elated!" said the man born absent a gift for small talk.

Like the wealthy Harvard freshman he had once been, Kennedy was checking out the young scholarship kid everyone was touting for quarterback, the gawky freshman with the haircut Billy Sutton said "he must have gotten in North Carolina somewhere!" In a matter of seconds, Jack Kennedy was also doing what he knew how to do almost better than anything else: convince someone he liked him.

The two ex–naval officers from the South Pacific theater would soon be sharing the same Capitol Hill billet. Like Kennedy, Nixon had been put on the pivotal Education and Labor panel, which was about to take on the unions. Years later, he would muse on the paradox of his drawing the shortest straw among freshman Republicans named to the committee, with Kennedy doing the same on the Democratic side. "By one of those curious coincidences of history," Nixon recalled, "another freshman assigned to that committee was a good-looking, good-humored young Democrat from Massachusetts named John Fitzgerald Kennedy. He and I shared the dubious distinction of sitting at the opposite ends of the committee table like a pair of unmatched bookends."

Thanks to the "Had Enough!" elections of the previous No-

vember, the Eightieth Congress was the first controlled by the
Republican party since the 1920s. Its new majority was primed to
ferret out the misdeeds of two decades of Democratic rule; or, as
one congressman put it, to "open each session with a prayer and
close it with a probe." Thirty-nine investigative committees and
subcommittees were poised to unearth suspected corruption in the
Roosevelt-Truman era. Communism was another target. In recent
months, the country's V-E Day euphoria had flattened. So had the
wartime goodwill toward Soviet Russia. With each new headline
from abroad the popularity of America's wartime ally plummeted.
So had the man on the street's estimate of those who had dealt
away the country's winnings at Yalta. Congress was looking for
the culprits. During the early weeks of 1947 a staffer like Billy
Sutton could peek into any hearing on Capitol Hill and watch
the hunt for "Reds" in progress. The Hill was, in Sutton's later
phrase, a "Stop 'n' Shop" of hearings on Communist subversion
in the film industry, in the labor unions, and in government itself.

RICHARD Nixon won a second, more dubious posting on the
anti-Communist front: the House Un-American Activities Committee (HUAC). Speaker Joe Martin of Massachusetts wanted
the thirty-three-year-old Californian on HUAC for what he was,
a lawyer, but also for what he was not, a crackpot. Such credentials were in short supply on a committee notorious for ignoring
civil liberties and tilting at windmills. Nixon brought another
talent to the committee table: an insatiable appetite for opposition research. That appetite had been whetted, not sated, by the
digging done on Jerry Voorhis, which produced the lethal NC
PAC memo.

The Honorable Richard M. Nixon, member of Congress, was
now hunting bigger game than Jerry Voorhis. He was out to catch
real Communists. Within days of joining the Education and Labor
Committee, he asked Wisconsin classmate Charles Kersten to find
him someone who could teach him about communism, something
that would take him beyond the bumper-sticker sloganeering of
his first campaign. Kersten mentioned John F. Cronin, whose research had guided Father Edward Duffy, the Catholic priest who

informally tutored candidate Jack Kennedy the summer before on Cape Cod. In love as ever with opposition research, Nixon went to work. Together, Nixon and Kersten began making pilgrimages to Baltimore for long discussions with Father Cronin about Soviet espionage.

Back in Washington, the Californian would now come face-to-face with his first Communist. A Fordham University economics professor and former U.S. Communist party member, Louis Budenz, told HUAC the name of the Soviet agent who was Moscow's direct line to the party: Gerhart Eisler, an Austrian-born Communist then being held on Ellis Island for illegal entry into the country. When the committee called Eisler to the stand, the witness refused even to take the oath. "I have to do nothing. A political prisoner has to do nothing." At this, the committee cited Eisler for contempt of Congress.

But the committee's junior Republican was not content; Dick Nixon smelled blood. How had a known Communist like Gerhart Eisler gotten through the immigration authorities in the first place? To get answers, he took a special subcommittee up to New York to find out. Two weeks later, he gave his maiden House address on the matter. Why, he demanded to know, did an "arrogant, defiant enemy of our government" like Gerhart Eisler, his record replete with criminal acts against the United States, from forgery to perjury to failure to register as an alien, get into the United States of America?

When the contempt motion against Eisler reached the House floor, only one member voted "nay": Vito Marcantonio, the Harlem congressman Nixon's allies had used as Jerry Voorhis's tar baby. Marcantonio relished the combat. Why was an "anti-Fascist" like Eisler being put on trial, he asked, by a House Un-American Activities Committee loaded with "pro-Fascists"? Cheered perhaps by Marcantonio's grand defense, his "anti-Fascist" later jumped bail and escaped to Communist-ruled East Germany.

Thanks to Father Cronin, Nixon had a far bigger target on his scanner. His mentor had written a report, "The Problem of American Communism," which listed several Communists who had risen to high government positions. One was the young State

Department whiz kid Alger Hiss, who had presided at the founding UN conference in San Francisco. For months, Nixon would keep this bit of opposition research to himself, much as he and Murray Chotiner had kept the NC PAC memo till the whites of Jerry Voorhis's eyes could be seen crossing the stage of the South Pasadena high school gym.

THE "Communist" issue continued to percolate. In March, President Harry Truman called on Congress to stop the Red advance across Europe by approving U.S. military aid to help governments in Greece and Turkey resist left-wing insurgencies. Speaking to a joint session, Truman called the move crucial to American security. To those on the political left, this new "Truman Doctrine" was an unwelcome 180-degree reversal from the pro-Russian policies of FDR. But for many of the young officers back from the war, the president was speaking just the right language.

Jack Kennedy thought stopping the Soviet advance in Europe was the only way to avoid repeating the mistake of not stopping the Nazi advance at the Munich Conference of 1938. Had Hitler been confronted before his deadly attack on Poland the following year, he might have retreated. Instead, it was the Allies who were thrown on the defensive. Having lived through prewar appeasement and its consequences, the World War II generation had come home from the South Pacific and Europe determined to prevent a sequel to the tragedy that had interrupted and harrowed their lives and erased so many others. This time, the dictator must be stopped in his tracks. To young men like Kennedy and Nixon, the Yalta Conference of February 1945, which divided up postwar Europe, had the stench of another Munich, another buckling under to an aggressor more subversive in his methods, more pervasive in his ambitions, than the one who died in his Berlin bunker.

To stop Stalin, Kennedy accepted the mission to seek out and destroy his allies here in the country. The day after Truman spoke to Congress, Russ Nixon (no relation to Richard) of the United Electrical, Radio and Machine Workers of America, a union known for its sizable Communist contingent, told the Education and Labor Committee that labor unions had as much right to be led by Communists as by Democrats or Republicans. When it came his turn to quiz the witness, Jack Kennedy said he was "impressed by the dexterity" the witness, a Harvard Ph.D. in economics who was Kennedy's instructor before joining the labor movement, had shown in fielding the earlier questions. Now he had some of his own. With a Mucker's relish, the student was about to grade the professor.

Was communism, he asked Nixon, "a threat to the economic and political system of the United States?" No, the labor official replied, the real threat to the country was its failure to meet the "basic economic problems of the people in a democratic way" as well as its failure to expand civil rights and meet "the problems of the Negro people."

Accepting those points, Kennedy cited what he called the Communist party's willingness to "resort to all sorts of artifices, evasion, subterfuges, only so as to get into the trade unions and remain in them and to carry on Communist work in them, at all costs."

Russ Nixon: I didn't teach you that at Harvard, did I?
Kennedy: No, you did not. I am reading from Lenin, in which is described the procedure which should be adopted to get into trade unions and how they conduct themselves once they are in.

His well-laid trap won Kennedy an instant salute from the press gallery. "A freshman House member with the coral dust of Pacific Islands still clinging to his heels," UPI's George Reedy reported in a radio broadcast, "stole the show from his older colleagues yesterday." With this one exchange, the young Irish-American lawmaker had cast himself as the veteran of one war ready, if necessary, to fight another.

Dick Nixon and Jack Kennedy were now positioned to go at each other for the first time. The question before Congress was how to cleanse the country's giant labor unions of both corruption and communism. As would become the case in other areas, their differences of view were not so wide as either chose to pretend. Publicly, Nixon spoke with the same cant he had used to woo the Committee of 100 prior to his 1946 congressional run. "I was elected to smash the labor bosses," he told a reporter on swearing-in day. "My only principle is to accept no dictation from the CIO PAC!" Privately, his position was more skeptical, closer to the center. He thought the massive Republican bill to be known as "Taft-Hartley" went too far.

Jack Kennedy also saw things differently than his party. The man who had run as a "fighting conservative" agreed with the Republicans that the power of big labor had to be tamed. Like most Americans, not just Republicans, Kennedy saw the excesses of a movement that had put 5 million men out on strike, but he could not flout the interests of Boston longshoremen and other working stiffs back home by backing the Republican bill. Instead, he decided to stake out a position apart from both parties.

Mark Dalton, called down from Massachusetts to help, was impressed that after just three months in office his freshman friend was offering a "dissenting opinion" not just to the landmark Republican measure but to the alternative put forth by his own party.

"John wanted to know what we—Billy Sutton was in the room —thought of the Hartley proposal and what he should do about it. We sat there and developed a position," recalled Dalton, who was the one at the typewriter. "People have always said to me, 'Was John Kennedy running for the presidency from the start?' The new congressman from Massachusetts, in his first months, filing a dissenting report and you asked, 'Was he thinking of the future?' "

He was also sizing up the competition. Dalton accompanied Kennedy when he testified before the Rules Committee about his labor-reform alternative. As they entered the cramped hearing room in the Capitol's top floor that morning, Christian Herter, the Massachusetts Republican, was in the chair. A young member Dalton hadn't met was speaking to the committee on the merits of the Republican bill. "Listen to this fellow," Kennedy whispered to his counsel. "He's going places." A few minutes later, the congressman who had spoken returned to take the seat next to Kennedy. "I'd like you to meet Richard Nixon of California," he told Dalton as they rose to greet him. Despite his personal belief that the Republican labor bill went "too far," the freshman from California had become its most eloquent advocate.

Within the week, Nixon and Kennedy went head-to-head in their first debate. A western Pennsylvania congressman, Frank Buchanan, had been asked by a civic group in McKeesport, a booming steel town, to pick the two hottest political prospects, one Republican, the other Democrat, to duke it out on the Taft-Hartley bill. Nixon had just turned thirty-four. Kennedy was about to have his thirtieth birthday.

The Washington travelers were greeted on their arrival at the Baltimore & Ohio railroad station and escorted to a local hotel, the Penn McKeesport. There, in a chandeliered ballroom, they offered a stark contrast in style. Nixon, a prize-winning debater at Whittier, drove a wedge through the audience. Ignoring catcalls from the blue-collar crowd, he warned that big labor's power was growing "by leaps and bounds." "The public was satisfied with labor laws on V-J Day. But in the year since then we have begun to see a shift in public opinion. We have had unprecedented labor strife—the automobile strike, the steel strike, the coal strike, and even the railroad strike, in which the president was forced to intervene." By evening's end, the jeers from the labor seats grew so bellicose that a local business leader felt called upon to apologize to the Republican congressman in writing.

Kennedy's impact on the room was markedly different. Looking more like a college kid than a U.S. congressman, the boyish Democrat from Massachusetts took a more conciliatory line. He said there was a lot of good in the Taft-Hartley bill, especially the provision outlawing "wildcat" strikes. He worried, however, that the bill would lead to a "war" between management and labor. "The way some of those provisions read, the unions can't even protect themselves from the competition of the sweatshop."

More telling than their argument, however, was the difference in manner. The Californian maintained a fighter's edge, challenging his more genteel seeming opponent on every point. The slender lawmaker with the slight limp focused on the audience, seducing the steel-town folk with his smooth delivery and youthful charm. While Nixon debated, Kennedy simply ignored his opponent, carefully making sure that the businessmen in the room understood his justified concern that the Republican's get-tough approach to labor might create more trouble, not less.

The battle between grit and charm scored points for both men with the audience. "Kennedy was smooth and genteel," said a lawyer who confessed to being "fascinated" by his quaint New England accent. The debate's moderator, a stockbroker, told his wife after the evening's matchup that Nixon was "going to go places." He had kind words for both debaters. "It was hard to tell who had come from the wealthy family and which had worked his way up. Neither could be called a stuffed shirt." But it was Kennedy who won the media battle. The next morning's editions of the *McKeesport Daily News* displayed a photo of a tanned, smiling Kennedy who could have been the captain of the local college football team. The picture of Nixon caught his eyes darting sideways with a hunted look, his defiant chin displaying a beard that had passed well beyond its five o'clock shadow. Even in the black-and-white photo, the charisma gap was stark.

But it was the way the two men hit it off personally, avidly discussing the new baseball season at the Star Diner afterward, that stuck most with the evening's organizers. A local Democratic party figure would remember Nixon and Kennedy as two "young fellows whom you could like" who showed what he took to be a "genuine friendliness."

Boarding the *Capital Limited* for home at midnight, the two ex-navy officers, the one who had gone to Harvard, the other who would have loved to, drew straws for the lower berth. Nixon won. Then, as the train rolled on toward Washington, the two spent the early-morning hours talking about their true interest, foreign policy, especially the rising standoff with the Soviets in Europe, which Bernard Baruch had just christened the "cold war."

ON the first day of May, Jack Kennedy went Red hunting. Education and Labor panelist Charles Kersten, who had helped Nixon get a grip on the issue of Communist subversion, was probing a suspicious 1941 strike against a huge defense plant in his Milwaukee district. The shutdown had occurred during the months prior to Hitler's invasion of Russia, when Joseph Stalin still enjoyed a nonaggression pact with Nazi Germany. Evidence tied the strike, which interrupted the flow of supplies to the U.S. Navy, to the plant's union leadership, which was believed to be taking orders from Moscow.

The witnesses before the Education and Labor Committee were Harold Christoffel and Robert Buse, both Communist party members, both leaders of the union that struck the Milwaukee defense plant in 1941 at a time when Soviet Russia was allied with Hitler.

"Would you call Russia a democracy?" Kennedy asked Buse, one of the suspect union's Communist leaders.

"I would not know. I do not think so."

Kennedy pressed. "I think I would like to inform you on what I believe to be the main difference between socialism in England and socialism in Russia: They have a freedom of opposition which they do not have in Russia," Kennedy zeroed in. "Do you think that is important?"

"I would not know if they have any opposition in Russia," Buse answered.

"Well, I do not think you are equipped to tell whether a member of your union is a Communist if you do not know any of the answers to any of the things that I have asked you."

At a later session, Kennedy went after Buse again. Why, he taunted the Local 248 leader, did the Wisconsin edition of the *CIO News* oppose "Roosevelt's War Program" prior to Hitler's invasion of Russia, then immediately thereafter run a banner headline "All Aid to Britain, Soviet Union"?

Kennedy had tougher evidence of the two men's collaboration with Moscow. Louis Budenz, the former Communist who had identified Gerhart Eisler, now testified to the committee that the 1941 strike of the Milwaukee plant was part of a "snowballing" of Communist-rigged strikes aimed at crippling the defense buildup. Budenz said that Buse and Christoffel were lying, that the American party was just a "fifth column" taking orders from Moscow. As Kennedy moved that the committee cite Christoffel for perjury, Kersten compared his young colleague's attack on the American Communist party to the opening shots of the Minutemen at Lexington and Concord. Christoffel was indicted, convicted, and given a five-year prison sentence. He later won an appeal to the Supreme Court on grounds that a quorum was absent the day of the perjury motion. Kennedy expressed his anger on the House floor. "What a travesty that a Communist witness testifies un-truthfully before a recognized committee of the House and then escapes the consequences of perjury by a technical claim that a specified number of congressmen were not present at a particular moment." Christoffel was later retried, convicted, and imprisoned.

THAT same month, Congress approved President Truman's call for Greek and Turkish aid, allotting additional money to help China's Chiang Kai-shek resist the Communist forces of Mao Tse-tung. Nixon and Kennedy both voted with the majority.

In June, Secretary of State George C. Marshall used the occa-sion of a Harvard commencement address to unveil an American escalation in the postwar battle between East and West: a massive plan for the economic reconstruction of war-torn Europe. Joseph Kennedy, Sr., thought it a terrible idea. It would be far shrewder, he calculated, to let the Communists grab Europe, creating eco-nomic chaos and thus greater opportunities for American business down the road. His son disagreed, having become an enthusiastic supporter of the Marshall Plan.

To promote the grand U.S. economic scheme, a bipartisan fact-finding delegation was dispatched to Europe. Led by Cong. Chris-tian Herter of Massachusetts, its mission was to verify the need for massive U.S. economic intervention. Nixon was named the committee's youngest member. He had won his spot with a hard sell in his isolationist district for the earlier Greek and Turkish aid bill. The trip, which was the Californian's first ever to Europe, would open his eyes to the world stage. "I think his whole life ambition in foreign policy started when he was on the Herter Committee as a young congressman," recalled Herb Klein, still with the *Alhambra Post Advocate*, who interviewed Nixon on his return home, where a poll showed three-fourths of Twelfth Dis-trict voters opposed to the Marshall Plan. An undeterred Nixon launched an ambitious speaking tour on its behalf.

Jack Kennedy, along with Charles Kersten, had cooked up a European junket of his own that summer. However, on a side trip to his ancestral home in Ireland, Kennedy fell desperately ill. A London doctor diagnosed his condition as Addison's disease, a failure of the adrenal glands that can prove fatal. On Kennedy's return to New York aboard the *Queen Elizabeth*, he was given the last rites of the church. Like so many others, Nixon had no clue as to the seriousness of the affliction that weakened his colleague's physique and yellowed his skin. That was something the fun-loving Kennedy let no one know.

As the Republican prepared to embark for Europe on the *Queen Mary*, the other famed British luxury liner, Nixon learned from secretary Dorothy Cox that his Massachusetts friend, who often stopped by the office for chats, had left a note for him. It contained the addresses of his sister and several other women to look up in Paris. Ms. Cox recounted the episode. "I don't think Mr. Nixon even took the numbers with him! He was far too embarrassed."

Chapter Three

While Kennedy Slept

Cong. Richard Nixon led a Dagwood Bumstead existence, a husband and father commuting each evening across the Potomac River to a Virginia subdivision known as Park Fairfax and described by his eldest daughter, Tricia, as "one of a row of identical duplexes teeming with small children and dogs." Jack Kennedy, ensconced in tony Georgetown, basked in a princely life, attended by a housekeeper, Margaret Ambrose, and a valet, George Thomas, who delivered a home-cooked hot lunch to his Capitol office each day. Press secretary Billy Sutton, with his own room tucked away on the top floor of 1528 Thirty-first Street, was Kennedy's comic in residence, "the firecracker." When Kennedy held receptions for his colleagues, including Nixon, his sister Eunice shared the host duties. More often, the comfortable town house was a base for its tenant's energetic romantic life. Sutton called the Thirty-first Street address a "Hollywood Hotel" for actress Gene Tierney and a regular stream of less famous beauties. "Thinking about girls is what kept Jack alive," Sutton explained.

For Jack Kennedy, staying alive was a serious concern. He managed the sweet life of the young bachelor despite his bad back, which often had him on crutches, and Addison's disease, which cast doubt over his longer-run prospects. "I sometimes wondered," Sutton recalled, "if he would make it, because I noticed physical changes and chemical changes in him: his complexion, his walk, his legs, his back." "Emaciated!" is how Miami congressman George Smathers remembers his frail 1946 classmate. "In your wildest dreams you'd never have guessed he would become president." Smathers, who had gotten to know Jack's father during the tycoon's frequent outings to Hialeah racetrack, recounts the hardship the young Kennedy experienced simply getting to the House floor. "Every time there was a roll call, he'd have to come over on his crutches." Smathers, a hall mate of Kennedy's, would stop by his colleague's office to help him on his painful journey across Independence Avenue to the Capitol.

Kennedy was "deeply preoccupied by death in those days," talking endlessly to Smathers on a Florida fishing trip about the best ways to die. He decided that drowning would be okay if you lost consciousness. "Quick"—that was the most important thing. "The point is, you've got to live every day like it's your last day on earth," he told him. "That's what I'm doing." What he didn't tell Smathers is that this same *carpe diem* philosophy explained their social partnership. "I love Smathers," Kennedy would say. "He doesn't give a damn!" Kennedy knew life's fragility. He had already lost his older brother, Joe, in a World War II bombing mission. In the spring of 1948, when he got word that his sister Kathleen had been killed in a plane crash, he just sat silently listening to the phonograph.

After his own brush with death, Kennedy maintained his easy-going approach to his congressional duties, which included bolting Capitol Hill on a Thursday or Friday for the weekend, dispatching orders over his shoulder as he disappeared in the direction of New York or Palm Beach. "You'll just have to work a little harder," he instructed Mary Davis when his secretary complained of the workload.

Congressman Kennedy's love of fun was not limited to his off-duty hours. Ted Reardon, who had thrown passes to his older brother, Joe, as a Harvard quarterback, now spent an impressive amount of office time throwing the football back and forth to

Jack. Thanks to Billy Sutton, a world-class mimic, the congressman in room 322 of the Old House Office Building was also able to pull off the occasional stunt worthy of his Muckers past. One day, Congressman Smathers was told he had a phone call from Vito Marcantonio. "I'm coming to your district," the caller said. "I would like to have you . . . I would like to have you introduce me."

Smathers, whose political ambitions depended on the archconservative voters of segregationist Florida, was terrified. "I came up with some excuse," he said, laughing, decades later, "said I had something to do . . . had to go to a funeral." It didn't work. As hard as he tried, Smathers couldn't shake what he now took as the New Yorker's pushy determination to be seen with the local congressman in Florida. Growing desperate, Smathers sought out Marcantonio at the next vote. Taking a seat next to the New Yorker, he began making excuses to a colleague who seemed to have no earthly idea what he was talking about. Only after several punishing moments of this did Smathers notice his pal Jack Kennedy, across the House floor, convulsed in laughter. It hadn't, of course, been Marcantonio on the phone, but Billy Sutton.

CONGRESSMAN Nixon had no time for such amusements. If Jack Kennedy was the class of 1946's charmer, Dick Nixon was its hardest worker. While Kennedy could use a fellow member of Congress like Vito Marcantonio as the prop in a practical joke, Nixon took everything and everyone on Capitol Hill seriously. "He was the most calculating man I ever knew," Smathers recalled. Just as the navy officer had scripted his lines for the Committee of 100, the freshman congressman now practiced the rituals of bonhomie to sell himself to colleagues. With Richard Nixon, every relationship was a well-rehearsed business relationship.

His dealings with the press were a prime example. UPI's George Reedy credits the freshman Californian with being the only member of HUAC whom reporters could trust for information. "Nixon was always supplying us with the red meat." Such reliability failed, however, to win Nixon much regard. "No newspaperman had any reason to complain about his relations with Nixon, and yet he was not popular with them. You didn't have to be around him very long without realizing that he was a formidable but also highly programmed man," Reedy recalled. "I had the impression he would even practice his inflection when he said, 'Hello.' "

Reedy remembered vividly his first close exposure to the Republican up-and-comer. It was at a small cocktail reception that Nixon had organized in his cramped "Attic" office in the Old House Office Building's fifth floor for the quartet of wire-service reporters covering HUAC. The host had made a point to brief himself on each guest beforehand, even to memorize each journalist's favorite drink. "Hi, George!" he greeted Reedy, whom he had never met, as the UPI reporter entered the suite. Reedy figured Nixon was trying to be one of the boys.

Bill Arnold, who ran Nixon's office in those early days, left behind this Dickensian portrait of his employer.

Mr. Nixon was always a restless soul carrying out his duties. He pushed himself hard, as all who worked for him were supposed to do. He never left his office to get to the airport or railroad station until the last possible moment, for fear of having to sit around and wait at a terminal. It was often my responsibility to drive him to such places and I always cautioned that we were going to miss a plane or train some time. One day this happened as we were attempting to cross the Potomac on the 14th Street drawbridge, which opened while we were en route to the airport to permit a boat to pass beneath. Sure enough, we missed the plane. But did we sit around and wait for the next one? We did not; instead we went back to the office to put in another hour's work.

By March 1948, Nixon's hard work earned him his first national publicity. When HUAC took up a bill to outlaw the Communist party, Nixon was ready with a substitute. Instead of banning Communists, the Nixon bill required party members to register with the government. It was the Nixon version that passed the House. The vote was 319–58. Still a freshman, he had succeeded in passing a measure Jerry Voorhis, the man he had tarred as a Communist dupe, introduced eight years earlier. In a further irony, the Nixon bill became the focus of a heated, misinformed, national radio debate between Minnesota's Harold Stassen and New York governor Thomas E. Dewey, the top candidates for the 1948 Republican presidential nomination. With 30 million listeners following his argument, Stassen applauded and Dewey opposed Nixon's bill for outlawing the Communist party, both debaters oblivious to the fact that the measure, a later version of which would be tied up in the courts for years, only required Communist party members to register.

By the summer of 1948, the national chill toward the Soviet Union had reached deep-freeze levels. First came the Communist coup in Czechoslovakia. The same country that had been sacrificed so cowardly to Hitler before the war was now firmly captive to Joseph Stalin. For daring to promote Czech participation in the Marshall Plan, Foreign Minister Jan Masaryk was thrown from a window to his death. In June, Communist East Germans cut off Western access to Berlin, requiring a three-month airlift by American planes before Moscow finally backed off. That same month, hard-liner Dick Nixon took advantage of California state law to enter both party primaries. Winning the Democratic nomination as well as that of his own party for a second term, he could ignore the November election and concentrate on matters in Washington. At thirty-five, Nixon was about to become America's most celebrated Communist-catcher.

ON August 3, 1948, a chubby, shabbily dressed senior editor from *Time* magazine named Whittaker Chambers made a stunning accusation to HUAC. He described having been a member of the Communist underground in the 1930s, of attending party meetings with figures now prominent in labor and government. He told of reporting these activities to Assistant Secretary of State Adolf Berle in 1939, at a time when Stalin was carving up Poland with Adolf Hitler. One of those Chambers identified was diplomat Alger Hiss, the State Department star who had been with Roosevelt at Yalta and later served as Secretary-General of the founding UN conference in San Francisco. Chambers accused Hiss of being an active Communist agent whose assignment was to infiltrate the

U.S. government and carry out espionage for the Soviet Union. Especially angering Nixon was what appeared to be the arrogant decision by the New Deal elite to protect its protégé. The cover-up demanded an investigation.

Two days later, an eager Alger Hiss testified before HUAC. Tall, slender, and elegantly dressed, the Harvard-trained lawyer stood before less-than-reputable HUAC as a member of the Washington elite. His defense was generously elaborate.

I am not and never have been a member of the Communist party. I do not and never have adhered to the tenets of the Communist party. I am not and never have been a member of any Communist-front organization. I have never followed the Communist party line, directly or indirectly. To the best of my knowledge, none of my friends is a Communist. To the best of my knowledge I never heard of Whittaker Chambers until 1947, when two representatives of the Federal Bureau of Investigation asked me if I knew him. I said I did not know Chambers. So far as I know, I have never laid eyes on him, and I should like to have the opportunity to do so.

A loud smack of applause rocked the room. Members of the committee suddenly were terrified that they had made a fatal mistake in airing Chambers's charges. How could anyone have believed such an unkempt fellow's denunciation of this distinguished man who sat before them? Instinctively, the room sided with the Franklin over the Orthogonian, except for Richard Nixon. He found Hiss's manner to be "rather insolent." When Nixon referred in passing to the witness having studied law at Harvard, Hiss took aim: "I understand yours was Whittier," he replied, sneering at the grocer's son.

George Reedy ran into the Californian that evening. "Nixon had a transcript of the Hiss testimony with him and went over it with me point by point." Nixon discovered that testimony which sounded hard, sharp, and categorical was nothing of the kind. All of Hiss's denials, including those about not knowing Chambers, had been hedged. It was always "to the best of my knowledge." Overcoming his colleagues' nervousness, Nixon took a HUAC subcommittee to New York to hear what Whittaker Chambers had to say now.

What Chambers had to say was spectacular. In place of the vague testimony of four days earlier, he offered a wealth of convincing detail about his relationship with Alger Hiss. He said that Hiss had contributed a car to the Communist party, had given him use of an apartment. Even more memorably, he recounted a bird-watching outing along the Potomac River during which Hiss had spotted a rare prothonotary warbler.

Nixon wanted further convincing. Three times he drove to Chambers's Maryland farm that week trying to work through his incredulity that the American diplomat who stood next to the president at Yalta had been a Communist agent. What finally convinced him was a small but telling detail. Chambers remembered that Hiss's wife, Priscilla, a Quaker, like both Nixon and Chambers himself, spoke in the "plain" language when alone with her husband. Nixon, raised in a family that also used "thee" and "thou" at home, recognized that only a close friend of the Hiss family would know such a thing. And if Hiss and Chambers knew each other, Hiss had been lying from the outset. "If the American people understood the real character of Alger Hiss," Nixon told Chambers one day at the barn, "they would boil him in oil."

Nixon wanted very much to expose that character. He showed the transcripts of Chambers's latest testimony to William Rogers, a Senate aide he had befriended, to Bert Andrews of the *New York Herald Tribune*, finally to John Foster Dulles and his brother Allen, top foreign policy advisers to Republican presidential candidate Dewey. All agreed he should keep up the fight.

On August 16, HUAC called Hiss to testify a second time. Sensing that the committee was closing in on him, he mentioned the name "George Crosley," whom he described as a freelance writer he once let stay in his home; he had also lent this "Crosley" a car, a Model A Ford. His denial of knowing Chambers passed within minutes from unconvincing to incredible when he confirmed his sighting of that prothonotary warbler along the Potomac. "Beautiful yellow head, a gorgeous bird!" he exclaimed.

However, when Nixon brought Hiss face-to-face with Chambers in New York's Commodore Hotel, Hiss again denied knowing the man. When Hiss challenged Chambers to reconcile his claim to have spent time in Hiss's apartment with a denial that he had paid rent, the witness confronted him starkly. "Alger, I was a Communist, and you were a Communist." At this, Hiss abruptly declared that the man before him was "George Crosley." "If he had lost both eyes and taken his nose off, I would be sure!" After being quizzed about Whittaker Chambers by the FBI since the year before, after having his career jeopardized by allegations of Communist activity, after signing a letter specifically denying any relation with Chambers, even after being confronted with his pictures, Hiss was now saying that, yes, he knew this fellow, but under another name.

On August 25, Chambers and Hiss faced each other in a public hearing. Thanks to tenacious research, Nixon had with him a copy of a D.C. Department of Motor Vehicles certificate proving Chambers's assertion that the accused had handed over a car to the party cause. Confronted with the document, Hiss became flustered. "I gave Crosley," he began, "according to my best recollection—"

Nixon pounced. "I don't want to interrupt you on that 'to the best of my recollection,' but you certainly can testify 'yes' or 'no' as to whether you gave Crosley a car. How many cars have you given away in your life, Mr. Hiss?" Laughter rocked the HUAC chamber. Nearly two hundred times Hiss would use the phrase "according to my best recollection."

Chambers, the Orthogonian, was now the convincing witness. "The story has spread that in testifying against Mr. Hiss I am working out some old grudge or motives of revenge or hatred. I do not hate Mr. Hiss. We were close friends, but we are caught in a tragedy of history. Mr. Hiss represents the concealed enemy against which we are all fighting and I am fighting."

Two days later, Chambers met Hiss's challenge to make his accusation outside of Congress, thus exposing himself to a libel suit. "Alger Hiss was a Communist and may still be," he said on *Meet the Press*. Later, the witness produced sixty-five documents, some of them in Hiss's own handwriting, that Chambers said Hiss had stolen from the State Department. Chambers had hid the microfilm of the documents in a hollowed-out pumpkin at his

Maryland farm. Nixon arranged for news photographers to take his picture studying the "Pumpkin Papers" with a magnifying glass. No newspaper spoiled the picture by noting that microfilm cannot be read that way.

For Nixon, there would be one last moment of doubt when word came that the Kodak film on which the State Department documents had been copied was not produced until 1945, years after the espionage was said to have been committed. "Oh, my god!" he exclaimed. "This is the end of my political career." Some torturous minutes later, the Kodak official called back to say he'd been wrong, a message that led Nixon and his chief counsel to begin waltzing around the room.

The most powerful evidence that the documents had actually been written on Mrs. Hiss's own typewriter would come later. In December the man who had presided at the founding UN conference was indicted on two counts of perjury: that he had lied to Congress about not stealing State Department documents and about not knowing Whittaker Chambers. The statute of limitations protected Alger Hiss from an espionage charge.

In beating Hiss, Nixon had also beaten the media. "None of us wanted him to be guilty," UPI's Reedy admitted. "We didn't want that committee to be right about anything. It was a committee that really made you cringe, it was so bad." At thirty-five, in his second year in Congress, Richard Nixon, the man who led the charge against the now-discredited Franklin, was now what he would remain for the next half century—a household name.

IF Nixon was at the center of the action for those early postwar years, Kennedy was, with the exception of his perjury motion against Harold Christoffel, out of it. He used what good health he had to enjoy himself. Yet beneath the fop's exterior lay something more tantalizing. "I'm going to debate Norman Thomas at the Harvard Law School," Kennedy told Mark Dalton on the telephone one day, "and I would like you to come up. I want to run some things by you." Dalton arrived at his friend's Boston apartment to find the congressman busy in his living room. "There was Kennedy sitting on the sofa. There were two or three books open there and six or seven books on the floor opened. Each one had been written by Norman Thomas."

On a rare occasion, Kennedy would invest the same zeal in his congressional work. Nor were his close aides the only people privy to Kennedy's furtive commitment to homework. Ted Reardon recalled an issue before the Education and Labor panel that triggered a sudden passion in his boss. "I'm going to dig into this thing," Kennedy informed his top aide, then headed down to the National Archives himself to retrieve the desired information. Many years afterward, Reardon would describe what happened next: "At the hearing, the thing I remember is when Jack started to talk, Dicky Boy sort of looked at him . . . with a look between awe and respect and fear."

CHAPTER
FOUR

The Castle or
the Outhouse!

FROM the time they arrived in the 435-member U.S. House of Representatives, Dick Nixon and Jack Kennedy shared a common ambition: escape. They and their 1946 classmate George Smathers engaged in regular one-upmanship over who would be the first to leave the rambunctious House and move up in status to the "world's most exclusive club."

Buoyed by the acclaim he had won in the Hiss case and worried the glow of fame would fade, Nixon decided to make his move in the summer of 1949. Quietly, he sought the advance backing of the *Los Angeles Times*, which had supported his first congressional race. But the connection to Hiss continued to pose a serious risk, for there remained the chance that the ex-diplomat might still be exonerated. This outcome became all too plausible when Hiss's perjury trial in New York ended that summer with a hung jury: eight for conviction, four for acquittal. Should the second trial yield a split jury or, worse yet, an acquittal, Nixon's political stock would plummet. Nervous about the outcome, the California congressman called for the appointment of a "special prosecutor," a step that, while never taken, would offer retrospective irony during a future, far wider probe of official misconduct.

As he awaited the results of the second trial, outside events made the country's most celebrated Communist hunter an even hotter political property. In September, President Truman stunned the country with news that the Soviet Union had detonated an atom bomb. Suddenly, Americans looked out beyond their border to a troubled world in which they no longer held a monopoly on the awesome weapon. The news from China that month added to the dark foreboding: Mao Tse-tung declared Communist sovereignty over the entire Chinese mainland, trapping America's World War II ally Chiang Kai-shek into what appeared permanent exile on the island of Formosa.

Reaction to the Asian situation was swift and angry even within Truman's own party. "The responsibility for the failure of our foreign policy in the Far East rests squarely with the White House and the Department of State," Cong. John F. Kennedy declared on the House floor in January 1949. "So concerned were our diplomats . . . with the imperfection of the democratic system of China after twenty years of war and the tales of corruption in high places that they lost sight of our tremendous stake in non-Communist China." The Truman policy "of vacillation, uncertainty, and confusion had reaped the whirlwind." The failure of the president and the State Department had left it to Congress to stop "the onrushing tide of communism from engulfing all of Asia," Kennedy said.

Against the darkening backdrop, Richard Nixon now drew the perfect cold war rival, one more vulnerable than Jerry Voorhis had been four years earlier. Cong. Helen Gahagan Douglas, actress-wife of Hollywood star Melvyn Douglas, close friend of the Roosevelts, and secret lover of that rising Texas star Sen. Lyndon Johnson, hoped to unseat Democratic senator Sheridan Downey in 1950. Unfortunately for her prospects, Mrs. Douglas had voted against President Truman's urgent call to stop the Communist advance in Europe through military aid to Greece and Turkey. Nixon, declaring his own candidacy in November, now charged that the Democratic party had been "captured and is completely controlled by a group of ruthless, cynical seekers of power and committed to policies and principles completely foreign to those of its founders. Call it planned economy, the Fair Deal, or social welfare—but it is the same old socialist baloney, any way you slice it!" "Socialist" would be one of the least offensive labels he would pin on Mrs. Douglas.

Nixon's luck held. In January 1950 a New York jury found Alger Hiss guilty of perjury in denying he had committed espionage for the Soviet Union. His chief congressional prosecutor now had validation of his charge that the whole New Deal establishment, including President Truman, had acted covertly to protect one of their own. "This conspiracy would have come to light long since had there not been a definite effort on the part of certain high officials in two administrations to keep the public from knowing the facts," he said in a lengthy speech on the House floor. Giving credibility to the charges of a cover-up was Secretary of State Dean Acheson's own steadfastness toward his convicted friend: "I do not intend to turn my back on Alger Hiss." Nixon called Acheson's remark "disgusting." The secretary of state suffered, he said, from "a form of pink eye toward the Communist threat in the United States."

Overnight, the issue of Communist subversion in the U.S. government was transformed from an indictment to a conviction. Joseph R. McCarthy, a heavy-drinking, politically desperate senator from Wisconsin, now escalated the anti-Communist probe from a question of *whether* there were fifth columnists in Washington to *how many* there were. Needing something to say to a Lincoln Day group of Republican women in Wheeling, West Virginia, McCarthy decided to crib from Nixon's speech in the *Congressional Record*. "The great lesson which should be learned from the Hiss case," the California congressman had told the House, "is that we are not just dealing with espionage agents who get thirty pieces of silver to obtain the blueprint of a new weapon . . . but a far more sinister type of activity, because it permits the enemy to guide and shape our policy." McCarthy stole this practically verbatim. "One thing to remember in discussing the Communists is that we are not dealing with spies who get thirty pieces of silver to steal the blueprint of a new weapon. We are dealing with a far more sinister type of activity because it permits the enemy to guide and shape our policy." Having plagiarized Nixon's words, the Wisconsin senator cloned the Hiss case into hundreds of other "cases." Whereas Nixon had found one Communist in the State Department, McCarthy now spoke of 205. Whereas Nixon had begun and ended his search with a single name, that of Alger Hiss, this medicine showman from Wisconsin was now pitching something more intoxicating: a *list*. Whereas Nixon, the old navy poker player, had held his stakes to risk all on Alger Hiss, McCarthy would bet on every hand. For four years the bluff worked.

NIXON's 1950 run for the Senate would exploit a deep left-right division in the Democratic party. When Senator Downey quit the race citing health reasons, Mrs. Douglas denounced Downey's explanation as a "cheap gimmick." He was dropping out, she charged, because he couldn't take the heat. With the Downey-Douglas rivalry festering, another Democratic candidate emerged on the right. Manchester Boddy, conservative editor of the *Los Angeles Daily News*, declared his wish to save California and the country from the Douglas campaign, which he called "a statewide conspiracy on the part of a small, subversive clique of red hots to capture, through stealth and cunning, the nerve centers of our Democratic party." He wasn't finished. "Mrs. Douglas gave aid and comfort to Soviet tyranny by voting against aid to both Greece and Turkey." Now the clincher: Helen Douglas had a "consistent policy of voting along with the notorious radical *Vito Marcantonio!*"

The Harlem congressman relished his West Coast notoriety. Hearing that the conservative Boddy had tied his voting record to that of Mrs. Douglas, he sent word to Nixon that it might be a "good idea" for him to do the same. "Tell Nicky to get on this thing!" he said, joining in the gang assault on the party colleague he delicately dubbed a "bitch."

An even more vicious Democratic primary was taking place in Florida, pitting veteran senator Claude Pepper, a New Deal liberal, against George Smathers in a contest to be forever known as the "Red Pepper" campaign. Pepper's vulnerability, which Smathers brutally exploited, lay in his having continued to back the Soviet Union after World War II was over. Like Mrs. Douglas, he had opposed Truman's 1947 call for aid to Greece and Turkey. He had added injury to insult by opposing his nomination in 1948. "Do me a favor," Truman instructed Smathers one day over the phone. "I want you to beat that S.O.B. Senator Pepper."

Smathers obliged with gusto. "Florida will not allow herself to become entangled in the spiraling web of the Red network," he said in announcing his challenge. "The people of our state will no longer tolerate advocates of treason." The Smathers knockout punch was a leaflet, distributed on primary eve, headlined "The Red Record of Claude Pepper." "I will never forget the feeling of revulsion that gripped me," Pepper recounted four decades later, "as my eyes fell on the cover, which was a dreadful, snaggle-tooth picture of me. I had never laid claim to being handsome, but this photograph was just indescribably ugly, monstrous, inhuman. That people who fancied themselves decent Americans would resort to such tactics to win an election defies belief to this day." But if Claude Pepper didn't like such cutthroat tactics, another Senate aspirant did. "Nixon Jubilant!" the *Los Angeles Herald Examiner* declared. "How'd you do it?" Richard Nixon quizzed Smathers on his Red Pepper tactics. Helen Douglas would soon be the "Pink Lady."

One day that summer, Jack Kennedy stopped by Nixon's office for a chat, as he often did in those early years. What made the visit different was the $1,000 he brought with him from his father. Learning that Nixon wasn't in, Kennedy handed the contribution to staffer Bill Arnold. "He explained that the check should be used in Nixon's campaign for senator, that its intention was due partly to admiration for Nixon and partly to a preference for Congressman Nixon over Congresswoman Douglas's pursuit of the senatorship." According to a secretary, Nixon was "flabbergasted." "Isn't this something," he said to aide Pat Hillings. "Isn't this something!" A Democrat had crossed the political aisle to help a Republican.

For Nixon, the breaks kept coming. Back in 1947, the *New York Daily Worker* had called Congresswoman Douglas "one of the Heroes of the 80th Congress." Also high on the list, predictably, was New York's own Vito Marcantonio. By January 1950, another Communist organ, the *Daily People's World,* was calling Nixon "The Man to Beat" in the California race. The Communist editors were right. Thanks to their fellow party members on the other side of the world, the California cold warrior would soon be invincible. In June, Communist North Korea attacked South Korea. Five days later, President Truman dispatched American troops. Two weeks after that, Americans Julius and Ethel Rosenberg were charged with stealing atomic secrets for the Soviet Union. These stories riveted the nation and brought with them a bone-chilling reassessment of Moscow's intentions. In an internal White House directive, Truman described the Soviet Union as "animated by a new fanatic faith, antithetical to our own, [that] seeks to impose its absolute authority over the rest of the world."

Foolishly, Helen Douglas felt the need to hit the Red button first, issuing a campaign document labeled "The Big Lie" that lambasted Nixon for having "voted with Representative Marcantonio against aid to Korea." In all, it cited five times where Nixon and the Harlem leftist had voted together. "On every key vote Nixon stood with party-liner Marcantonio against America in its fight to defeat Communism." Mrs. Douglas called Nixon and the other Republicans in the class of 1946 a "backwash of young men in dark suits," a reference to Mussolini's Fascists.

Murray Chotiner, a master at this game, struck back. "How can Helen Douglas, capable actress that she is, take up so strange a role as foe of communism? And why does she when she has so deservedly earned the title of 'the Pink Lady'?"

Nixon's own campaign now took to the road. He rode up and down California in a wood-paneled Ford station wagon; his mission: to alert the townsfolk to the threat posed by Helen Gahagan Douglas. As the Woody arrived on the main drag of each hamlet, a loudspeaker would blare out "If I Knew You Were Comin' I'd a Baked a Cake." Advance man Ace Anderson, cigar in mouth, would urge passersby to gather around and hear Dick Nixon, candidate for the U.S. Senate. When a crowd had gathered, Ace would yell into the Woody, "Okay, Dick, you can get out now." Nixon would emerge, take his place on the car's roof, and tell voters why it was imperative that they now send him to an even bigger job in Washington. At every stop, his favorite topic was Alger Hiss—how he had unmasked him, how the Democrats had tried to cover up Hiss's perfidies.

The Douglas campaign was able to enjoy a few small victories that fall. A student at the University of California at Santa Barbara named Richard Tuck managed to get himself named a Nixon advance man. His assignment was to prepare a campus location where the congressman would address the student body. The basic strategy in advancing such campaign events is to rent a small room, saturate the campus with posters, blast the local airwaves with radio spots, then pack as large a number of students as possible into the smallest space, thereby creating the greatest possible excitement about the visit. A Douglas mole, Tuck gleefully did the opposite, renting a cavernous room, then inviting practically no one to a speech he billed as a discussion on "the International Monetary Fund." Nixon gave, according to Tuck's gleeful report, "one of the most disjointed speeches I ever heard." On leaving the giant empty hall, Nixon rendered his decree. "Tuck, you've made your last advance!"

Nixon, no stranger to the game, worked his own psychological tricks. Each time he encountered Mrs. Douglas on the stump, he executed the same velvet-gloved jab, always with a look of sadness. "It's awfully hard on a woman, this campaigning."

But Nixon refused to trust either the course of events or the sentiments of the voter. He called his opponent worse than a bad risk for the task of fighting communism: Far from being the solution to the Communist challenge, she was part of the problem. "During the past six years she has been in Congress, she consistently supported the State Department's policy of appeasing Communists in Asia, which finally resulted in the Korean War." Then his attacks took an intimate turn. "She's pink right down to her underwear." Responding in kind, Mrs. Douglas threw one nickname after another at her rival—"Pipsqueak," "Peewee"—finally finding one that stuck: "Tricky Dicky!"

As he had four years earlier, Nixon made a practice of sending out spies. He wanted to know precisely what his opponent was saying about him. After hearing one Douglas speech in northern California, aide Bill Arnold returned with an account of her remarks he recalled as "somewhat unflattering to Nixon." "Did she say that?" Nixon erupted. "Why, I'll castrate her!" Advised as to the impossibility of such a punishment in a woman's case, Nixon was undeterred. "I don't care," he stammered, "I'll do it anyway!" To sew up his victory, Nixon resorted to the nastiest trick of the campaign, the infamous "Pink Sheet," which listed more than three hundred times that Mrs. Douglas had voted with the New York pariah Vito Marcantonio. The "Douglas-Marcantonio Axis," the headline would read. It was a California version of "The Red Record of Claude Pepper."

The election, if not decided already by the Korean War, was to move further in Nixon's direction when Communist Chinese troops attacked U.S. troops in Korea the last week of October. Nixon demanded that Mrs. Douglas state categorically whether she supported letting Red China into the United Nations. When she refused to give a categorical "No," Nixon went in for the kill. "This is the last straw. I know my opponent was committed to the State Department policy of appeasement towards Communism in the Far East, but I never dreamed she would stick to it even after we were *attacked!*"

Just before the election, the Nixon campaign pulled a final coup. It involved the state's most prominent Republican governor, Earl Warren. Despite his loss as Thomas E. Dewey's running mate in 1948, Warren retained great prestige, which he was unwilling to dilute by endorsing the man with whom he shared the top of the 1950 GOP ballot, Richard Nixon. Congresswoman Douglas was respecting his neutrality by refusing to back the Democratic candidate for governor, James Roosevelt.

To smash the Douglas-Warren neutrality pact, the Nixon campaign detailed an operative to query Mrs. Douglas at each of her press conferences whether she backed Roosevelt. Having exhausted her restraint, Douglas let fly with her endorsement: "I hope and pray he will be the next governor, and he will be if the Democrats vote for the Democratic ticket!" Ecstatic, the Nixon camp passed the Douglas remark to a reporter covering Warren. After first remaining aloof, the governor now exposed his position. "In view of her statement, I might ask her how she expects I will vote when I mark my ballot for the United States senator next Tuesday?" Murray Chotiner made it official. "Every voter in California who reads her statement will realize that Earl Warren intends to mark his ballot for Dick Nixon on election day."

It worked, but at a high price. Nixon won by 600,000 votes but in the process incurred a brutal reputation and a legion of enduring enemies. Once again, his take-no-prisoners campaign methods made future rivals all that more determined not to be taken alive.

One Democrat remained in Dick Nixon's corner. In a postelection meeting with a Harvard graduate seminar, Jack Kennedy told the students how pleased he was that Richard Nixon had won the California Senate race. Helen Douglas was "not the sort of person he'd like working with on committees," he explained. Kennedy repeated the judgment in a letter to Paul Fay, telling his navy buddy to look up his fellow Californian, whom he described as "an outstanding guy [who] has the opportunity to go all the way."

To give California's new senator a jump on his job, Sheridan Downey resigned his seat right after election day. This made Richard Nixon, at thirty-seven the youngest member of the Senate, the first to break the ribbon in his race with Smathers and Kennedy for who would precede the other two in the move up from the House. In a strange twist, one of Nixon's first exploits as a U.S. senator was protecting a famous newsman from being beaten up by a drunk. The victim was the muckraker Drew Pearson; the soused assailant was that reckless hunter of Communist subversives Sen. Joseph R. McCarthy. "Let a good Quaker stop this fight," Nixon told the two as he forced himself between McCarthy and the man he was madly punching in the stomach at the checkroom of Washington's Sulgrave Club. When the referee got McCarthy outside, he realized that his Wisconsin colleague had forgotten where he had parked his car. Dutifully, Nixon spent a half hour searching the Dupont Circle area until he found it.

Both Richard Nixon and Jack Kennedy had been giving wide latitude to McCarthy's dizzying assault on domestic communism. One reason was that they liked him personally. Another was that they disliked his enemies. Nixon shared McCarthy's resentment of the New Deal and foreign-service elite. Kennedy enjoyed his contempt for them. The Wisconsin senator "may have something," Kennedy said in the same off-the-record Harvard seminar during which he had cheered Nixon's Senate win. He felt a kinship with his loutish fellow Irishman, whom his sister Pat had dated, his father had befriended and defended, and whose soul contained a powerful strain of the Mucker. Nixon, on the other hand, liked McCarthy for the basic reason that the social elite of Georgetown despised him.

But the sympathy toward McCarthy shared by both men owed as much to ideology as it did to any personal factors. On the most vital issue of post–World War II American politics—communism—they knew which side they were on. Those who pretended neutrality or, worse yet, cast a blind eye to the struggle were worthy of neither power nor respect. Those who, whatever their shortcomings or excesses, fought the enemy were worthy of both. This included Joseph McCarthy. In February 1952, a speaker at an anniversary evening at Kennedy's Harvard club told the gathered alumni how proud he was that their college had never produced "a Joseph McCarthy or an Alger Hiss."

Kennedy jumped to his feet. "How dare you couple the name of a great American patriot with that of a traitor!" Angry, he left the dinner early.

It was hard to find a more committed Cold Warrior in either party than the thirty-four-year-old from Massachusetts. "The political point of the Kennedy speech," the *Haverhill Gazette* remarked after hearing his attack on the Democratic administration's foreign policy in August 1950, "is that the Republicans should try to sign him up for a job with their speaking bureau." Jack Kennedy advocated aid to Franco's Spain, attacked Great Britain for its "trade in blood" with Communist China, and criticized Mississippi congressman Jamie Whitten for daring to push pork-barrel spending at a time when the country faced so great a threat from abroad. "I think we ought to spend money this year only when it has defense implications," Kennedy told his colleagues.

To inform himself about the global threat, Kennedy left in the fall of 1951 for a seven-week tour of the Far East that would include a stop in Hanoi. Arriving in the colonial capital, he could see the weakness of the French position. Whereas its army was fighting for French imperialism, Ho Chi Minh and his Viet Minh army were seen as fighting for Vietnamese independence. The issue was not so much ideology as nationalism. Appearing on *Meet the Press* upon his return, he told moderator Lawrence Spivak that France's only realistic course was for Paris to abandon its colonialist ambitions and build up a nationalist "native army" to fight the "native armies" on the Communist side, an eerie precursor of the later Nixon attempt to "Vietnamize" the struggle.

But the big news of that Sunday broadcast centered on the thirty-four-year-old's own career plans:

Spivak: When I was in Boston last week, I heard a good deal of talk about you. There were many who thought that you would be the Democratic nominee for the senatorship against Henry Cabot Lodge. Are you going to run?
Kennedy: Well, uh, I'd like to go to the Senate. I'm definitely interested in it. I think most of us in the House who came in after the war—some of them have already gone to the Senate, like George Smathers and Nixon and others, and I'm definitely interested in going to the Senate, and I'm seriously considering running.

"I'm going to run!" he exulted to a skeptical George Smathers, who thought Lodge's position impregnable. "I'm going to use the same kind of stuff," pointing to his Florida pal's assault on Claude Pepper. Though still on crutches most of the time, regular cortisone treatments for his Addison's disease had improved Kennedy's overall health. The last thing he wanted now was to be left behind while Nixon and Smathers strode Capitol Hill as U.S. senators. Kennedy had begun to look upon members of the House as "worms." "I'm not going to stay in the House," Kennedy told new aide Larry O'Brien, whom he recruited to organize Massachusetts for him town by town. "It's up or out." His father sized up the risk-laden appeal of a statewide run with greater color. "For the Kennedys, it's either the castle or the outhouse! Nothing in between."

Many Massachusetts voters were anxious for somebody named

Kennedy to finally get the castle. After years of dutiful hat tipping to well-born Protestants, the Irish of Massachusetts were ready to elect an aristocrat of their own. Kennedy gave the Catholic voters the opportunity to elect a senator from among their sons whose polish matched that of the Yankee ruling class. "Kennedy represented a new generation, a new kind of Irish politician," as O'Brien assessed it. "One who was rich and respectable and could do battle with the Lodges and the other Yankee politicians on their own terms."

Like Nixon before him, Kennedy placed great faith in personal appearances. By the end of 1951, the map of Massachusetts on the bedroom wall in the Boston apartment was covered with pins showing the hundreds of towns he had visited. To prepare for the planned bombardment of Lodge, Ted Reardon had begun assembling an inventory of the senator's voting record. This carefully documented file, entitled "Lodge's Dodges," would provide the ammunition for the coming assault on the respected Brahmin rival, a man who had been Jack Kennedy's schoolboy hero. Reardon's loose-leaf book, each page covered in sheer plastic, offered ammunition for a two-front assault on the confident incumbent. It would appeal to the regular Democratic voter by showing Lodge as overly conservative on domestic issues and to anti-Communist conservatives in both parties by painting Lodge as a shirker in the global struggle against Russia and Red China. The approach would prove masterful enough for Kennedy again to use it against another centrist Republican eight years later.

HENRY Cabot Lodge was preoccupied in these latter months of 1951 by a grander enterprise than his own reelection. On a July tour of NATO headquarters in Paris, the senator, who had suspended his political career to fight with Eisenhower's forces in Europe, now urged the man commanding the postwar military alliance to seek the Republican presidential nomination in 1952. The general refused. Lodge ignored the rebuff. On returning home, he took his plea public, telling a *Meet the Press* audience that Ike would make a great president. In October, the *New York Herald Tribune*, for whom Lodge once wrote editorials, declared

Eisenhower the perfect man to lead the nation. A month later, an Ike-for-President group led by New York governor Thomas Dewey named Lodge to manage the campaign. In January, acting on his own authority, Lodge wrote New Hampshire governor Sherman Adams asking that Eisenhower's name be entered in the March Republican presidential primary. Behind the scenes, he won Ike's commitment not to debunk the fledgling effort. Eisenhower didn't and won, defeating the conservative favorite, Ohio's senator Robert Taft, who had been the front-runner for the nomination. The victory in New Hampshire, followed by a huge write-in vote in the Minnesota primary, brought a wave of excitement to the Eisenhower effort. Lodge, who had engineered the drive from the start, told fellow senator Richard Nixon that if he helped bring the California delegation aboard at the national convention in Chicago, the vice presidency could be the prize.

Nixon had ties to both Republican camps, that of the war hero Eisenhower and Taft, favorite of the party's old guard. The California senator's backing of the Greek and Turkish aid bill, and later of the Marshall Plan, marked him as an internationalist in the Eisenhower-Lodge mold. His harsh criticisms of Truman's Far East policies and his success with the Hiss case had made him a hero among Taft conservatives. His problem was Earl Warren. Defeated along with Dewey as the Republican's vice presidential candidate in 1948, the proud California governor was holding to his favorite-son candidacy and, with it, his dreams of a Taft-Ike deadlock that would deliver the nomination to him.

Nixon had other plans. Having not forgotten Warren's aloofness toward his 1946 House and 1950 Senate races, he used his free Senate mailing privilege to survey the state's thousands of Republican precinct workers on who they thought would be "the strongest candidate the Republicans could nominate for president." Ike won. The man called "Nick" in all those wartime poker games saw his chance to raise the stakes. Boarding the California delegation's train to Denver, he spent the rail time to Chicago nudging passengers toward the candidate his poll had shown to be the best man. By the time the train reached Chicago, the California delegates emerged from the station to see buses awaiting them decked out with "Eisenhower for President" banners. Murray Chotiner, as outrageous as ever, had worked his magic.

With Ike headed for victory, only the nomination for vice president remained a mystery. Nixon, meeting *New York Times* photographer George Tames at the Blackstone Hotel, said he thought Lodge himself would get it. What he didn't say is how ready he was to grab the offer should it come. Pat Hillings, the Nixon campaign worker who replaced him in Congress, was in Nixon's suite when the call came. Herbert Brownell, the campaign strategist who would be Eisenhower's attorney general, was on the line. "It's Nixon!" Hillings heard Brownell tell someone at the other end. *"Wake up, Dick! It's you!"* Hillings yelled to his friend. Seven years after Nixon had received the note from Herman Perry in his Baltimore apartment, the men around Eisenhower had found their man. Dick Nixon was to be the vice-presidential running mate of the most grandly popular figure in America. "The general asked if you could come see him right away in his suite," Brownell told him when he got on the line. Dwight Eisenhower, the five-star victor of World War II, wanted Dick Nixon to be his running mate.

Back in Washington, Senator Nixon found a two-page handwritten letter.

Dear Dick:

I was tremendously pleased that the convention selected you for V.P. I was always convinced that you would move ahead to the top —but I never thought it would come this quickly. You were an ideal selection and will bring to the ticket a great deal of strength.

Please give my best to your wife and all kinds of good luck to you.

Cordially,
Jack Kennedy

That same month, the Massachusetts congressman won a prize of a different sort. Three hundred Capitol Hill news correspondents voted him the "handsomest" member of the House. He first heard the news while in the midst of taking a special CBS course in how to use television. It was the opinion of the course's director that Kennedy's "natural approach" came over especially well on the new medium. Nixon had shown his ability to play politics at the highest levels; Kennedy, his gift for the decisive new medium. Salieri had learned the powers of craft; Mozart had begun to discover his talent.

CHAPTER FIVE

Cloth Coats and Lace Curtains

THE Democrats, who nominated Adlai Stevenson, the eloquent governor of Illinois, to run against Eisenhower, got their first break in September. Following an appearance on *Meet the Press*, Richard Nixon was asked by a journalist about a "fund" that a group of California businessmen had raised for him. Nixon explained that the money was strictly for campaign purposes and that the columnist should contact his treasurer, Dana Smith. When Nixon's train stopped in Bakersfield four days later, an unconcerned vice-presidential nominee pounded away at the ticket's number-one selling point: "Who can clean up the mess in Washington?" he led the crowd. "Ike can!" Across the continent, the headlines of the archliberal *New York Post* screamed "Secret Nixon Fund" from its front page: "Millionaire's Club Allows Candidate to Live Good Life." The Republican vice-presidential nominee, it told readers, was getting money for his private use from fat cats back home wanting influence in Washington; the crusader was a crook like the rest of them.

Richard Nixon was being taken to public account for the patronage of California businessmen like those who had set him up politically in late 1945. Suddenly, he found himself facing the first scandal of his career, one that could cost Dwight Eisenhower the presidency. Without warning, he had come under assault from the kind of sneak attack he had himself executed against Voorhis and Douglas. "When it hit us, coming out of nowhere, we couldn't believe it," recalled Pat Hillings, the Californian who had won Nixon's old congressional seat and was traveling with the vice-presidential candidate. Not even a Nixon-ordered audit showing that none of the contributed money had gone to his private use could appease Eisenhower. "What was the use of campaigning against the business of what has been going on in Washington," he added with lethal candor, "if we ourselves aren't as clean as a hound's tooth?"

Other Republicans were less conditional in their backing of the beleaguered nominee. "I am in your corner 100 percent. Fight to the finish just as you did the smears by the Communists when you were proving charges against Alger Hiss. I will personally welcome you in Grand Rapids or any other part of Michigan." Cong. Gerald Ford's loyalty would one day be grandly repaid.

But as the rumors of the "fund" spread, the outlook for Nixon grew dark. The *New York Herald Tribune*, an exuberant backer of Eisenhower, called for Nixon to resign his nomination. New York governor Dewey, Ike's most influential adviser, then reached Nixon in Portland with firm marching orders from the general himself. He was to go on television and defend himself. Ike, grabbing the phone, confirmed the mission. "Tell them everything there is to tell, everything you can remember since the day you entered public life. Tell them about any money you have ever received."

Would there be a thumbs-up or thumbs-down decision on his fate following the broadcast? Ike answered Nixon's desperate query with one of his own. "I'm having a tough time deciding this; it's about how people perceive it." Hearing this five-star waffle, the former junior navy officer could not contain himself: "There comes a time in matters like these when you have to either shit or get off the pot."

* * *

THE goal was now to get the largest possible audience for Nixon's televised apologia. Initially, the Republican National Committee hoped to get the Monday slot right after *I Love Lucy*. When CBS would not sell them the time, the Tuesday night slot following Milton Berle was booked on NBC. On a postmidnight flight to Los Angeles, Nixon grabbed some souvenir postcards from the seat pouch in front of him and began jotting down notes. "Pat's cloth coat. . . . Checkers." All the next day he wrote and rewrote in his room at the Ambassador Hotel. He knew that an appeal for compassion would not do the job. The hurdle had been set higher than that. Unless the audience response was 90 percent in his favor, he had been warned by the men around Eisenhower, he was a political cadaver. Found unfit for national office by Ike, he could hardly expect the people of California to confirm him as their U.S. senator come the next election.

Pat Hillings, traveling with Nixon, later painted a stark portrait of the vice-presidential candidate at this low moment. "Dick was sitting in a huge leather chair, his arms stretched out, his hands dangling in that characteristic way of his. His brooding face and his posture reminded me of the statue in the Lincoln Memorial in Washington. I knew I was in the presence of total despair."

But the final blow was still to come. Ike now demanded license to dump Nixon without soiling his own nice-guy reputation. An hour before the live nationwide broadcast, Governor Dewey called from New York with an ultimatum. Not yet president, the great general was engaging in a practice chief executives regularly use for dirty jobs: plausible deniability. He had given an instruction he could later deny. "There has been a meeting of all of Eisenhower's top advisers," Dewey told Nixon. "They've asked me to tell you that in their opinion at the conclusion of the broadcast you should submit your resignation to Eisenhower." Nixon said nothing. Dewey plunged the knife deeper, offering Dutch uncle advice that Nixon should resign his Senate seat and run again in a special election, a risky gambit meant to reinforce his electorate mandate back home. Nixon again said nothing.

Dewey: Hello, can you hear me?
Nixon: What does Eisenhower want me to do?

Dewey: What shall I tell them you are going to do?

Nixon: Just tell them that I haven't the slightest idea what I'm going to do and if they want to find out they'd better listen to the broadcast! And tell them I know something about politics, too.

That night he proved it. Nixon's speech employed all the craft gained since his student days at Whittier organizing the Orthogonians. He began by listing his modest assets, describing how he and Pat were like other returned-GI couples: a car in the driveway, young kids in school, a mortgage on the house. "I should say this—that Pat doesn't have a mink coat. But she does have a respectable Republican cloth coat." The slash was twin-edged, striking at both the well-off New Deal liberal establishment and at a recent scandal involving one of Truman's White House cronies.

He now went after the muckrakers. Nixon told his national audience that a supporter had sent his daughters a cocker spaniel, that Tricia had named the dog "Checkers," and no matter what *"they,"* alluding to the Pharisees in the media, said about it, the Nixons were going to keep the dog.

It was the well-honed Nixonian appeal: resentful, emotional, square. If the sophisticates thought it mawkish or corny, it mattered little. He was talking to all the people out in the country who had to struggle, who were tired of being talked down to by the elite New Dealers. And he got to them. The Depression and the war were over. The striving middle class no longer needed to take orders from the privileged few in New York and Washington. "Eisenhower is a great man," Nixon reminded his audience in farewell, "believe me, he is a great man." But he told viewers to write or wire the Republican National Committee, not the general. He would abide by the party's judgment.

For several minutes, Nixon had no idea how well his broadcast had gone. Jittery, he had insisted that Hillings, Murray Chotiner, and friend William Rogers be out of the studio before the ON-AIR light flashed. Hillings recalled Nixon's tears when they joined him onstage afterward. He was emotionally distraught at his failure to give himself enough time to tell the huge audience the address of the Republican National Committee. "He broke down a little bit, and he couldn't get off the set." Anxious to get the nationwide reaction to what, by his reckoning, was a smashing performance by Nixon, Hillings rushed to check his reaction with the NBC switchboard. "We're just swamped!" said a woman operator who sounded to Hillings as if she'd been crying.

The eyes of a more influential woman, those of Mamie Eisenhower, also had moistened during the broadcast. "Tonight I saw an example of courage," her husband declared to a packed Cleveland auditorium that had just watched Nixon's speech on a large screen. He had seen "many brave men in tough situations" and compared his running mate to Gen. George Patton, another officer of his who had once "committed an error." Eisenhower was placing the Nixon fund on the same level of wrongdoing as Patton's slap of an enlisted man. "I believed the work of that man was too great to sacrifice . . . but . . . certainly George Patton justified my faith."

Like "Old Blood and Guts," Nixon was being found guilty but worthy of Ike's absolution once he had suffered sufficient mortification. Just as the Supreme Allied Commander had made Patton apologize to his entire command, Nixon had been made to do the same before the voters. Riding back to the hotel, feeling the full weight of the verdict to come, Nixon noticed a large Great Dane running alongside the car. "Well, we made a hit with the dog world, anyway," he muttered.

But still there was no clear decision from Ike on Nixon's status. Despite the wild success of the Checkers broadcast, it did not seem enough to convince the man who had chased the Wehrmacht back to Berlin. Back at the Ambassador, Nixon decided to dictate a telegram to secretary Rose Mary Woods telling Ike he was resigning from the ticket. Murray Chotiner wisely tore it to shreds; Nixon's performance was playing well in the country. Fifty-eight million Americans, the greatest television audience in history, had seen the gritty young politician defend himself, his generation, his class.

Eisenhower, in the end, had little choice but to ratify Nixon as his "boy." But the deficit in trust that required Nixon to give the Checkers defense had poisoned forever his faith in other politicians and the press. Before this humiliating episode, he had counted many reporters his friends, taken for granted the brotherly loyalty of fellow Republicans. That faith was now destroyed. Nixon now knew that people were fully prepared to believe the worst about him. While he now knew television's power for going over the heads of the press, he had also learned the weakness of political friendship. He would never be the same man. Just as he would later pay for his persecutions of Jerry Voorhis, Helen Gahagan Douglas, and Alger Hiss, so would he also pay for the us-against-them stance exploited in the Checkers speech. Dick Nixon had won, as his friend Jack Kennedy put it, and held his place at the "top," but at a terrible price.

In the same weeks that Nixon was personally experiencing the terrors of "attack" politics, Kennedy was showing a new degree of ruthlessness. Mark Dalton, who had held the job of Kennedy campaign manager in 1946, had been given it again for the 1952 Senate race. The ally who had volunteered his services for six years, paying his own expenses, was now on the Kennedy payroll, a change of status that brought certain implications. The first trouble came after candidate and top aide attended a meeting at a Fall River club and were heading past the bar. "Three guys who were feeling no pain," as Dalton described them, boisterously surrounded Kennedy as Dalton went to get the car. The candidate did not appreciate being left behind. "He got in the car, turned around, and stuck his finger in my belly," Dalton recalled with anger. " 'Don't you ever let that happen to me again!' "

Dalton, a Harvard law graduate, son of a prominent Irish-Catholic family, was learning that people who worked for the Kennedys *worked* for the Kennedys. "I was to take care of him with drunks. I was his caretaker, his bodyguard." He would never get over the slight, recalling it aloud again and again years later: "That son of a bitch! Right in the belly. 'Don't you ever!' " It was the beginning of the end of their friendship. The final straw came at a strategy meeting where Kennedy's father humiliated Dalton in front of the assembled campaign team, the candidate included. When Jack refused to stand up for his campaign manager, Dalton had no choice but to quit.

Certainly it was hard for anyone, least of all his son, to question

Joseph Kennedy's abilities. In addition to unlimited money, the former film producer was a master at the Hollywood buildup. "In all my years of public life, I've never seen a congressman get so much press while doing so little work," Tip O'Neill would say. To win the endorsement of the conservative *Boston Post*, Kennedy senior now unblinkingly lent its pliable publisher $500,000. His father had to "buy a fuckin' newspaper" for him to get his Senate seat, Jack later would joke. But there were greater possibilities to exploit than mere cash and Dad's readiness to spend it. There was also the fury of Republican party conservatives in Massachusetts at Henry Cabot Lodge for hijacking the party's presidential nomination from the worthy hands of "Mr. Republican" Robert Taft that summer. Joe Kennedy took several calculated steps to exploit the feud. He organized "Independents for Kennedy" and found a pro-Taft Republican banker to chair the front group. Next, he got the pro-Taft publisher of the *New Bedford Standard Times* to, first, reprint the *Reader's Digest* article on his son's PT-109 exploits, then to endorse the Democratic candidate Kennedy outright. When young Kennedy attacked Lodge's absenteeism from the Senate, the newspaper dutifully repeated the Democrat's charges in its editorials. When Lodge charged Kennedy himself with a poor voting record, the *Standard Times* refused to even publish it. As they had in 1946, the Kennedys showed the will, the smarts, and the clout to bend the media to their purposes.

To pound home Lodge's weakness among Taft Republicans, Congressman Kennedy accused him of being a "100 percent" supporter of Truman's "appeasing administration policy in China and the Far East." He further ridiculed Lodge for "straddling" on Senator McCarthy's charge of Communist subversion in the State Department.

The one man who might have saved Lodge refused to help. When someone from Lodge's campaign called McCarthy urging that he go to Boston and make a speech on behalf of the incumbent senator, the Wisconsin senator demurred. He told conservative columnist William F. Buckley, Jr., in whose Connecticut home he was staying, that Lodge had always opposed him, while he counted young Jack Kennedy a covert supporter. McCarthy told Buckley that he had made Lodge a counteroffer he would surely refuse. "I told them I'd go up to Boston to speak if Cabot publicly asked me to. And he'll never do that; he'd lose the Harvard vote!"

The Kennedy campaign, meanwhile, presented its own man as every inch an anti-Communist crusader as any Republican. When Adlai Stevenson made a campaign stop in Springfield, Sargent Shriver sent word to him that "up there, this anti-Communist business is a good thing to emphasize." The future Kennedy brother-in-law let it be known in a briefing paper what the Kennedy people wanted the Democratic presidential candidate to say about the local boy: It was Cong. John Kennedy, not his Republican colleague from California, who was the first to expose Communists in organized labor. He "was the man . . . that got Christoffel . . . not Nixon."

Such issues as who was the fiercer anti-Communist would not alone decide the Kennedy-Lodge fight. As in the 1946 campaign, Jack Kennedy's looks and charm were exploited without shame. Thousands of women answered personal invitations to a series of formal "teas" hosted with lace-curtain pomp by "Ambassador and Mrs. Joseph P. Kennedy." Their son's sex appeal was such a tremendous asset, another aide, Bob Griffin, recalled, that Kennedy would routinely visit the Tremont Street campaign headquarters late each night, thereby causing all the women volunteering to stuff envelopes to stick around and stay busy until closing. But Tip O'Neill recalled a moment when charm was the very opposite of what the Kennedys were dispensing in the rough campaign to unseat Lodge. O'Neill, the Democratic candidate to take Jack Kennedy's congressional seat, was asked to substitute for him on an election-eve radio broadcast. Though the format called for Lodge to speak first, he let O'Neill go ahead of him. The script from Kennedy headquarters had not arrived. When it did, arriving at the studio seconds before airtime, it "kicked the living hell out of Henry Cabot Lodge," O'Neill would recall to his chagrin. Lodge, outraged by the ambush, told O'Neill's wife, Millie, exactly what he thought of it, reminding her, "The Kennedys would never give a speech like that for him. And I would never say the things about Jack Kennedy that he's saying about me."

If Dick Nixon was displeased by Kennedy's reach for glory or the discomfort his attainment of it caused Republicans generally, it didn't show. From the steps of a Boston hotel, the campaigning vice-presidential candidate one day saw Jack Kennedy drive by in an open convertible. When he began waving with excitement, his wife, Pat, worried at the pictures the news photographers would snap, told Nixon to cool his public show of affection. "Remember, he's running against Lodge." It would not look good for the Republican rising star to be wagging his hand so excitedly at the young Democratic congressman about to beat the man who had engineered Dwight Eisenhower's run for the presidency.

The irony is, Kennedy and Nixon were campaigning with the same message. Nixon said that Truman had "covered up the Communist conspiracy." Kennedy tied Lodge to Truman's "appeasing" foreign policy.

On election day, the Eisenhower-Nixon ticket carried the country by 7 million votes, winning a majority in the House of Representatives and a 48–48 tie in the U.S. Senate, which the new vice president could break in the Republicans' favor. But in Massachusetts, where Adlai Stevenson suffered a crushing defeat, Jack Kennedy won by seventy thousand votes. For the noble Lodge, it was a humiliating defeat. With the ballots in, Lodge could not bring himself to wish the winner well. From the window of his Tremont Street headquarters, Kennedy watched the proud Yankee's car drive by on its way into the night. Only then, exhausted and suffering from the effects of his Addison's disease, would Kennedy have himself taken to the hospital. Once again, he had made the political grade set by his father without an ounce of energy or will to spare.

CHAPTER SIX

Hall Mates

JOHN Fitzgerald Kennedy, thirty-five years old, was sworn in as a U.S. senator on January 3, 1953. He was assigned room 362 of the Senate Office Building, across Constitution Avenue from the Capitol. Richard Milhous Nixon was sworn in as vice president, the second youngest in history, on January 20, 1953, and assigned room 361, directly across the hall. "It was a busy corridor between those two offices," Kennedy secretary Evelyn Lincoln would recall. "The two of them were continuously tripping over cameras. You couldn't get through. Hardly a day went by, when Nixon was in Washington, that all kinds of cameras and press equipment were not lined up outside his door. Kennedy was a new celebrity. He got tremendous publicity. There was a steady stream of people passing his door trying to catch a glimpse of him."

A few days before the Inauguration, Nixon's secretary, Rose Mary Woods, told Mrs. Lincoln that there might be some standing-room tickets available if any of the Kennedy staff would like them. When the day came, she handed Mrs. Lincoln a pass to sit in a prize location, on the platform supporting the recording machines and amplifiers, directly in front of the stand where

General Eisenhower and Woods's boss were to take their oaths. "We had a very nice relationship," Mrs. Lincoln said of her ties with Nixon's personal secretary. "Rose Mary Woods and I were very friendly."

So, apparently, were their bosses. When Kennedy applied for membership in the all-male Burning Tree golf club that year, Nixon wrote a letter sponsoring him. "I have known Senator Kennedy for a number of years as a personal friend and I feel he would make an excellent addition to the membership," he vouched in a note sent to the club's admissions chairman.

Just as the two freshman congressmen were thrown together in the same committee back in 1947, they now faced each other across the same hallway. For the next eight years, the two men would work and plot their ambitions within a few feet of each other.

One reason for the across-the-hall cordiality was that while Kennedy and his staff assumed even back then that the 1960 Republican presidential nomination was Nixon's to lose, the vice president had little reason to suspect Kennedy as a rival. Just turned forty, Nixon was now the dynamic national figure of his generation. Thanks to the Hiss case and the Checkers melodrama, he was one of the few public figures known by every voter in the country. More than that, he had become the gritty symbol of a postwar middle class nervous about Communist aggression abroad and uneasy, closer to home, about big labor and the entrenched liberal governmental elite. Kennedy, on the other hand, was a bachelor navy hero enjoying what seemed to be an indefinite shore leave, a man whose tenuous health had taken him to death's door; a Roman Catholic in a Protestant country that had been electing Protestant presidents since the first peal of the Liberty Bell. Add to that Kennedy's health: the strange losses of weight, the stark changes in his coloring, the absences. If these reasons were not sufficient to bar a Kennedy presidential shot, there was Kennedy's youth. At thirty-five, he barely met the minimum constitutional age for the office. By all outward appearances, he seemed a genial dilettante destined for a long, no-heavy-lifting career in the Senate, something in the well-trod Yankee footsteps of Henry Cabot Lodge.

Kennedy had a grander adventure in mind. The ex–navy skipper, who saw relationships as an array of tightly sealed compartments—girls, political colleagues, social friends, aides—was filling out the crew. He interviewed and hired as his legislative assistant a young liberal Nebraskan of Protestant and Jewish background named Theodore Sorensen. For the first time he had someone on his payroll whom neither his father nor his late older brother would have picked in a million years—a horn-rimmed intellectual, the kind who hated and were hated in return by tribal Irish types like Joe Kennedy and Joe McCarthy. Sorensen would be Jack Kennedy's "intellectual blood bank," imparting to his new boss's utterances the Churchill-like quality we now associate with him. "I never had anyone who could write for me until Ted came along," a satisfied Kennedy would later say to Tip O'Neill.

But there was cruelty in this crisp changing of the guard. Before Sorensen arrived, Kennedy's speeches had been written by his former Harvard tutor Joe Healy, who had remained devoted to him. Such substitutions became a familiar JFK pattern. For years Billy Sutton had filled the sidekick role. Later, Dave Powers assumed the role. Once Mark Dalton had been the trusty campaign manager. In 1952, Larry O'Brien got the job of putting pins on the map. Ted Reardon, who served with Kennedy from beginning to end, recognized the Machiavellian guile at work. "Jack had the ability to have guys around him who personally he didn't give a damn about. Some . . . he wouldn't give a dime for as a pal, but he was able to get what he needed from them." Larry O'Brien also sensed early on the cold utility with which Jack Kennedy manipulated his staff and long resisted joining him for that reason. "If you work for a politician," he said after the upset victory in 1952, "he tells you what to do, but if you maintain your independence, you can now and then tell *him* what to do."

In the spring of 1953, one compartment in John Kennedy's life remained to be filled. If he was to advance politically, he would have to shed his playboy image and acquire for himself a wife. Fortunately, a pal had already come up with an especially attractive prospect for the empty slot. Two years earlier, columnist

Charles Bartlett had asked Kennedy to dinner, hoping to match him with another guest, Jacqueline Bouvier, a twenty-two-year-old George Washington University senior. She had already interviewed both Kennedy and Nixon for her job as "Inquiring Camera Girl" on the *Washington Times-Herald*. Bartlett's hunch proved sound. "I leaned across the asparagus," Kennedy would later joke, "and asked for a date."

"I gave everything a good deal of thought, so I am getting married this fall," he now wrote to Red Fay in San Francisco. "This means the end of a promising political career, as it has been based up to now almost completely on the old sex appeal. Let me know the general reaction to this in the Bay area." Kennedy was serious about the public relations fallout. He managed to keep secret his engagement to Miss Bouvier until after the *Saturday Evening Post* had run a long-planned feature: "Jack Kennedy: The Senate's Gay Young Bachelor." Later, without telling his fiancée, he invited a *Life* photographer along on a sailing trip that his bride-to-be had imagined would be a twosome.

The Kennedy-Bouvier wedding, that September in Newport, celebrated by Boston archbishop Richard Cushing and the front page of the *New York Times*, engendered an even bigger publicity blitzkrieg. Chuck Spalding, Red Fay, George Smathers, and Charlie Bartlett were groomsmen, each told by pal Jack that he was best man. Joe McCarthy was among the Senate guests. Richard Nixon, asked to spend a once-in-a-vice-presidency social and golf weekend with President Eisenhower in Denver, had to turn down his invitation.

As Jack Kennedy acquired this last political necessity, an impressive marriage, his eyes were already gazing on the same prize as the man out in Colorado absorbing fairway wisdom from the general. Looking out over Long Island Sound, the groom made an assessment that, coming from any other man of his age, might have seemed either presumptuous or fantastic. "That would be a helluva place to sail in the presidential yacht."

* * *

IN 1953, the question of Indo-China entered the American political debate. Barry Goldwater, a Republican senator from Arizona, proposed cutting off all U.S. aid to the French forces fighting Communist leader Ho Chi Minh's insurgency unless Paris agreed to the country's independence. Jack Kennedy liked Goldwater's approach. His visit two years earlier had shown him that Communist insurgents enjoyed real popularity in Indo-China because of their nationalist appeal. But he would not let a difference in policy divide the anti-Communist cause. "If we do not stand firm amid the conflicting tides of neutralism, resignation, isolation and indifference," he declared at Boston College, "then all will be lost, and one by one the free countries of the earth will fall until finally the direct assault will begin on the great citadel—the United States."

In late 1953, Nixon got his own eyewitness look at Indo-China. Sent on a Far East fact-finding trip by Ike, he deliberately divided his time between the French and native Indo-Chinese, quickly discovering that these were two separate worlds, with the French treating the Vietnamese people with disdain, refusing to integrate them into their elite society. Whereas Jack Kennedy had sensed the nationalism cutting off colonist from colonized, Nixon noticed class resentment. Officers looked down even on those Vietnamese fighting in their regiments. "The French had forfeited their loyalty by not talking to them" was Nixon's verdict. Ho Chi Minh was "far more appealing as a popular leader," he discovered, than the figurehead installed by Paris. "The French, if not losing the war, did not know how to win it," he decided.

Like Kennedy, Nixon kept his doubts to himself. In a December radio broadcast, he clung to the parlance of the global game board, skipping over the inconvenient realities he had seen in-country. "If Indo-China falls, Thailand is put in almost an impossible position. The same is true of Malaya. . . . The same is true of Indonesia. If Indo-China goes under Communist domination, the whole of Southeast Asia will be threatened, and that means that the economic and military security of Japan will inevitably be endangered also. That indicates to you, and to all of us, why it is vitally important that Indo-China not go behind the Iron Curtain." Caught up in the "who lost China?" syndrome, he and

Kennedy continued to speak of Southeast Asia with the same simplicity Ike had employed when he compared its countries to a row of dominoes.

When the Viet Minh surrounded the French army at Dien Bien Phu, Nixon grew more hawkish still, telling news editors he supported sending "American boys" to replace them. He backed a secret plan, "Operation Vulture," to drop atom bombs on Ho Chi Minh's forces should the French forces get overrun. "We simply cannot afford further losses in Asia," he said. The Democrats had lost China. The Republicans could not afford to lose Indo-China. For the first time, however, Kennedy broke with the hard line. "To pour money, material and men into the jungles of Indo-China without at least a remote prospect of victory would be dangerously futile and self-destructive. I am frankly of the belief that no amount of military assistance in Indo-China can conquer an enemy that is everywhere and at the same time nowhere."

With France's final capitulation, which forced a division in Vietnam between a Communist North and pro-Western South, Nixon, too, had second thoughts. In a *US News & World Report* article written after the decisive French defeat at Dien Bien Phu, he said that no added American aid would have changed the outcome. "What Indo-China proves is that where the will to resist does not exist it is not possible to save the people from coming under Communist domination. In other words, military strength, mutual-defense treaties, military assistance operating together will not do the job alone unless the people are on your side."

Jack Kennedy now saw the non-Communist South Vietnamese as a people worthy of American help. "Vietnam represents the cornerstone of the Free World in Southeast Asia, the keystone in the arch, the finger in the dike," Kennedy said. "It is our offspring. We cannot abandon it, we cannot ignore its needs." He became a founding member of the Friends of Vietnam, a personal backer of South Vietnam's president and fellow Roman Catholic, Ngo Dinh Diem. It would prove to be a dangerous liaison for both men, especially Diem.

Each in his own way, Kennedy and Nixon had seen the soft ground beneath the French position, the hard foundation of Ho's.

Each now failed to see their own country marching inexorably into the same quicksand.

NIXON and Kennedy each faced a more personal trauma in 1954. For Nixon, the problem was emotional. He talked to Murray Chotiner during 1954 about getting out of politics altogether. It had not been the same. "I resented being constantly vilified as a demagogue or as a liar. As the attacks became more personal, I sometimes wondered where party loyalty left off and masochism began," he would write years later with rare introspection. "My heart wasn't really in the battle. For the first time, I realized how much the agony of the fund had stripped the fun and excitement of campaigning from me." Tormented, he had already made several visits to a New York specialist in psychosomatic illnesses, who later said he had treated the vice president for the "stresses of his office."

One stress was Joe McCarthy. When the Wisconsin senator first began making his wild accusations of Communist subversion in 1950, Nixon warned that the real beneficiary would be the American Communist party. What he didn't say was that, with all his bluster, McCarthy appealed to Nixon's old Orthogonian spirit. Here was an uncouth lout from the heartland raining terror on the "Hiss types." And doing it with panache, referring to Truman's secretary of state, Dean Acheson, for example, as "the Red dean of fashion."

But McCarthy knew no loyalty. Republicans hoped he would conclude his charges of Red infiltration after Ike's victory. Instead, the often intoxicated marauder simply turned his sights on the Eisenhower team. Though Nixon, as well as Kennedy, attended McCarthy's wedding in the fall of 1953, they could see that Mc-Carthy had not retired his crusade; had escalated it. In a national television address, the groom declared that communism in government was going to be a major issue in the 1954 congressional elections.

At Eisenhower's request, Nixon invited McCarthy to visit him and his family in Key Biscayne that Christmas. Along with his friend Bill Rogers, now deputy attorney general, the vice president tried talking McCarthy into shifting his fire to a more partisan target. Why not investigate Truman's use of the Internal Revenue Service to reward allies and punish political enemies? Why not call off this probe of Communist subversion in the U.S. Army, he urged his houseguest? That was Ike's turf.

When McCarthy took no heed of such appeals, the Democrats saw their opportunity. Adlai Stevenson, still honored as his party's leader, slyly attacked the Republican administration as "half Mc-Carthy and half Eisenhower." Ike asked Nixon to give the television response, which he wanted to include a clear whack at McCarthy. Nixon, he said, was one politician immune to the Wisconsin demagogue for the simple reason that no one, not even Joe McCarthy, would appear credible calling Nixon *"pink."*

In his national TV address, Nixon's first target was the previous Democratic administration. "Isn't it wonderful that finally we have a secretary of state who isn't taken in by the Communists, who stands up to them? We can be sure that the victories our men win on the battlefields will not be lost in the future by our diplomats at the council table." Nixon balanced his harsh shot at the State Department set with a squeamish rebuke of McCarthy. "When you go out to shoot rats, you have to shoot straight, because when you shoot wildly . . . you make it easier on the rat." Unchastened, McCarthy declared he was sick and tired of all the "yack-yacking . . . from that prick Nixon."

For Jack Kennedy, McCarthy's crazed attack on the army caused a more personal conflict. The tie between the two Irish Catholics was strong and tribal. When a reporter asked the Massachusetts Democrat how he could be friendly with someone of McCarthy's politics, Kennedy brushed off the question. If he could get along amiably enough with Vito Marcantonio, he said, there was nothing so surprising about his genial relations with Joe McCarthy. What he didn't say was that he liked McCarthy personally, that he relished the pyrotechnics of this most outrageous of Muckers, much as Nixon had been warmed by the man's deep-burning Orthogonian resentment.

As the months of 1954 passed, however, the McCarthy connection became more and more embarrassing. Jack Kennedy had ambitions in a national Democratic party that now perceived

McCarthy as the archvillain. The Army-McCarthy hearings, televised day after day from the Senate Caucus Room, had given the
country an eyeful of the senator's boorishness.

The McCarthy crisis coincided with an even more fateful reckoning for Kennedy. "We used to ride home together every night,"
Ted Reardon recalls, thinking of one afternoon in particular. "It
was a bright, shiny day. We had the top down in the car. Out of
the blue, he said, 'What do you think is the best way of dying?' "
George Smathers recalled a similar conversation with Kennedy
on a fishing trip. "He was always talking about dying, about ways
of dying, how drowning would be good. 'If he gets unconscious,'
Kennedy said, giving the experience of the drowning man some
thought, 'okay.' "

Unknown to those outside his well-guarded circle, Jack Kennedy was still a man in poor health. "At least half of the days that
he spent on this earth were days of intense physical pain," Bob
Kennedy would say years later of his brother. "He had diphtheria
when he was very young and serious back trouble when he was
older. In between, he had almost every conceivable ailment.
When we were growing up together we used to laugh about the
great risk a mosquito took in biting Jack Kennedy—with some of
his blood the mosquito was almost sure to die."

Each health problem was treated as a political problem, to be
spun. He had developed, in fact, a reliable smoke screen. When
he needed crutches, it was because of the "wartime injury." When
he turned yellow or took sick because of Addison's disease, it was
billed as a recurrence of malaria, another reminder of wartime
service.

By May 1954, Kennedy was once again on crutches. "Please
call the vice president's office and tell them that we will not be
able to come to the dinner," he told Evelyn Lincoln on one
occasion. "Tell them I am having a little trouble with my back."
By August his condition had grown stark. He had dropped from
180 pounds to 140. So bad was the back pain that he needed to
remain on the Senate floor in between votes rather than make
the horrendous struggle back and forth from his office. There was
scuttlebutt in the Capitol about Kennedy's impending death and
how the appointment of his successor by Massachusetts governor

Christian Herter, a Republican, might shift the delicate party balance in the Senate.

In October, Kennedy checked into New York's Hospital for Special Surgery. "This is the one that kills you or cures," he told Larry O'Brien. Complications set in. Evelyn Lincoln recalled getting the dreaded call. "The doctors did not expect him to live until morning." The death watch was even reported on television. For the second time in his life, Kennedy was given the last rites of his church.

The reaction from the vice president across the hall was dramatic. Lincoln recalled Nixon racing into Kennedy's office, an odd look on his face, wanting to know if the reports were true, that her boss lay mortally ill. "That poor young man is going to die," Secret Service agent Rex Scouten would recall Nixon saying on the way home one evening, his eyes filling with tears. "Poor brave Jack is going to die. Oh, God, don't let him die."

Kennedy pulled through. "The doctors don't understand where he gets his strength," Lincoln was told when she called the hospital the following morning. "He rallied during the night." To cheer him up, friends got Grace Kelly to play a Mucker's trick. "I'm the new night nurse," the young movie star whispered into groggy Jack's ear.

Kennedy rallied, but on December 2, 1954, the Senate closed the curtain on Sen. Joseph McCarthy, voting to condemn him for conduct that brought discredit on the Senate itself. While he would live two and a half years longer, both his anti-Communist crusade and his political significance had ended. The lone senator who refused to take a public position on the condemnation vote was John F. Kennedy of Massachusetts. It was a privilege of the sick that he relished in full. "You know when I get downstairs, I know exactly what's going to happen," he told friend Chuck Spalding upon leaving the hospital a few days before Christmas. "Those reporters are going to lean over me with great concern, and every one of those guys is going to say, 'Now Senator, what about McCarthy?' Do you know what I'm going to do? I'm going to reach for my back and I'm just going to yell 'Oow!' and then I'm going to pull the sheet over my head and hope we can get out of there."

Even as he moved to woo the Democratic liberal establishment, Kennedy could never bring himself to side fully with McCarthy's enemies. "I had never known the sort of people who were called before the McCarthy committee. I agree that many of them were seriously manhandled, but they represented a different world to me. What I mean is, I did not identify with them, and so I did not get as worked up as other liberals did." It was a telling observation. Kennedy's contempt toward those Nixon called "Hiss types" was as real as Nixon's resentment. "They're not queer at State, but . . ." he told Charlie Bartlett. "They're sort of like Adlai." Kennedy hated being grouped with such people in the public mind. "I'd be very happy to tell them I'm not a liberal," he declared in a *Saturday Evening Post* interview the year before. "I never joined the Americans for Democratic Action or the American Veterans Committee. I'm not comfortable with those people."

Kennedy's harrowing back surgery would now cost him an eight-month absence from the action on Capitol Hill. "One thing about Nixon, God bless him," Ted Reardon recalled, "every few days he'd stop in and ask, 'How's Jack getting along?' He really admired Jack." To take the pressure off Kennedy, Nixon even took Ted Sorensen aside to suggest an unusual offer. He wanted Kennedy to know that he, the constitutional president of the Senate, would refuse to exploit Kennedy's absence. If the Democrats won a one-seat majority in the Senate that November, the vice president would refuse to "break the tie in favor of the Republicans." Whether the gesture was valid or not—two Democratic absences would have been required to forfeit a 49–47 majority—Jacqueline Kennedy took the gesture to heart.

December 5, 1954

Dear Mr. Vice President,

I could never describe to you how touched and appreciative Jack was at the message you sent him through Ted Sorensen—that you won't let his not being there in January affect the reorganization of the Senate—

If you could only know the load you took off his mind—He has been feeling so much better since then—and I can never thank you enough for being so kind and generous and thoughtful—He was having such a difficult time and I know one of the reasons was he just felt so frustrated and hopeless—cooped up in the hospital and wondering if it would affect everything in Washington.

I don't think there is anyone in the world he thinks more highly of than he does you—and this is just another proof of how incredible you are—

Thank you so very much—that sounds so inadequate—all the thanks in the world wouldn't be enough—Every good wish from us both to you and Mrs. Nixon—

Very Sincerely, Jacqueline Kennedy

Two months later, Nixon found an excuse to write Kennedy.

February 5, 1955

Dear Jack:

Last Saturday Pat and I took our youngsters to the Ice Capades and we were delighted to find that Jackie's mother was sitting behind us. We didn't realize it until we were about ready to leave but we did enjoy chatting with her for a few minutes.

As you know, we are all looking forward to your being back with us in the very near future. I can assure you that they are working hard over there because I have stuck my head in a couple of times when I have gone home at a rather late hour and somebody is usually still there!

When you return I want you to know that my formal office will be available for you to use anytime you have to stay near the Floor. I do not use it myself except just before the session opens and I think you will find it very convenient to handle your appointments or other business which you have to take care of when you find it necessary to attend a session.

Pat joins me in sending our very best wishes to you and Jackie.

Sincerely, Richard Nixon

"It made Jack feel very good," Ted Reardon would remember, for another politician to assure him that his staff was working "double hard," taking care of problems back in the state. Kennedy, who had won narrowly in 1952, knew the reelection hazard of the "absenteeism" issue. It was the charge he had used against Henry Cabot Lodge to win his seat.

In February, Kennedy went back to the hospital for a second, more successful operation. With the help of physical therapy, a corset, and a rocking chair, the young senator was set to proceed gingerly with a career that had hung, along with his life, in the balance. Pale and limping, he returned to Capitol Hill in late May, more sensitive than ever to the public relations of his condition. When a Senate page, Martin Dowd, saw the long-absent senator approaching on crutches and opened the Senate chamber door for him, Kennedy tore into him. "Shut the door!" Kennedy yelled at the crushed seventeen-year-old. Unwilling to drop the matter, he confronted Dowd a moment later. "Don't you touch that door until I tell you to!"

Others were more delicate in recognizing what Kennedy had been through. Greeting the Massachusetts senator on his first day back at the office was a basket of fruit sitting on his desk with a card attached. "Welcome Home!" it read. "Dick Nixon."

CHAPTER
SEVEN

Profiles in Ambition

In June 1954, Vice President Nixon stood on the tarmac at National Airport as Britain's wartime leader Winston Churchill walked right past him to the microphones. The young American vice president had lost the chance to deliver to his hero a welcoming speech he had sweated the entire night to prepare.

A summer later, Kennedy suffered a similar dose of Churchillian disregard. The occasion was an evening dinner aboard Aristotle Onassis's opulent yacht, *Christina*. Excited at the chance to exchange big-picture observations with the great world statesman, Kennedy found himself totally ignored by the guest of honor. Afterward, Jacqueline Kennedy couldn't resist teasing her husband, who had made a point of wearing a starched white dinner jacket for the occasion. "I think he thought you were the waiter."

THAT fall, Nixon came closer to the vision of glory shared by both young men than even his ambitious schedule for advancement had allowed. President Eisenhower suffered a heart attack. Operating coolly only "a heartbeat away" from the nation's highest office, Nixon won praise for grace under pressure. Yet one man's approval would be conspicuously absent. The day after Christmas, Dick Nixon sat in the Oval Office listening in disbelief as Eisenhower suggested to him that he think about another line of work. Ike even asked his vice president if he would like a cabinet post, couching the proposal as a useful career move, a chance to bolster his management credentials. In February, Eisenhower repeated the unwanted advice, again urging Nixon to seek the maturity that could come only from a position of command. Running a government department would leave him far better placed for a presidential run come 1960, Ike told him. "However, if you calculate that I won't last five years, of course that is different," he coldly added.

In March, the people of New Hampshire presented the vice president with a write-in vote in the state's Republican primary. Eisenhower still refused to commit to a second Nixon term. "The only thing I have asked him to do is to chart his own course and tell me what he would like to do," he told the press. Privately, he turned the screws tighter, deputizing Republican chairman Leonard Hall to ask Nixon if he would step aside for Frank Lausche, the conservative Democratic senator from Ohio. Unknown to his vice president, Ike was intrigued by Lausche's religion. "I'd love to run with a Catholic," he confided to friends, "if only to test it out." Nixon's liberalism on civil rights was another factor. Eisenhower had gotten a report from press secretary James Hagerty that his number-two man's aggressive stance was hurting the ticket in the South.

Nixon responded to Ike's message carrier just as he had to Governor Dewey when he had phoned before the Checkers broadcast with the disheartening request that he, Nixon, submit his resignation from the Republican ticket. Taking the same shrewd tack he had used to shuck off the 1952 call, Nixon said absolutely nothing to the party leader's entreaty, waiting to hear the bad news directly from Ike. In April, more pressure was applied. Asked in a press conference if his vice president had charted his course, Ike again refused to bite. "As far as I'm concerned," he decreed, "I will never answer another question on this subject until after August." With that command decision, he ordered any further scuttlebutt about Nixon's fate off-limits until the Republican convention that August in San Francisco. Or so he hoped. Nixon was uniquely alert to the danger behind the former general's stalling. Given the chance to name a vice president at the eleventh hour, Ike might well choose to stampede the delegates. Understanding this, the vice president made his move. Getting an appointment with Ike, he entered the Oval Office with the upbeat news that he had carried out the assigned orders. The Supreme Commander had told him to "chart his course." He had charted it: The right thing for him was to run for reelection as vice president. It was a bold move, and it worked. Eisenhower, realizing that he'd been outflanked, sent Hagerty out to announce how *delighted* the boss was with his young vice president's decision.

I N addition to overcoming Ike's stubborn conviction that his vice president lacked the "maturity" for the top job, Nixon needed to stand tough against the Democrats' belief that playing the Nixon card was the way to bring about the defeat of the still-popular Ike in 1956. Robert Kennedy, now chief counsel to the Senate Government Operations Committee, opened an investigation of lobbyist–political consultant Murray Chotiner for possible conflict of interest. Called to testify, the combative Chotiner managed to land a *so's your own man!* slap at the Kennedys. He suggested that in the course of examining potential influence peddling, Kennedy might "explain whether any influences were used in connection with his own appointment as attorney for a subcommittee of a committee of which his brother is a member." However, committee chairman John McClellan soon ruled that the Chotiner probe was too overtly partisan for an election year.

Meanwhile, Jack Kennedy was preparing a more direct challenge to the vice president's position. He had begun a quiet campaign to snag Nixon's job for himself. Former House colleague Gerald Ford recalls bumping into him at a Washington black-tie affair. When Ford asked how things were going over in the Senate, Kennedy said he had "bigger plans."

His first step was to secure for himself more of an "intellectual" aura within the ranks of a Democratic party that revered Adlai Stevenson's erudition and wit. While recuperating from his back operation the previous spring, Kennedy had enlisted Ted Sorensen, wife Jacqueline, and what amounted to an entire faculty of historians in a book project about members of the Senate who had taken principled, courageous positions at odds with their constituencies. The book's publication was intended to identify Kennedy as a politician of stature, moral as well as mental. "Where else, in a non-totalitarian country, but in the political profession is the individual expected to sacrifice all—including his own career—for the national good?" it asked the reader.

The Kennedys, father and son, had great hopes for *Profiles in Courage*, regarding it as a tool for transforming a first-term New England senator into a figure of national prominence, a young politician into an emerging statesman, and an "author" at that. Joseph Kennedy was ready to try almost anything to propel *Profiles in Courage* into bestsellerdom. With Ted Sorensen still polishing the manuscript, Senator Kennedy himself called the book's editor, Evan Thomas, with a query about the publication date, which he followed by an astounding declaration. "We've got the Pulitzer!"

In January 1956, Jack Kennedy hand-delivered copies of *Profiles* to every member of the U.S. Senate, including its constitutional president.

Dear Jack:

I found a copy of your book, *Profiles in Courage*, on my desk yesterday morning, and I want to thank you for your thoughtfulness in giving me an autographed copy of your latest success.

My time for reading has been rather limited recently, but your book is first on my list and I am looking forward to reading it with great pleasure and interest.

It is mighty nice to know that you are back at your desk again.

Dick Nixon

JACK Kennedy's next task on the road to the vice-presidential nomination was to get control of politics back home in Massachusetts. It was just the kind of messy, parochial fight he had side-stepped in his rise to the senate. William "Onions" Burke, a tavern keeper and central Massachusetts farmer, had been elected chairman of the state Democratic committee. He was the kind of clubhouse Democrat for whom Kennedy had contempt—a fat, patronage-loving *pol*. Worse yet, Onions was fervently opposed to Adlai Stevenson's winning the 1956 nomination. In the April primary Burke organized a write-in campaign for his ally, House majority leader John McCormack, that outpolled Stevenson 20,969 votes to 13,377, embarrassing the state's junior senator in his own backyard. If Jack Kennedy couldn't deliver Massachusetts in the primary, how could he be counted on at the convention in Chicago? And if he couldn't deliver, why should Stevenson even consider him as a running mate?

But Onions overreached. Alger Hiss, just released from federal prison, had been invited to speak at Princeton, his alma mater. "Anybody who's for Stevenson," Burke said, lumping Kennedy into the far-left crowd, "ought to be down at Princeton listening to Alger Hiss." Having dared to tie him to a man Kennedy had publicly called a "traitor," Onions had to go.

In order to knock Burke out of the chairmanship, Kennedy needed to switch from the *wholesale* politics of media manipulation—his father's and his specialty—to the *retail* politics of the clubhouse. He ordered his staff to run a personal check on every member of the state Democratic committee. "Find out everything about them. Who do we know who knows them? What time do they get home from work at night? I'm going to ring their doorbells and talk to each one of them personally." Armed with this intelligence, Kennedy traveled the state, visiting every one of the eighty committeemen.

Two weeks before the state convention in May, the victory assured, Kennedy invited Onions to a Saturday morning breakfast on his own Northampton turf to tell him he was through. Echoing 1946, the loser's protest that many of the committeemen had been bought went ignored. "He and his millions don't know what honor and decency is," Burke complained after members of the state committee, lobbied personally by the charming young senator on the way into their meeting, voted Onions out. Kennedy had risen to the occasion, done exactly what was necessary, changing his tactics to suit the situation, ambushing his complacent rival on his home terrain.

Kennedy's next bit of maneuvering in his bid to become Adlai Stevenson's running mate involved converting his Roman Catholicism from a debit to a credit. Ted Sorensen prepared a memorandum toting up the Electoral College votes of those states with large numbers of Catholic voters. By putting a Catholic on the Democratic ticket, it reasoned, the divorced Stevenson might win back those millions of Catholics who had switched to Eisenhower-Nixon in 1952. To give Sorensen's memo greater credibility, the Kennedy people circulated it across the country as the work of the Connecticut party chairman, John Bailey. The Kennedy selling document thus gained currency in Democratic circles as the "Bailey Memorandum."

Jack Kennedy now undertook the final assault. To win the affection of the Stevensonian liberals among the Democratic convention delegates in Chicago, he struck at the man in the office directly across the hall. On a personal level, Kennedy and Nixon had kept their dealings cordial. When asked on *Face the Nation* that July if he would "advise the Republicans to replace Mr. Nixon in view of the president's health problem," Kennedy resisted the easy shot. He said a dump-Nixon move "might split the Republican party open."

But Kennedy now needed the support of Adlai's followers, not to mention their hero himself. To woo the keepers of the New Deal flame whom he had been bashing over Yalta and China, those liberals he said he did "not feel comfortable with," he needed to do some genuflecting. After years of deriding the soft-line foreign policy of the old Roosevelt crowd, from Henry Wallace to Alger Hiss to the State Department's China hands, young Senator Kennedy would now pay court to the New Deal grande dame and Stevenson mentor Eleanor Roosevelt herself.

She would not make it easy. "I am troubled by Senator K.'s evasive attitude on McCarthy," Mrs. Roosevelt had written. The Kennedy-Roosevelt meeting in Chicago, elaborately orchestrated, was a disaster. When Mrs. Roosevelt raised the McCarthy issue, Kennedy said it was "so long ago" it didn't matter, quibbling that the time to censure the Wisconsin senator had been when he was being reseated for a second term in January 1953. FDR's widow was having none of it. She berated Kennedy before everyone present, including other politicians who kept coming and going throughout the discussion. To win over the liberal crowd, Kennedy would have to do something that would convince them he was one of them, that he shared their sensibilities as well as their party.

When asked to make the formal nominating speech for Stevenson, Kennedy and aide Ted Sorensen worked until six o'clock in the morning. That afternoon, he went before the Democratic National Convention a full-fledged loyalist to "the man from Libertyville," a liberal partisan who shared the Stevenson crowd's hostility for one Republican in particular. Derided by the *New York Times* for overreliance on a "cliché dictionary," Kennedy nonetheless delivered a genuine rouser. He warned that the Democratic ticket would be facing fierce opposition in the fall from "two tough candidates, one who takes the high road and one who takes the low road." The stab at Nixon was unmistakable. For the first time in a decade of peaceful coexistence, one of the two men was using "attack" politics on the neighbor across the hall.

Kennedy understood well the intensity with which partisan, liberal Democrats hated Richard Nixon. Ike's heart attack, combined with his enormous popularity, exaggerated the emotion. If the president were to die during the next four years, Richard Nixon would be president. Since the liberals dreaded this prospect, it was easy to convince themselves that the country's uncommitted voters did as well.

Having received his party's nomination, Stevenson moved to exploit the anxiety about the nation's number-two slot. At eleven o'clock at night, the Democratic presidential candidate went before the convention to say that he would not pick a running mate. Rather, he wanted the convention to do it. Seven of the country's thirty-four presidents had risen to the office because of an incumbent's death. Bluntly implying this could happen again, Stevenson told the assemblage that he wanted the decision made by the party rather than a single man. "The nation's attention has become focused as never before on the . . . vice presidency," he ex-

plained, making pointed reference to Eisenhower's medical crisis
of the year before. The Democratic candidate for that office
should be "fully equipped" to "assume, if need be, the highest
responsibility." He wanted the party to pick its number-two man
"through the same free processes" by which it had chosen him.
What he didn't voice was the hope of party strategists that the
huge media fuss created by the race for the second spot on the
ticket would shift the focus of the fall campaign itself to the vice
presidency, from "Ike" to "Dick." His speech cloaked an even
deeper truth: Plagued by indecision, Stevenson was using Richard
Nixon, the man Democrats loved to hate, as his excuse for not
naming Jack Kennedy his vice-presidential nominee. Instead, he
made the young Massachusetts senator enter what would now be
a twenty-four-hour campaign for the honor.

"George, old pal" came the 1:00 A.M. phone greeting to George
Smathers, the "old pal" being a sure signal to the Florida senator
of impending unpleasantness. "Do me a favor; nominate me for
vice president. Adlai has thrown the nomination open to the
convention." Smathers wondered what he, a southern conservative, could say that would help Kennedy. "Just talk about the war
stuff," his early-morning caller instructed. For the class of 1946,
World War II was still the "greatest campaign manager." As his
taxi headed toward the convention hall that dawn, a sleepless
Kennedy was clenching his fist, whispering again and again to
himself: "Go! Go! Go!"

As balloting commenced, Kennedy mustered surprising
strength, especially in the South. "Texas proudly casts its fifty-six
votes for the fighting sailor who wears the scars of battle," Senate
Majority Leader Lyndon Johnson hollered when his state's delegation was recognized. The first ballot count was John F. Kennedy,
304 delegates; Tennessee senator Estes Kefauver, 483½; Sen. Albert Gore, also of Tennessee, 178; 686½ delegates were needed
for the required two-thirds majority. With the second balloting,
the momentum shifted to Kennedy. Once again, he was drawing
far more than expected from among the southern delegates. "I'm
going to sing 'Dixie' for the rest of my life," the candidate promised aloud as the states reported their counts to the podium. With
646 delegates, victory seemed assured.

"The senator was convinced, and so were most of us on the floor," recalled Kenny O'Donnell, "that he had more than enough votes to win the nomination." He didn't. The convention chairman, Speaker of the House Sam Rayburn of Texas, would not recognize several delegations that wished to switch to Kennedy. Instead, Rayburn called on Senator Gore, who then threw his own dwindling number of delegates to his fellow Tennessean, Kefauver. The Kennedy team correctly sensed the resistance of party bosses, including Rayburn, to the thirty-nine-year-old's upstart candidacy. "If we have to have a Catholic," the gruff speaker had told Stevenson, "I hope we don't have to take that little pissant Kennedy."

Loss came as a shock to a confident Jack Kennedy. One moment, he had been headed toward the convention floor; the next, he was absorbing the fact of defeat. It was the first political setback of his life. As wife, Jacqueline, and his aides gathered around him in his Stockyards Inn suite, Kennedy refused to be cheered by those who said the close defeat was the best possible outcome, that he had made a name for himself without having to endure the defeat in November everyone expected for the Stevenson ticket. "He hated to lose anything, and he glared at us when we tried to console him by telling him that he was the luckiest man in the world," O'Donnell remembered.

The defeat brought Kennedy to a sober reckoning. He now believed that whatever lip service they paid to tolerance, the main party leaders, like Rayburn, would simply not let him— young, independent, and Catholic—become their nominee. The 1956 experience also marked Kennedy's metamorphosis from dilettante to professional. "I've learned that you don't get far in politics until you become a total politician," he told his aides. "That means you've got to deal with the party leaders as well as with the voters." The Kennedy team learned another lesson from the loss: While a candidate's Senate colleagues may be big shots in Washington, they cannot be counted on to deliver votes at a convention. The true power lay elsewhere. To win a presidential nomination, Jack Kennedy and his organization realized, they needed to get out and win support in the country itself.

In this coming fight, John F. Kennedy would have a clear edge.

Something had changed out in that vast territory beyond Capitol Hill. As the country had listened to the Democratic balloting, from its car radio, it had caught a race to the finish between the well-known Estes Kefauver and this new political name, "Kennedy." Those who watched on television had seen something more dazzling. In a sea of gray faces, the camera had lingered on the handsome countenance of Jack Kennedy. It had spotted, too, his radiant spouse: Anyone with Jacqueline Kennedy at his side could hardly be counted among life's losers. Moreover, Jack Kennedy in defeat had found the electoral edge that would carry him to victory four years later: the sense by millions of Catholics that one who shared their faith had been denied something he had justly deserved.

THE Republican convention opened in San Francisco the following week with the vice-presidential nomination still in doubt. Just days earlier, former Minnesota governor Harold Stassen had called for the nomination of Massachusetts governor Christian Herter to run with Ike. Stassen ignored the fact that Nixon had outpolled Herter in a nationwide opinion survey 83 percent to 10 percent! Once again, Ike was allowing his veep to sweat. Though Herter himself dubbed Stassen's effort a "comic opera," the silence emanating from 1600 Pennsylvania Avenue lent the stop-Nixon campaign a certain stature. "I can't understand how a man can come so far in his profession," Ike wondered aloud about his loner vice president, "and not have any friends."

Not until he reached San Francisco did Ike consent to take Nixon off the hook. While much of the country would continue to idolize his tormenter as a kindly grandfather, Nixon knew the Ike secret. So did Jack Kennedy. "He's a terribly cold man," he said of the great general before whom political necessity forced Dick Nixon once again to bow.

ADLAI Stevenson would spend much of the general election attacking Richard Nixon. "Our nation stands at a fork in the political road. In one direction lies a land of slander and scare;

the land of sly innuendo, the poison pen, the anonymous phone call and hustling, pushing, shoving; the land of smash and grab and anything to win. This is Nixonland." Taking the low road himself, the second-time Democratic nominee went on to predict ominously that Eisenhower would not live out the term. "Every piece of scientific evidence that we have indicates that a Republican victory would mean that Richard Nixon would probably be President within the next four years."

Shrewdly, Nixon refused to respond. This caused a desperate Stevenson, in turn, to mock him for the nasty tactics he had abandoned. "The vice president has put away his switchblade and now assumes the aspect of an eagle scout." Bobby Kennedy, who was traveling with the Stevenson campaign, saw the fault in the strategy. "The subject of Nixon came up, and I was strongly against making the campaign built around an attack on him." It was obvious to him, if not to the liberals surrounding the Democratic candidate, that the Stevenson people were deluding themselves into thinking that the country's undecided, swing voters shared their contempt for the Republican vice president. Bobby knew better; the Nixon haters and the Stevenson lovers were one and the same. They constituted a minority of the electorate. The Democrats' only hope, such as it was, against the immensely popular Republican president lay with those Catholic and other conservative Democrats who had switched to Ike in 1952, voters who not only lacked the liberals' contempt for the vice president but, in many cases, identified more with Nixon's grit than with Stevenson's eloquence.

The disdain of the younger Kennedy for Stevenson extended well beyond campaign strategy. "I came out of our first conversation with a very high opinion of him. Then I spent six weeks with him on the campaign and he destroyed it all." On election day, Robert Kennedy voted without fanfare for the Republican ticket of Dwight Eisenhower and Richard Nixon.

CHAPTER EIGHT

Two Men on Third

UPON publication in 1956, *Profiles in Courage* garnered impressive reviews for its senator-author. The *New York
Times* declared that a "first-rate politician" had written "a
thoughtful and persuasive book about political integrity." To Joe
Kennedy, good notices were not enough. Defying the word of
mouth that his son had received substantial help in producing the
inspiring book on political courage, he wanted greater legitimacy
still. He wanted the Pulitzer Prize.

Crony Arthur Krock, the *Times* columnist, began working quietly to secure for his friend's son the award for biography. Robert
Choate, the member of the Pulitzer advisory board he lobbied,
was skeptical. "Give me some reasons why the Kennedy book
might be considered among the biographies," the *Boston Herald*
publisher wrote back. Choate told Krock that the prize's jurors for
biography had not even mentioned the Kennedy book. When
Krock made a second pitch for the book, this time for the history
category, Choate said it had been ignored by those screeners as
well.

Wishing to be helpful, Choate now gave Krock the names of

the Pulitzer screening board and suggested that Krock contact them directly. "I am quite confident that Joe would be glad to see it went to a Democrat," he kidded Krock, referring to the prize's namesake, Joseph Pulitzer. Choate expressed his full confidence that the New York Times men would keep their dealings confidential.

Here again the Kennedys proved their agility at surmounting barriers. In May 1957, the Pulitzer Prize was awarded to *Profiles in Courage*. In an extraordinary move, the full committee, of which Choate was a member, disregarded the judges' recommendation and presented Sen. John F. Kennedy with the award for biography. Rose Kennedy frankly credited the triumph to her husband's "careful spade work." Joseph Kennedy had learned "who was on the committee and how to reach such and such a person through such and such a friend." It was a simple matter, she said, of doing what was necessary to win. "Things don't happen; they are made to happen," she said.

By year's end, however, the authorship of the book and Senator Kennedy's Pulitzer had *both* become controversial. Influential columnist Drew Pearson went on Mike Wallace's popular ABC program to allege that *Profiles* was "ghostwritten," that Senator Kennedy's willingness to accept the prize for the book therefore constituted a public fraud. Fearful that the publicity would cripple his presidential buildup, Kennedy paid an emergency call on Washington superlawyer Clark Clifford. As he sat in Clifford's office explaining his plight, the telephone rang. "Sue the bastards!" It was Kennedy's father yelling through the receiver. "For fifty million dollars! This is a lie! They are trying to destroy Jack." Clifford, with a cooler head, explained that a lawsuit would only focus greater attention on Pearson's accusation. Instructing Kennedy to gather together any notes showing his personal involvement in producing the book, anything to indicate he had done more than simply let his name be put on the cover, Clifford then traveled to New York, where, in a face-to-face confrontation, he forced ABC executives to retract the "ghostwritten" allegation. While never persuaded that the senator had done any significant amount of the actual writing, Kennedy's knowledge of the subject matter convinced Pearson that he had been seriously involved in the project. Decades later, Mike Wallace would call the ABC retraction a "craven" buckling to a Kennedy "bluff."

"The author is the man who stands behind what is on the printed page," Ted Sorensen would argue loyally. "It's his responsibility to put his name to it and to put it out." While Jack Kennedy may have lacked the requisite zeal for the lonely toil of drafting and redrafting manuscripts, he would prove adequate to the writer's more public role of promoting the finished work.

"THERE'S no question that Jack played the game of politics by his own rules," Massachusetts colleague Tip O'Neill noted, "which is why his fellow politicians were so slow to take him seriously." Always fascinated by the personal magnetism of movie stars like Cary Grant, Kennedy now possessed it himself. Thanks to his concession speech at the 1956 convention and his Pulitzer, he had become a figure of glamour around the country, and thanks to his ex–movie mogul father, he would now get the buildup accorded a new Hollywood matinee idol. His PT-109 exploits were chronicled on the TV series *Navy Log*. He was the subject of a *Time* cover story. Reaching a more passionate, if narrower, audience, the magazine of the Knights of Columbus, the Catholic fraternal organization, informed readers that a Roman Catholic, indeed a brother Knight, might soon be running for president. Senate colleague Hubert Humphrey watched it happen. "He had the publicity. He had the attraction. He had the *it*."

Kennedy was determined to maximize that "it," understanding that what seemed effortless could never be left to chance. There was the long day spent at the Manhattan studio of photographer Howard Conant, a photographer famed for his portraits of Grace Kelly and other stars. Conant worked with Kennedy from different angles, then carefully studied the contact proofs. The result was the dashing, sideways Jack Kennedy glance into the distance that would adorn a hundred thousand buttons and placards in the years ahead.

Now, as Humphrey and his Democratic rivals passed legislation in the halls of the Capitol, Kennedy crisscrossed the map of the country. While the pack at home logrolled legislation in Senate committee hearings, his campaign plane, the *Caroline*, logged 110,000 air miles carrying the junior Massachusetts senator to meet voters. Ted Sorensen was compiling a card file of thirty thousand Democrats known to have local election-day clout in their district. What amazed Larry O'Brien, who was also criss-crossing the country organizing local Kennedy efforts, was the loneliness of the mission. Where was everyone else? No one representing Senators Johnson or Humphrey or Symington or any other 1960 presidential hopeful ever seemed to be anywhere around. The Kennedy strategy was working. "The thing that amazes me is that we had the field almost entirely to ourselves," O'Brien recalled.

Majority Leader Johnson, Humphrey, and the others slowly realized that their younger colleague had already beaten them in the race to capture control of the modern media apparatus. Thanks to both his and his father's cunning efforts, Kennedy had leapfrogged the Democratic pack for the 1960 presidential nomination. "Now I admit that he had a good sense of humor and that he looked good on television, but his growing hold on the American people was simply a mystery to me," Johnson was to confess.

The upstart from Massachusetts was now being compared to his ultimate rival himself. "Kennedy has been regarded by many as the Democratic counterpart for the GOP's Richard Nixon," the *Winchester Evening Star* declared in February 1958. "Nixon, probably, is basically a moderate conservative, though with some liberal tendencies," the Virginia newspaper noted with approval. "Kennedy is basically a moderate liberal, but with many conservative leanings. Neither is an extremist in any sense." The editorial earned a thank-you note from the polished Massachusetts senator. "Once he started in 1956, he told me he was going to cultivate reporters," remembers Smathers. To get more TV appearances, he told producers of the Sunday interview programs to count on him as a substitute if an invited guest failed to appear.

As he had in 1956, Kennedy now focused the full power of his charms on his party's liberal wing. Beginning with his "one takes the low road" knock at Nixon in Chicago, he engaged in a step-by-step campaign to woo Democratic intellectuals who took pride in having twice run the "egghead" Stevenson against the Philistines. The Pulitzer had been the first important move. His next curtsy to the Democratic Left would take the form of a speech aimed at convincing liberals that he had departed from his rigid Cold Warriorism, that he shared their more sophisticated perspective on world affairs.

On the Senate floor in July 1957, Kennedy called boldly for revision of the Eisenhower administration's Eurocentric foreign policy. America, he said, should end its automatic alliance with its colonialist World War II Allies and recognize instead the rising aspirations of the developing world. "The most powerful single force in the world today is neither communism nor capitalism, neither the H-bomb nor the guided missile," he began. "It is man's eternal desire to be free and independent." The immediate target was French colonial rule in Algeria. Kennedy explained that France's 1954 defeat at Dien Bien Phu had not resulted from a shortage of military power. In his opinion, the French would have lost the war in Indo-China even if it "could afford to increase substantially the manpower already poured into the area." In the long run, it was a prophetic warning to the country that would soon inherit France's military commitment in Southeast Asia. In the short run, it was an affront to the Allies. "His words annoyed the French, embarrassed the American administration and almost certainly would not satisfy Algerian nationalist leaders," the London Observer tartly noted at the time. "But they did one thing: They introduced Kennedy the statesman."

Lou Harris, Kennedy's newly recruited pollster, admits that the Algeria speech had in fact been customized to win over the wing of the party whose backing his client needed. It was meant to show the liberals just how far Joe Kennedy's boy had come! The irony, Harris argued, was that Kennedy actually read a good deal more and was a good deal more informed than those on the Democratic left into whose political bed he was trying to climb.

The Algerian speech contained a direct shot at Nixon. "Instead of recognizing that Algeria is the greatest unsolved problem of Western diplomacy in North Africa today, our special emissary to that area this year, the distinguished vice president, failed even to mention this sensitive issue in his report." In the next paragraph,

Kennedy took the occasion to zero in on another old rival. "Instead of recognizing France's refusal to bargain in good faith with nationalist leaders or to grant the reforms promised, our ambassador to the UN, Mr. Lodge, in his statement this year, as previously . . . expressed firm faith in the French government's handling of the entire matter." "I do not criticize them as individuals," Kennedy added out of courtesy to the pair who would head the Republican national ticket three years hence, "because they are representing the highest administration policy."

Nixon was quick to react. He informed Republican congressional leaders that the only way to proceed in Algeria was to work "quietly, behind the scenes, to get the French to take a reasonable position and to work to prepare the Algerians for independence." A quick pullout, he warned, would mean a bloodbath between the Algerians and the million French nationals in the country. Pushing for it now, as Jack Kennedy had rashly proposed, would "only harden the French determination."

Continuing his efforts to bolster the respectability of his foreign policy views, Kennedy began to assemble a brain trust that included Harvard professor Henry Kissinger and a defense planner named Daniel Ellsberg. He also assembled a Labor Advisory Committee, naming as its chairman Harvard law professor Archibald Cox. For economic wisdom he drew on Paul Samuelson, John Kenneth Galbraith, and Walt Whitman Rostow; for history, Arthur Schlesinger, Jr. A Roper poll taken in 1957 favored Kennedy far ahead of Majority Leader Lyndon Johnson as the most admired member of the U.S. Senate. "He never said a word of importance in the Senate," Johnson would admit in dismay, "but somehow, with his books and his Pulitzer Prize, he managed to create the image of himself as a shining intellectual."

For those observing the rise of John Kennedy, it was hard not to resent the ease with which he achieved his new eminence. At a 1958 luncheon honoring Eisenhower envoy Max Raab, the Lodge aide who had won a key position in the Eisenhower White House, Kennedy offered a light yet eloquent tribute sprinkled with several Latin phrases. Nixon, speaking next, felt compelled to administer a tweak. "I might have used a Latin phrase but I didn't go to *Harvard.*" For some, memories of this revelatory moment would linger. "I recognized that day his resentment against the whole Kennedy-Harvard monied establishment," a young aide to Massachusetts senator Leverett Saltonstall, Charles Colson, said of Nixon's performance. "It came out as a joke, but in the humor was the truth." The charming fellow across the hall had become a threat to Dick Nixon's career plans.

One important Democratic figure was still carefully keeping her distance from the popular Kennedy. Eleanor Roosevelt, along with many of her devotees, continued to dislike him, if for no other reason than the undeniable fact that he was not one of them. The feeling was mutual. "I always had a feeling that he always regarded them as something apart from his philosophy," Charles Bartlett recalled. "I think he regarded the liberals as the sort of people who ran like a pack." Benjamin Bradlee, at the time the *Newsweek* bureau chief in Washington, whom Kennedy had met through Bartlett, agrees with the assessment. "He *hated* the liberals."

Kennedy was being cagey. Whereas he seduced the Democratic left with urbane commentary on colonialism, he protected the southern strength he had shown in his failed vice-presidential bid. Whatever maneuvers he slyly executed in order to win over the liberals, he kept himself positioned as the best hope of moderate and conservative Democrats, which included those southerners still holding fast to segregation. In the same year he gave the Algeria speech, Kennedy broke with his fellow northern Democrats to support an amendment to the 1957 Civil Rights Act requiring jury trials for local officials charged with contempt of court. The segregationists, whom Kennedy joined on the measure, believed no southern, presumably all-white, jury would ever vote to convict a defendant in such tinderbox cases. Kennedy's deft positioning on the jury-trial question earned him a rebuke from the NAACP but also the warm regard of his colleagues below the Mason-Dixon line. There was even talk of pairing Kennedy with a southerner on a Dixiecrat ticket.

Meanwhile, Dick Nixon was assuming a quite different posture on the civil rights bill. In Ghana for that African state's independence ceremonies, Nixon met another American guest, Dr. Martin Luther King, Jr. When they returned home, the quiet NAACP member became allies with King on civil rights legislation. When the jury-trial amendment passed the Senate 51–42, with Kennedy among the majority, the Republican vice president denounced the decision as "a vote against the right to vote." Their contrary positions on civil rights in 1957 would add one more odd twist to the presidential campaign to come.

I N October 1957, the country became suddenly uneasy about the grandfather-like leadership of Dwight Eisenhower. The launching of the Soviet space satellite *Sputnik* sent an ugly shiver down the spines of complacent citizens long convinced of their country's enduring edge against the Soviet menace. "Artificial satellites will pave the way for space travel," the Soviet news agency Tass explained to the humiliated West. Moscow was justified in its self-assurance. *Sputnik* was, after all, nine times the weight of the satellites the United States had been trying, with a discouraging lack of success, to launch. If Communists could beat us in the technology of the future, they might also defeat us ideologically as well. The emerging "third world" might decide to look to Moscow rather than Washington for aid and guidance in their struggle for economic development.

As the national mood shifted uneasily from the "Peace and Prosperity" boosterism of the 1950s, the two politicians on the third floor of the Old Senate Office Building continued their minuet of ambition. While the country at large perceived them as operating in wholly different spheres, they were, in Kennedy secretary Evelyn Lincoln's phrase, "two men on third," each continuing to eye home plate while keeping a wary eye on the other. "Their doors were opposite each other," remembers veteran Hearst reporter Bob Thompson, who spent a year working for Kennedy in the late 1950s. "Every so often Nixon would come out of his door, and Kennedy would come out of his." The vice president's reaction was visceral, Thompson recalls, his body tensing each time. "Nixon was always a little bit in awe," Thompson says.

To his more glamorous colleague, however, Nixon continued to show goodwill in matters political and personal. When John

"Black Jack" Bouvier died in August 1957, Nixon composed a gracious note to Jacqueline. "Parents are always special people," he wrote, "it's hard to let them go no matter when." Jacqueline Kennedy replied warmly. "With all you have to do, I have to tell you it was appreciated more than I can say." When Caroline Bouvier Kennedy was born in November of that year, Nixon wired an exuberant telegram to Jack at the Kennedys' Park Avenue apartment:

Welcome to the Father-Daughter club. Pat joins me in sending our best to you, Jackie and Caroline Bouvier.

Again, Jackie responded with care to the gesture. "That was so thoughtful of you, with all that must weigh on your mind at this trying time. Jack greatly appreciated your invitation to join you in the Father-Daughter Club and is already acting slightly ridiculous about belonging to it! Just think how thrilled this baby will be when she can read—and I show her your telegram—which I will always save."

The thing weighing most heavily on the vice president's mind that month was the stroke President Eisenhower had just suffered, which again put Nixon in the same uneasy position he had found himself in two years earlier at the time of Ike's heart attack.

Making allowances for the occasional partisan shot, relations between the two base runners remained cordial. Using Smathers as a go-between, Nixon let Kennedy and a handful of other moderate-to-conservative Democrats up for reelection in 1958 understand that "under no circumstances" would he campaign for their Republican rivals. Just as Kennedy had crossed partisan lines to help Nixon in 1950, Nixon now refused to attack Kennedy. He would concentrate his fire on the Democratic left. Despite a growing possibility that he and the senator might soon be locked in struggle, the vice president was also the only outsider invited to Kennedy's office birthday parties. Dave Powers, forever the loyalist, remembers Nixon once standing in the back of the room during the festivities "as if wondering why no one would ever have a party like this for him."

But the confident Kennedy staff, still retaining cordial ties with the Nixon people across the hall, fully expected that the long cease-fire between the two politicians was about to end. Their man would take the Democratic nomination; Nixon would almost certainly win the Republican. Though the two men still greeted one another warmly, Evelyn Lincoln observed, "that didn't mean that each side wasn't watching with an eagle eye for points to be used if they were both nominated."

Behind the scenes, the effect one had on the other was less predictable. Several times, on social occasions, Kennedy refused to join in the fashionable ridicule of the vice president. One fall day, Jacqueline Kennedy invited McLean neighbors Joan and Arthur Gardner to dinner the next night. The guests would include the two couples plus Rose Kennedy, who was stopping by on her way south to Palm Beach for the winter. Over dinner, Mrs. Gardner made a crack about the "dreadful" Richard Nixon, fully expecting the Democratic senator from Massachusetts to chime in his agreement. He didn't. "You have no idea what he's been through," Kennedy shot back. "Dick Nixon is the victim of the worst press that ever hit a politician in this country. What they did to him in the Helen Gahagan Douglas race was disgusting." But if he was staying on good terms personally with the inhabitant of room 362, he was publicly separating himself. Kennedy told the author of a *New York Times Magazine* profile that he hardly knew Richard Nixon. As a gauge of his candor, Kennedy claimed in the same interview to have the same political outlook as liberal icon Adlai Stevenson. His new identification with the party left and his eschewing of any comfort with Nixon was a useful posture to compensate for the residual embarrassment of his tribal tie to liberal archvillain Joe McCarthy. In an October 1958 speech to the Richmond Junior Chamber of Commerce, Kennedy took a direct shot at the presumed GOP nominee. "When Mr. Eisenhower talks about the party of the future, he is talking about the party of Richard Nixon. And I cannot believe that the majority of American voters would want to entrust the future to Mr. Nixon."

Clearly, Kennedy did not wish to be caught by certain people in Nixon's company. Arriving at a 1959 social event at which Nixon had reason to expect him, Kennedy decided it would be impolitic to enter. Later, he stopped by the vice president's office with an apologetic message that he "did make it out there but at the last minute a crisis arose." He explained that he had to avoid someone leaving just as he was coming. Kennedy summed up his view of the man he now had to beat for the presidency: "Nixon is a nice fellow in private, and a very able man. I worked with him on the Hill for a long time, but it seems he has a split personality and he is very bad in public, and nobody likes him."

CUBA was viewed by most Americans as a Caribbean playground, a haven for prostitution and gambling and the home of *I Love Lucy* costar Desi Arnaz. The party came to an end on New Year's Eve in 1958 when dictator Fulgencio Batista fled, leaving the country to the rebel forces of Jesuit-trained radical Fidel Castro. The United States greeted the new leader as a hero, only to watch in dismay as he gave orders throwing more than five hundred people before firing squads. During an eleven-day U.S. tour in April 1959, however, Castro told American newspaper editors that he supported a free press and promised the Senate Foreign Relations Committee he would not expropriate U.S. property in Cuba. On *Meet the Press*, he declared his opposition to communism and his backing of democracy, and he piously laid wreaths at the Lincoln and Jefferson memorials.

Not everyone believed it. On a warm, rainy Sunday, Vice President Nixon received the fatigue-clad Castro in his Capitol office. As always, he loved the chance to spar. Why don't you hold free elections? he asked. "The people of Cuba don't want free elections; they produce bad government," Nixon would report his guest as replying. Why not trials for your political enemies? "The people of Cuba don't want them to have fair trials. They want them shot as quickly as possible," Castro answered calmly.

After the three-and-a-half-hour meeting ended, Nixon quickly sent a memo to President Eisenhower, Secretary of State Christian Herter, and CIA director Allen Dulles with his assessment. Castro, he wrote, had "that indefinable quality that, for good or evil, makes a man a leader. Whatever we may think . . . he is going to be a great factor in the development of Cuba and very possibly in Latin affairs generally. He is either incredibly naive about Communism or under Communist discipline—my guess is the former . . . because he has the power to lead . . . we have no choice but at least to orient him in the right direction."

For whatever reason, Nixon was being cautious in front of Eisenhower and the others. With his staff, he was more bluntly suspicious, telling press secretary Herb Klein afterward that the Cuban leader was an "outright Communist and he's going to be a real danger." For his part, Castro was offended by the vice president's coolness. "That son of a bitch Nixon, he treated me badly," the smarting dictator told a Havana magazine. Decades later, Castro would confide to an American visitor, in one of his famed all-night conversations, his wonder that Nixon alone had guessed at his Communist loyalties. "How did he know?"

NIXON had a much more celebrated encounter with a Communist that year: his "Kitchen Debate" with Soviet party chairman Nikita Khrushchev. The face-off came at an American trade exhibition in Moscow, where the pair argued the relative merits of the two countries' latest technological breakthroughs. "There may be some instances where you may be ahead of us," Nixon said, parrying Khrushchev's bluster, "in the thrust of your rockets. There may be instances where we are ahead of you—in color television." More vivid than any words spoken between the two, however, was the news photograph of the American vice president poking his finger hard into the fat Ukrainian's chest. The show of strength was actually a publicity trick. What the wirephoto didn't show was that at the moment of his finger-pointing, Nixon was actually giving Khrushchev the banal information that the speech the Soviet leader was about to make would be carried on American television. Anyone reading the next day's newspapers might have guessed that Vice President Nixon was getting the better of the tough Soviet leader on a more consequential point. Prior to the Kitchen Debate, Nixon trailed Kennedy 61 percent to 39 percent in the Gallup poll. A poll taken afterward would show him leading the popular Democrat 53 percent to 47 percent.

* * *

As the months passed, Dick Nixon still didn't believe the junior senator from Massachusetts had what it took to be nominated and thus continued to underestimate him. Like others who had spent their lives in the Capitol's corridors, he let his vision be distorted by the daunting presence of Lyndon Baines Johnson. Right up until the West Virginia primary, Nixon firmly believed Kennedy would be stopped, that Johnson would be anointed the candidate by Speaker Sam Rayburn and other party kingmakers, as Kefauver had been in the 1956 nomination fight for vice president.

Pat Hillings observed from up close Nixon's attitude toward Kennedy's bid. "I never heard Nixon say, 'Well, he's no good,' or, 'He's a pushover.' Nothing like that. But we just didn't think he was a heavyweight. Also, we just didn't think he would work that hard. We never thought of him as the effective guy he turned out to be on the campaign trail, because, you see, I had served with him in the House. We kept thinking Hubert or somebody would stop him. In the House, for instance, he really didn't do much. He really wasn't much on legislation, and then he was gone for long periods of time, illness and other things. He was sick . . . [there were] disclosures that Addison's disease might have killed him."

Nixon was not alone in underestimating Kennedy. In June 1959, the *Congressional Quarterly* polled senators and members of Congress on who would be the "strongest possible" Democratic presidential candidate in 1960. Fifty-four percent named Lyndon Johnson; 20 percent, John F. Kennedy; and 14 percent, Adlai Stevenson. Capitol Hill insiders simply accepted the conventional wisdom that Kennedy's bid, no matter how rousing, would eventually be stymied by voter concerns, especially in the Bible Belt, about his religion. That same month, the *Methodist Christian Advocate*, the denomination's official publication in Alabama, criticized Gov. John Patterson for backing the Massachusetts senator. "It is cause for regret that Governor Patterson is willing to ignore harsh lessons of history to give support to a Roman Catholic for the highest office in the United States." While calling Kennedy "an admirable man, undoubtedly brilliant, successful and courageous," the Methodist newspaper warned Patterson that he would discover "to his sorrow that the people of Alabama, whose attitudes are basically Protestant, do not intend to jeopardize their democratic liberties by opening the doors of the White House to the political machinations of a determined, power-hungry Romanist hierarchy."

It was just this kind of talk that made Nixon think Kennedy would be stopped, just as he had in 1956. Tip O'Neill would recall the Wednesday nights he played cards with a "gregarious and talkative" vice president during this period. Before one such evening, Nixon sent word to O'Neill that he hoped the Democratic congressman could come early so that the two might have a private conversation. Nixon wanted to talk about Massachusetts, a state Ike had carried twice. "They tell me you know Massachusetts politics," he began. "I don't want to go with the old guys who've been around a long time. Give me the names of some young fellas I ought to take into my organization."

O'Neill resisted. "Well, you're wasting your time. Kennedy's going to be the Democratic nominee in 1960, and you won't have a chance of carrying Massachusetts."

"Kennedy's got no chance," Nixon retorted. "I'm running against Johnson. You're not going to be able to stop him."

Eventually, after failing to convince the Republican vice president he was off-base, O'Neill acceded, producing the names of a number of young GOP comers, including that of Sen. Leverett Saltonstall's gung-ho top staffer: Charles Colson.

As he began campaigning cross-country for the Democratic nomination, Sen. John F. Kennedy had a standard icebreaker he used to establish common ground with the local partisans, most of whom had fought the two bitter, losing campaigns against the Eisenhower-Nixon ticket. To set up the punch, he would say that the reason for his visit to the area was to taste some culinary exotica unique to the locale and that he had brought Richard Nixon along to join him in the food tasting. "If we both pass away, I feel I shall have performed a great public service by taking the vice president with me." This cornball quip was meant to perk up the fervor of those pro-Stevenson Democrats in the audience who were by definition Nixon haters as well. In private, the candidate's feelings toward Nixon were still hard to figure. A *Washington Post* editorial cartoon of August 1959 showed the two of them peeking out their office doors at one another across the corridor. "Currently they are on a 'Hi! Dick' and 'How are you, Jack?' basis, but they no longer stop for a chat when they meet in the hall," explained an accompanying article by Scripps Howard reporter Andrew Tully. After Kennedy obtained the original, he got Nixon to inscribe it. "To my friend & neighbor Jack Kennedy with best wishes for almost everything!" Nixon wrote.

"Before the 1960 Kennedy-Nixon debates, JFK didn't dislike Nixon, to the annoyance of many of his card-carrying anti-Nixon friends," Ben Bradlee recalls. Longtime journalist-friend Charles Bartlett and wife, Martha, spent New Year's Eve 1959 with Jack and Jackie Kennedy. Something Kennedy said that night caused Bartlett to write a note to himself the following morning. "Had dinner with Jack and Jackie—talked about presidential campaign a lot—Jack says if the Democrats don't nominate him he's going to vote for Nixon." Bartlett recalls his reaction to his friend's surprising remark. "After that I figured that's the kind of thing memoirs are made of." Out of loyalty to his politician-pal, he decided not to keep one.

JOHN F. Kennedy knew from the 1956 experience that in order to win the nomination he had to beat the party bosses at their own game. He must force them to take him. After all, he was neither a leader in Congress nor a member of the party's liberal establishment. Of necessity, his strategy was to gain delegates by winning primaries, convincing the backroom boys by proving to them that his nomination was inevitable. "You think I'm out here to get votes?" he said, sitting in a Wisconsin diner one morning early in the campaign. "Well, I am, but not just for their vote. I'm trying to get the votes of a lot of people who are sitting right now in warm, comfortable homes all over the country, having a big breakfast of bacon and eggs, hoping that young Jack will fall right on his face in the snow. *Bastards.*"

Instinctively, he understood how it was possible to end-run the bosses. One route was to exploit his glamour with the print media. "You could go to the A & P store. You could go to any grocery store," primary opponent Hubert Humphrey of Minnesota observed with a touch of envy. "You'd pick up a women's magazine —there would be a wonderful article: good pictures. Nice things, always, everything . . . from the *Foreign Affairs Quarterly* to the family magazine. It didn't make any difference what it was, it was a good, solid piece." With his publicity machine humming along, Kennedy also enjoyed a secret edge as he entered each state primary: He had commissioned private polling data on local attitudes and concerns peculiar to local voters. He knew what people had on their minds, what arguments would win their interest. It was a breakthrough technique. "I believe to this day that certain issues fit certain candidates," Lou Harris would observe. In 1960 the pollster and his candidate made sure they matched the issues to the primary voters, a practice that became part of modern campaigning.

As before, Kennedy also had the money—unlimited amounts of it—and the willingness to play rough. An example was the campaign's use of a forty-six-year-old, gravelly voiced hatchet man, Paul Corbin. A onetime Communist who had become a fan of Joe McCarthy's, Corbin was the complete political acolyte, reputedly capable of doing anything for a Kennedy victory, whether that meant replicating the "teas" that had so charmed the voters during the 1952 Senate effort in Massachusetts or distributing spurious anti-Catholic literature where it would do the most good—in the mailboxes of Roman Catholic voters. What better way to get out the vote of Kennedy's coreligionists than to convince them that the 1960 Democratic presidential contest was a tribal war and that their tribe was playing defense?

Despite a surprise attack from liberals for the $1,000 contribution he had delivered to Nixon in 1950—an episode his aides were under instructions to deny—Kennedy scored a big victory in Wisconsin's April primary, winning 478,901 votes to Humphrey's 372,034. Yet the press preferred to put a religious spin on the results: Kennedy had won in six of the state's ten congressional districts, it was decreed, because Wisconsin's Republican Catholics had crossed over to vote for him on the Democratic ballot. The Catholics had simply rallied to their own. Wisconsin, so went the media line, proved nothing.

The Kennedys were furious at the dismissal of their hard-fought

victory. When CBS's Walter Cronkite asked Kennedy that primary night about the Catholic vote, the candidate showed his
cold fury. His campaign manager was more vocal. "I'm going to see
you never get another interview," Robert Kennedy told Cronkite.
After all the trudging through the snow, the hand shaking, and
the speech making, the victory in Wisconsin was being denied
him. He would now have to win in heavily Protestant West Virginia.

It didn't look good. The focus on Kennedy's religion had hurt.
Lou Harris's numbers, which had been giving Kennedy the lead,
70–30 in West Virginia, now showed Humphrey ahead 60–40.
An anti-Kennedy landslide loomed. In Washington, the odds-
makers, including Nixon, were betting that he couldn't pull it off.
The nomination would have to be brokered, after all, at the
convention in Los Angeles, a scenario that tallied with Lyndon
Johnson's own game plan. The Senate leader could get together
with the delegates and woo them in the same tried-and-true manner he used on senators before a key vote. He'd work the states
one at a time, using his allies from the Hill as local kingmakers.
When the time came to pick a presidential nominee, the convention would choose a candidate who could actually win in November—not a Catholic, not a young backbencher who had never
done much of anything where it counted: on Capitol Hill.

Around this time, Lyndon Johnson called on Tip O'Neill in his
office. The Senate leader said that he understood O'Neill's first
loyalty was to his colleague from Massachusetts but that "the boy"
would falter after not getting it on the first ballot. He lobbied
O'Neill for his commitment on the second ballot. But there never
was one.

IN West Virginia, Kennedy rewrote the game plan for Johnson
and all future presidential campaigns. Henceforth, the battle of
strength and tactic would be in the primaries, not in Capitol
offices. Having influenced Catholics in Wisconsin to back Kennedy out of religious solidarity, the new Kennedy spin was designed to convince West Virginia's Protestants that bigotry was
the only reason a person could have for opposing him. Another

was to exploit Hubert Humphrey's major weakness, his lack of military service during World War II. To guarantee that no voter remained unaware of who had served and who had not, the Kennedys undertook a comprehensive education program. Souvenir PT-109 insignia emblems of Jack Kennedy's wartime heroism were put on sale at the affordable price of a dollar. Franklin Roosevelt, Jr., son of the man who led the country in World War II, now condemned the senator from Minnesota for ducking it. A letter back from FDR, Jr., was conspicuously postmarked Hyde Park to give the impression that FDR himself was endorsing the young candidate from beyond the grave.

Finally, there arrived the U.S. cavalry of every campaign: greenbacks. West Virginia was a state, after all, where county chairmen expected pay for service. The decisive swing to the handsome young senator from Massachusetts came on election eve, when the largest amounts yet of Kennedy cash started falling into outstretched hands. Humphrey could do little but complain. "I'm being ganged up on by wealth. I can't afford to run around this state with a little black bag and a checkbook." Nixon aide Charles McWhorter, a native of the state, got a taste of things to come in the general election. "They went through West Virginia like a tornado, putting money—big bucks!—into sheriffs' races. You were either for Kennedy or you weren't. The Kennedy people just wanted the gold ring. They were ruthless in that objective. That scared the shit out of me."

William Rogers, U.S. attorney general and close Nixon friend from the Hiss days, began quietly looking into the Kennedys' West Virginia operation.

To diminish the impact of a possible defeat in West Virginia and also to escape the pressure, Kennedy went searching on primary night with Ben Bradlee for a downtown Washington movie. After trying another theater, they ended up at a porno film showing around the corner from the White House. The diversion didn't work. "Kennedy's concentration was absolutely zero," Bradlee recalled. "He left every twenty minutes to call Bobby in West Virginia." Finally, word came that Kennedy had won. After watching the returns from the safety of Washington and thereby hedging his bets, Kennedy flew in his private plane to the scene of his big victory. Nothing stood between him and the Democratic presidential nomination.

Nixon staffers remember the abrupt change in the relations between the two Capitol Hill offices that occurred after West Virginia. While it didn't faze Kennedy a bit to now confront the Republican vice president, the same could not be said for his new rival. "It bothered Nixon plenty," their mutual friend George Smathers recalled. Dick Nixon and Jack Kennedy were now set against each other in a zero-sum game. For one to win, the other had to lose. For one man's dream to become reality, the other's had to become a nightmare.

CHAPTER
NINE

Kennedy
Versus Nixon

RICHARD Nixon had reason to believe that, had Kennedy failed in the primaries, his wealthy father would quietly support the GOP ticket in the November election. The pugnacious Joe Kennedy had told him as much. Pat Hillings, traveling with Nixon those early months of 1960, overheard a revealing conversation while aboard a commercial airliner headed for Los Angeles. Seated on the aisle next to Nixon, Hillings saw Joseph Kennedy, Sr., heading toward them. "I want to talk to you, Dick," the elder Kennedy said as he came within speaking distance. Giving up his seat, Hillings heard what Kennedy had to tell the vice president. "I just wanted you to know how much I admire you and what you've done in the Hiss case and in all the anti-Communist activity of yours." Then, after a few minutes more of conversational pleasantries, the ambassador laid out his fallback position for 1960. "Dick, if my boy can't make it, I'm for you."

His boy could. "It was the goddamndest thing," Lyndon Johnson complained about the 1960 Democratic front-runner. "Here was this young whippersnapper . . . malaria-ridden, yallah . . . sickly, sickly." Johnson knew full well that the young man rolling up delegate totals at the Los Angeles convention was suffering from health problems far worse than malaria, and the majority leader had no desire to keep that knowledge to himself. Hoping to shake some of Kennedy's delegate strength, a Johnson ally, John Connally, called a press conference to let reporters know that Jack Kennedy had been diagnosed with Addison's disease, a dysfunction of the adrenal glands that, absent regular doses of cortisone, would eventually kill him. The Kennedys were enraged by the Connally gambit. Press secretary Pierre Salinger indignantly called the statement "despicable." Worse than that, it was true.

But the Kennedy juggernaut that had piled up a 7–0 primary sweep was not to be stopped either by the machinations of Lyndon Baines Johnson or by those of the old liberal crowd that now packed the convention galleries for Adlai Stevenson. Eleanor Roosevelt could ardently beseech the delegates to "let it go to a second ballot" all she wanted. Kennedy had it clinched on the first. Their "operation was slick, well financed, and ruthless in its treatment of Lyndon Johnson's southerners and the uncredentialed mob that was trying to stampede the convention for Stevenson," reported John Ehrlichman, then a young Nixon campaign worker who had sneaked into the Kennedy nerve center. He came away with enormous respect for the organization he was spying on.

Richard Nixon himself couldn't help but be impressed by the cold cunning his opponent displayed, especially in selecting a running mate. The Democratic nominee had seen what he needed most—the South—and set about recruiting the strongest possible vice-presidential candidate to win it. If Lyndon B. Johnson was a politician nasty enough to raise the harsh specter of Addison's disease, he was also the best man for the job Kennedy so desperately needed done: shore up Dixie while the presidential candidate himself energized the liberal, Catholic, ethnic, black, and other voting blocs up North. Instead of getting angry or getting even, the candidate understood how to use his defeated foe to get ahead.

If there was a weakness in the Kennedy performance in Los Angeles, it lay with his acceptance speech. Except for its catchy reference to a "New Frontier," it was not viewed as a statesmanlike performance. Watching the closing-night ceremonies at the Los Angeles Coliseum, Richard Nixon decided that Jack Kennedy could be bested. He would now make the single most momentous calculation of the campaign. He would forgo the protection of high office and greater name recognition and meet his lesser-known rival in open combat. He would accept the broadcast networks' offer to host a series of four face-to-face debates between the two presidential candidates.

When the Republicans convened in Chicago in late July, Nixon won the nomination handily. To add a needed measure of drama, Tom Dewey, Nixon's old mentor, roused the delegates with a contemptuous keynote appraisal of the Democratic candidate. "Senator Kennedy has already disappointed his followers. In his first formal address he made regrettable, *smart-aleck* attacks upon the president and the vice president of the United States. Now, while age alone is not an issue, this irresponsible behavior makes people wonder whether the senator really is *grown-up* enough to be president," Dewey bellowed to loud applause. With the delegates cheering his every assault, Dewey, the failed 1944 and 1948 Republican nominee, went after Kennedy with the very weapon that Franklin Roosevelt had once used on him with such devastating effectiveness: ridicule. He scathingly recounted the forty-three-year-old Democrat's reaction to the suggestion that he might be too young for the presidency. "Kennedy, of course, disagreed. He modestly announced that, like Abraham Lincoln, he was *ready*. With further modesty, he then proposed to associate himself with George Washington, Thomas Jefferson, Alexander Hamilton, James Madison, Christopher Columbus, Alexander the Great, and Napoleon. The only ones he left out were Julius Caesar and Hannibal."

Had the Republican candidate himself chosen to adopt a similar tone, had Nixon decided to run against Jack Kennedy as he had against Voorhis, Douglas, and Stevenson, the 1960 campaign might have taken a different course. Due to strategy or the lack of it, Nixon played it positive. He chose as his running mate Henry Cabot Lodge, the former senator who had been Ike's highly respected ambassador to the United Nations. The Republicans would emphasize "experience," especially in foreign policy. It was a risky but necessary choice for a man whose startling victories of the past had resulted from gambles. But in saluting Lodge's stolid defense of U.S. interests at the United Nations, Nixon could hardly have forgotten his weak defense of himself against Jack Kennedy in the 1952 Senate race. Though generous in his public remarks about the rival nominees, Kennedy delighted in the bizarre pairing of middle-class hero and New England aristocrat. "That's the last Nixon will see of Lodge. If Nixon ever tries to visit Lodge at Beverly," a reference to the family's North Shore estate, "they won't let him in the door."

Yet Nixon had little choice but to play the foreign policy card. The Kennedy advantages—which included a running mate with roots in Texas and a regional appeal to the rest of the Democratic South plus a partisan edge with Jewish, Catholic, and other big-city voters in New York, Michigan, Illinois, and Pennsylvania—made it essential that Nixon run the election on global concerns. After three recessions in eight years, a battle centering on domestic issues would give a decisive edge to the challenger. With a strong plurality of Americans preferring the Democratic party to the Republican party—the Gallup poll had it 47 percent to 30 percent—a Nixon decision to run on a party label would have been foolhardy. As the choice of Lodge displayed, Nixon understood that the most useful strategy available to him was to prove that he, *not* John Fitzgerald Kennedy, was the best possible steward of foreign policy, that he and Lodge, not Kennedy and Johnson, were the most seasoned men to confront the Soviets. He would need to make the 1960 presidential election into a national referendum on the Cold War.

"Our next president must tell the American people not what they want to hear but what they need to hear," Nixon said in his acceptance speech. "Why, for example, it may be just as essential to the national interest to build a dam in India as in California." When read with historical hindsight, his best line dealt with the cold war. "Mr. Khrushchev says our grandchildren will live under communism. Let us say his grandchildren will live in freedom." Nixon would later call his words that evening "the single most effective political address" he ever made. Ted Sorensen, architect of Kennedy's acceptance speech, later called the Nixon acceptance speech "brilliant."

*　*　*

OUT from under Ike's shadow, for the first time Nixon set a solid pace for the general election, moving slightly ahead in the polls. A Gallup poll showed him leading Kennedy 53 percent to 47 percent. Then disaster. A reporter asked President Eisenhower what he thought of the Nixon backers who were claiming that Ike's vice president "had a great deal of practice at being president?" Could he give an example of a "major idea" of Nixon's that had been adopted? Eisenhower's reply was lethal: "If you give me a week, I might think of one. I don't remember." One staff member describes the blow as virtually an emotional concussion for the vice president.

Nixon tried his best to minimize the damage, emphasizing the chain of command, the U.S. Constitution, etc. Appearing on the *Jack Paar Show*, Nixon reminded viewers that "only the president can make the great decisions." What he could not say is that Dwight D. Eisenhower had simply made a thoughtless, selfish, rotten statement about his loyal junior partner of eight years.

On the same Paar show, Nixon was queried about his relations with the Democratic presidential nominee. "Are you friendly with Jack Kennedy?" Amid the audience's laughter, Nixon said that he was. "You two have offices near each other?" the host continued. "Well, we certainly do," Nixon came back. "We're members of what we call 'the Club.' Anybody who has ever been a member of the Senate is a member of a club." He then turned to his relations with Kennedy himself. "And while we have very definite differences on great issues and we have very different views on how this election should come out, I would say our relations on a personal basis are friendly. That means we couldn't disagree more on some great issues, but I don't believe this campaign will be a personal campaign from the standpoint of personal animosity. I would hope not." Asked by Paar if he'd seen Kennedy recently, Nixon said he had bumped into him on the Senate floor the day before. "You don't meet at the water cooler or anything," Paar prompted him, speculating that such encounters might pose "a problem." Nixon allowed that, yes, their meetings were, in fact, becoming a bit uncomfortable.

The competition was, in fact, becoming entirely personal. Commentator Eric Sevareid wrote:

> The case that there is no real difference in the election begins with the personalities of the candidates themselves. They are both "cool cats," we are told, men devoid of deep passions or strong convictions, sharp, ambitious, opportunistic, with no commitments except to personal advancement. They are junior executives on the make, political status seekers, end products of the Age of Public Relations. Their genius is not that of the heroic leader but of the astute manager on his way up. They represent the apotheosis of the Organization Man. The "managerial revolution" had come to politics, and Nixon and Kennedy are its first completely packaged products. The Processed Politician has finally arrived.

Like Fitzgerald's Jay Gatsby, both Nixon and Kennedy had, in fact, made themselves into public figures they could admire—one, the gritty champion of the square; the other, the ageless Mucker, the first truly hip candidate to seek the presidency.

There was artifice in both cases, but Kennedy recoiled at Sevareid's rough pairing. He especially mocked his rival for aping Ike's two-handed *V* sign, as he did watching the exultant Nixon respond to the crowd's cheers from his hard-won place atop the Republican convention podium. "If I have to stand up before a crowd and wave my arms over my head like that in order to become the president of the United States," he said of his rival's clumsy body language, "I'll never make it."

Yet Kennedy was not above shaping himself to the task in other ways. Just as he had once spent hours in a Manhattan fashion photographer's studio trying out his most dashing poses, he had also driven up to Baltimore week after week to study speed-reading. In order to equip himself with the right voice, he had been coached to bark for hours like a seal. One campaign worker, stopping by Kennedy's home one evening, caught his candidate listening to the booming voice of Winston Churchill on his record player. The pupil was studying the master.

The most important part of Kennedy's transformation, however, was physiological. More than save his life, the cortisone he had taken during the 1950s had transformed his face, fleshing out his features until they coalesced into the radiant handsomeness, the familiar JFK image, that would linger on in the nation's fantasy years later. Billy Sutton, who had lived with Kennedy those early years in Washington, would remark that he never looked better than he did in those months of running for president against Richard Nixon.

But having an edge in the attractiveness department didn't keep Kennedy from running scared. Throughout the fall campaign, Dave Powers, the campaign's "body man," would employ a standard method for waking up his exhausted candidate. Each morning he would walk into Jack Kennedy's hotel or motel room, pull open the curtains, and begin his tuneless serenade: "I wonder where Dick Nixon is this time of day. I wonder how many factories he's been to, how many events he's had already." It was the ideal reveille for a man who had watched his fellow World War II vet and 1946 House classmate win all the early battlefield promotions so far. Nixon's ambitions had become the sharpest possible prod to Kennedy's own, for he had shown the country and Kennedy what a person of their generation could achieve.

I n late August, with the campaign just under way, Kennedy was offered an unexpected advantage when his rival was suddenly forced to limp to the sidelines. In Greensboro, North Carolina, the forty-seven-year-old front-runner injured his left knee so badly that it soon became infected. He was ordered by his doctors to spend three weeks in a hospital. As he lay in bed, Kennedy doggedly kept on the campaign trail. Rejecting newspaper editorial pleas that he cease campaigning until his opponent was back in the race, he sent Nixon a get-well message instead.

Western Union Telegram   August 29,   7:50 PM
To: Vice President Richard M Nixon
        Walter Reed Army Hospital
I am extremely sorry to hear of the necessity of your being hospitalized for treatment of your knee. I hope your stay in the hospital will be of short duration and that you will make a speedy and

effective recovery. I look forward to seeing you on the campaign trail. With every good wish I am sincerely,

John F Kennedy

Nixon responded to the pro-forma greeting:

Western Union Telegram   August 31,   3:41 PM
To: The Hon John F Kennedy
It was most thoughtful of you to wire me as you did. I hope you have no similar accident. Much against my will, I am trying to do what the doctor orders. I hope to be back on the campaign trail before too long. Sincerely,

Dick Nixon

On the hustings, Kennedy was slyly unpleasant. "Well, I said I would not mention him unless I could praise him," he announced, "so I have not *mentioned* him." When a few hecklers responded by yelling, "We want Nixon!" Kennedy didn't miss a beat before shooting back, "I don't think you're going to *get* him!"

ONE great irony is that Jack Kennedy, of all people, should have had his religion become a political issue. Joe Kennedy had not raised his boys to master their theology at Holy Cross or Notre Dame but to cut a swath across Harvard Yard. According to him, the church had but one role to play in the lives of the male Kennedys: to bless their political ambitions and stay out of the way.

By this standard, the church was far from infallible. Lou Harris recalls a December 1, 1959, precampaign strategy session. Just days earlier, on November 25, the Catholic bishops had issued a strong letter attacking "population alarmists" advocating birth control. "They know I'm going to announce in a month," Jack tersely told the group. "It's a dagger in my back." Turning to his father, he made his displeasure even more explicit. "And you tell your friends, the bishops, that if I'm so lucky to get elected in spite of all their obvious opposition to me, it will take a redwood tree to knock down the door of the White House if they try to get into it."

It had been the Democratic primary in Wisconsin that first exposed Kennedy to the perils of the religion issue. The same sharp, unsentimental vision that had led him to pick Lyndon Johnson and that four years earlier had inspired Ted Sorensen to ghostwrite the Bailey Memorandum arguing the case for a Catholic on the national ticket drove him in the late summer of 1960 to the bold decision to flaunt rather than submerge the matter of his religion, to follow his brother Robert's all-purpose admonition to "hang a lantern on your problem." Sorensen's political math underwrote the decision. But Kennedy also knew the power his religion gave him. While just one voter in four was Catholic, these voters had sizable leverage in the states with the largest electoral votes. If Kennedy could manage to bring back the Catholics who had voted for Eisenhower, the Democrats might take New York, Massachusetts, Rhode Island, Connecticut, Pennsylvania, and Illinois. And if he could woo those who had started to vote Republican during the 1940s, the Democrats could get New Jersey, Minnesota, Michigan, California, Wisconsin, Ohio, Maryland, Montana, and perhaps New Hampshire. Such a scenario would decisively undercut Nixon, a politician whose anticommunism and "cloth coat" antielitism had held a gritty appeal to Catholic voters.

Kennedy thus had twin goals: minimize the anti-Catholic vote by tagging any Protestant vote against Kennedy as a vote based on "bigotry"; meanwhile, maximize his ethnic support by convincing Catholics, Jews, and other religious minorities to circle the wagons. He needed to mobilize the Catholic issue among Catholics while making Protestants uncomfortable with the issue. Nixon had no choice but to go along. In a September appearance on *Meet the Press*, he assured listeners that he had "no doubt whatever" about Kennedy's "loyalty to his country and about the fact that . . . he would put the Constitution . . . above all other consideration . . . even, substantially, on religious grounds."

The Republican candidate hoped, of course, that Catholic voters would not vote their religion. But he could hardly say that directly. "The best way the candidates can keep it out of the campaign is not talking about it," he admonished. "I've issued orders to all the people in my campaign not to discuss religion . . . not to allow anybody to participate in the campaign who does so on that ground. I will decline to discuss religion. I feel that we ought to have a cutoff date on its discussion. I would hope that Senator Kennedy would reach the same conclusion."

Kennedy, for his part, played the issue masterfully. When Harry Truman told the Republicans in mid-October to "go to hell," earning him a pious rebuke from Nixon, Kennedy dispatched a whimsical telegram to the crusty ex-president:

Dear Mr. President, I have noted with interest your suggestion as to where those who vote for my opponent should go. While I understand and sympathize with your deep motivation, I think it is important that our side try to refrain from raising the religious issue.

Before dropping the matter, JFK first wanted to shape the battlefield for the coming months. He traveled to Houston for a confrontation with the city's organization of Protestant ministers. Several calculations figured in the Houston meeting. To impress the clerical participants as well as those voters following the event through the media, Kennedy walked into the meeting room alone, the Christian striding unafraid into the lions' den. To make sure the television cameras knew who was who, advance man Robert S. Strauss picked the "meanest, nastiest-looking" ministers to put in the front row. By opening his campaign on the religious front, the Democratic candidate showed he had nothing to hide. Assuming the role of the defendant in the argument, he offered respect to serious citizens with doubts about his loyalties. The invited ministers had a perfect right to question him, he was saying. But having satisfied themselves as to his sincerity, they also had a responsibility to move on; other issues needed examination.

Kennedy's opening statement in Houston was his best of the campaign. "It is apparently necessary for me to state once again not what kind of church I believe in, for that should be important only to me, but what kind of *America* I believe in. I believe in an America where the separation of the church and state is absolute, where no Catholic prelate would tell the president—should he be a Catholic—how to act and no Protestant minister would tell his parishioners for whom to vote." And he concluded with an extraordinary commitment: He would resign the presidency if his conscience, presumably meaning his religious or philosophical principles, ever conflicted with his oath to uphold the Constitution. Up until that time, it must be remembered, no president in history had ever resigned the office; it was, in effect, an unimaginable circumstance.

Not only did Kennedy speak eloquently; he carried himself impressively, displaying a kind of elegant pugnacity. Had Nixon seen *this* Kennedy in Los Angeles, he might never have agreed to meet him in debate. "He's eating them blood-raw!" yelled Sam Rayburn, whom the Kennedy camp saw sabotage their man's vice-presidential run in 1956. The Kennedy team had played the event perfectly. By answering all reasonable questions, the young Democratic candidate had left his opponents with only unreasonable questions. He could henceforth campaign as if the ministers, whom the Kennedy people had cast as judge and jury, had not only heard their case but closed it in their favor.

Even Nixon, who hoped for the issue to be dropped from the headlines, agreed that Kennedy's self-defense in Houston "should be accepted without questioning." But as his brother's rival prayed for the issue to go underground, Robert Kennedy barnstormed through the Catskills telling Jewish voters that an attack on one religion presaged an attack on another. Brazenly, the Kennedys were encouraging such voters to unite against intolerance even as they themselves made a bluntly tribal appeal to those same conservative Irish Americans who had cheered on Joseph McCarthy. The pincer maneuver was as effective as it was outrageous.

CHAPTER TEN

The Great Debate

DESPITE his early success with the Checkers speech, Richard Nixon didn't understand the power of TV. "Television is not as effective as it was in 1952," he told the *New York Herald Tribune's* Earl Mazo prior to the 1960 race. "The novelty has worn off." With that odd mind-set in play, the first presidential debate between Nixon and rival Kennedy was set for September 26 in Chicago, the city of Nixon's selection as the vice-presidential candidate in 1952 and Jack Kennedy's melodramatic run for the same office four years later. With the country awaiting the televised confrontation between the two men, their positions in the Gallup poll had frozen. An August 16 poll gave Nixon 47 percent, Kennedy 47 percent; an August 30 poll had it Nixon 47 percent, Kennedy 48 percent. A September 14 survey showed Nixon at 47 percent, Kennedy 46 percent. The electorate was waiting until it saw the two gladiators in the same arena, saw how they handled each other, how each reacted to the sight and power of the other man.

Two weeks before the Great Debate, Nixon was asked a deflating question by CBS's Walter Cronkite. "I know that you must be aware . . . that there are some . . . who would say, 'I don't know what it is, but I just don't like the man; I can't put my finger on it; I just don't like him.' Would you have any idea what might inspire that kind of feeling on the part of anybody?" Nixon, who did not seem put off by the query, answered that it was hard for "the subject of such a reaction" to be objective. He then chalked it up to politics. "In my public life, I have been involved in many controversial issues. As a matter of fact, that is why I am here today." Finally, he raised the matter of cosmetics. "Then, of course, another thing might be the fact that when people take pictures of you or when you appear on television, you may not make the impression that they like. Oh, I get letters from women, for example, sometimes—and men—who support me, and they say, 'Why do you wear that heavy beard when you are on television?' Actually, I don't try, but I can shave within thirty seconds before I go on television and still have a beard, unless we put some powder on, as we have done today."

But if Nixon was also concerned about his notorious five o'clock shadow, a feature long satirized in editorial cartoons, Kennedy was already moving to exploit what he knew to be his own telegenic advantage. "Kennedy took the thing much more seriously than Nixon," recalled Don Hewitt, the CBS producer assigned to direct their first encounter. The Democrat had asked Hewitt to meet with him a week earlier in a hangar at Chicago's Midway air terminal. "Where do I stand?" he wanted to know, pressing for details. "Where do I stand?" he repeated, hungry for some idea of the setup in advance.

Kennedy and his team were aware that Nixon had a history of debating successes and that, if cornered, he could turn very nasty. In preparation, they commandeered the two top floors of Chicago's Ambassador East Hotel. Lou Harris recalls the candidate lying on his bed, braced by a pair of pillows, his discarded tray beside him. Dressed in a terry-cloth robe, Kennedy had a fistful of cards in his hand, each with a probable question and its staff-prepared answer. Drilling him were the invaluable Ted Sorensen and his other legislative assistant, Mike Feldman. To offer further backup, Kennedy and his briefers had the help of a hefty research and speechwriting operation headed by Prof. Archibald Cox, on leave from Harvard Law School and now working for the campaign full-time. According to Harris, after each card had been dealt with, Kennedy would throw it on the floor. As a backup document for the prep session, Feldman had produced a "Nixopedia" of the vice president's positions and statements over the years. It was a variant of the Lodge's Dodges catalog aide Ted Reardon had compiled for the first Senate race eight years earlier.

At noon on the day of the first debate, Robert Kennedy interrupted the cramming. Aware, as were other family members, that the candidate's talk of "vigah" was just that, he insisted that his brother take a nap. But it was not to be. "I will never forget going in after that so-called nap," Harris remembers. "I go by his door and he's obviously up because he's playing Peggy Lee records. So I asked him if he'd taken a nap. He said 'no' and asked where Bobby was. So I went next door and had a hell of a time getting Bobby up. Bobby had taken a nap, which was typical. Bobby was a true believer."

The candidate understandably was keyed up for this, the biggest test of his career. According to Harris, "he came out and spent the rest of the waiting time in his robe. I'll never forget; he was out on the terrace, there was sunlight on him. Whenever he was nervous, he would hit his fist. There he was, walking back and forth, hitting his fist." Kennedy kept asking his pollster how he went about the business of calculating public opinion, much as he had regularly grilled Tip O'Neill on the voting habits of the Irish, Italians, Jews, and Armenians back in his old congressional district.

CAMPAIGN manager Bob Finch was there for Richard Nixon's own hectic hours of September 26, 1960. Instead of resting or prepping, the candidate had spent the night before addressing rallies in five different Chicago wards, then getting up the morning of the debate for a speech to the Carpenters Union. "He was upset, because he had insisted on doing those last-minute car stops. He hadn't gotten his strength back from being in the hospital."

Nixon refused to engage in the kind of practice session being held at the Ambassador East, Finch revealed in frustration. "We kept pushing for him to have some give-and-take with either somebody from the staff . . . anything. He hadn't done anything except to tell me that he knew how to debate. He totally refused to prepare. After all, he was the master debater. Who were any of us to presume to insist?" Going back to that first tussle with Jerry Voorhis and on through the Hiss case, the Checkers speech and the Kitchen Debate, Richard Nixon had proven himself fully capable of pulling off another triumph.

Now came the greatest miscalculation. Already handicapped by his hospital pallor and lack of warm-up, the Republican candidate chose the wrong strategy. Attorney General William Rogers, Nixon's counselor since the Hiss case, coaxed him to be "the good guy," to be tolerant of Kennedy's shortcomings rather than reproachful. Then, minutes before heading to the studio, Nixon received further reinforcement for the soft sell. Henry Cabot Lodge, his vice-presidential running mate, who had already lost one race to Kennedy, cautioned Nixon to avoid being his own Herblock caricature, the swarthy bully of Alger Hiss and Helen Douglas. "Erase the *assassin* image!" Lodge exhorted. The advice could not have been worse. Had Lodge's message been as brutal as the one delivered by Governor Dewey the night of the Checkers speech, Nixon's short fuse of resentment might have been ignited, giving him the angry focus he needed to dominate the night.

Jack Kennedy would have appreciated the ironies of Lodge's advice. He had told John Kenneth Galbraith that his rival had to decide, in every circumstance, whom to present himself as. According to Galbraith, Kennedy "felt sorry for Nixon because he does not know who he is, and at each stop he had to decide which Nixon he is at the moment, which must be very exhausting." Had Nixon known how polished and prepared Kennedy would be for the meeting, his predebate decision to go easy on his rival would have been different; as he had understood in the case of Alger Hiss, trying to outgentleman a gentleman is a foolish strategy. The only safe road to victory against young Jack Kennedy lay in a direct, unrelenting attack aimed at piercing the armor of his enemy.

* * *

In 1950 one in ten American families had a television set. By 1960 that number had increased to nine in ten. Anyone running for president should have realized what these figures meant: The audience, watching the first debate between Richard M. Nixon and John F. Kennedy, would be the largest yet assembled.

The Republican candidate's arrival at Channel 2, the CBS affiliate in Chicago, was marked by bad luck. "He was in the right seat, I was in the left seat in the back," recalled Herb Klein, who was with Nixon in the car. "When he got out of the car, he bumped his knee bad. It was the knee that had been infected." Others saw Nixon's face go "chalk white."

His discomfort didn't stop Nixon from making an ostentatious display of good fellowship when he met with the phalanx of CBS executives, including CBS president Frank Stanton, who formed a reception committee for the two candidates. Despite the knee, Nixon seemed in lively spirits, taking time to banter with the men snapping pictures. "Have you ever had a picture printed yet?" he cruelly kidded one of the hardworking photographers.

Then it happened, the moment that would forever shake Nixon's confidence. "He and I were standing there talking when Jack Kennedy arrived," Hewitt remembers. Tanned, tall, lean, well tailored in a dark suit, the younger candidate gleamed. Photographers, seizing their chance, abandoned Nixon and fluttered about their new prey like hornets. The senator bore no resemblance to the emaciated, wan, crippled, yellow figure he'd once been. "He looked like a young Adonis," Hewitt would recall.

The psychological battle was on. Kennedy, asked to pose with his rival, appeared barely to notice him. His well-practiced Yankee chill froze the air between the two. "I assume you guys know each other," Hewitt said. At this, the two shook hands, "not warmly," Hewitt recalled, "not coldly," but as prizefighters "about to enter the ring."

"How're you doing?" Kennedy asked.

"You had a big crowd in Cleveland," Nixon rejoined.

They could have been strangers for all the interest Jack Kennedy showed in the colleague he'd known since 1947. Nixon, for his part, seemed intimidated. From the moment Kennedy strode in, hijacking the attention of the photographers, Nixon was not the same man. Visibly deflated by his rival's matinee-idol aura and seeming nervelessness, Nixon slouched in his chair, his head turned away, a man in retreat.

"Do you want some makeup?" Hewitt asked Kennedy. Hearing the Democrat's "no," Richard Nixon also declined, ignoring the fact that his opponent had just spent days campaigning in the California sun while he himself had been hospitalized. On an impulse, he discarded his long reliance not just on television makeup itself but on a particular blend of shades specified for TV makeup. Hewitt, worried about the stark difference in the two men's video appearances, called CBS president Stanton into the control room. He wanted him to see how bad Nixon looked. Stanton then called Nixon's television adviser, Ted Rogers. Assured by Rogers that the Nixon aide was "satisfied" with what he saw on the screen, Stanton motioned Hewitt to join him outside the control booth. "If they're happy, who are we to make any changes?"

Herb Klein had an explanation, years later, for Nixon's refusal to use the cosmetic help he so desperately needed. His candidate had heard Jack Kennedy's derision of Hubert Humphrey for wearing heavy makeup in their joint television appearances during the Wisconsin primary campaign. "To Nixon this made it look like he lacked macho, and Nixon was a very macho man." It was a manhood thing. Intimidated, Nixon relied on the Lazy Shave an aide ran out to buy on Michigan Avenue, the same "beard stick" he had used to cover his five o'clock shadow prior to the famed Kitchen Debate the year before in Moscow. Richard Nixon would learn, to his horror, that it was easier to look good next to Nikita Khrushchev than to Jack Kennedy.

Both candidates now retired to separate rooms. Ten minutes before the broadcast, however, Nixon was back in Studio B, nervously awaiting airtime. Lawrence O'Brien, whose candidate was still in his holding room, watched the vice president pacing up and down the back wall of the set. "He went onto the platform a time or two. He mopped his brow with his handkerchief. Even from across the studio I could see . . . he was in unbelievable shape. The countdown commenced over the loudspeaker. 'Five minutes to airtime.' " Nixon was staring at the studio door. Now there were only three minutes left. "Nixon was still watching the door, as tense a man as I had ever seen. By then, I was sure that no one had summoned Kennedy, and I was about to dash after him, when the door swung open. Kennedy walked in and took his place, *barely glancing at Nixon*. Kennedy had played the clock perfectly. He had thrown his opponent off stride." He had set his rival up for the kill.

"THE candidates need no introduction," moderator Howard K. Smith announced to 80 million Americans. Richard Nixon, for his part, looked like an ill-at-ease, unshaven, middle-aged fellow recovering from a serious illness. Jack Kennedy, by contrast, was elegant in a dark, well-tailored suit that set off his healthy tan. Kennedy sat poised, his legs crossed, his hands folded on his lap; Nixon had his legs awkwardly side by side, his hands dangling from the chair arms. Their faces presented an even starker contrast. "I couldn't believe it when the thing came on and he looked so haggard," Bob Finch recalls. Nixon's campaign manager also noticed something else. "I saw he didn't have any makeup on."

Too late. The debate was under way. By agreement, the focus of this first encounter was to be domestic policy. Believing that the audiences for the four debates would grow, the Nixon people had saved foreign policy until last. But in his opening statement, Kennedy made clear he could not only handle a foreign policy debate, he relished it. "Mr. Smith, Mr. Nixon," he began, slyly equating the status of a two-term vice president and a television newscaster. "In the election of 1860, Abraham Lincoln said the question is whether this nation could exist half slave or half free. In the election of 1960, and with the world around us, the question is whether the world will exist half slave or half free, whether it will move in the direction of freedom, in the direction of the road that we are taking, or whether it will move in the direction of slavery."

Then he dispensed with the rules to extol his global agenda.

"We discuss tonight domestic issues, but I would not want . . . any implication to be given that this does not involve directly our struggle with Mr. Khrushchev for survival." He had cold-cocked his rival by introducing precisely the topic Nixon had agreed to postpone. His reference to the Soviet leader, who Kennedy noted was "in New York" (as if Nikita Khrushchev's current trip to the United Nations were a symbolic invasion of the country), was that of the classic Cold Warrior. The United States needed to be strong economically, Kennedy declared, not just to maintain the American standard of living but because economic strength buttressed our fight against the Communists. "If we do well here, if we meet our obligations, if we are moving ahead, I think freedom will be secure around the world. If we fail, then freedom fails. Are we doing as much as we can do?" he teased an anxious country. "I do not think we're doing enough." Was America to be led by the gutsy GI generation back from the Pacific or by slackers ready to let things slide?

To bolster his indictment of the White House, Kennedy recited a long list of national shortcomings: steel mills operating with unused capacity, West Virginia schoolkids taking their lunches home to hungry families, and the poor prospects facing the "Negro baby." Then he posed the challenge. "The question now is: Can freedom be maintained under the most severe attack it has ever known? I think it can be, and I think in the final analysis it depends upon what we do here. I think it's time America started moving again."

No matter that John F. Kennedy had delivered this selfsame appeal scores of times before. His words now carried a martial cadence in the ears of his largest audience ever. In eight minutes a lean, smartly tailored young gentleman had made a proposal to the American man and woman sitting in the family parlor. In doing so, he had shown himself as infinitely more appealing than the fellow who had been vice president of the United States for eight years. There wasn't a word of his opening presentation that anyone could have argued with, not a sentiment that his fellow citizens couldn't share. No, the country was not meeting its potential. No, we were not the same nation of doers who had ended World War II. Yes, the country *could* do better. And, yes, we needed to "get the country moving again." Kennedy was playing a hawk on foreign policy, the activist at home, the same strategy he had used in the 1952 Senate race that sent Lodge packing. By going to his rival's right on foreign policy and to his left on domestic policy, Jack Kennedy would leave Nixon scrambling for turf.

After observing this tour de force, Nixon began to betray the hunted look of a man dragged from a five-dollar-a-night hotel room and thrust before the unforgiving glare of a police lineup, a man being charged with a crime of which he knew himself to be guilty. Afraid to project the "assassin image," he was stymied. "Mr. Smith, Senator Kennedy, there is no question but that we cannot discuss our internal affairs in the United States without recognizing that they have a tremendous bearing on our international position. There is no question that this nation cannot stand still, because we are in a deadly competition, a competition not only with the men in the Kremlin but the men in Peking." Finally: "I subscribe completely to the spirit that Senator Kennedy has expressed tonight, the spirit that the United States should move ahead."

Incredibly, Nixon was agreeing with his challenger. Yes, domestic policies affect the country's foreign situation. Yes, we cannot afford to "stand still." Yes, Kennedy has the right "spirit" to lead. His only concern was that Kennedy's statistics made the situation appear bleaker than it was.

Regarding Kennedy's call for medical care for the aged: "Here again may I indicate that Senator Kennedy and I are not in disagreement as to the aim. We both want to help old people." Minutes later: "Let us understand throughout this campaign that his motives and mine are sincere." And, after a small reminder that he knew "what it means to be poor," he offered yet another genuflection to Kennedy's goodwill. "I know Senator Kennedy feels as deeply about these problems as I do, but our disagreement is not about the goals for America but only about the means to reach those goals."

Only? The race for the presidency is "only" about "means"? With staggering humility, Nixon was telling the largest American political audience ever assembled that his rival was not only a man of unquestioned sincerity but one of unassailable motive. It was merely a matter of method that separated the two applicants for the world's most exalted position. To avoid the "assassin image," Dick Nixon was presenting himself as Jack Kennedy's admiring, if somewhat more prudent, older brother.

He committed a second tactical error. Just as he had at McKeesport thirteen years earlier, Nixon ignored the audience and fixed his attention exclusively on Kennedy. He seemed intent on getting Kennedy himself to agree that when it came to goals, there really wasn't much difference between them. Worse still, he seemed to crave Kennedy's *approval,* even to the point of rebuking his own administration. "Good as a record is," he averred, "may I emphasize it isn't enough. A record is never something to stand on. It's something to build on."

As the incumbent vice president of the United States dealt with each of his opponent's points, he tried desperately to elevate himself to an Ike-like pedestal, one from which Kennedy was just as determined to knock him off. Asked about Nixon's campaign charges that he was "naive and sometimes immature," Kennedy explained how the two men had come to Congress together in 1946 and how both served on the Education and Labor Committee. "I've been there now for fourteen years, the same period of time that he has, so our experience in government is comparable." Thus, Nixon's me-too approach seemed to validate the claim of equal seniority. Why wasn't a man running on the slogan "Experience Counts" talking as if he believed in his own campaign rhetoric?

Yet at least one important listener thought the Nixon approach was working. Lyndon Johnson, following the proceedings on his car radio, gave most of the points to the Republican; so did the millions of others who followed the sound but not the picture.

The wound inflicted by President Eisenhower's late-August denial of any vice-presidential role in his executive decision making was about to have its scab ripped. Reporter Sander Vanocur noted with brutal force that the "question of executive leadership" had become a major campaign issue. How did Nixon square this with President Eisenhower's "If you give me a week, I might think of one" reply after being asked to cite a single case of when he'd acted on a Nixon idea? "I am wondering, sir, if you can clarify which version is correct, the one put out by Republican campaign leaders or the one put out by President Eisenhower."

Summoning all his self-control, Nixon tried for the best plausible set of answers:

Explanation 1: "Well, I would suggest, Mr. Vanocur, that if you know the president, that that was probably a facetious remark."

Explanation 2: "I think it would be improper for the president of the United States to disclose the instances in which members of his official family had made recommendations."

Explanation 3: "I do not say that I have made decisions, and I would say that no president should ever allow anybody else to make the major decisions."

Finally: "I can only say that my experience is there for the people to consider. Senator Kennedy's is there for people to consider. As he pointed out, we came to the Congress in the same year; his experience has been different from mine. Mine has been in the executive branch; his has been in the legislative branch. I would say that the people now have the opportunity to evaluate his against mine, and I think both he and I are going to abide by whatever the people decide."

In a rare reversal, Kennedy's retort was now oddly defensive, as if he himself recognized the advantage Nixon's eight years as vice president gave him. "Well, I'll just say that the question is of experience, and the question also is what our judgment is of the future and what our goals are for the United States and what ability we have to implement those goals." He then offered the sort of ironic observation that contrasted so well with Nixon's sad defense. "Abraham Lincoln came to the presidency in 1860 after a rather little known session in the House of Representatives and after being defeated for the Senate in 1858 and was a distinguished president. There is no certain road to the presidency. There are no guarantees that if you take one road or another that you will be a successful president."

But more than either contestant's words, it was their images, projected on millions of black-and-white Admiral and General Electric televisions, that affected the American judgment. Each time Kennedy spoke, Nixon's eyes darted toward him in an uncomfortable mix of fear and curiosity, the same look Kennedy aide Ted Reardon had spotted more than a decade before at a House committee meeting. When Nixon was on, Kennedy sat, sometimes professorially taking notes, at other moments wearing a sardonic expression as he concentrated on his rival's answers. Sargent Shriver would note that it was his brother-in-law's facial language, more than anything he said, that decided the results of the Great Debate. By raising an eyebrow at Nixon, he had shown he had the confidence to lead the country.

The fight was becoming personal. With the broadcast ended, Nixon tried to repeat the feint he had used so successfully with Khrushchev. Pulling Kennedy aside for what seemed a private conversation, he kept poking his right index finger into his hall mate as if he were lecturing him on something. The photographers clicked away. Having just spent an hour on national television treating Nixon like a lower form of life, Kennedy was getting the other end of the stick, however belatedly.

But in the hours that followed, the challenger was convinced he had won. "Right after the debate, he called me up at the hotel," Lou Harris recalled. *"I know I can take 'im. I know I can take 'im!"* Kennedy had exulted. He was not alone in the assessment. A despondent Henry Cabot Lodge, who had given Nixon the misguided advice to go easy on his rival, watched the last minutes of the debate with dismay. "That son of a bitch just lost the election."

Lodge's running mate headed back to his hotel unsure of how the night had gone. As he arrived, an apparent Nixon booster ran up, loudly consoling him for all the microphones and reporters to hear: "That's all right. You'll do better the next time!" The woman had been put up to the prank by Dick Tuck, the dirty trickster who had humiliated Nixon with the empty university hall in his Senate race a decade earlier.

This night, too, was a debacle. After weeks of parity in the polls, one candidate now moved into a clear lead. A Gallup survey taken in the days following the Great Debate found Nixon with 46 percent, Kennedy pulling ahead to 49 percent. Who had "won" the debate? Forty-three percent said Kennedy; 29 percent called it even. Just 23 percent gave it to Nixon.

Nixon partisans were furious. What could this man have been thinking of, with all that unctuous nonsense of his about Kennedy's motives being sincere, about the two men having similar goals? Why the soft soap? The "old Nixon," the hard charger of the Voorhis and Douglas races, the Hiss case and all the other street fights since, would have drubbed the young swell standing across from him. For the rest of his life Nixon would refuse even to *look* at the tapes.

1

John F. Kennedy and Richard Nixon both served as junior navy officers during World War II. When Kennedy's PT boat was rammed in the Solomon Islands, supply officer Nixon was operating "Nick's Canteen" a hundred miles away. Kennedy returned a war hero, Nixon with a $10,000 kitty, much of it won at poker. Both were elected to Congress on the basis of their war records. Kennedy aide Billy Sutton would say years later that "World War II was their greatest campaign manager."

Both Kennedy and Nixon lost their political virginity in 1946. Kennedy's father tried bribing one rival out of the race and reduced another's vote by paying a man of the same name to file for the same office. Nixon tied his liberal rival to the left-leaning CIO-PAC despite the Democrat's open criticism of postwar strikes and Soviet aggression in Europe.

3

4

Dick Nixon and Jack Kennedy join for a group photo with other freshman congressmen in 1947. Nixon would compare the two to a "pair of unmatched bookends." Their mutual friend, George Smathers of Florida, is standing to Kennedy's right. The three shared an intramural competition to see who would be the first man promoted to the Senate.

5

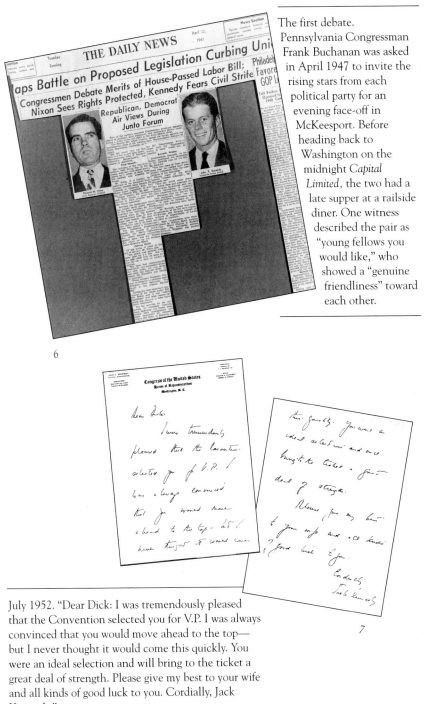

The first debate. Pennsylvania Congressman Frank Buchanan was asked in April 1947 to invite the rising stars from each political party for an evening face-off in McKeesport. Before heading back to Washington on the midnight *Capital Limited*, the two had a late supper at a railside diner. One witness described the pair as "young fellows you would like," who showed a "genuine friendliness" toward each other.

6

7

July 1952. "Dear Dick: I was tremendously pleased that the Convention selected you for V.P. I was always convinced that you would move ahead to the top—but I never thought it would come this quickly. You were an ideal selection and will bring to the ticket a great deal of strength. Please give my best to your wife and all kinds of good luck to you. Cordially, Jack Kennedy."

8

Though invited to attend the "wedding of the year," Nixon accepted President Eisenhower's once-in-a-vice-presidency offer for a weekend of golf in Denver.

9

(*Right, above*) "Don't get mad; get even." As chief counsel to the Senate Government Operations Committee, Robert Kennedy opened a 1956 investigation of Nixon aide Murray Chotiner. As attorney general five years later, he began a quiet probe of the $205,000 loan by Howard Hughes to Nixon's brother.

(*Right, center*) Jack and Jacqueline Kennedy chatting with the vice president after an accidental rendezvous at Chicago's airport in June 1959. Kennedy is holding Allen Drury's hot new political novel *Advise and Consent*. Jacqueline would recall the friendly encounter at a private 1971 White House dinner with then-President Nixon.

(*Right, below*) Jack Kennedy, in Room 362 of the Senate Office Building, asked the vice president, across the hall in Room 361, to write something on this *Washington Post* cartoon showing each of the two 1960 hopefuls keeping a watchful eye on the other man. It came back with: "To my friend and neighbor Jack Kennedy with best wishes for almost everything! Sincerely, Dick Nixon."

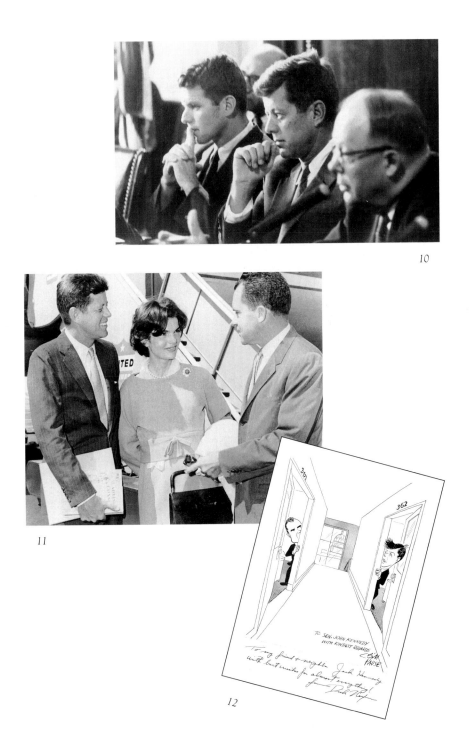

10

11

12

TO SEN. JOHN KENNEDY
WITH KINDEST REGARDS

The Great Debate. The two candidates stand for picture-taking prior to the first debate of the 1960 campaign. Before Kennedy's arrival, Nixon was the star. Confronted by his rival's stunning appearance, the Republican vice president seemed physically overwhelmed. "He looked like a young Adonis," CBS director Don Hewitt recalled.

13

Jack Kennedy passes the final moments in a New York studio before the third presidential debate; Richard Nixon has taken his seat in Los Angeles. The only encounter in which the two candidates spoke from different locations, it was also the only debate that Richard Nixon clearly won.

14

15

On January 6, Nixon performed a ritual duty of the Senate's constitutional president. He stood at the rostrum of the House of Representatives for the official balloting of the Electoral College. The roll call completed, the count stood 303 for Kennedy, 219 for Nixon, 15 for Virginia senator Harry Byrd. After announcing the results, Nixon said: "This is the first time in a hundred years that a candidate for the presidency announced the results of an election in which he was defeated. I do not think we could have a more striking and eloquent example of the stability of our constitutional system."

The Monday after election day, Nixon received Kennedy in Key Biscayne. "It was the difference between night and day," said Nixon press secretary Herb Klein as he recalled the euphoria that swept over his defeated boss when he heard that Kennedy wanted to meet him.

Nixon watches as Kennedy takes the oath of office. Nixon loved the cold war rhetoric of the new president's inaugural address. He also believed "until the day he died" that the election had been stolen from him.

16

17

18

"I just saw a crushed man today." Nixon consoles Kennedy on the failure of the 1961 Cuban invasion. The president tells his guest how California governor Pat Brown is worried about Nixon running against him in 1962. It was a rare reprise of their long-ago cordiality amid the bitterness born of the 1960 election. Nixon spent the rest of the day asking political allies to stand behind Kennedy.

On the eve of his 1969 inauguration, Richard Nixon is reminded by an Oliphant cartoon that he is not the only politician awaiting his turn in the Oval Office.

(*Below*) Senator Robert Dole offers his emotional tribute at the Nixon grave site in 1994. The two met in 1964 when the former vice president campaigned through Kansas. He shared Nixon's "cloth coat" Republican roots and resentment toward the liberal elite.

(*Bottom*) The Watergate and the Kennedy Center sitting beside each other along the Potomac River—like unmatched bookends.

"Next!" January 1969.

19

20

21

CHAPTER ELEVEN

Bearing Any Burden

KENNEDY'S triumph in the first debate made him the country's number-one box office attraction. Traveling through Ohio the next day, he was confronted by a new phenomenon in the political world—the "jumper"—the teenager or young woman who literally jumped up in the crowds to get a better look at the most exciting male sex symbol since the debut of Elvis Presley. On Thursday, Jack and Jackie Kennedy were given genuine *star* treatment on CBS's *Person to Person*. Taped at the Kennedy home in Georgetown, the program was basically a television advertisement for the glamorous young couple. "How does he keep fit?" host Charles Collingwood asked Mrs. Kennedy.

She answered: "He doesn't sleep; he doesn't eat; he doesn't do anything to keep fit, but he thrives on it. It's something that amazes me. He looks wonderful, I think."

The interview showed the Democratic candidate's new level of confidence: John Kennedy had begun to speak like a president. Asked by Collingwood to offer up his thoughts on the "political qualities of leadership," the candidate's response was impromptu and impressive. "I think the principal quality is to have some vision into the future about what you want this country to do and then have an opportunity to communicate that vision. I think that Wilson and Franklin Roosevelt did that particularly well. They set the public interest before the people, the unfinished business. Actually only the president can do that. He is at the center of our constitutional system, the leader of the majority party. The leader of the country, he is able to make a judgment as to what the country must do, what the public interest requires and then, I think, ask the people to do it, and I don't think the people have ever failed to respond to that kind of leadership."

Nixon had no time for such grand appraisals of the presidential office. Having survived the political equivalent of a train wreck, he was engaged in damage control, devouring four milk shakes a day in an attempt to fill out his shirt collar and trying vainly to minimize the event's significance. Like any other team behind in points, what he now needed most was for the other team to fumble.

On October 1, Nixon got his break. During an interview at Hyannis Port, Kennedy offered a foreign policy judgment that would throw him on the defensive. It concerned the offshore Chinese islands of Quemoy and Matsu, which, since the 1949 Communist takeover, had been occupied by the forces of Chiang Kai-shek, leader of the holdout Nationalist government on Formosa. The Communists had been shelling the tiny islands, demanding the evacuation of Chiang's forces. Kennedy told NBC's David Brinkley that helping the Nationalists defend the islands made no strategic sense to him. "It seems to me that we should draw the line very exactly and precisely so that any aggressor knows that if he moves into this area it would mean war. Under the Eisenhower doctrine and the interpretation it has been given, we have stated that we would defend Quemoy and Matsu if it was part of an attack on the island of Formosa. How are we going to make that judgment? On what basis? Quemoy and Matsu are not essential to the defense of Formosa."

These words gave Nixon ammunition for the second debate on October 7. Arriving at the NBC studio in Washington wearing a better-fitting dark suit, the milk shakes having done their work, Nixon clearly had learned from his mistakes. He had even engaged an expert to apply his makeup before he left home. Most important, he was poised to attack. This time, when Kennedy spoke of the need to "bear any burdens" in defending freedom around the world, he would be ready.

Nixon's men were also prepared on the environmental front. Newsman John Harter, then a young NBC page, recalls Bobby Kennedy entering the studio and complaining about the cold temperature, the goal of which was to keep Nixon from sweating as heavily as he had in Chicago. The younger Kennedy quickly headed to the control room, demanding to know what was going on.

When debate number two was under way, Nixon showed that he had been preparing himself not simply to look better than in the first encounter with Kennedy but to fight better as well. "I should point out here," Nixon said, after being asked a general question, "that Senator Kennedy has attacked our foreign policy. He's said that it's a policy that has led to defeat and retreat, and I'd like to know where have we been defeated and where have we retreated? In the Truman administration, six hundred million people went behind the Iron Curtain, including the satellite countries of Eastern Europe and Communist China. In this administration we've stopped them at Quemoy and Matsu. We've stopped them in Indochina. We've stopped them in Lebanon. We've stopped them in other parts of the world." Nixon's reference to Quemoy and Matsu was impossible to ignore.

Kennedy's tortured response to a question on the Chinese islands made him even more vulnerable on the subject. "We have never said flatly that we will defend Quemoy and Matsu if it's attacked. We say we will defend it if it's a part of a general attack on Formosa, but it's extremely difficult to make that judgment." Then he started to backpedal. "I would not suggest the withdrawal at the point of the Communist gun; it is a decision finally that the Nationalists should make, and I believe that we should consult with them and attempt to work out a plan by which the line is drawn at the island of Formosa."

A happy Nixon pounced. "The question is not these two little pieces of real estate—they are unimportant. It isn't the few people who live on them—they are not too important. It's the principle involved. These two islands are in the area of freedom. We should not force our Nationalist allies to get off of them and give them to the Communists. If we do that, we start a chain reaction. In my opinion, this is the same kind of woolly thinking that led to disaster for America in Korea. I am against it. I would not tolerate it as president of the United States, and I will hope that Senator Kennedy will change his mind if he should be elected."

For the first time in the debates, Nixon had scored a hit. He had wounded Kennedy where the Democratic candidate himself knew his party was vulnerable. It was, after all, a target Kennedy himself had shelled back in the "Who lost China?" days. He knew firsthand the potential firepower of the issue: if the Democrats found themselves positioned again as the party of "appeasement" in Asia, they were finished.

In the days ahead, Nixon continued to hit Kennedy for his craven willingness to cede territory to the enemy. "I think it is shocking for a candidate for the presidency of the United States," he said in speech after speech, "to say that he is willing to hand over a part of the Free World to the Communist world. The woolliness of the foreign policy thinking of the opposition party has already cost America tragically in the loss of China to the Communists and in the Korean War. Let me say this to you: If you elect me president, I assure you that I will not hand over one square foot of the Free World to the Communists." Finally, Nixon had a way to attack Kennedy for sharing the same party with the Achesons and Stevensons and all the "woolly thinking" State Department types.

Republican polls now showed that Nixon's new aggressiveness was having an effect, that the Kennedy advantage from the first debate could, in fact, be chipped away at. Unfortunately, Nixon's comeback had been staged before an audience 20 million viewers smaller than the earlier Great Debate.

Kennedy, meanwhile, was trying desperately to stay on the offensive, hoping to make Nixon's emphasis on Quemoy and Matsu appear jingoistic. "Mr. Nixon is not interested in policies of caution in world affairs," he told a supportive crowd at the Waldorf-Astoria. "He boasts that he is a 'risk taker' abroad and a conservative at home. But I am neither. And the American people had a sufficient glimpse of the kind of risks he would take when he said in 1954, 'We must take the risk now of putting our boys in Indo-China on the side of the French if needed to avoid further Communist expansion there.' That is a foolhardy and reckless decision. How much wiser it would be to follow the president's original recommendation—to persuade the Chinese Nationalists to evacuate all military personnel and any civilians who wish to go—now, when we would not be seeming to yield under Communist pressure, before real pressure is put on again."

Jack Kennedy faced two hurdles as he headed into the third debate on October 13. One was that his statements continued to peg him as the squeamish candidate, ready to pull back in Asia, while Nixon remained the vigilant contender, prepared to hold the line. Another problem, perhaps more serious, was the new debate format, which placed the Democrat in a studio in New York and his Republican opponent three thousand miles away in Los Angeles. With an entire country between them, Kennedy's ability to intimidate his rival, so crucial a factor in their first encounter, would be gone.

NBC's Frank McGee posed the first question, asking Kennedy about his charge that Nixon was being "trigger-happy" in regard to Quemoy and Matsu. He wondered if Kennedy would be willing to take military action to defend Berlin. Ignoring the Asia reference, Kennedy limited his answer only to a commitment regarding Berlin. But when Nixon took his turn, he swiftly moved the issue back to the offshore Chinese islands. "As a matter of fact, the statement that Senator Kennedy made was . . . to the effect that there were trigger-happy Republicans, that my stand on Quemoy and Matsu was an indication of trigger-happy Republicans. I resent that comment." On the attack, he challenged Kennedy to come up with the name of a Republican president who had led the country into war. Boldly, Nixon cited the pre–World War II legacy of Munich, comparing Kennedy's position to the appeasement policy toward Hitler's Germany his father had supported as ambassador to Britain. "This is the story of dealing with dictators. This is something that Senator Kennedy and all Americans must know. We tried this with Hitler. It didn't work. He wanted, first, we know, Austria, and then he went on to the Sudetenland, and then Danzig, and each time it was thought this is all he wanted."

Before a national television audience, Richard Nixon was reminding Jack Kennedy of his father's disgrace. "Now what do the Chinese Communists want?" he asked, building dramatically to his climax. "They don't want just Quemoy and Matsu. They don't just want Formosa. They want the world."

Kennedy's response was to cite a letter from President Eisenhower to the chairman of the Senate Foreign Relations Committee promising that the United States would not act militarily "merely in the defense of Quemoy and Matsu." His opponent, he said, was promising to defend the islands under any circumstances. This, Kennedy said, was brinkmanship.

However, when it came his turn, Nixon kept at it. "The president has always indicated that we must not make the mistake of dealing with the dictator or indicating that we are going to make a concession at the point of a gun. Whenever you do that, inevitably the dictator is encouraged to try it again. So, first it will be Quemoy and Matsu. Next, it may be Formosa. What do we do then? My point is this: that once you do this, follow this course of action, of indicating that you are not going to defend a particular area, the inevitable result is that it encourages a man who is determined to conquer the world to press you to the point of no return—and that means war." Nixon called the islands "a symbol of freedom."

NBC's John Chancellor asked the vice president if he intended to keep talking about Quemoy and Matsu. Nixon said the Chinese islands would remain a campaign issue as long as Kennedy persisted in "a fundamental error. He can say now that he no longer believes that a line should be drawn leaving these islands out of the perimeter of defense. If he says that, this issue will not be discussed in the campaign."

Nixon was setting terms. Kennedy's only escape would be to fashion a *mea culpa,* of the sort required from the soft-liners a decade earlier. But the well-prepared Democrat found another route. He accused Eisenhower himself of sending envoys to Chiang asking that he quit the offshore islands. "I challenge you tonight to deny that the administration has sent at least several missions to persuade Chiang Kai-shek to withdraw from these islands."

Time ran out. It had been, nonetheless, the Republican candidate's strongest performance. If the first debate turned the election, the second and third, with their focus on holding the line against Asian communism, would one day drive American foreign policy.

Quemoy and Matsu remained hot. On the October 16 edition of *Meet the Press*, moderator Lawrence Spivak hit Kennedy with question after question on the subject. Trying to deflect the issue, Kennedy cited the Eisenhower policy of fighting for the islands only if the Chinese tried taking them in an all-out grab for Formosa. The dispute, he charged, was actually between Nixon and Ike. But Kennedy's own discomfort with the Quemoy and Matsu issue was manifest. He wanted it dropped.

Strangely, Nixon complied. Kennedy's people approached Secretary of State Herter with a plea that the Democratic candidate didn't want to give any Communists the impression that America was divided on the China front. They told him that Kennedy was even prepared to change his position in order not to appear out of step with administration policy. Nixon agreed to a moratorium on discussions of Quemoy and Matsu.

Kennedy covered his retreat with a shot at his advancing rival. He said he was happy "the politics of a presidential campaign will not risk war by recklessly committing us in advance to the defense of every inch of another nation's territory!" But this is precisely what the presidential debate over Quemoy and Matsu did: commit whoever won to the defense of "every inch" of non-Communist Asia.

THE focus of the Cold War debate was now moving closer to home—Cuba. That March, CIA deputy director Richard Bissell had briefed Vice President Nixon on "dirty tricks" being perpetrated against the Cuban leader. One scheme involved spraying Castro with a drug similar to LSD just prior to one of his planned radio broadcasts, thereby causing the dictator to become disoriented in the midst of his harangue. Another far-fetched plan involved contaminating Castro's cigars with a chemical that would cause his beard to fall out.

Nixon recognized that the weirdness of such pranks belied the very real political danger of having a Communist regime ninety miles off the American coast. He placed far greater reliance on the CIA's creation of a paramilitary force to unleash against the Castro regime. As one of the few people outside of Eisenhower's staff and the CIA itself to know about the covert project, he counted on an invasion, initially set for September, as his political trump card, an election-eve coup that would loudly trumpet the Eisenhower-Nixon supremacy in matters of foreign policy. The vice president's confidence was short-lived; to his exasperation, the CIA plan began to unravel. In April, Nixon sent a memo to his national security adviser, Maj. Robert Cushman, that the agency brass "ought to get off their tails and do something" about Castro. All summer and into the fall campaign, he pushed Ike to act on Cuba, only to be told that the CIA-backed operation was not ready to be put into place. Moreover, Eisenhower was insisting that in advance of the invasion a Cuban government-in-exile first be established. The responsibility for this task was assigned to CIA agent E. Howard Hunt, operating as "Eduardo."

In late summer, the CIA escalated its covert operations against Castro from attempts to embarrass the Cuban leader to plots to assassinate him. In August, Bissell used middleman Robert Maheu to open contact with Chicago crime leader Sam Giancana and other mob figures still angry at the loss of their lucrative gambling and prostitution operations in Havana. That same month, Bissell struck up a relationship with Jack Kennedy, whom he met at a Georgetown dinner party given by columnist Joseph Alsop. Bissell, who had asked Alsop to arrange the meeting, flirted with the notion of quitting the CIA and joining JFK's campaign.

Fidel Castro himself spent much of September 1960 in New York, using the United Nations as his pulpit for spouting anti-American rhetoric. In one memorable episode, the Cuban exuberantly embraced Soviet leader Nikita Khrushchev, who had recently made his own publicity waves banging his shoe on his country's Security Council desk to protest further the U-2 espionage plane that had been shot down several months before over Soviet territory.

In early October, Nixon was driven to ask Republican party

chairman Leonard Hall to encourage Ike to move ahead more speedily on Cuba. Desperately, he went to the president himself, pleading with him to impose a trade ban on the island. Complaining to his aides that the State Department types were too worried about offending "left-wingers" at the *New York Times,* he was forced to play Ike's good soldier. As much as he detested the go-slow policy toward Castro, he had to defend it.

For Richard Nixon, the whole get-Castro effort was moving with lethal slowness. As the election crept closer, Kennedy began to push harder and harder, blaming the Eisenhower administration for the 1959 Communist takeover of Cuba. Like Nixon, he saw the irony of his public position. "Of course, we don't say how we would have saved Cuba. What the hell, they never told us how they would have saved China!" he told liberal speechwriter Richard Goodwin, conveniently forgetting that he, Jack Kennedy, was one of those who had been yelling at Truman the loudest. But if Kennedy saw the paradox in his position, Nixon felt personally damaged by the administration's reluctance to act. "Are they falling dead over there?" he complained to his military aide about the CIA invasion plan. "What in the world are they doing that takes months?"

For Nixon, forced to play dove to Kennedy's hawk, the mutual masquerade grew more and more humiliating. At first, Kennedy merely criticized the Republican administration for failure to compel Castro to hold free elections. Then, in mid-October, after the Cuban leader had raised the ante by nationalizing about four hundred American businesses, Kennedy turned the screw on his rival further by saying that Nixon could talk all he wanted about Quemoy and Matsu; Americans cared much more about events in their own backyard. "The people of the United States would like to hear him discuss his views on an island not four miles off the coast of China but ninety miles off the coast of the United States —Cuba."

Finally, two weeks before the election, the administration declared an embargo on all trade with Cuba except medicine and food. In a further slap at Castro, Eisenhower recalled his ambassador.

Lou Harris was pushing Kennedy, too, to "do something about

Castro." The written questions the Kennedy entourage solicited at evening campaign stops included more uncertainty about Castro and Cuba than about any other foreign policy matter. This triggered a Kennedy demand for tougher sanctions, propaganda, increased support for exile groups. Yet the Democrat stopped short of calling for a U.S.-backed armed invasion by the anti-Castro forces. Having been briefed by the CIA on its plans, he did not want to be blamed for giving away the operation. "Kennedy felt it imperative that he not reveal, even by indirection, the secret knowledge with which he had been entrusted," Richard Goodwin recalled.

But he also refused to be outgunned. In response to Eisenhower's get-tough stance, Kennedy decided to escalate his demands. He told Goodwin to prepare a "real blast at Nixon." He did just that. "We must attempt to strengthen the non-Batista, democratic forces in exile and in Cuba itself who offer eventual hope of overthrowing Castro. Thus far, these fighters for freedom have had virtually no support from our government." When he called the Carlyle Hotel, where Kennedy was staying, Goodwin found his candidate asleep. After checking with other staff members, none of whom was willing to wake him, he went ahead and released the statement to the press.

"Kennedy Advocates U.S. Intervention in Cuba, Calls for Aid to Rebel Forces in Cuba" ran the headline the next morning, which was the same day as the two candidates' final televised debate. Knowing that Kennedy had been briefed by CIA director Allen Dulles, a furious Nixon believed his opponent had betrayed the administration's trust. The Democrat was attacking Eisenhower for not helping the anti-Castro Cubans with military training and equipment, knowing the CIA was doing just that. He was calling on the administration to do something he well knew Nixon could not admit doing. "I could hardly believe my eyes," Nixon would write later. "For the first and only time in the campaign, I got mad at Kennedy *personally.* I thought that Kennedy, with full knowledge of the facts, was jeopardizing the security of a United States foreign policy operation. And my rage was greater because I could do nothing about it."

Nixon was particularly furious at Allen Dulles. At a meeting of the National Security Council, the vice president exploded when the CIA director told those around the table of his meeting with Kennedy. What neither Nixon nor Dulles knew was that there was a second source of information regarding the CIA's plans. Gov. John Patterson of Alabama, a Democrat and close Kennedy ally, had been approached by a CIA official seeking recruits from the state's National Guard to help with a Cuban invasion force. The official told him that President Eisenhower had given his full approval to the operation. Patterson decided to alert his party's presidential candidate, arranging a secret New York meeting through Kennedy brother-in-law Stephen Smith.

Preparing to meet Kennedy in their fourth debate, Nixon was still fuming over Kennedy's "fighters for freedom" statement. When the first question of the final debate concerned Cuba, he threw everything he had at the Democrat, calling Kennedy's recommendations "dangerously irresponsible." He cited a handful of treaties with Latin America, including the charter of the Organization of American States, in which the United States agreed not to intervene in the internal affairs of any other American country. He also cited the UN charter's decree that "there be no intervention by one nation in the internal affairs of another." "Now I don't know what Senator Kennedy suggests when he says that we should help the exiles and those who oppose the regime in Cuba, but I do know this: that if we were to follow that recommendation, we would lose all of our friends in Latin America, we would probably be condemned in the United Nations, and we would not accomplish our objective. I know something else: It would be an open invitation for Mr. Khrushchev to come in, to come into Latin America and to engage us in what would be a civil war and possibly even worse than that." Rather than extend this "invitation" to the other nuclear-armed superpower to come to the defense of Cuba, Nixon recommended the moderate course of economic sanctions. Adlai Stevenson could not have expressed the sentiments better.

Now it was Kennedy's turn to get angry. Knowing of CIA efforts to help the "fighters for freedom," he watched Nixon deride the very notion of such help, mocking Kennedy's immaturity for proposing it. The *New York Times*'s James Reston now added to the insult, calling the senator's comments "probably his worst blunder of the campaign." But Kennedy knew, and he knew Nixon knew, that no American administration, whatever it said publicly, could avoid doing everything it could to clear its backyard of Fidel Castro.

IN their final debate, Kennedy executed a broader line of attack: the growing sense in the country that America was falling behind the Soviets in space and strategic weaponry. Kennedy scoffed at Nixon's assertion, made in the Kitchen Debate, about the Soviets being ahead in rocket thrust but the United States being ahead in color television. "I think that color television is not as important as rocket thrust." The notion that the United States suffered from a "missile gap" would become a powerful metaphor for Kennedy's taunt that America was slipping behind. Many of the nations of Africa, Latin America, and Asia were moving toward the Soviet camp, and according to the Democratic candidate, there was little reason to be confident "that we will be the strongest military power by 1963."

Here was another case where Nixon felt himself undercut by the "Old Boy" foreign policy establishment. Briefing Kennedy, CIA director Allen Dulles had failed to refute the Democrat's "missile gap" charge, thus tacitly endorsing Kennedy's skepticism about America's long-presumed military superiority.

Another Kennedy point of attack was a secret government poll showing a decline in American "prestige" around the world. When Walter Cronkite asked Nixon about it in the fourth debate, Nixon broke the ice with a light joke about being, of course, aware of such a document because he paid such close attention "to everything Senator Kennedy says." The camera caught Kennedy responding with a good-natured laugh. Then, to his rival's face and in front of the entire country, Nixon suddenly revealed the full extent of his bitterness toward the man he believed had betrayed his country's trust with his exploitation of the CIA briefing on Cuba. "America's prestige abroad will be just as high as the spokesmen for America allow it to be," Nixon declared. "Now, when we have a presidential candidate, for example, Senator Kennedy, stating over and over again that the United States is second in space . . . When he states that we're second in education, that we're second in science. . . . When he says . . . we have the worst slums, that we have the most crowded schools, that we have seventeen million people go to bed hungry in this country every night . . ." Millions of voters watching the debate now saw Kennedy reacting angrily in the background.

"When he makes statements like this, what can it do to American prestige?" Nixon continued. "It can only have the effect of reducing it. Let me make one thing very clear. Senator Kennedy has a responsibility to criticize those things that are wrong, but he has also a responsibility to be right in his criticisms. On every one of these items I have mentioned he has been wrong. Dead wrong. And for that reason, he has contributed to any lack of prestige." Flashing Kennedy a smile, he said American leaders should be adding to the nation's "dignity," as Eisenhower was doing, "not running down America the way Senator Kennedy has."

Kennedy took the shot as it was meant, *personally*. "I really don't need Mr. Nixon to tell me about what my responsibilities are as a citizen. I served this country for fourteen years in the Congress and before that in the service. I have just as high a devotion, just as high an opinion . . . What I downgrade is not the country but the leadership the country is getting. . . . Anyone reading the papers and any citizen of the United States must come to the conclusion that the United States no longer commands the same image of a vital society on the move, with its brightest days ahead, as it carried a decade or two decades ago."

Jack Kennedy, harking back to the wartime energies of the 1940s, was promising to *get the country moving again*. Having risen high in the 1950s, Dick Nixon was obliged to defend the somnolent decade.

CHAPTER TWELVE

The Verdict

WITH the fourth and final debate with his charismatic rival behind him, Richard Nixon had reason for optimism: He now had two weeks to concentrate his message of superior Cold War experience and thus overcome Kennedy's 49 percent to 45 percent lead in the Gallup poll. Sadly for the vice president, the nation's civil rights struggle did not conform to his electoral timetable.

On October 19, a group of seventy-five African Americans had politely asked for service at the Magnolia Room in Rich's, the grand Atlanta department store. It was a whites-only restaurant. Among those arrested and charged with trespassing was the Reverend Martin Luther King, Jr. While the other participants in the sit-in were soon released, a judge denied King bail, sentencing the civil rights leader to six months at hard labor. The charge: violating probation on an earlier conviction for driving with an out-of-state driver's license.

Coretta Scott King feared with good reason that her husband, a black man, might not get out of jail alive. The pregnant wife's fears grew to horror when she learned that her husband had been awakened at night, placed in handcuffs and leg chains, then driven hundreds of miles into rural Georgia, never knowing whether or not he was about to be lynched. Mrs. King shared her worry with longtime friend and civil rights activist Harris Wofford, then working for the Kennedy campaign.

After discussing the situation with fellow Kennedy aide Louis Martin, Wofford persuaded Kennedy brother-in-law Sargent Shriver to take the case for action to the candidate. "Why don't you telephone Mrs. King and give her your sympathy," Shriver argued. "Negroes don't expect everything will change tomorrow no matter who's elected, but they do want to know whether you care. If you telephone Mrs. King, they will know that you understand and will help. You will reach their hearts and give support to a pregnant woman who is afraid her husband will be killed."

Despite his yearning for the continued confidence of the conservative southern Democrats who had backed his 1956 vice-presidential run, Kennedy made the call. Mrs. King would later recount his words to her friend Wofford. "I want to express my concern about your husband. I know this must be very hard on you. I understand you are expecting a baby, and I just wanted you to know that I was thinking about you and Dr. King. If there is anything I can do to help, please feel free to call me." From Mrs. King, the press quickly learned about John Kennedy's expressions of sympathy. "It certainly made me feel good that he called me personally and let me know how he felt. I had the feeling that if he was that much concerned, he would do what he could so that Dr. King was let out of jail. I have heard nothing from the vice president or anyone on his staff. Mr. Nixon has been very quiet."

Beyond the hearing of the press Kennedy worried out loud that even his little gesture had been too much. When a reporter asked him about the call to Mrs. King, he appeared irritated at the leak. Campaign manager Robert Kennedy was downright furious. "Do you know that this election may be razor close and you have probably lost it for us!" he scolded Wofford and Shriver. Yet a day later, the younger Kennedy, nimble enough to exploit the political turn of events, called the judge who had sentenced King to ask for his release on bail. Louis Martin, an African American, was elated when his friend Bobby Kennedy phoned in the early-morning hours with news of his successful mission. "You are now an honorary brother."

Nixon, meanwhile, was silent. Despite his pro–civil rights record and Quaker's commitment to the cause of black equality and opportunity—a Whittier friend recalls the vice president being quite passionate on the topic over a beer one afternoon—the King arrest had brought no reaction from the Republican candidate. There were reasons for this, among them Nixon's hope to make inroads, as Eisenhower had done, among white southern-ers. "At least we're going to give the people down there a choice, something that they sometimes have not had in previous times." Just the week before, Nixon had publicly disavowed a commit-ment by running mate Henry Cabot Lodge that a black would be named to the cabinet. The flip-flop had its predictable effects, the initial promise disturbing southern whites, the ultimate denial disappointing hopeful blacks. Nixon now feared that his involve-ment or interference in the King matter would, as he told press secretary Herb Klein, "look like he was pandering." Baseball hero Jackie Robinson tried and failed to elicit a Nixon statement when he caught up with the Republican vice president on a whistle-stop tour through the Midwest. "He thinks calling Martin would be grandstanding," Robinson tearfully said after meeting the man who had until that moment been his candidate. "Nixon doesn't understand."

For his failure to act, Nixon would pay dearly. Martin Luther King, Sr., like his son a prominent Atlanta minister, now decided to endorse Kennedy publicly despite the religious difference be-tween them. "I had expected to vote against Senator Kennedy because of his religion," the elder King somberly told his flock in the Ebenezer Baptist Church during the exultant welcome-home service held for his rescued son. "But now he can be my president, Catholic or whatever he is. It took courage to call my daughter-in-law at a time like this. He had the moral courage to stand up for what he knows is right. I've got my votes, and I've got a suitcase, and I'm going to take them up there and dump them in his lap."

Up at Kennedy headquarters in Washington, Harris Wofford and Louis Martin were about to make history. Collecting all the appreciative and admiring comments pouring in from black leaders and others praising the Kennedys' efforts on behalf of the Kings, they found a pair of Philadelphia ministers willing to sponsor publication of a pamphlet, "The Case of Martin Luther King," which laid out the story of the Kennedy-King episode in bold language. "*No Comment* Nixon Versus a Candidate with a Heart, Senator Kennedy," one caption read. "I earnestly and sincerely feel that it is time for all of us to take off our Nixon buttons," the Reverend Ralph Abernathy, a King ally, was quoted in the document. "Since Mr. Nixon has been silent through all this, I am going to return his silence when I go into the voting booth."

The pamphlet, 2 million copies of which were printed on light blue paper and delivered to black churches the Sunday before election, would be dubbed "the blue bomb." Yet it never stirred even the mildest alarm among conservative white voters, who would remain loyal to the national Democratic ticket. In a silent coup, black America was being moved overnight to the Democratic side of the ballot, from the party of Lincoln to that of the Kennedys. Martin Luther King, Jr., summing up the episode's meaning, was eloquent: "There are moments when the politically expedient can be morally wise." Murray Chotiner himself could not have worked the gambit better.

DESPITE the King episode, which for many added to Kennedy's moral stature, and despite the advantages of his newly celebrated glamour, Jack Kennedy was losing momentum by late October and Nixon was gaining, even as the most potent Republican weapon still lay covered in the armory. President Dwight D. Eisenhower—the general who had accepted the Nazi surrender papers—was at last ready to hit the road for Nixon and defeat the Democrat he sarcastically called "that young genius." "Listen, dammit," he told an Oval Office guest, "I'm going to do everything possible to keep that Jack Kennedy from sitting in this chair."

But he could have done more than he did. On October 31, Nixon was invited to lunch with the president and his speech-writers. Despite at last having his boss on his side and willing to help, Nixon was behaving a bit oddly. When Eisenhower described enthusiastically his plans for expanding his campaign schedule on behalf of his vice president, the candidate seemed reluctant to share Ike's ready-for-battle fervor. Infuriated, the president lashed out. "Goddammit, he looks like a loser. When I had an officer like that in World War II"—he demonstrate by hunching his shoulders and bending his head down—"I relieved him." Only years later did Nixon reveal the serious warning he had received at the time, first from a concerned Mamie Eisenhower and then seconded by the president's physician, that too vigorous a campaign effort would threaten Ike's weakened heart.

Another explanation for his unwillingness to send the general into action may have been that Nixon was again taken in by Kennedy's taunts. Just as his rival's refusal of makeup in the first debate had prodded him to do the same, he was now determined again to prove himself the better man, foolishly forfeiting his own greatest advantage. According to Pat Hillings, "he had stood in Ike's shadow for eight years and suffered a lot of humiliation. Now he wanted to win on his own."

Had Nixon been able to judge his situation with clearer eyes, he would have seen Ike as the deal maker between him and the hundreds of thousands of voters who remained uncommitted as the election approached. Abdicating his position as Ike's partisan successor was like Jack Kennedy deciding to reject some of his father's money or to minimize his telegenic appearance in order to prove himself the better man. The final Gallup poll, taken October 30 through November 1, showed Nixon with 48 percent and Kennedy with 49 percent. The Republican candidate was taking a needless gamble in rejecting the 100 percent help of the man who, despite having treated him so roughly during the Checkers and "dump Nixon" episodes, was now squarely on his side.

* * *

ENTERING the campaign as he did at the most critical moment, like a blue-coated cavalry charge from the hills, Ike was nevertheless an awesome presence. "Now I've heard complaints about the country not moving," the president said, mocking Kennedy's favorite mantra to a Westchester, New York, airport crowd. "Of course you can move easily. You can move back to inflation. You can move back to deficit spending. You can move back to the military weakness that allowed the Korean War to occur. No trouble at all." Ike's impact on the enemy was immediate. "Unlike a lot of Republicans," Ken O'Donnell noted later, "Kennedy felt that Nixon was right in keeping Eisenhower out of the campaign as long as possible. If Nixon had brought Eisenhower into the campaign earlier, Kennedy would have charged him with hiding behind Ike's favorable image and being unable to stand on his own record and merits."

To counter the impact of the five-star general's emergence, Kennedy's team settled on a delicate strategy. They decided to treat Ike with all proper respect, at the same time ridiculing Nixon for being so desperate as to resort to Ike's intervention on behalf of his sputtering candidacy. "I don't care how many rescue squads they send," the Democratic candidate scoffed. "You've seen those elephants in the circus. They have a long memory but no vision. When they move around the ring, they have to grab the tail of the elephant in front of them so they'll know where to go. Dick grabbed the tail of the elephant ahead of him in 1952 and 1956, but now, in 1960, he's the one who is supposed to be running, not President Eisenhower."

But if the pro-JFK crowds lining his own parade routes and the local politicians cheering his every cliché believed this bravado, the candidate himself knew better. Jack Kennedy could feel the old general's popularity working its magic. "Last week Dick Nixon hit the panic button and started Ike," Kennedy told San Francisco pal Red Fay as the candidate soaked in his Palace Hotel bathtub. "With every word he utters, I can feel the votes leaving me. It's like standing on a mound of sand with the tide running out. If the election were held tomorrow, I'd win easily, but six days from now, it's up for grabs."

Eisenhower's speeches were breathtakingly direct, tearing into the Kennedy complaints about Castro and allusions to a missile gap. "A nation needs leaders who have been immersed in the hard facts of public affairs in a great variety of situations, men of character who are able to take the long-range view and hold long-range goals, leaders who do not mistake minor setbacks for major disasters," he said to cheering applause, "and we need leaders who by their own records have demonstrated a capacity to get on with the job. This is why I am so wholeheartedly in back of Richard Nixon and Henry Cabot Lodge."

Ike's economic policy was not so helpful. While his late entry into the campaign counted as a definite plus, his tight-fisted fiscal policy was a clear minus. From 5.9 percent in August, the nation's jobless rate rose to 6.4 percent in October, its highest since the previous recession. Between the conventions and election day, 330,000 people were thrown out of work. Not many of those hundreds of thousands of pink-slipped workers were in a mood to cheer Republican "peace and prosperity."

Despite the huge presence of Eisenhower in the campaign's closing week, Kennedy morale stayed high. No longer the newly minted nominee of the late summer, the maturing, more seasoned JFK was suddenly statesmanlike, explaining to audiences how it was the "president's responsibility to set before the American people the unfinished business of our society, to rally them to a great cause." Even when things went wrong on the campaign trail, Kennedy kept on enjoying himself. When a microphone went dead at a Los Angeles stop, he didn't miss a beat. "That never happens in the vice president's campaign. I understand everything's in perfect order all the time," he told the laughing crowd. "They don't get the votes, but it's well organized." When an electrician arrived and began fumbling with the microphone, Kennedy joked that the man was actually the local Republican congressman. "You all know Pat Hillings, don't you?" he said to loud applause.

With the end near, Kennedy openly flaunted his contempt for the other side. "I stand tonight where Woodrow Wilson stood and Franklin Roosevelt and Harry Truman stood," he proclaimed in Buffalo. "Dick Nixon stands where McKinley stood, where Harding and Coolidge and Landon stood, where Dewey stood.

Where do they *get* these candidates?" The Nixon people wanted the press to focus on the far sexier topic of Jack Kennedy's private life. Pat Nixon was especially frustrated by what seemed a media conspiracy to package their opponent as a devoted husband. She had not counted on this wall of protection around her husband's rival. "I knew Kennedy too well to think that the country would elect him."

Just as Kennedy had now turned his politics of contempt on Nixon, Nixon now targeted his politics of resentment on Kennedy. "You know, it's not *Jack's* money they're going to be spending!" It was a shot Kennedy would never forget. His references to his rival became withering. "The first living creatures to orbit the earth in space and return were dogs named Strelka and Belka, not Rover or Fido—or Checkers." Backing up his charge that Dick Nixon, his rival, had been standing still, Kennedy offered himself as an on-the-spot eyewitness. "I know because I've been there with him for the past fourteen years."

It grew hotter still. To a Nixon accusation that he was a "barefaced liar," Kennedy retorted: "Having seen him in close-up—and makeup—for our television debates, I would never accuse Mr. Nixon of being barefaced." Away from the microphones and reporters' notebooks, he could be nastier still. "He's a filthy, lying son of a bitch and a very dangerous man," Richard Goodwin heard him say once. Enraged at his rival's charge that he was out to "wreck" Social Security, Nixon could only fume: "Now the first time you say something wrong like that, it's a mistake. The second time you say it, it's a bad mistake. The third time you say it when you know it's wrong, it's a falsehood or lie, and that's what I call it tonight."

Kennedy's attacks on Nixon's character were now underscored by a timely bit of muckraking. Two weeks before the election, columnist Drew Pearson, whom Nixon had saved from Joe McCarthy's inebriated assault a decade earlier, reported that the vice president's brother, Donald, had borrowed $205,000 from billionaire Howard Hughes a few years earlier. Technically lent to Nixon's mother, the money was to finance an expansion of his parents' old grocery store in Whittier. Capitalizing on the family name, Donald Nixon had added, among other touches, a drive-in restaurant featuring "Nixonburgers." Questions about the "Hughes loan," so reminiscent of the 1952 "fund" episode, would haunt Nixon for the rest of his days.

Kennedy, too, worried about dirt, waiting for Nixon's people to hit him with a charge, perhaps even hard evidence, of what JFK privately called his "girling." But they never did. Voters would never catch so much as a glimpse of *that* Jack Kennedy. One Nixon aide, watching a news film of Jack and Jackie in the final hours of the campaign, suddenly was struck by the power of the beautiful couple's allure. *Good God,* he would recall thinking to himself, how do you run against *that!*

For whatever reason, Nixon never once unleashed the kind of scorched-earth raid on the enemy that had made him such a ferocious campaigner in the past. After a weak attempt at getting Ike to force public revelation of his opponent's Addison's disease —presidential press secretary James Hagerty thought it indecent for Eisenhower to ask the candidates to do what he himself had done four years earlier, following Ike's heart attack—Nixon backed off and let the matter rest. The man warned to avoid the "assassin image" never did get all that tough with Jack Kennedy.

ON election day, November 8, Nixon escaped the country, driving with an aide down to Mexico, where he and Pat had driven after that first great victory in 1946. Kennedy awaited the returns at his father's house at Hyannis Port. Before dinner he placed a call to Chicago mayor Richard Daley. "Mr. President, with a little bit of luck and the help of a few close friends," Kennedy quoted Daley to *Newsweek's* Ben Bradlee minutes later, "you're going to carry Illinois." The Democrat would carry the pivotal state by a scant 8,858 votes. "Later, when Nixon was being urged to contest the 1960 election," wrote Bradlee, "I often wondered about that statement." One Chicago voter totally in the dark about the mayor's success was Ed Myles, whose ballot was cast in the Fourth Ward, Thirty-first Precinct. The late Mr. Myles was part of Richard Daley's loyal "cemetery vote."

By 11:30 P.M. California time, the results were clear. At the

Ambassador, the same Los Angeles hotel where he had prepared for the Checkers speech eight years earlier, Richard Nixon now told his two daughters, Tricia and Julie, he had lost. There remained only a remote chance of victory. He would need to carry his home state of California plus two of the three states—Minnesota, Michigan, and Illinois—still undecided. "If the present trend continues," Richard Nixon told the loyal crowd waiting in the hotel ballroom, his arm around Pat, who was holding back tears, "Senator Kennedy will be the next president of the United States." As supporters shouted out that he not concede, Nixon doggedly kept on. "Certainly if the trend continues and he does become our next president, he will have my wholehearted support."

"Does this mean you're president, Bunny?" Jackie Kennedy asked her husband back in the Hyannis Port compound.

"Why don't you give up?" someone else in the room exhorted the face on the television screen.

"Why should he?" Kennedy jumped in. "I wouldn't in his place."

JOHN F. Kennedy had won the election with 303 votes in the Electoral College to Nixon's 219. At forty-three, he was the youngest person ever elected president. Nixon's press secretary, Herb Klein, read the concession statement: "I want to repeat through this wire the congratulations and best wishes I extended to you on television last night. I know that you will have the united support of all Americans as you lead the nation in the cause of peace and freedom during the next four years."

"Your sincere good wishes are gratefully accepted," Kennedy wired back. "You are to be congratulated for a fine race. I know that the nation can continue to count on your unswerving loyalty in whatever new effort you undertake and that you and I can maintain our long-standing cordial relations in the years ahead." The Kennedy telegram cloaked the winner's contempt for his rival's refusal to concede in the venue that had decided the election: television. "He went out the way he came in," Kennedy remarked. "No class."

Adding to Kennedy's anger was growing scuttlebutt of voter

fraud in Illinois and elsewhere. Such talk could undermine the legitimacy of his election. What Kennedy now needed, as rumors spread of voting-booth shenanigans in Chicago and in Lyndon Johnson's Texas, was certification of his mandate to lead the country. Only one man could give him that.

CHAPTER
THIRTEEN

If

| Kennedy | 34,226,731 |
| Nixon | 34,108,157 |

RICHARD Nixon would spend the rest of his life examining the many factors that could have reversed the 1960 presidential election results. If Lyndon Johnson had not been on the Democratic ballot and his allies not in unchallenged control of the Texas election machinery, the state wouldn't have given the Democratic ticket its 46,000 plurality. If the twenty-seven electoral votes of Illinois and the twenty-four of Texas had been switched from Kennedy's column to Nixon's, the final tally in the Electoral College would have been 270–252 for Nixon instead of 303–219 for Kennedy.

Nor did Nixon's people believe ballot theft was limited to those states. They had enough reports of "irregularities" elsewhere to challenge the outcome even without Texas. They figured a fair count in Arkansas, whose eight electoral votes Kennedy had won by 30,541 votes, or Missouri, whose thirteen electoral votes Kennedy got with less than 9,980 votes, or New Mexico, whose four electoral votes the Democrat had won with a skimpy 2,294 votes, could have combined with Illinois to give the Republicans an outright victory.

There were still other possibilities. Had Nixon gotten Illinois, Arkansas, and New Mexico but not Missouri, Kennedy would have fallen short of the required 269 electoral votes; the election would then have to be decided by the House of Representatives. There, with each state delegation getting a single vote, Nixon's victories in the majority of states might have proven decisive.

Unfortunately, the Chicago ballots, on which all else depended, had been quickly destroyed. Texas presented a different problem, since its law had no provision for a recount. Still, if Nixon had chosen to fight, possibilities remained. "We had enough evidence. We had all kinds of affidavits. It did not all turn on Chicago," campaign manager Bob Finch would argue. Texas, its government and election apparatus firmly in Democratic hands, remained the stumbling block. Moving the state legislature in Austin to review the balloting, investigate charges of fraud, and review the count would have required a heroic effort. It would have kept the American government and its Cold War leadership on hold for months. Nixon decided to accept the verdict as it was. Without success, he urged the *Herald Tribune*'s Earl Mazo to kill a series of stories on voting fraud in Chicago's and Texas. The country, he said, could not afford to be without a leader.

Richard Nixon's sense of being robbed of a deserved victory, which never left him, would one day be joined by a colder, broader political assessment. The loser would come to believe that he had lost a game of political hardball at which his opponent had come better prepared to do precisely what was necessary for victory. The vote stealing evidenced in Chicago, Texas, and other Democratic strongholds was simply due to the other side's tougher skills. His rival had simply been better at the game than he.

I had been through some pretty tough campaigns in the past, but compared to the others, going into the 1960 campaign was like moving from the minor to the major leagues. I had an efficient, well-financed and highly motivated organization. But we faced an organization that had equal dedication and unlimited money, that was led by the most *ruthless* group of political operatives ever mobilized for a presidential campaign. Kennedy's organization approached dirty tricks with a roguish relish and carried them off with an insouciance that captivated many politicians and overcame the critical faculties of many reporters. The way the Kennedys played politics and the way the media let them get away with it left me angry and frustrated. From this point on, I had the wisdom and wariness of someone who had been burned by the power of the Kennedys and their money and by the license they were given by the media. I vowed that I would never again enter an election at a disadvantage by being vulnerable to them—or anyone—on the level of political tactics.

On the Saturday after the election, the Kennedys were ensconced in Palm Beach, expecting Nixon to demand a recount. Even the vice president's silence was a problem. There needed to be a formal, public validation of the country's decision.

Richard Nixon was in no condition for such rituals. Not yet. As he had after every election since 1950, when George Smathers first suggested the refuge, the exhausted vice president had flown to Key Biscayne for rest and emotional refueling. Never had he needed them more. In the same hours that Jack Kennedy puzzled at the narrowness of his victory, Nixon felt the knife-edge of defeat. Herb Klein recalls both the heavy mood that Saturday and the fascinating development that was to lift it.

"Nixon was, in my opinion, more unresponsive than at any time I had known him. He was completely depressed and had finally realized, four days later, that he'd lost the election." The Nixon party, which included the vice president, Pat, Bob Finch, Klein, their wives, Nixon pal Bebe Rebozo, and secretary Rose Mary Woods, had assembled for drinks at the Key Biscayne Hotel. When the group moved to the Jamaica Inn for dinner, the maître d' said there was a call for the vice president. As the defeated candidate moved with the others to their reserved table, Klein was delegated to take the call. He found Herbert Hoover on the line waiting to speak to Nixon. The former president had just gotten a call at his Waldorf Towers apartment from Joseph Kennedy, who had asked if he would see if Nixon would be willing to meet with the president-elect "about what to do with the country divided." Once again, the senior Kennedy was enlisting his vast contacts into his son's service. He had found the perfect conduit to the defeated Dick Nixon, a former president who had himself recovered from harsh electoral defeat.

Nixon would quote Hoover in his memoirs: "Hello, Chief!" Nixon said to his old mentor, then listened as Hoover did precisely what his wealthy crony had requested. "The ambassador has just called me and suggested that it would be a good idea for you and the president-elect to get together for a visit. If you approve of the idea, the president-elect, who is now in Palm Beach, would like to phone you to make the necessary arrangements. I think we are in enough trouble in the world today that some indications of national unity are not only desirable but essential."

What Nixon would not record was how thrilled he was with the Kennedy call. In a fit of despair just moments before, the defeated vice president was now euphoric. "It was the difference between night and day," Klein remembers. Back at the table, Nixon, Finch, and he resolved that a meeting with Kennedy "would be a good thing" but that first Nixon should telephone President Eisenhower, who told his number-two man not to sign off on any Republican serving in the Kennedy cabinet. He didn't want the new administration painting itself with the "color of coalition." Young Kennedy had been ambitious to have the daunting duty of the presidency. Now he had it.

Jack Kennedy was too anxious to wait. As Nixon talked to Ike on the public pay phone, the maître d's phone rang for the vice president. "He was very, very chatty," recalled Klein, who had gotten to know the senator during those many years spent working across the hall. He said how well Nixon's press secretary had presented himself on television the morning after the election, saying he wished that his own spokesman, Pierre Salinger, dressed as well. Finally, Kennedy got to the point. He wanted a meeting.

When Nixon called back, using the number the president-elect had left him, Kennedy said he would be more than glad to come down to Key Biscayne that Monday, "if it won't interfere with your vacation." Kennedy was worried, figuring that a single wrong word could trigger Nixon into demanding recounts. But his supplicatory tone wasn't necessary.

"I would be glad to come up to Palm Beach to call on you," Nixon assured him. "After all, that's the proper thing to do in view of last Tuesday's results."

Kennedy laughed. "No, I have a helicopter at my disposal, and it would be easier for me to come to you." About to succeed Dwight Eisenhower as the country's commander in chief, he already held a token of the arsenal.

WHEN the appointed time for the Kennedy-Nixon meeting arrived, the defeated man, surrounded by reporters and photographers, was forced to stand a long, humiliating watch outside the Key Biscayne Hotel. Kennedy, once again, was late, just as he had been arriving to the Great Debate. Nixon would recall the scene decades later. "First the Dade County police escort came heading up the hotel drive. Behind them was the Secret Service car. In the next car, a convertible, was Kennedy sitting in the backseat looking almost lonely."

Greeting him, Nixon suggested that the two ex–junior officers observe navy protocol, with the president-elect walking on the right, befitting his higher rank, the vice president on the left. Then, after making Kennedy comfortable on the porch of one of the hotel's villas, he went inside to get him and his guest some Cokes.

"Well, it's hard to tell who won the election at this point," Kennedy began. When Nixon refused to take the bait, Kennedy told his defeated colleague that he would welcome his advice on putting together the administration. Nixon responded with two suggestions. First, he noted that the CIA might successfully be split in two, with one entity responsible for gathering intelligence, the other for covert action. The second area of Nixon counsel dealt with the status of China. He had heard from Smathers just

the day before that some of Kennedy's liberal advisers were pushing him to admit the Communist Chinese to the United Nations.
This, Nixon told Kennedy, he would oppose vigorously.

Kennedy also mentioned that he was thinking of Henry Cabot
Lodge, among other Republicans, for a foreign policy post. Kennedy wondered if Nixon himself might like some sort of "tempo-
rary" overseas assignment. Sensing that the offer was actually
more ritual than real, Nixon declined.

Kennedy never raised Nixon's apparent decision not to contest
the election results. He didn't have to. The meeting had created
just the picture of victor meeting victim that his impresario father
had hoped to stage. Just as Nixon had tricked Kennedy during
the photo opportunity at the Great Debate, making him appear
subservient, so Kennedy was now having his way with his rival,
listening obligingly to Nixon's advice for the sole purpose of
getting Nixon's television picture paying court to him as the
president-elect.

The intent was made clear in a later meeting with reporters.
"Ladies and gentlemen, I just wanted to say that the vice president and I had a very cordial meeting. I was delighted to have a
chance to see him again. We came to the Congress the same day
fourteen years ago, and both served on the Labor Committee of
the House of Representatives. So I was anxious to come here
today and resume our relationship, which had been somewhat
interrupted by the campaign." Asked whether he had offered
Nixon an appointment, Kennedy was curt. "We did not discuss
that." Had the two discussed the campaign during their hour-long
meeting? "I asked him how he took Ohio, but he did not tell me,"
Kennedy joked. "He is saving it for 1964."

Back in Washington, the lame-duck vice president soon was
busy personally signing an enormous batch of thank-you letters to
campaign workers. "My only regret," he wrote to a California
supporter, "is that I could not have done that extra bit which
would have assured victory nationally for all of you who worked
so hard for our cause." But he never did call for a recount. If Jack
Kennedy felt gratitude for the vice president's graceful acceptance
of defeat, he never voiced it to Nixon or anyone else.

In late November, Kennedy was briefed by the CIA's Allen

Dulles on plans for the upcoming invasion of Cuba, plans Nixon had been pushing for months. The president-elect showed neither surprise nor a wish to change course. His mind was on picking a cabinet. Hearing his son grouse one day in Palm Beach about his problems matching cabinet slots with the powerful egos who sought to fill them, Joe Kennedy reminded his son of the thin line separating victory from defeat. "Jack, if you don't want the job, you don't have to take it. They're still counting votes in Cook County."

THE narrowness of the verdict—Kennedy 49.7 percent, Nixon 49.5 percent—was as profound as the decision. Half of those entering the voting booths had responded to the younger man's call to "get the country moving again." As *Time* observed: "Kennedy had done it all not with any specific program, or even any specific catalogue of faults. He had done it by driving home the simple message of *unease*, of things left undone in the world where a slip could be disastrous. But most of all, he had done it by the force of his own youthful and confident personality, which seemed to promise freshness and vigor. The U.S. had literally taken Jack Kennedy at face value."

Half the United States, that is. Despite all the mythmaking to come later, roughly the same number of Americans chose Nixon as his far more appealing rival. They'd done so with little encouragement from Nixon's party, whose congressional candidates ran four points behind him. "Nixon was more popular than his party," Kennedy aide Ted Sorensen wrote later, "and more able and likeable than his enemies portrayed him." Colleague Dick Goodwin went further: "As a result of our hostility, we underestimated Nixon. Admittedly, he was clever, certainly he understood politics, the art of acquiring votes and power. But we thought he did not know, thus could not reach, the country he aspired to govern. We were wrong. He knew a lot about America. He could reach, with uncanny intuition, the buried doubts, the secret dreads, the nightmare panic of the threatened soul."

The close call affected both men. Nixon, feeling himself the victim of an ambush, would spend the rest of his career trying to avoid another. Kennedy, stunned by the close split, would remain embittered toward his rival, who had convinced half the country he was Jack Kennedy's better. "I can remember him telling me, 'If I've done nothing for this country, I've saved them from Dick Nixon,' " pal Red Fay recalled of those Palm Beach days after the election. It marked, as his old PT boat pal logged it, a "180-degree reversal" in Kennedy's attitude toward his Republican colleague. He had joined the Nixon haters.

ON December 22, three days before Christmas, Nixon received an ironic communication in his capacity as president of the U.S. Senate. Addressed to "Richard N. Nixon," it was a copy of Kennedy's letter to the governor of Massachusetts resigning his position. And in a more dramatic twist, Nixon was next forced to preside over Kennedy's ascension to the nation's highest position. On January 6, 1961, a blustery, snowy day in Washington, Nixon stood at the rostrum of the House of Representatives for the quadrennial balloting of the Electoral College. He was to officiate at his own political requiem.

The first state to be counted, Alabama, showcased the narrow division in the popular vote two months earlier. Five Alabama electoral votes were cast for John F. Kennedy. Six, those of the unpledged electors, went to the segregationist Sen. Harry F. Byrd of Virginia. "The gentleman from Virginia is now in the lead," Nixon remarked to a roar of laughter, exhibiting the wry humor that would forever be associated with his rival.

The roll call of the fifty states completed, the count stood Kennedy, 303; Nixon, 219; Byrd, 15. Without notes, the candidate with the 219 electoral votes spoke to the assembled senators and members of the House.

This is the first time in one hundred years that a candidate for the presidency announced the result of an election in which he was defeated. I do not think we could have a more striking and eloquent example of the stability of our constitutional system and of the proud tradition of the American people of developing, respecting and honoring institutions of self-government. In our campaigns, no matter how hard fought they may be, no matter how close the election may turn out to be, those who lose accept the verdict and support those who win. It is in that spirit that I now declare that John F. Kennedy has been elected President of the United States.

Democratic and Republican members gave Nixon a standing ovation.

O N January 19, the day before the inauguration, Jack Kennedy went to the White House for one last meeting with the great World War II general he would succeed. Clark Clifford, who had piloted him through the controversy over authorship of *Profiles in Courage* and was now advising him on the transition, accompanied the president-elect and took notes. The two critical topics were Cuba and the Communist threat in Southeast Asia. The Eisenhower policy toward Fidel Castro, Ike told Kennedy, was to seek his overthrow. While "no specific plans for an invasion have yet been made," he said, "they should be as soon as a government-in-exile is formed." Eisenhower regarded Laos as the most serious potential problem facing the United States, according to Clifford. The old soldier was uncharacteristically passionate about the inland country, which was under more immediate threat than neighboring South Vietnam. "If we permit Laos to fall, then we will have to write off the entire area." Promising support of Kennedy on foreign policy, he made a single exception. It was the same point on which Nixon had taken a stand at Key Biscayne. Ike put his successor on notice that he would rally public opinion against any recognition of Communist China.

A s he had in January 1947, Jack Kennedy arrived in frigid Washington with a Palm Beach tan. For drama, he endured the inaugural ceremonies without a topcoat, warming himself instead with long underwear. But if he and wife Jacqueline's glamour offered a stark contrast to the gray face of the preceding administration, his address from the east front of the Capitol underlined their similarities. Except for his admonition to "ask not what your country can do for you; ask what you can do for your country," a hard Republican-sounding slap at the welfare state, Kennedy devoted the entire address to the subject his rival had emphasized in the campaign: foreign policy.

The new president's martial cadences were more synchronized with his rival's career than his own. Gone was the cautious stance of the Quemoy and Matsu debate, the unorthodox nature of his Algeria speech. "Let every nation know, whether it wishes us well or ill, that we shall pay any price, bear any burden, meet any hardship, support any friend, oppose any foe to assure the survival and the success of liberty." He was giving the other candidate's speech. "Let the word go forth from this time and place, to friend and foe alike, that the torch has been passed to a new generation of Americans, born in this century, tempered in war, disciplined by a hard and bitter peace, proud of our ancient heritage, and unwilling to witness or permit the slow undoing of those human rights to which this nation has always been committed, and to which we are committed today at home and around the world."

With this stirring call to arms concluded, Nixon, who loved the brazen Cold War rhetoric, jumped from his chair, paused patiently as the new president accepted the congratulations of others, then gingerly tapped his old colleague, now the president of the United States, on the back. He then clutched Kennedy's hand in exultant tribute for giving the sort of Cold War call to arms that saluted both men's worldviews. But Kennedy's stiff body language suggested little relish for the eager tribute. His use for his adversary at an end, the new leader met Nixon not as a hearty club member he had just taken in golf but as a social discard, a gentleman finessing a gate-crasher. The last thing Kennedy needed was a prominent news photo of a sportsmanlike Richard Nixon graciously congratulating the winner while validating his own new role as leader of the loyal opposition.

HOURS later, as John F. Kennedy basked in the glow of the inaugural balls, Nixon made a sentimental journey. Forced to surrender his car and driver at midnight, he went for one last ride through the nation's capital.

"No one noticed as we drove past the White House and headed through the streets toward Capitol Hill," where his rival had just become president.

I got out and walked up the broad stone stairs. A surprised guard let me in, and I walked past the entrance to the Senate chamber and down the long corridor to the Rotunda, the dome of the Capitol rising above it. The only sound was the echo of my heels on the bare stone floor. I opened a door and went out onto the balcony that looks out across the west grounds of the Capitol. I had stood there many times before. It is one of the most magnificent vistas in the world and it never seemed more beautiful than at this moment. The mall was covered with fresh snow. The Washington Monument stood out stark and clear against the luminous gray sky, and in the distance I could see the Lincoln Memorial. I stood looking at the scene for at least five minutes. I thought about the great experiences of the past fourteen years. Now all that was over, and I would be leaving Washington, which had been my home since I arrived as a young congressman in 1947. As I turned to go inside, I suddenly stopped short, struck by the thought that this was not the end, that someday I would be back here. I walked as fast as I could back to the car.

CHAPTER FOURTEEN

Bay of Pigs

FROM the moment they arrived at the White House, the Kennedys fashioned a mystique of seemingly effortless elegance and sophistication about the new presidency. They invited cultural icons like cellist Pablo Casals to give White House concerts for small groups. Though he joked to a pal about not knowing exactly what instrument the Spaniard played, Jack Kennedy instinctively understood that such guests added an air of style and assurance to the New Frontier. "It's not what you are," his father had taught, "it's what people think you are that counts."

Backstage from the black-tie cello concerts and other trappings of entitlement, Kennedy could not forget the bitter political score. "Don't get mad; get even" was still the Kennedy credo. His irritation at Nixon's campaign tactics was palpable. *New York Times* photographer George Tames recalled going to the White House to shoot a photo of Kennedy with his sparring partner from the previous year's Democratic primaries, Minnesota senator Hubert Humphrey.

"Wait till I'm ready, George," Kennedy said, moving uncomfortably close to Humphrey and poking him hard in the stomach.

"For chrissake, Jack. What are you doing?" his guest demanded, backing away.

"Just a little trick I picked up from Nixon," Kennedy said, chuckling at the distasteful memory of Nixon's stage gimmick. "Not only do you keep him off balance, but you upstage him."

Keeping Richard Nixon off balance remained high on the Kennedy agenda. Within months of taking office, the new attorney general, Robert Kennedy, ordered a Justice Department investigation of the Nixon family's loan from Howard Hughes. He dropped the matter only when he could not find any evidence with which to prosecute.

Beneath the New Frontier's confident exterior there lay, of course, the inescapable narrowness of its electoral mandate. No matter what Kennedy said, felt, or thought about his defeated rival, Richard Nixon had fought the Kennedys practically to an even draw. One thing Kennedy particularly dared *not* do was feed the impression Nixon had created of a young Democrat unprepared and perhaps even unwilling to stop the Communists in Asia. Though he told Ben Bradlee he saw no problem letting Communist China into the United Nations, he also insisted that this particular flash of New Frontier vision be kept out of print. He intended to go to great lengths to honor the sober warning he had gotten from both Nixon and Ike. At one point he got several African countries to support keeping Communist China out of the United Nations if America and Taiwan voted to let Mauritania and Outer Mongolia in. Having watched his party burned alive by the "Who lost China?" issue since 1949, having been scorched himself by Quemoy and Matsu in the campaign, the young candidate who had questioned a rigid, hold-the-line stand in Asia was becoming, as president, its strongest advocate. Within days of taking office, he signed a national security directive stating U.S. policy toward South Vietnam in the starkest possible language: "Defeat Communist insurgency." Meanwhile, outside the White House, Richard Nixon could be heard beating the drum for an even harder Asian line: "Some commentators say Kennedy is afraid to start a war."

Of more immediate concern was Vietnam's inland neighbor, Laos, a beleaguered, rural land Ike had called "the cork in the bottle." Instinctively sensitive to public relations, Kennedy felt that one cause of America's trouble in Asia was its "Ugly American" image; U.S. diplomats were still as elitist as those he had met on his first 1951 trip to the region. Facing a group of new ambassadorial appointees, the young president cited a recent *New York Times* article that accused American diplomats of hanging around the embassy compound and not getting out in the countryside. Hoping to reverse the practice, he issued orders: "Remember, you're ambassador to the country, to the whole country. Don't get deskbound."

As Kennedy accustomed himself to life in the Oval Office and basked in a 78 percent approval rating, the only program that grabbed his attention was space. It was a matter of national image. Kennedy saw the global struggle with the Soviets and Chinese much like a political campaign in which the third world was the *swing* vote. To impress the Asian, African, and Latin American masses, the United States had to overtake the Russians in space. With Soviet cosmonauts orbiting the earth and American rockets crashing on takeoff, Kennedy asked the National Aeronautics and Space Administration (NASA) if the United States could possibly "leapfrog" the USSR to the moon. To improve the third world in its daily life, he created the Peace Corps. He would send Americans not just to the moon but to far-off lands like Swaziland.

LEAVING his wife and two daughters behind in Washington to complete the school year, Richard Nixon assumed a Los Angeles law practice. Taking an apartment on Wilshire Boulevard, he cooked his meals and avoided social events. The one thing he craved was the latest scuttlebutt from Washington. Luckily for him, it was an appetite the Republican National Committee (RNC) was eager to sate. Soon after the inauguration, the RNC hired Eisenhower speechwriter Stephen Hess to help keep the former president and vice president up-to-date on political news. Hess's new clients displayed vastly different appetites for his service. "The RNC wanted to keep Eisenhower alive for political purposes, to use him in campaigns and so forth," he recalled. "Eisenhower just wanted to have a nice time in Gettysburg."

Nixon was different. Hess could see that his heart and mind had never made the move from Washington. Eager to meet Nixon's need for news, the twenty-seven-year-old Hess began sending regular political updates from the capital to Los Angeles. "I'm writing a newsletter once a week. Because I was reading all these newspapers, I would keep a list each month of people who had gotten an honor, like an honorary degree, or been appointed to a ... board of directors. I drafted these little letters." Again, Nixon and Ike had different reactions. "Eisenhower was signing them like crazy. He loved them. All over town people would say, 'Hey! I got this terrific note from Ike.' Nixon says to me, 'Don't bother sending me those letters anymore. I don't want to be known as a guy who remembers people's birthdays!' "

A grander vocation tugged at Nixon. Even as he settled in at the law firm of Adams, Duque and Hazeltine, he and those close to him knew that he remained the Republicans' obvious candidate to challenge Kennedy in 1964. "I traveled with him after the election to Chicago, Washington, and New York," Bob Finch recalled. "We knew that he had enough support if he wanted to get the nomination." The man who believed he had gotten the most votes in 1960 even had a slogan ready: *Reelect Nixon.* What scared the once-and-future candidate, Finch said, was being seduced by party leaders, as Adlai Stevenson had been, into a second drubbing, losing twice to Kennedy, a spectacle that would make him, still in his fifties, a political cadaver. "He was mortally afraid of that."

JOHN Kennedy had an affinity for the Central Intelligence Agency (CIA). Its style was nothing like the effete diplomats at Foggy Bottom. "The State Department takes four or five days to answer a simple yes or no." The CIA was more to Kennedy's liking, more like James Bond, the suave and deadly agent 007, whose adventures Kennedy had enticed his countrymen into sharing. The CIA got things done.

Or so Kennedy was led to believe. CIA efforts to kill Castro had been a pathetic failure. At first, the agency had asked mobsters Johnny Roselli and Sam Giancana to carry out a gangland-style assassination of the Cuban leader, having a hit man shoot him down in the street. Giancana insisted on a subtler method: poison. By March 1961, that plan was also going nowhere. Roselli returned poison pills given him by the CIA, and the mob's contact lost the job that had given him access to Castro.

That same month, the CIA deputy director, Richard Bissell, briefed Kennedy on the planned invasion of the island. Anti-Castro exiles, drawn from the huge Cuban community in Miami, were being trained in Guatemala. Pilots from the Alabama National Guard were teaching the Cubans to fly some B-26s the CIA had recovered from government surplus. The new president's prime concern was that the operation not create so much international "noise" that it triggered a Soviet grab for always-vulnerable West Berlin. But "noise" was precisely what the CIA planners believed was needed to transform an invasion into an insurrection against Castro; that and the complete elimination of the Cuban air force.

Almost from the outset, however, the CIA's goals grew well beyond the resources and risks the president was willing to invest. The original strategy of infiltrating the island with small units lost favor because such commando groups kept getting caught. This led to the plan for a full-scale invasion. Troop readiness was another problem. While some of the Cuban recruits had military experience under the old Cuban regime, many in the brigade were middle-class sons of professionals, more adept at winning arguments in cafés than in amphibious assaults. The CIA had failed, moreover, to establish an exile government of Cubans with sufficient appeal to their compatriots on the island. When the assigned agent, E. Howard Hunt ("Eduardo"), failed to organize a credible group, Bissell replaced him. A more basic problem lay with the military plan itself. When the exiles asked the Americans how such a small force could defeat a 200,000-man army, they were assured by the CIA that an "umbrella" of air cover would keep every Cuban car, truck, tank, or airplane from moving the day of the attack. "It was on this premise that all related plans were made," CIA agent Hunt insisted. Unfortunately, that particular promise had never come from the top.

On Sunday morning, April 16, the operation was under way. B-26 bombers, taking off from Nicaragua, struck at the Cuban air force, but with minimal success. Only a handful of planes had been disabled. With fifteen hundred exiles prepared to land at the Bay of Pigs, Kennedy, worried about Moscow's reaction, called off a second air strike. From Nicaragua there would be no more strikes, the White House ruled, until the exiles had secured a takeoff strip in Cuba, thereby giving the invasion the plausible cover of being a covert act by Cuban defectors. "I thought Kennedy was tough," the CIA's deputy chief Richard Bissell said later, "that he wouldn't cancel air strikes and lose his first main effort."

When distress calls came from the landing beach, Bissell and the military chiefs urged Kennedy to commit U.S. forces immediately to the attack, navy jets to give air cover to those pinned down on the beach and naval artillery to destroy Castro's tanks. The young commander in chief rejected the plea, believing that the invasion did not justify the risk of a Soviet countermove in West Berlin, a confrontation that could trigger nuclear war.

Kennedy's partial commitment to the Cuban invasion incurred the wrath of both the left and right. A group called Fair Play for Cuba picketed the UN in New York, yelling: "Cuba, sí! Yankee, no!" At the CIA war room in Washington, a group of gung-ho agents, including Hunt, were screaming in four-letter language, pleading for an air strike. What they and the rest of the agency had stubbornly refused to admit was that the invasion had never stood a chance without a far greater American role than the one Kennedy had approved. Without a full-scale invasion, a people's revolt against Castro was not in the cards. And if the United States was not going to enter big and win the fight, and if it had little expectation of the Cuban populace rising up, certainly the small forced landing at the Bay of Pigs could not do the job.

The effort to topple the Cuban leader, Kennedy's first enterprise as president, was thus a debacle. Used to victory, he took the defeat hard. For the first time, people witnessed him in tears. "All my life I've known better than to depend on the experts," he said, denying that the central failure had been his. The new commander in chief had backed a military effort that required greater resources than he was ready to commit, greater risks than he wanted to take. He'd been "given to believe," he told George Smathers, that Castro would be assassinated, creating "pandemonium" on the island as the exiles hit the beach. But the person controlling the main operation, giving the go-ahead, and then calling off the second air strike had been the president.

By happenstance, Richard Nixon had requested and been granted a foreign policy briefing by Allen Dulles on April 19. It was to prepare him for a May speaking tour. The two men met, as scheduled, at Nixon's Washington home. Prospects for the Cuban operation were still being publicly portrayed as murky. But when the host asked Dulles if he wanted a drink, the CIA director had showed the strain. "I certainly would—I really need one. This is the worst day of my life." Dulles then revealed to Nixon for the first time that the long-planned invasion of Cuba had failed. The decisive factor, Nixon recalled him saying, was the unwillingness to make full use of America's military power in the operation. It had been mindless to proceed halfheartedly, to hold back from completely supporting the mission.

The next day Kennedy had Nixon, as well as Eisenhower, to the White House for separate meetings. "JFK called," said the note Nixon found left by daughter Tricia. "I knew it! It wouldn't be long before he would get into trouble and have to call on you to help." The two men greeted each other in the Oval Office with solemn handshakes. After Vice President Johnson left the room, Nixon took a seat on a small sofa. Kennedy was in his rocking chair. It was "the worst experience of my life," he said of a meeting he had just had with the Cuban exile leaders, many of whom had lost sons in the disaster. Both politicians knew the irony at work: Nixon had been secretly supporting the Cuban invasion plan throughout the previous year, at the same time publicly declaring such a move as wrong. Kennedy had pitched for bold action against Castro while privately aware the invasion was already in the works.

Now, for the first time since their early days in the House, Nixon and Kennedy stood momentarily united. "I was assured by every son of a bitch I checked with, all the military experts and the CIA, that the plan would succeed," the young president raged, Nixon relishing his venom. "His anger and frustration poured out in a profane barrage. He jumped from his chair and began pacing back and forth in front of his desk," the former vice president wrote in an article for *Reader's Digest* years later. "Pacing around the room cursing, using his down-to-earth Irish vocabulary rather than his Harvard vocabulary, he told me how disappointed he had been in the advice he had received."

Kennedy asked what he, Nixon, would do. "I would find a proper legal cover, and I would go in." But Kennedy reminded his guest of the danger: An open move against Castro would free the Soviets to grab West Berlin. That could mean war. The Russians only respond to strength was Nixon's response. "I will publicly support you to the hilt if you make such a decision with regard to either Laos or Cuba," he promised in words laced with the threat of criticism should the Democrat choose an alternative course. For his part, Kennedy did his best to charm his 1960 rival. "It really is true that foreign affairs is the only important issue for a president," Kennedy allowed, resuming the banter of the Senate cloakroom. "Who gives a shit if the minimum wage is $1.15 or $1.25 in comparison to something like this?"

Kennedy encouraged Nixon in the writing of his memoirs, reciting his father's views on the public relations value of having one's name on a book jacket. "There's something about being an author which really builds the reputation of a politician."

Then Kennedy shared with Nixon a nugget of political news from the West Coast. Gov. Pat Brown was worried, he told him, by polls showing Nixon could beat him were he to run for governor of California in 1962. Flattered by Kennedy's rare display of intimacy, Nixon proceeded to spend the rest of the day urging Republican leaders to back the administration during the Cuban crisis. "He kept making call after call while I waited for nearly an hour," an eyewitness recalled. "Some he asked. Others he begged. Some he even threatened. He was telling them not to attack Kennedy on this thing."

"I just saw a crushed man today," Nixon was heard to say. "He needs our help. I told him to go upstairs and have a drink with his wife and avoid making any decision until the thing brightens up a bit."

Nixon, who was struck by how "alone" Kennedy must have felt, remained buoyed by the meeting. A week later, he wired the White House: "I greatly appreciated the message which Pierre

Salinger transmitted to me in California this morning," he wrote. "You may be sure that I shall continue to urge bipartisan support for programs of effective action to meet the threats to United States security presented by direct and indirect Communist aggression in Cuba, Laos and other areas of the world. Regards, Dick Nixon."

KENNEDY'S angry Oval Office outburst divulged a deepening passion. "There can be no long-term living with Castro as a neighbor," Robert Kennedy and JFK's military aide Maxwell Taylor wrote in a June memorandum to the president.

"Bobby is a wild man on this," the CIA's Bissell recalled of the months after the Bay of Pigs. "Get off your ass about Cuba!" the attorney general barked at another CIA official. "No time, money, effort or manpower is to be spared." The attorney general himself was to head the operation. In November he "chewed out" Bissell for what he saw as inaction on the Castro front. That month "Operation Mongoose" was created. Its mission—help someone inside Cuba do the dirty work. Richard Helms, who had replaced Bissell as head of covert operations and reported directly to Bobby on a daily basis, said there were to be "no limitations" placed on methods. A CIA report would later note the "severe pressure" from the Kennedy administration. Bissell later pronounced it "inconceivable" that the president himself hadn't known about the plotting.

THE pressure to rid the hemisphere of the Red blotch just ninety miles from Florida heightened after the Bay of Pigs. "The worst thing that can flow from our failure in Cuba is that this failure may discourage American policy makers from taking decisive steps in the future because there is a risk of failure," Richard Nixon warned in a May speech to the Executive Club of Chicago. "We should not start things in the world unless we are prepared to finish them." The former vice president told a reporter it was "near criminal" for Kennedy to have called off the air cover once the invasion was launched.

Cuba was not the president's only source of pain. That month the president made his first foreign trip, meeting with Canadian prime minister John Diefenbaker in Ottawa. After speaking to the Canadian Parliament, the visitor participated in a local groundbreaking ceremony. As he lifted a silver shovel of dirt, Kennedy suddenly wrenched his weak back so terribly that he grabbed his forehead in anguish. Back in Washington, he needed crutches to get from the helicopter to the White House. Ignoring the severity of his rival's condition, Nixon made the injury the occasion for humor. Interviewed as he moved his family out to California, he described the tedious chore of packing up his household and heading West. "Now I've got something in common with President Kennedy," he told journalists at the airport. "A sore back."

By early June, Kennedy was recovered enough to head for Europe and his first summit meeting with Nikita Khrushchev. In Paris, press secretary Pierre Salinger released, to his subsequent horror, the first report that Dominican Republic dictator Rafael Trujillo had been assassinated. Having armed the plotters, the U.S. government had good reason not to show itself so well informed on such murderous matters.

Introduced to Khrushchev, Kennedy now tried breaking the ice with an approving reference to Foreign Minister Andrey Gromyko. "My wife says that Gromyko looks so kind, so pleasant, that he must be a nice man."

His eyes fixed on his doleful diplomat, Khrushchev seemed puzzled. "Really? Some people say Gromyko looks like your Richard Nixon."

Khrushchev boasted that he had cost Nixon the presidential election by delaying the release of Gary Powers, the U-2 pilot captured during a spy flight over the Soviet Union. Had he released Powers before the election, the Soviet leader announced, Kennedy would have lost by at least 200,000 votes. "Don't spread that story around," the American parried.

The meetings in Vienna confirmed Kennedy's worst fears about Soviet intentions toward West Berlin. The Soviet premier was intent on recognizing East Germany, a step seen as denying America and its allies access to the surrounded city. "The USSR will sign a peace treaty, and the sovereignty of the GDR [East Germany] will be observed," Khrushchev said in a formal pronouncement. "Any violation of that sovereignty will be regarded by the USSR as an act of open aggression. If the U.S. wants to start a war over Germany, let it do so."

Kennedy believed the enemy meant business. Nixon and others could sound off back home about the need to call the Soviets' bluff. But Nikita Khrushchev looked nothing like a bluffer.

But Kennedy also knew the political price of softness. "There are limits to the number of defeats I can defend in one twelve-month period," he would say later in his presidency. The new president could also hear the calls for a tougher stand from the man he had defeated the previous November. "Vice President Nixon seems to be taking a dim view of your administration. He said in a speech yesterday that never in American history has a man talked so much and acted so little. Do you have anything to say about this?" a reporter asked at a June White House press conference. Kennedy countered with a wicked slap at his rival's evacuation to Los Angeles. "No. I wouldn't comment on Mr. Nixon. He has been engaged and busy, and I sympathize with the traveling problems he has been having and other problems. I don't have any response to make. We're doing the best we can and will continue to do so until 1964, and then we can see what the situation looks like." He was daring Nixon to run against him.

Nixon was facing the first long summer away from Washington in fifteen years; his worst problems were tedium and irrelevance. Quietly reading a book one Saturday morning, former congressman Pat Hillings got a telephone call. "Pat, what are you doing?" Nixon asked from his office in downtown Los Angeles. When Hillings said he was relaxing around his pool, Nixon said he needed to talk. Shaved, showered, and dressed, Hillings entered Nixon's office to find his friend alone and distressed. "Where is everybody? There's no one here. Look at the street down there. There's no one down there. Doesn't anyone do anything around here?" Informed that it was a summer Saturday in a part of the country where people did such things as play tennis, go to the beach, and hang around swimming pools, Nixon was indignant. "Don't they realize they'll all become vegetables?"

IN August the Soviets made their long-threatened move on West Berlin. Fortunately for the world, the Soviets and East Germans had found a solution to stop the tide of refugees to the West—a wall. To Kennedy, the news came as a secret relief. "Why would Khrushchev put up a wall if he really intended to seize West Berlin?" Kennedy asked. "There wouldn't be any need of a wall if he occupied the whole city. This is the way out of this predicament. It's not a very nice solution, but a wall is a hell of a lot better than a war."

But the calm White House reaction drew criticism. "Mr. Nixon has called the movement of American troops into West Berlin a useless gesture which Mr. Khrushchev might interpret as weakness rather than strength," a reporter challenged Kennedy at an August press conference. "At the same time, the Republican national chairman has said that your administration's attitude in general is one of appeasement toward communism throughout the world. Do you have any comment on this criticism by top spokesmen of the opposition party?"

Only his contempt was apparent. "No, I don't. We are in a situation in Germany which is fraught with peril, and I think that anyone who is aware of the nature of the destructive power that's available to both sides should, I would think, be careful in attempting to make any political advantage out of our present difficulties.

"It would seem to me, and I think at the time, that the West Berliners would benefit from a reminder of that commitment, and it was for that reason that those troops were added to the garrison of West Berlin. I don't really see how that weakens our commitment. If troops were withdrawn, would that strengthen it?"

SETTLED in California, Nixon was anxious to regain some political strength of his own. In September, Ted Sorensen traveled to

Los Angeles to be honored among the "Ten Outstanding Young Americans" by the Junior Chamber of Commerce. He would recall a comical backstage moment with the event's master of ceremonies, Richard Nixon.

As emcee and honorees awaited their cue to enter the hotel ballroom, an elderly waiter walked past carrying a large tray. To the others' amazement, Nixon made a great fuss over the gentleman, asking after his wife, his family, his health. Knowing that the lively familiarities had caught the group's interest, Nixon waited for the elderly gentleman to pass before offering a well-timed mock explanation: "He was one of *last* year's winners."

Just as Kennedy had surmised in their April meeting, the vice president was intent on challenging Gov. Edmund G. "Pat" Brown in 1962. While the opportunity looked sound—he was leading Brown in the polls five to three—there was an obvious risk that if Nixon lost, his political career would be over. No one could ever run for president who had been rejected by his own state.

Kennedy thought a Nixon run made no sense. As a former vice president, he enjoyed durable status that would enable him to run for president again without ever having to seek another lower office. "Why is he running?" he asked Ken O'Donnell. "He hasn't got a chance, and the risk of getting beaten by Brown far outweighs any advantage he could win from being elected." What Kennedy couldn't imagine was Nixon's fear of being trapped into a futile rerun against an incumbent Kennedy in 1964. That would be hopeless. The only president beaten for reelection in the century had been Herbert Hoover, the man blamed for the Great Depression. "The important thing, in terms of Nixon's career, is that he chose to run for governor of California so that he *wouldn't* have to run against Kennedy in '64," aide Stephen Hess recalls. "The irony of the whole thing is that he was attacked successfully as using the statehouse as a stepping-stone for the presidency. He actually wanted to use it as a bomb shelter." Pat Hillings had a similar recollection. "Nixon was still a very young man. Our biggest problem was that the man who beat him was also a very young man. What was Nixon going to do for eight years?"

Nixon would explain his decision years later: "My own political judgment at that point told me that Kennedy would be almost unbeatable in 1964. If I ran for governor, I felt I would have to pledge to spend the full term in Sacramento. That would leave someone else to square off in 1964 against Kennedy, his money and his *tactics*." But the real prod to Nixon's running for governor was that he lacked Kennedy's confidence in his own political staying power.

In late September, Nixon made his announcement: He would *not* seek the presidency in 1964 but would run instead for governor of California, committing himself to serve a full four-year term. "Despite all the talk about drafts," he said of the possibility the party might want him to challenge Kennedy in 1964, "there has never been one in history. The candidate has always worked for it, and I will not." Nixon made the decision, he told his aides, despite the knowledge he would be facing the all-out opposition of the man who had beaten him a year earlier. Nixon knew that anger over the administration's civil rights stance in the South would make California vital to Kennedy in 1964. Nixon knew that Kennedy was aware that his rival's winning control of the state would create a serious obstacle to Kennedy's prospects. "There would be the all-out opposition of the Kennedy family," he told Bob Finch. "They would do everything they could to stop me from getting a new political lease on life by winning the governorship."

For Nixon, the governor's race started badly, with Governor Brown accusing him of using California's highest office to advance his national career. "He sees the governorship of this state only as a stepping-stone for his own presidential ambitions." President Kennedy, visiting Los Angeles for a November Democratic fund-raiser, reminded his audience that Brown knew the state, a reference to the fact that his rival did not. For weeks it appeared that Nixon might have to endure a fight for his party's nomination with the former governor, Goodwin Knight.

From three thousand miles away, Jack Kennedy relished the prospect. He was sitting at the stern of the *Honey Fitz*, daiquiri in hand, the sun coming down at the end of a beautiful Newport day. "What do you feel at a moment like this? What is it like to be president?" his pal Charles Bartlett asked.

Kennedy smiled and dropped an ash from his Cuban cigar. "Well, I tell you one thing, this beats the hell out of mucking around in California with Goodie Knight."

CHAPTER FIFTEEN

Coup de Grâce

HAVING made the leap into the gubernatorial race, Nixon realized the depths of his misjudgment. For one thing, he saw from crowd reactions just how popular his recent rival, Jack Kennedy, had become in his inaugural presidential year. Nor was JFK's popularity based on any one achievement. After the Bay of Pigs, he was more beloved than ever. People who had voted for Nixon were now telling pollsters they had voted for his opponent. Realizing he could not compete with such star quality, the former vice president tried co-opting it. "I was in the navy in the South Pacific but wasn't in a PT boat," he told his California audiences. "That's why I'm here and not in Washington." He paid more subtle tributes. When the Nixons' new house was completed, he arranged for his wife to give a televised tour like the one Jacqueline Kennedy had just given of the White House.

Yet his bitterness was thinly disguised. "My little daughter, Tricia, says she doesn't blame the people who voted for Kennedy," he said. "She blames the ones who counted the votes in Chicago." When his memoirs, which he entitled *Six Crises*, were published in the spring of 1962, he quoted his younger daughter Julie on the

1960 election count. "Can't we still win? Why can't we have a recount in Chicago?" he recalls her asking him every day from the election until Kennedy's inauguration. Kennedy got the message. When Ben Bradlee asked Kennedy if he had read the book, he got a testy answer. "Just the 1960 campaign stuff, and that's all I'm going to read. I can't stand the way he puts everything in Tricia's mouth. It makes me sick. He's a cheap bastard; that's all there is to it."

Six Crises also reopened the controversy over the CIA's 1960 briefing of Kennedy. The White House released a statement denying Nixon's charge that candidate Kennedy had gotten a heads up on the planned Cuba invasion. When Allen Dulles denied giving Kennedy actual CIA "plans," the author was furious. Once again, Kennedy was being shielded. When the president and his attorney general, Bobby, paid simultaneous visits to California, Nixon let loose. "We welcome them. In November we're going to show these carpetbaggers a thing or two."

Asking Kennedy about Nixon's rocky race for governor became a favorite sport at televised presidential press conferences. "Mr. President, you once told us you had an opinion as to whether Mr. Nixon should enter the race for the California governorship, but you never did tell us what that was. Could you tell us about it?" a reporter asked Kennedy in March.

"Well, I think I said at the time I'd be glad to confide it to him, and he has not yet spoken to me about it."

Riding the laughter, a reporter brought up the 1960 debates. "Mr. Nixon in his book has indicated that he feels he won three of the four debates. In view of this, do you think that future debates are advisable?"

For Kennedy it was an easy setup. "Well, I would think that they would be—they'd be part of the '64 campaign. I've already indicated I'll be glad to debate even if I did, as the vice president suggested, lose three of the four."

That spring, Kennedy showed how far he had come in the raw use of power. Determined to fight inflation, he jawboned both industry and labor to hold the line on price and wage hikes. Executives of the steel industry and the United Steelworkers agreed at a White House meeting in March to hold off any pay increase that might trigger a new cycle of higher prices. But a month later, Roger Blough, chief executive officer of U.S. Steel, asked to see Kennedy. He began the Oval Office meeting by saying: "Mr. President, I want to ask your permission to raise the steel prices."

Kennedy was swift in his response. "Mr. Blough, what you are doing is in the best interest of your shareholders. My shareholders are every citizen of the United States. I'm going to do everything in the best interest of the shareholders, the people of this country. As the president of the United States, I have quite a bit of influence."

Kennedy was about to give Big Steel the Onions Burke treatment. "You find out about these guys in these steel companies, where they have been on vacation, who they have been with on vacation." The next day, Robert Kennedy announced that he had ordered a grand jury investigation under the antitrust laws of the steel price hike. Subpoenas to produce documents were served on U.S. Steel. Defense Secretary Robert McNamara ordered that the Pentagon buy steel "where possible" from companies that had not raised prices.

By the next night, eight steel companies that had announced price hikes canceled them. Two months later, Kennedy joked over dinner how a steel company president, Jim Patton of Republic Steel, had complained to him that day about the telephones of the steel executives being tapped and their tax returns being checked. "I told him that was totally unfair, that the attorney general wouldn't do such a thing." Pause. "And, of course, Patton was right!"

Kennedy suspected Richard Nixon's hand in the steel crisis. "It looks like a double-cross," he told Ben Bradlee. "I think steel made a deal with Nixon not to raise prices until after the election. Then came the recession, and they didn't want to raise prices. Then, when we pulled out of the recession, they said, 'Let Kennedy squeeze the unions first, before we raise prices.' They kicked us right in the balls. And we kicked back. Are we supposed to sit there and take a cold, deliberate fucking?" Two years later, Robert Kennedy admitted that he and his brother had used rough tactics to intimidate the steel executives. "We looked over all of them as individuals . . . we were going to go for broke . . . their expense accounts and where they'd been and what they were doing. I picked up all their records. . . . I told the FBI to interview them all, march into their offices the next day! We weren't going to go slowly. . . . So all of them were hit with meetings the next morning by agents. All of them were subpoenaed for their personal records. I agree it was a tough way to operate, but under the circumstances, we couldn't afford to lose."

In May, Kennedy celebrated his forty-fifth birthday in New York's Madison Square Garden with a gala fund-raising evening featuring Marilyn Monroe. After hearing the actress, wearing a skintight dress, coo "Happy Birthday, Mr. President," Kennedy couldn't resist a shot at Nixon. It came in a mock tribute to the Kennedy children's affection for Macaroni, their pet pony. "Actually, there's another speech, given by a former vice president of the United States, in 1952, which is even more pertinent. It was just a little pony, and you know the kids—like all kids, loved it. And I just want to say this right now, that regardless of what they say about it, we are going to keep it. And I feel about Macaroni the way the vice president did about Checkers." It was a devastating lampoon of Richard Nixon's most celebrated performance.

In June, Nixon won the Republican nomination for governor, defeating conservative state assemblyman Joseph Shell by more than 600,000 votes. Two days later, Kennedy ridiculed Nixon's defeat of a political unknown. "I think he emerged from a tough one," he told White House reporters.

At a July press conference, the political banter continued. "Mr. President, Governor Brown is coming here to see you this afternoon. I wonder if you have any advice for him in the contest with Mr. Nixon and what your overall view might be of the campaign in California?"

Again, Kennedy was ready. "I would not advise Governor Brown. I think this is a matter for the people of California. He seems to be doing very well. He was running far behind in the beginning. And now he is leading in the polls by substantially more than I led at the end of the election."

In August, the press and Kennedy were still at the game. "Mr.

President, a day after you left California last week, the proposed debate between our governor and Mr. Nixon blew sky-high, and it's been suggested since, in public speculation, that you advised our governor to avoid this kind of confrontation. As the reigning champion in this field, I wondered if you would like to tell us whether or not you did discuss this with Governor Brown and also if maybe the time has come when you would tell us what you once suggested you would have advised Mr. Nixon?"

Kennedy denied giving Nixon's California rival any debate strategy. "I understand that Governor Brown is suggesting the format which was used in the '60 campaign . . . and which I think is very satisfactory. But they have to work out those details. In answer to your last . . . I will be glad to tell you in November."

To warm Nixon's own relations with reporters, Nixon's aides convinced him to throw a party. Aide Stephen Hess recalls the scene: "Got a ballroom. Lots of good food. The press is gathered around. And Nixon starts telling a story about if you want a fresh salad in a restaurant, ask the waiter to slice the tomato against the grain. He had all these jobs as a kid, and he worked in a kitchen. He was explaining that in the middle of the afternoon you prepare the salads and they have been sitting there for three hours when you order your salad. The reporters are gasping. They're coming up for air. This is the small talk of this guy!"

Nixon's ineptitude at chitchat was now the least of his problems. Pat Brown was proving far tougher than expected. Nixon couldn't find anything to throw at him. There was no "meat" around, no PAC issue, no voting record to compare with Vito Marcantonio's. And unlike his challenger, Brown was a perfect fit for the governor's chair. Even Nixon's close advisers admitted that their candidate could not match the governor's zeal for the issues of daily interest to California voters. As press secretary Herb Klein confessed, the former vice president was beyond bothering with "peaches or produce."

Brown also turned out to be a more appealing opponent than expected. One day, Nixon staffers were gathered in front of the television at the candidate's house, enjoying the governor's on-air fumbles, when Nixon joined the group. "How did he do, boys?" After everyone had chimed in, slamming the performance, Julie Nixon came into the room. "You're all wrong. He was terrific." Nixon's youngest daughter had intuitively recognized what the professionals didn't: the decency of the man her father was running against.

The Hughes loan had also made an unexpected comeback. That $205,000 Donald Nixon had borrowed in 1956 to expand the family store in Whittier was never repaid. At a joint Nixon-Brown press conference, the closest Nixon would come to a debate, liberal editor Tom Braden raised the devilish issue. "I want to ask you whether you, as vice president, or as a candidate for governor, think it proper for a candidate for governor, morally and ethically, to permit his family to receive a secret loan from a major defense contractor in the United States?"

Nixon was indignant. "Now it is time to have this out. I was in government for fourteen years. I went to Washington with a car and a house and a mortgage. I have made mistakes, but I am an honest man." He dared his rival to make an issue of it. "Governor Brown has a chance to stand up as a man and charge me with misconduct. Do it, sir!" But the issue survived Nixon's stagecraft. A few days later, a more confident Brown demanded that Nixon defend the unpaid loan from Hughes Tool. Nixon never did and paid for it at the polls.

But a far greater voter concern about the former vice president was the suspicion he was only using Sacramento as a refueling stop. Desperate, the Nixon forces trotted out the familiar anti-Communist pitch. "Is Brown Pink?" a bumper sticker coyly asked. "The Committee for the Preservation of the Democratic Party in California," a front organization financed with Nixon campaign money, mailed 500,000 postcards to registered Democrats claiming that Pat Brown was in bed with the Communists. Nixon tried giving the smear credibility by demanding that Communist speakers be banned from University of California campuses. He spoke of the "mess in Sacramento," trying to resurrect the old Ike-and-Dick crusade against "the mess in Washington." The staleness of Nixon's act suffered from the dramatic change in backdrop. The nation was now in the youthful embrace of the New Frontier, not the death throes of the Truman era.

One of the president's own political chores that fall was bequeathing his old Senate seat to his youngest brother, Ted. Having failed to buy out rival Edward McCormack, using Tip O'Neill as the middleman, the Kennedys succeeded in blasting him out. By October, the confident president was back in McKeesport, Pennsylvania, campaigning for the Democratic party nationally, recalling an earlier stop there. "The first time I came to this city was in 1947, when Mr. Richard Nixon and I engaged in our first debate," he quipped to an outdoor crowd. "He won that one, and we went on to other things." The fight was still on, he said. "And that's why I am here in this community, sixteen years later, still debating Mr. Nixon and his confreres on which party should hold office in 1962 and in this decade."

To help finish off his 1960 rival, Kennedy dispatched a half-dozen cabinet officers to California to stump for Pat Brown. "The administration is really loading the defense contracts into this area and getting maximum publicity every time," Nixon wrote backers. "With all their faults, we will have to agree that they play their politics to the hilt." Kennedy had made Fred Dutton, an old Pat Brown hand, his back-channel liaison with Sacramento during the race. As in the Cuban invasion, his goal was plausible deniability. The idea, as Dutton explains, was to get Nixon "tripped up without Kennedy being involved in it." Even if his old rival managed to eke out a victory, Kennedy wanted to "dent him enough so he wouldn't be back for a rerun of 1960."

SINCE the Bay of Pigs, Fidel Castro had been a vivid emblem of Kennedy indecision, incompetence, and failure. "We need a man on horseback, and many people think you are riding Caroline's bicycle," E. M. Dealey of the archconservative *Dallas Morning News* had scolded the president to his face in a public meeting with publishers the year before.

Kennedy refused to be bullied. "I'm as tough as you are, Mr. Dealey. I have the responsibility for the lives of 180 million Americans, which you have not. I didn't get elected by arriving at soft judgments."

No right-wing voice outside the administration could have matched its own behind-the-scenes passions. Not even the most adversarial newspaper publisher could have conjured up the image of an American president sharing a mistress, as Kennedy did until warned off by FBI director J. Edgar Hoover, with Sam Giancana, the same Mafia don the CIA had contracted to kill Fidel Castro. But neither could the Kennedy brothers' most Communist-hating critics have imagined their zeal to kill off the Communist leader who had humiliated them the spring before. "Robert Kennedy ran with it, ran those organizations," CIA covert chief Richard Helms would one day testify of the anti-Castro plotting. The attorney general's only concern, voiced after he had been given a thorough briefing on the assassination effort, was that he be kept informed. His orders to "get rid" of Castro were unrelenting.

In October, New York senator Kenneth Keating charged that the Russians were constructing missile bases in Cuba; worse yet, the president was covering up the threat. "Intelligence authorities must have advised the president," the New York Republican declared, "that ground-to-ground missiles can be operational within six months." Two weeks before the November elections, Kennedy took action. "This government, as promised, has maintained the closest surveillance of the Soviet military buildup on the island of Cuba," he told a national television audience, the aerial photographs at hand. "Within the past week, unmistakable evidence has established the fact that a series of offensive missile sites is now in preparation on that imprisoned island. The purpose of these bases can be none other than to provide a nuclear strike capability against the Western Hemisphere." The missiles had to go, Kennedy said, declaring a naval blockade of all ships carrying offensive weapons or missile-firing equipment to Cuba. Any such vessel would be stopped and turned back.

"It shall be the policy of this nation to regard any nuclear missile launched from Cuba against any nation in the Western Hemisphere as an attack by the Soviet Union on the United States, requiring a full retaliatory response to the Soviet Union." He then recited the Cold War canon. "The 1930s taught us a clear lesson: Aggressive conduct, if allowed to go unchecked and unchallenged, ultimately leads to war."

Richard Nixon watched the speech from the Edgewater Hotel in Oakland. "It's over," he said as Kennedy declared the blockade. "There's no way that anyone is going to pay any attention to a

California governor's race now. I just lost the election." Behind in his race, Nixon knew he could not possibly catch the California voters' attention, much less turn them against Brown. His last hope, a thin one, was to capitalize on his historic connection to Kennedy. "What he did decide to do was immediately talk about support for the president and what we ought to do in pressuring other countries," Herb Klein recalled. "He immediately wanted to talk about national security, not California issues. He thought it was the only way to chime in, to get any attention at that time."

Within the week, Kennedy had won Khrushchev's agreement to remove the missiles. The crisis had ended. A nation that had lived for days with the prospect of nuclear war could now breathe easy. "If Kennedy never did another thing," said British prime minister Harold Macmillan, "he assured his place in history by this single act." Using precious campaign funds, Nixon now bought television time to declare that the president's success in the Cuban Missile Crisis "demonstrates again that when you stand up to Communist aggressors, they back down." Desperate, he was trying to capitalize on Kennedy's feat by reminding voters that he and the heroic president had once competed in the same league.

But the rivalry, with its visceral shenanigans, played on. Democratic prankster Dick Tuck would recollect with a chuckle years later:

We're in LA and we hear that Dick Nixon is doing a thing in Chinatown. I decide maybe we can smoke Nixon out on the $205,000 unsecured loan that Howard Hughes gave to his brother Don. I get to the event and I make up a big sign that says, in Chinese characters, "How about the Hughes Loan?" Above that, I write "Welcome Nixon" in English. There's one TV news crew there, and I tip them off that Mr. Nixon may be about to do something interesting. So Nixon's standing there, posing with this kid holding up my sign, when a Chinese elder suddenly says, "No! No! No!" Nixon says, "What do you mean, no! no! no?" When the man explains what the Chinese characters say, Nixon grabs the sign out of the kid's hand and tears it up. Right there on camera!

Once, when candidate Nixon was speaking from the back of a whistle-stop campaign train in San Luis Obispo, a man dressed as a conductor signaled the engineer to start the train. As the candidate stood on the platform speaking to the crowd, he watched his audience slowly disappear into the distance. "The crowd went out like the morning tide," a proud Tuck would brag.

Voters came gradually to suspect that Richard Nixon didn't really want to be California's governor, that he was simply using the Sacramento office as a rest stop to the White House. "When I become pres—" the candidate began one answer in his election-eve telethon. The slip surprised no one. Running for an office in which he had never shown interest before, the former vice president of the United States could see the loss coming long before the balloting ended. On election day, with many of the votes still to be cast, Steve Hess asked the candidate if he was still pessimistic about the results. "Yes," Nixon answered, "but at least I am never going to have to talk about crap like dope addiction anymore."

NIXON was right. On November 6, Pat Brown beat him by 297,000 votes. His anticipation of the voters' verdict didn't protect the loser from a long, brutal night, a feeling of public rejection beyond any he had experienced.

With the bright light of the next day, things had only grown bleaker. Groggily awaking in his Beverly Hilton suite, Nixon confronted the public hell of his second electoral defeat in two years. In the ballroom below, the press pack was hungry for blood.

"They're all waiting," Herb Klein said.

"Screw them," Nixon said. When Klein and the others said Nixon had no choice but to offer a concession statement, the candidate wouldn't budge. "Screw them."

Klein tried again. "I told them you'd make a statement."

"You make the statement!" Nixon retorted. "You make it!"

Hillings recalls Nixon's condition. "He had a scotch or two. He was exhausted, bitter, unhappy, but he was not drunk. He was unshaven and was sitting there in his robe with the world going down around him." "To hell with the bastards," Nixon grumbled.

Realizing that the defeated candidate was in no mood to make an appearance, his aides decided that Nixon should slip out while his press secretary read a statement to the press. The plan's fault lay with the candidate. "Why doesn't he make the statement himself?" a reporter screamed at Klein. Watching the television up in his room, Nixon grew furious. Instead of ducking out of the hotel as planned, he headed for the elevator and the ballroom. The stage was now set for the most infamous press conference in history.

"Now that Mr. Klein has made a statement, now that all the members of the press are so delighted that I lost, I would just like to make a statement of my own," a morose Nixon began. First came his sledgehammer blow at how the California press corps had covered the race. That done, he could not resist a dig at Jack Kennedy. "This cannot be said for any other political figure today, I guess. Never in my sixteen years of campaigning have I complained to a publisher, to an editor, about the coverage of a reporter." Unlike JFK, he had not canceled a subscription to an offending newspaper, as JFK just had to the New York Herald Tribune. "And as I leave the press, all I can say is this: For sixteen years, ever since the Hiss case, you've had a lot of fun—a lot of fun—that you've had an opportunity to attack me, and I think I've given as good as I've taken. . . ."

Regaining his global statesman's voice to offer a backhanded compliment to an old foe, Nixon predicted that President Kennedy would confront the continuing Cuban threat. "If he has his own way, he will face up to them; if he can only get those who opposed atomic tests, who want to admit Red China to the United Nations, all of the woolly-heads around him—if he can just keep them away from him and stand strong and firm with that good Irish fight of his, America will be in good shape in foreign policy."

His own political career was, of course, kaput. "One last thing: What are my plans? Well, my plans are to go home. I'm going to get acquainted with my family again [a promise Kennedy had made after *winning* in 1960]. And my plans, incidentally, are, from a political standpoint, of course, to take a holiday. It will be a long holiday. I leave you gentlemen now, and you will now write

it, you will interpret it, that's your right. But as I leave you I want
you to know—just think how much you're going to be missing
me." Brightening, he let loose with his kicker: "You won't have
Nixon to kick around anymore, because, gentlemen, this is my
last press conference."

Stepping off the stage and away from the ears of the presss,
Nixon shared his actual sentiments with aide Bob Haldeman. "I
finally told those bastards off. And every goddamn thing I said
was *true*."

"Exit Snarling," the *Washington Star*'s Mary McGrory headed
her column on the "last press conference." The losing candidate
himself savored his outburst. "Nixon never wavered in his personal satisfaction with that incident," Haldeman recalled years
later.

But for a man who had devoted his life to politics, no measure
of backbiting could soothe the pain of what seemed the final
defeat. Back at home the day after the election, he and his wife,
Pat, were both in tears. It was the first time their daughters could
ever remember their both losing control of their emotions at the
same time.

The following Saturday, President Kennedy and Supreme Court
justice Earl Warren flew together to the funeral of Eleanor Roosevelt. Both Nixon rivals were in high spirits. During the flight they
were relishing accounts of the "last press conference." Kennedy
got a special joy from the Nixon jab, obviously meant for him,
about never having canceled a newspaper subscription. The president congratulated Mary McGrory: "That was a nice story you
wrote about Nixon."

"It would have been hard to say, watching their faces," the
columnist wrote in a follow-up, "who had enjoyed the downfall
more, the chief justice or the president of the United States. They
had their heads together over the clippings and were laughing
like schoolboys."

JACK Kennedy was not the only one who thought Nixon was
finished. "Barring a political miracle," *Time* magazine reported,
"his political career ended last week." The Sunday after the elec-

tion, ABC News broadcast a nasty half-hour special entitled "The Political Obituary of Richard Nixon." The program was a diabolical version of *This Is Your Life*, with the devil as spirited moderator. One of the guests was Alger Hiss. The implication was that Nixon, not Hiss, had been the one convicted and sentenced. Many viewers saw it as overkill, however, by a press corps long tilted toward the liberal Democratic line. Eighty thousand Americans wrote to complain about ABC's decision to let a convicted perjurer criticize a former vice president for losing an election. Sponsors threatened to cut their advertising.

Nixon encouraged the buzz. "What does an attack by one convicted perjurer mean when weighed . . . against the thousands of wires and letters from patriotic Americans?" he asked in an open telegram to major newspapers. He was hardly alone in his thinking about the "Obituary" program. Lyndon Johnson, watching the ABC program with fellow Texan Jim Wright, thought that it was "mean and unfair" to Nixon.

Typically, Jack Kennedy had two responses to the "Political Obituary" of his rival: one for the public, one for his pals. "How do you feel about the appearance of Alger Hiss on a television program on the career of Richard Nixon?" a reporter asked at the next White House news conference. Dodging, Kennedy said that he agreed with the FCC commissioner that the wisdom of putting on a person such as Alger Hiss was not up to the sponsors but "for the public to decide." Privately, Kennedy had a different reaction. Although he thought Nixon now "beyond saving" and his last press conference "sick," he retained his Mucker's contempt for the network's decision to have Alger Hiss dance on Nixon's grave. He called the program "a typical demonstration of phony liberals."

CHAPTER
SIXTEEN

Diem

Nixon spent the three weeks after the defeat in the Bahamas, walking up and down the beach. At forty-nine, the young man who had seen his ambitions so quickly and brilliantly realized was a political has-been. "It was the system that produced him," *New York Times* columnist James Reston decreed the day after the 1962 election. "He came to power too early and retired too soon."

BUT by New Year's a striking metamorphosis was under way. Nixon visited Tom Dewey in New York. The former governor, twice-beaten Republican presidential candidate, lawyer, and elder statesman, would be his new role model. Soon another New York law firm had a prominent political name in its partnership. With the move eastward came a fresh energy to Nixon's stride. Before him loomed the twenty-four-hour-a-day excitement of the big city. Behind him, happily, was the slower pace of his native Southern California. "If I have to play golf one more afternoon with Randy Scott," Nixon said of his too many hours sharing the tee and cart with the former cowboy star, "I'll go out of my mind."

His new life in a new place did not hide Nixon from his enemies. In February 1963, the Internal Revenue Service initiated three successive audits on the former vice president's income tax returns, scrutinizing them again and again for possible wrongdoing. The Kennedy fingerprints were unmistakable. Amid the painful investigation, however, the Nixons established themselves in New York, renting an East Side apartment and enrolling their daughters in the Chapin School, Jacqueline Kennedy's alma mater. By spring, Tricia and Julie's father was ready for his own coming-out party.

Appearing, once again, as a guest on the *Jack Paar Show*, Nixon this time was a hit. As he chatted amicably with the popular host, the former vice president came across as someone with neither politics in mind nor tricks up his sleeve. When Paar inquired about the early friendship between his guest and the president, Nixon allowed, somewhat hesitantly, that this had "certainly" been the case. "When we came to Congress . . . we were low men on the totem pole in the Labor Committee. We stayed low men till we ran for president. Now he's up, and I'm down." The studio audience loved it.

"Can Kennedy be defeated in '64?" Paar asked.

"Which one?" came Nixon's answer, a snappy reference to a trio of high-profile brothers that included the attorney general and the new junior senator from Massachusetts.

"Boy, I hate a smart-aleck vice president," the host responded, underscoring the irreverent mirth of the broadcast.

So debonair was Nixon's performance that media guru Marshall McLuhan declared that had he shown this "cool" side of himself in 1960, he would have won. Later that month, Nixon polished his new credibility in a speech at the annual meeting of the American Society of Newspaper Editors. He opened with a frontal defense of his "last press conference" of the previous autumn. "I felt like returning for sixteen minutes some of the heat I had been taking for sixteen years," he said to laughs, then applause. Journalists, he admonished his audience, should be able to take what they dish out. "If you can't stand the heat," he quoted Harry Truman, "stay out of the kitchen."

Nixon now turned to his main topic: John F. Kennedy. "If the United States had dealt with Castro effectively in the Bay of Pigs, Khrushchev would not have miscalculated a year later in the Cuban Missile Crisis. Khrushchev, like all aggressors, all dictators, interpreted indecision as weakness. The way to avoid miscalculation is never give them a moment when they think you're weak." Nixon would not let Kennedy's success in October 1962 cover up his debacle of April 1961.

Asked about Nixon's criticisms at a press conference, Kennedy tried to shove the problem back at him. "I know there is a good deal of concern in the United States because Castro is still there. I think it was unfortunate that he was permitted to assume control in the 1950s, and perhaps it would have been easier to take action then than it was now. But those who were in positions of responsibility did not make that judgment. Now, coming to the question which is rather sidestepped, that is, if the United States should go to war in order to remove Castro. It would seem to me that we have pretty much done all of those things that can be done to demonstrate hostility to the concept of a Soviet satellite in the Caribbean except take these other steps which bring in their wake violence and may bring a good deal of worldwide difficulty."

The positions of the two men on Cuba had now shifted 180 degrees. Since 1960, Nixon, an outsider, as Kennedy had once been, could afford to play hawk. Kennedy, having stared Khrushchev in the face, lacked that luxury. He had no choice but to see nuclear war as a deadly, tangible prospect.

Jack Kennedy was not the only American disturbed by Nixon's hawkish stance on Cuba. On the morning of April 21, Russian-born Marina Oswald recalled her husband, Lee, a self-styled "Marxist," heading out to buy the Sunday newspaper, the *Dallas Morning News*. That day's edition contained a banner headline: "Nixon Calls for Decision to Force Reds Out of Cuba." The former vice president was calling on Kennedy to rid the hemisphere of Fidel Castro. Oswald, who had immigrated to the Soviet Union out of sympathy for communism, then returned disillusioned, was a passionate defender of the Cuban leader. Within minutes, his wife would testify before the Warren Commission, he was dressed in gray slacks, white shirt, tie, jacket, and pistol. "Where are you going?" his Russian wife asked.

"Nixon is coming to town. I am going to have a look." Marina Oswald recoiled. "I know what your *looks* mean!" Acting quickly, she lured her husband, a former marine, into the bathroom and slammed the door behind him. "How can you lie to me after you gave me your word? You promised me you'd never shoot anyone else, and here you are starting in all over again." Two weeks earlier, Oswald had shot at and missed retired general Edwin A. Walker, a leading spokesman for the American right. He had used a secondhand Manlicher-Carcano rifle mounted with a four-power telescope. Refusing to let him out of the bathroom, Marina Oswald convinced her husband to hand over his gun and drop his planned "look" at Richard Nixon. She told him she was tired of his "pranks." Only later did it become clear that it was the expected arrival in Dallas of Lyndon Johnson, the current vice president, that had combined with the Nixon headline on Cuba to trigger her husband's confused but deadly conduct.

LIKE all politicians, John F. Kennedy had a Janus quality. A part of him worried about the basic questions of winning elections, gaining and holding power; the other face looked to the larger vision of what he could do to improve the world. As president, Jack Kennedy had to meet the grand concerns of humanity as well as the dictates of politics.

In one month—June 1963—John F. Kennedy gave three of his greatest speeches. The first, a commencement address at American University, was conciliatory. He used the occasion to call for a limited nuclear-test-ban treaty with the Soviets. Within four months he would sign the historic accord into law. His goal was peaceful relations between the United States and the USSR, between communism and the West. "What kind of peace do I mean?" he asked his audience, including his adversaries in the Kremlin. "Not the peace of the grave or the security of the slave.

I am talking about genuine peace, the kind of peace that makes life on earth worth living, the kind that enables men and nations to grow and to hope and to build a better life for their children—not merely peace for Americans but peace for all men and women—not merely peace in our time but peace for all time."

Kennedy was talking about protecting the world he so relished from destruction. He spoke of peace not as a retreat into weakness but as a challenge, like the race into space, a test of man's ingenuity. "Our problems are man-made; they can be solved by man. And man can be as big as he wants. No problem of human destiny is beyond human beings. Man's reason and spirit have often solved the seemingly unsolvable—and we believe they can do it again."

Richard Nixon, touring Europe, expressed his skepticism toward the emerging dialogue between West and East. "We must be under no illusions that this indicates any change in his basic objective, which is to impose communism on the Western world," he said. But after lunching in Paris with President de Gaulle, one of the few world figures who still believed in Nixon's political potential, the tough cold warrior called on Republican senators to support Kennedy's test-ban treaty, which he pointed out was initially proposed by Eisenhower. He continued to question, however, the highly discussed split between the Soviet Union and the world's other major Communist power, China. "Too many people today are gloating publicly because the Chinese Communists and the Soviet Communists are having an argument. What they fail to realize is that this argument is not about how they can beat each other but how they could beat us."

Kennedy's second memorable address that month concerned civil rights. The day after Kennedy's American University speech, two black students attempted to enroll at the University of Alabama. Both were blocked by order of Gov. George C. Wallace, who had sworn, during his most recent gubernatorial campaign, to prevent such desegregation. Kennedy was now forced to call out the National Guard in order to force the students' admission. That night, he went on national television to commit himself and his administration to the right of every citizen to enter public institutions as well as restaurants, hotels, and other places of public accommodation. Calling civil rights "a moral issue . . . as old as the Scriptures and . . . as clear as the American Constitution," he framed it in the context of the cold war. "Today we are committed to a worldwide struggle to promote and protect the rights of all who wish to be free. And when Americans are sent to Vietnam or West Berlin, we do not ask for whites only. We preach freedom around the world, and we mean it." For the first time, the voice and spirit of the presidency was behind the struggle for civil rights.

Later that month, *Newsweek*'s Benjamin Bradlee watched Kennedy struggling to rehearse some German sentences he intended to use in West Berlin. He knew of his friend's difficulties with languages. But the next day, two-thirds of the people of West Berlin crowded into the street greeting him with chants of *Ken-nah-dy; Ken-nah-dy*. John Kennedy delivered his triumphant challenge in the plaza of West Berlin's city hall. "Two thousand years ago the proudest boast was '*civis Ro manus sum*,' he told the massive crowd in front of him. "Today, in the world of freedom, the proudest boast is '*Ich bin ein Berliner!*' " It conveyed all the contempt for the Communists Kennedy and his country had within them. Not only did he embrace the people of the surrounded capital, he said he was one of them! It was the finest speech of the Cold War. "There are many people in the world who really don't understand, or say they don't, what is the great issue between the Free World and the Communist world. Let them come to Berlin. There are some who say that communism is the wave of the future. Let them come to Berlin. And there are some who say in Europe and elsewhere we can work with the Communists. Let them come to Berlin. And there are even a few who say that it is true that communism is an evil system but it permits us to make economic progress. *Lass' Sie nach Berlin kommen*. Let *them* come to Berlin. Freedom has many difficulties, and democracy is not perfect, but we have never had to put a wall up to keep our people in. All free men, wherever they may live, are citizens of Berlin, and therefore, as a free man, I take pride in the words '*Ich bin ein Berliner*.' "

* * *

By autumn of 1963, Nixon had settled in as a commentator on the New Frontier. He was producing articles on a wide range of subjects for *Reader's Digest*, the *Saturday Evening Post*, and the *Los Angeles Times* syndicate. Stephen Hess, the ghostwriter with whom he was splitting the magazine payments fifty-fifty, recalled Nixon as a "terrific boss," a generous employer who "really didn't have that much interest in money." But if the former vice president didn't care about the writing fees, Nixon did care that attention be paid to his increasingly hawkish line. By October 1963, his policy stance had shifted markedly to the right, as had that of his party. Stopping communism was not enough; we needed to lift the Iron Curtain. In a *Saturday Evening Post* article he warned against a "sell-out of the right of ninety-seven million enslaved people in Eastern Europe to be free.... Nothing less than to bring freedom to the Communist world" would now satisfy him.

Too weakened by his California defeat to be a candidate in 1964 himself, Nixon planned to write a book, with Hess's help, on the race. It would be modeled after *The Making of a President*, Theodore White's groundbreaking description of the 1960 race. By the fall of 1963, the Kennedy White House was growing touchy about such political books. When Victor Lasky's *Kennedy: The Man and the Myth* mentioned the $1,000 contribution Congressman Kennedy had delivered to Richard Nixon's office thirteen years earlier, the White House denied the episode altogether. Circumstances had rendered it inconvenient for the Democratic president, headed toward reelection, to admit even so ancient an alliance with the enemy.

IN 1963, there were twelve thousand American military "advisers" in South Vietnam defending the government of President Ngo Dinh Diem. A Roman Catholic leader, Diem had enjoyed support from his American coreligionists, including John F. Kennedy, since Vietnam's partition in 1954. But in addition to the Vietcong, the Communist guerrilla movement Saigon had been fighting since 1959, Diem confronted his country's hostile Buddhist majority. This placed the United States in conflict with both a Communist insurgency in the countryside and a Buddhist uprising in the cities. It was hard enough standing up to the hardships of the jungle. How could a country that ensured religious liberty support the South Vietnamese government in a civil war against its own religious majority?

During his first two years as president, Kennedy had played for time in Southeast Asia. He had cut a face-saving deal with the Soviets on Laos and then increased the number of American advisers in Vietnam. But he had drawn a line: He resisted calls by President Diem, beginning in 1962, to introduce American combat troops into Vietnam. He had taken to heart the advice given him by World War II leader Gen. Douglas MacArthur about the folly of committing GIs to a "ground war in Asia." But there was a sharp limit to such a policy. Kennedy knew that he could not abandon South Vietnam to the Communists and expect to get reelected. He had seen Truman's Fair Deal destroyed by the cry of "Who lost China?" He didn't want the New Frontier to suffer the same fate. Jack Kennedy could not afford to "lose" Vietnam.

His problem, Kennedy decided, was President Diem, a once-impressive leader now believed captive to the influence of a brother, Prince Ngo Dinh Nhu, and sister-in-law, known in the West as "Madame Nhu." Nhu was failing to prosecute the war vigorously and was suspected of plotting a secret deal with the Communist enemy. Of more immediate concern was his embarrassment of America before the world by his brutal repression of the Buddhists. On a June morning in 1963, the heat from South Vietnam became insufferable. American reporters in Saigon were handed a statement from a seventy-three-year-old Buddhist monk. "Before closing my eyes to Buddha," it began, "I have the honor of presenting my words to President Diem, asking him to be kind and tolerant toward his people and to enforce a policy of religious equality." Sitting in the lotus position, the elderly monk proceeded to burn himself on a bustling street corner, providing a horrified American public thousands of miles away with a news photo more incendiary than the million words printed in the *New York Times*.

Kennedy acted. His first step was to name as his personal ambassador to South Vietnam the man he had defeated for the Senate in 1952, then as Richard Nixon's 1960 running mate, Henry Cabot Lodge. Detecting Lodge's interest in the post, Kennedy quickly saw the advantages of the unusual appointment. It gave him a man in Saigon who was (a) totally unsentimental toward Diem personally and able to do the dirty work of discarding the longtime U.S. friend; (b) an agent equipped by background and experience to act decisively, unconstrained by bureaucratic control or protocol; (c) someone with a direct line to Kennedy personally; and, finally, (d) a politician with the ego to straighten out the situation in Saigon for the stark, powerful reason he was posted there.

The Lodge appointment revealed Kennedy's instinctive compartmentalization, his aptitude for pursuing his separate ambitions without letting one leak into another. To handle the hellish situation in South Vietnam, he now had a brand-name Republican to make the hell bipartisan. Lodge's Brahmin disdain was another plus: He was a WASP grandee with no motive whatever to prop up the corrupt regime of the Roman Catholic mystic in Saigon.

By late summer of 1963, the pictures coming out of South Vietnam had turned more menacing. They showed the Vietnamese Special Forces raiding Buddhist pagodas in Saigon and other South Vietnamese cities, ruthlessly placing the monks and nuns who attended under arrest. The raids were carried out by forces jointly directed by Diem and Prince Nhu. Those within the Kennedy administration who had been lobbying for an anti-Diem coup saw their chance. Assistant Secretary of State for Far Eastern Affairs Roger Hilsman drafted a cable from Kennedy to Lodge: "We must . . . tell key military leaders that the U.S. would find it impossible to continue support GVN [government of Vietnam] militarily and economically unless steps are taken immediately, which we recognize requires removal of the Nhus from the scene."

Getting rid of Diem's brother and sister-in-law, those on the scene knew full well, meant eliminating Diem himself. Averell Harriman, Kennedy's undersecretary of state for political affairs, immediately endorsed the Hilsman draft, as did National Security Council staffer Michael Forrestal, who sent it to Hyannis Port, where Kennedy was spending the late August weekend. The South Vietnamese generals wanted a signal that Washington would recognize a coup. Hilsman, Harriman, and Forrestal were urging the White House to send it.

Kennedy gave Lodge the go-ahead. "U.S. government cannot tolerate situation in which power lies in Nhu's hands," the August 24 cable read. "Diem must be given chance to rid himself of Nhu and his coterie and replace them with the best military and political personalities available. If, in spite of your efforts, Diem remains obdurate and refuses, then we must face the possibility that Diem himself cannot be preserved. You will understand that we cannot from Washington give you detailed instructions as to how this operation should proceed, but you will also know we will back you to the hilt on action to achieve our objectives."

But the administration was divided. Back at the White House that Monday, Kennedy heard Rusk, McNamara, and his military aide Maxwell Taylor accuse Hilsman, Harriman, and Forestal of pulling an end run of sending a cable sure to trigger an anti-Diem coup. "It shocks and saddens me," McNamara would write three decades later, "to realize that action which eventually led to the overthrow and murder of Diem began while U.S. officials in both Washington and Saigon remained deeply divided over the wisdom of his removal." Lacking a clear notion of who would rise to replace Diem, Kennedy had signed onto a coup that his team, including his secretary of state and secretary of defense, did not support. "My God!" Kennedy told Charles Bartlett on hearing of the dispute. "My government's coming apart!"

Lodge made clear in a cable to Washington five days later that he took the August 24 cable to be a direct presidential order to encourage an anti-Diem coup. "We are launched on a course from which there is no respectable turning back: the overthrow of the Diem government. We should make an all-out effort to get generals to move promptly. If generals insist on public statement that all U.S. aid to Vietnam through Diem regime has been stopped, we would agree."

Lodge reaffirmed his position the next day. The best chance of reaching American objectives in South Vietnam, he wired Washington, was "by the generals taking over the country lock, stock, and barrel." The day after that, a Lodge cable reported that Diem was cutting his long-feared deal with the Communists and would soon order the United States to leave his country.

Diem now posed a double jeopardy to Kennedy. He might lose the war to the Communists, having already alienated the majority Buddhist population. Or he might sign a separate peace with Hanoi, making the United States look not only weak but irrelevant. Kennedy had sized up the predicament to Charles Bartlett: "We don't have a prayer of staying in Vietnam. Those people hate us. They are going to throw our asses out of there at almost any point. But I can't give a piece of territory to the Communists and then get the American people to reelect me." To ensure plausible deniability about his role, he ordered his people to destroy all records of cable traffic between Washington and Saigon, starting with the fateful August 24 order he had approved in Hyannis Port.

Kennedy needed to conduct the nasty business with Saigon personally. To the nervous generals, plotting their coup, he had to declare his dissatisfaction with Diem and the desire for a change in leadership. He accomplished this mission in a September 2 interview with CBS's Walter Cronkite. "It is *their* war," Kennedy said of the South Vietnamese government. "They are the ones who have to win it." His second message was to those Americans worried that the Democratic president might not stick out the fight. He compared the struggle in South Vietnam to the successful U.S. effort to save Western Europe from communism after World War II. "What I am concerned about," he told NBC's David Brinkley a week after the Cronkite interview, "is that Americans will get impatient and say, because they don't like events in Southeast Asia or they don't like the government in Saigon, that we should withdraw. I think we should stay." In a press conference three days later, he made the point more sharply. "We have a very simple policy. We want the war to be won, the Communists to be contained, and the Americans to go home. That is our policy. We are not there to see a war lost."

On the morning of November 1, with the coup set for noon, a cold-blooded Lodge had breakfast with Diem. When the Vietnamese president said he sensed a plot, the American ambassador said he had nothing to fear. Hours later, with the U.S.-backed rebellion under way, Diem called the U.S. embassy asking for the American government's position. Lodge waffled. Everyone was asleep at that hour in Washington, he said, and his only communication was from the generals, who he had heard were offering Diem safe passage out of the country if he agreed to resign. What Lodge didn't tell Diem was that the coup leader, Duong Van Minh —"Big Minh"—had already made clear his desire to kill members of Diem's family. And the United States had no plans to stop him from doing whatever he wanted to Diem himself. When Lodge offered to help with the threatened president's physical safety, Diem reminded him that he was still his country's leader. "I am trying to reestablish order; after all, I am a chief of state," he said. "I have tried to do my duty. I believe in duty above all."

Taken from a Catholic church, where they had gone to hear an early-morning mass, Diem and his brother Nhu were thrown into an armed personnel carrier, their hands tied behind their backs. "Big Minh" asked the CIA, at this point, to get him a plane able to take his prisoners out of the country and into exile. He was told it would take twenty-four hours. For Minh that was too long to wait. "We can't hold them that long," he told Lucien Conein, the CIA agent who was working with the coup leaders. Diem and Nhu were then taken from the armed personnel carrier, shot repeatedly, and stabbed to death.

The killings were useful to both coup partners. "We had no alternative," General Minh rationalized. "They had to be killed. Diem could not be allowed to live because he was too much respected among simple, gullible people in the countryside." Henry Cabot Lodge spoke with similar contentment of the assassinations. "What would we have done with them if they had lived?" he told author David Halberstam. "Every Colonel Blimp in the world would have made use of them." When a younger Diem brother, Ngo Dinh Can, took refuge in the U.S. consulate in Hue, Lodge tricked him out of the consulate under the pretense he would be flown to asylum in the Philippines. Instead, the American plane carrying him to promised safety stopped at Tan Son Nhut Air Force Base, where Can, laden with cash, was turned over to the coup leaders, who then executed him by firing squad.

* * *

THOUGH a willing collaborator in the coup, Kennedy seemed stunned by the graphic account he received in the Cabinet Room of how Diem and Nhu had been removed from the church and killed. Military aide Maxwell Taylor recalled Kennedy rushing from the room with a pale and shocked look on his face which he had never seen before. "What did he expect?" Taylor asked the group. When Roger Hilsman, the State Department person who had plotted Diem's demise, tried defending the coup leaders' claim that Diem and Nhu had committed suicide, Kennedy was skeptical. He didn't believe that the Vietnamese leaders, both Roman Catholics, would ever have considered such a course of action. Taylor dryly pointed out that it was uncommon for people to shoot and knife themselves with their hands tied behind their backs. Meanwhile, Kennedy's representative in Saigon got nothing but praise. Kennedy sent an "Eyes Only" cable to Lodge commending his "leadership in pulling together and directing the whole American operation in South Vietnam. You should know that this achievement is recognized throughout the Government." One person outside the Kennedy team disagreed. "The Diem murder was the most disgraceful deed to date in our mixed-up foreign policy record," Richard Nixon wrote a Republican senator.

Yet the killing of Diem and the end of the embarrassing repression of the Buddhists were greeted as the most dramatic display yet of the young president's ability to cut through any political obstacle that lay before him. Suddenly, he had a military government in Saigon with the clout and motive to destroy the Vietcong. What Kennedy, his agent Lodge, and their country could not see was that the last leader of South Vietnam with the independence to tell the United States to get out of his country was also the last one with the legitimacy to ask it to stay.

While Kennedy had gotten past his earlier political contests with Lodge to the point of plotting a deadly coup with him, his differences with Nixon remained personal. With the exception of their meeting after the Bay of Pigs, the ex–vice president was *persona non grata*. Their early friendship had been a casualty of electoral war. "I like him, too," Kennedy said when told by author

Theodore White that a prospective 1964 challenger, New York Governor Nelson Rockefeller, held a warm regard for him. "But that's not important. He'll get to hate me. That's inevitable."

B Y November 1963, Kennedy's 1960 rival also loomed, despite all expectations to the contrary, as a credible Republican presidential candidate the following year. General Eisenhower praised him on *Face the Nation* as a "courageous type of guy." James Reston, who had penned an obituary the year before, now wrote that Nixon possessed a "ready-made strategy" for challenging Kennedy. "He lost to Kennedy by only 113,000 votes, and he could argue with considerable force that Kennedy's performance has fallen far short of all the promises he made." Reston reminded readers that Kennedy's 1960 claim of a "missile gap" would allow Nixon to say in 1964 that he had lost their first contest thanks to JFK's deception. "Richard Nixon suddenly seems to be the Republican whom everybody is talking about for his party's 1964 Presidential nomination," *Time* declared.

Jack Kennedy's prognosis was proving correct. Dick Nixon hadn't needed that humiliating 1962 run for governor of California to stay alive politically. He had gained enough stature from his eight years as vice president to survive even the live burial of the year before. With an election year before him, Nixon was talking very much like a partisan politician.

"Contrary to what the pundits say and write, it's what *others* have done which has caused this Nixon talk. The others are active and running. I am not. And it's because there is disillusionment with Kennedy," Nixon told *Time* in an extended interview. He mentioned the "increasing possibility" that Kennedy could be beaten. "As the possibility increases, so does the interest in getting a Republican who can win. I find there is a correlation between Kennedy's failures and interest in me."

Nixon was beginning to probe Kennedy's moral responsibility for his role in the overthrow and death of President Diem. He told *Time* that the Kennedy-backed coup against Diem might take on importance in 1964 should the war against the Vietcong take a turn for the worst. "If it goes well, Vietnam won't be an issue."

Asked to gauge his party's chances of beating Kennedy, Nixon showed the scars of the 1960 defeat. "Running against him next time will be running against all his money, the federal Treasury, and all kinds of public relations. Kennedy will shoot the works."

These remarks appeared in the issue of *Time* dated November 22, 1963.

CHAPTER

SEVENTEEN

Dallas

ON November 18, 1963, President Kennedy gave a tough anti-Castro speech in Miami. "A small band of conspirators has stripped the Cuban people of their freedom and handed over the independence and sovereignty of the Cuban nation to forces beyond the hemisphere," he told a meeting of the Inter-American Press Association. "This, and this alone, divides us. As long as this is true, nothing is possible. Once this barrier is removed, everything is possible." Good relations between Cuba and the rest of the hemisphere would return when Fidel Castro was gone.

On November 20, Richard Nixon flew to Dallas, Texas, to attend a board meeting of the Pepsi Cola Bottler's Association. He was accompanying Donald Kendall, president of the soft-drink company, a major Nixon client. The next day, November 21, he summoned a group of reporters to his hotel room. The president was coming to town, and his old rival wanted to work some mischief. Aware of the fierce anti-Kennedy sentiments in the city he had carried by over 60 percent in 1960, Nixon called on the people of Dallas to give a "courteous reception" to the president and vice president. Just days before, Adlai Stevenson, Kennedy's UN ambassador, had been spit upon by an angry resident. But Nixon couldn't resist inflaming the city's volatile mood. He said that Kennedy might dump his Texan vice president from the 1964 ticket if it suited his purposes. "Nixon Predicts JFK May Drop Johnson" was the next day's headline in the *Dallas Morning News*.

> Former Vice President Richard M. Nixon predicted here Thursday that President Kennedy will drop Lyndon Johnson from the No. 2 spot on the Democratic ticket if a close race appears likely next year.
>
> Nixon said that Johnson is becoming a "political liability" to the Democratic party.
>
> "President Kennedy has stated he intends to keep Lyndon as the vice-presidential nominee. The fact they are coming to Texas together, I believe, indicates the President means what he said.
>
> "But we must remember that President Kennedy and his advisers are practical politicians. I believe that, if they think the race is a shoo-in, they will keep Lyndon. Otherwise, I think, they will choose someone who can help the Democratic ticket."

"DAMN it!" Kennedy had told his Florida pal George Smathers as they headed up from Palm Beach that Tuesday. "I hate to go to Texas. Johnson's got it all fouled up." Back at the White House, he asked Tip O'Neill about the old gang back in the Eleventh Congressional District. "How's Billy doing?" Could O'Neill make sure that he was taken care of? Charles Bartlett, the columnist-buddy who introduced him to Jackie, was on the phone chatting with the president the night before he left for Dallas. Chuck Spalding figured the calls he kept getting and missing from the White House were from Kennedy, trying to invite him for the weekend in Virginia after he returned from his Texas swing.

Kennedy had politics on his mind. To carry Texas in 1964, he needed to boost his own approval rating, which was down to 38 percent in the state. He also needed to patch up the state party, badly fractured between conservatives and liberals. Money, too, was a reelection necessity. Texas was a wealthy state, and even a moderately liberal Democratic president needed to get his share.

The president awoke that Friday morning at the Hotel Texas in Fort Worth. The first formal event was a chamber of commerce breakfast. At the urging of local congressman Jim Wright, Kennedy agreed to begin the day with an outdoor rally in the hotel parking lot, something for blue-collar workers headed to the 8:00 A.M. shift. Emerging into an early-morning drizzle, Kennedy succeeded in whipping up the appreciative outdoor crowd. His high spirits continued when he joined the business group inside. A local television crew caught him sitting at the head table of the chamber of commerce event, kidding back and forth with Johnson as the two endured the familiar tedium of hearing the name announced of every local dignitary with a ticket.

Mentally, Jack Kennedy was busy that morning with his accustomed exercise of trying to figure out what makes voters, in this case Texans, tick. Just as he had once checked the voting patterns of Italian, Jewish, and Armenian voters back home in Cambridge with Tip O'Neill, he was now intrigued with the difference in politics between two Texas cities. Riding to the airport, he asked Wright and Connally to account for the extreme rightward tilt in Dallas. What made it so different from the Democratic stronghold of Fort Worth? Wright chalked it up to the archconservative *Dallas Morning News,* which that morning carried a vicious ad accusing the president of Communist sympathies. Connally gave an economic explanation. Unlike Fort Worth, Dallas was a high-rise boomtown of banks and insurance companies, all filled with men wearing white shirts to work. Unconsciously, the Democratic governor, with an 81 percent approval rating, was divulging his own careful calculations of where the state—and John Connally —were headed. He had earlier made clear he did not want to be seen locally as a "Kennedy man."

The forty-six-year-old president landed in Dallas at noon. His first stop was a luncheon at the Texas Trade Mart, where former vice president Nixon had spoken to the Pepsi people the day before and where twenty-five hundred people were now waiting to hear him. He was just five minutes from the mart when his limousine passed Dealey Plaza and a Manlicher-Carcano rifle, equipped with a four-powered telescope, aimed down from a window of the Texas Book Depository.

JOHN F. Kennedy died as he had lived, riding in an open convertible, a loving, beautiful woman beside him, charming everyone in sight. He died as he had told George Smathers he had wished—quickly. He was shot by a troubled loner infatuated with Fidel Castro's Cuba, disgusted with Russia, and angry at his own country. He died his father's son, campaigning to hold the great prize of honor he and his family had won. He was at the end what he was those first months after V-J Day: a Cold Warrior. "Without the United States, South Vietnam would collapse overnight," he had said at the Fort Worth breakfast.

AMERICAN Airlines Flight number 82, with Richard Nixon aboard, had departed Dallas's Love Field three hours before *Air Force One* arrived. After speaking briefly to a group of reporters at New York's Idlewild Airport, he took a cab into Manhattan. Stopping at a red light on the Queens side of the Fifty-ninth Street Bridge, he saw a stranger rush from the curb. "Do you have a radio in your cab? I just heard that Kennedy was shot." Nixon was incredulous. Maybe the guy on the curb was a nut or a prankster. Maybe Kennedy had only been wounded.

Nixon aide Stephen Hess was having lunch that day in New York with the editor of the book the former vice president and he were planning to write on the 1964 presidential campaign. As word moved through the restaurant of the grim events in Dallas, Hess telephoned Nixon's secretary, Rose Mary Woods. What should he do? Woods said Nixon would, given the dire circumstances, go home rather than to his law offices. Arriving at the Fifth Avenue apartment, Hess was stunned to see his boss himself answer the buzzer. "Nixon opens the door, he's jacket-less, not tie-less but jacket-less, which is very informal for him. And he is really shook up and he tells me that he heard the news. His reaction seemed to be 'There but for the grace of God go I.' There is no doubt that that's how he greeted me. What he did was open his attaché case. He quickly showed me a copy of that morning's *Dallas Morning News* with Nixon's front-page sentence urging the people of Dallas to afford Kennedy 'a courteous reception.' He wanted to show me that because he was worried that people would think that Kennedy was killed by a right-winger and that somehow he would be blamed for it."

Erase the assassin image, Henry Cabot Lodge had warned him.

Soon Nixon would learn, to his relief, that police suspected someone from the other political extreme.

NIXON canceled a golf match set for that afternoon with Roger Blough, the U.S. Steel executive with whom Kennedy had suspected the former vice president had conspired to hold down steel prices during the 1960 campaign. He had also planned to attend the opera that evening with his mentor, Tom Dewey. Instead, he stayed in, watching the networks' hastily-thrown-together profiles of John F. Kennedy's life and career, with himself cast as the foil. Later, after Rose Mary Woods had invited Nixon's local political allies together for a meeting with him the next morning, Nixon sat in front of his fireplace long after the ashes had cooled in the fire composing a letter to his rival's widow:

> Dear Jackie,
>
> In this tragic hour, Pat and I want you to know that our thoughts and prayers are with you.
>
> *While the hand of fate made Jack and me political opponents I always cherished the fact that we were personal friends from the time we came to the Congress together in 1947.* That friendship evidenced itself in many ways including the invitation we received to attend your wedding.
>
> Nothing I could say now could add to the splendid tributes which have come from throughout the world.
>
> But I want you to know that the nation will also be forever grateful for your service as First Lady. You brought to the White House charm, beauty and elegance as the official hostess of America, and the mystique of the young in art which was uniquely

yours made an indelible impression on the American consciousness.

If in the days ahead we could be helpful in any way we shall be
honored to be at your command.

Sincerely,
Dick Nixon

CHAPTER EIGHTEEN

Eternal Flame

PRIOR to an interview on the Kennedy assassination, CBS producer Don Hewitt, who had directed the Great Debate three years earlier, asked guest Richard Nixon if he wanted the makeup person, Frances Arvold, to prepare him for the broadcast. Nixon accepted. Hewitt could not resist kidding, "If Frannie had done your makeup three years ago, you'd be president now." Nixon's reply was equally macabre.

"I would be dead now, too," he said.

The New Year would bring a warm reminder of the long and complicated relationship he had shared through so many Capitol corridors, hotels, and campaigns.

Dear Mr. Vice President—

I do thank you for your thoughtful letter—

You two young men—colleagues in Congress—adversaries in 1960—and now look what has happened— Whoever thought such a hideous thing could happen in this country?

I know how you feel—so long on the path—so closely missing the greatest prize—and now for you, the question comes up again, and you must commit all your and your family's hopes and efforts again— Just one thing I would say to you—if it does not work out as you have hoped for so long—please be consoled by what you already have —your life and your family.—

We never value life enough when we have it—and I would not have had Jack live his life any other way—though I know his death could have been prevented, and I will never cease to torture myself with that—

But if you do not win—please think of all that you have— With my appreciation—and my regards to your family. I hope that your daughters love Chapin School as much as I did—
                              Sincerely Jacqueline Kennedy

Included in the envelope was a mass card from St. Matthews cathedral.

THE young widow's intuition of another Nixon presidential run was correct, just as her husband's had been in predicting that his 1960 rival had no need to run for governor in 1962 to remain a live presidential prospect. The first Gallup poll, taken with Lyndon Johnson in the White House, showed Nixon with 29 percent and the previous front-runner, conservative senator Barry Goldwater of Arizona, with 25 percent. Nixon's former running mate, Ambassador Henry Cabot Lodge, received 16 percent, New York governor Nelson Rockefeller 13 percent.

Jacqueline Kennedy had inherited a part for herself in the political arena. The Sunday after her husband was killed, she began to play it. "And there's going to be an eternal flame," she said amid the plans for the funeral arrangements. Sargent Shriver worried about the protocol. "We'll have to find out if there's one at the Tomb of the Unknown Soldier, because if there is, we can't have one." The grieving First Lady was adamant. "I don't care if one is there. We're going to have it, anyway." Shriver, whom the Kennedy family had deputized to manage the grand ceremonies, tried to finesse the question. "I think the only places with eternal flames are Paris and the one already out at Arlington. I want to be sure you're not subjecting yourself to criticism. Some people might think it's a little ostentatious," he explained.

"Let them," the president's widow replied.

The tragedy in Dallas had transformed the Kennedy personality from a slain president to a clan whose every member had been touched with his glamour. Despite the proud Lyndon Johnson's feudalistic oath to "continue" the dead president's legacy, the Kennedys and their loyalists were not ready to yield the scepter of national leadership won in 1960. Henceforth, they would treat all other claimants to the presidency as caretakers or, worse yet, usurpers. "Camelot," the poignant conceit Jacqueline Kennedy now confected, *colorized* the career of John F. Kennedy much as film distributors would some years later transform vintage black-and-white movies. People would absorb it so deeply into their memories of the New Frontier period as to make it seem contemporary. "Camelot" came to symbolize a mass longing not limited to partisan Democrats for a return of something beautiful and lost, the honoring of a dynastic claim. What John Kennedy had won through democratic election his family now demanded as hereditary rank.

Jacqueline Kennedy's instrument for imprinting "Camelot" onto the nation's psyche was Theodore White, the same author whose *Making of the President* had celebrated John F. Kennedy's coming to power. A week after the assassination, she invited White up to Hyannis Port. There was something she wanted to tell him about her husband, something that was not being written in the newspapers.

When the *Life* correspondent arrived at the Kennedy summer home, his hostess dismissed Chuck Spalding and another guest, Franklin Roosevelt, Jr., from the room. She wanted to talk with her selected chronicler alone.

It was raining outside that night. Above her gray pullover sweater, Jackie's face was drained and pale. "History! History! It's what those bitter old men write," she railed when the conversation began at 8:30 P.M. By midnight she got to the reason she had summoned her influential guest. "I've got to talk to somebody, I've got to see somebody, I want to say this one thing, it's almost an obsession with me, all I keep thinking of is this line from a musical comedy, it's been an obsession with me. At night before we'd go to sleep . . . we had an old Victrola. Jack liked to play some records. His back hurt, the floor was so cold. I'd get out of bed at night and play it for him, when it was too cold getting out of bed . . . on a Victrola ten years old—and the song he loved most came at the very end of this record, the last side of *Camelot*, sad *Camelot*: . . . 'Don't let it be forgot, That once there was a spot, For one brief shining moment that was known as Camelot.' Jack loved history so . . . history made Jack what he was . . . this lonely, sick boy . . . this little boy sick so much of the time, reading in bed, reading history . . . reading the Knights of the Round Table . . . and he just liked that last song. For Jack history was full of heroes. And if it made him this way, if it made him see the heroes, maybe other little boys will see."

White spent two hours knocking out his story. At 2:00 A.M., he gave Jacqueline Kennedy a carbon copy of what he had written. After she had volunteered her changes, he went to the kitchen phone and began dictating to his editors in New York. When Mrs. Kennedy walked in and heard White fighting his editor's objection that there was too much "Camelot" in the article, Jacqueline Kennedy shook her head insistently. "She *wanted* Camelot to top the story," White wrote years later in his memoirs. He knew that he had let his sentiments be manipulated, knew that the analogy was "a misreading of history." "The magic Camelot of John F. Kennedy never existed," he confessed. "Of all the figures of the New Frontier," he believed John F. Kennedy to be the "toughest, the most intelligent, the most attractive—and inside, the *least romantic.*" Voices from the Kennedy inner circle shared in the admission. "Camelot is a fraud," Pierre Salinger would say. Roger Hilsman, who had played his own hard role in the toppling of Ngo Dinh Diem, said: "Camelot was an invention of my good friend Teddy White, using Jackie's romanticism after the president's death. If Jack Kennedy had heard this stuff about Camelot he would have vomited."

EARLY in 1964, Jacqueline Kennedy acted to shield her husband's public legacy. She commissioned author William Manchester to write about the assassination, with the proviso that she would review the final manuscript.

Robert Kennedy operative Paul Corbin undertook a more immediate claim on the JFK legacy. He secretly promoted a vice-presidential write-in campaign for the attorney general in the New Hampshire Democratic primary. "You always had some of the Kennedy supporters who thought it wasn't legitimate unless you had a Kennedy in the White House," said Johnson's press secretary, George Reedy, summing up the impulse. Ted Sorensen, the man Jack Kennedy christened his "intellectual blood bank," said that Bobby Kennedy, anxious for the number-two spot on the 1964 Democratic ticket, was not out to serve Lyndon Johnson's place in history but to recover his brother's. "He wanted to be there to carry on the legacy of the previous president, not the incumbent president."

Johnson was furious at the subterfuge, telling Kennedy to get Corbin out of New Hampshire and off the Democratic National Committee payroll. "He was loyal to President Kennedy. He'll be loyal to you," Kennedy argued. "I know who he's loyal to," Johnson snapped back. "Get him out of here." Johnson later phoned Bobby to tell him that he had fired Corbin personally. He was not about to share the 1964 ticket with Jack Kennedy's brother.

VIETNAM was a far more treacherous piece of the Kennedy legacy.

In taking the presidential oath aboard *Air Force One*, Lyndon Johnson took custody of a war to which Jack Kennedy had committed sixteen thousand troops. On the morning of November 22, Kennedy had predicted that South Vietnam would fall overnight if the United States lessened its commitment; Secretary of Defense Robert McNamara, just back from Saigon, now offered an even more troublesome report to the new president. "Current trends, unless reversed in the next two months, will lead to a neutralization at best and more likely to a Communist-controlled state." Just as critics of the November 1963 coup had feared, the generals Kennedy helped topple Ngo Diem were considerably less impressive leaders than the man they had deposed and killed.

Johnson held Kennedy personally responsible for Diem's death, believing he had pulled the strings while protecting his own "plausible deniability" in the episode. The conviction that Diem

had been eliminated with JFK's complicity created a fateful rea-
soning on his successor's part. "Could the United States engineer
the assassination of a nation's leader," LBJ aide Joseph Califano
explained, "and then walk away from its commitment to that
nation on the ground that the legitimate leader of the people was
no longer in power?"

In January 1964, Nixon called together his veteran strategists,
Bob Finch, Bob Haldeman, and Steve Hess, for a meeting at the
Waldorf Towers. They agreed that Nixon's best stance, for the
time being, was to lay low. The consensus was that their man was
not in a position to run openly for president but that he could
turn out to be an acceptable compromise between the party's left
and right should that summer's convention in San Francisco reach
a deadlock. By March, the scenario seemed plausible. Henry
Cabot Lodge, Nixon's former running mate and the American
ambassador to South Vietnam, won the New Hampshire Republican primary with 33,000 write-in votes, defeating the two front-
runners, Barry Goldwater and Nelson Rockefeller. Richard
Nixon, also not on the ballot, received 15,600 write-ins, a significant portent for a politician whose career had seemed finished.

The former vice president now departed for a trip to the Far East
to visit some of his firm's international clients. Saigon was on the
itinerary. Before leaving New York's newly christened John F.
Kennedy International Airport, he declared he was on a "holiday
from politics." Would Vietnam be an issue in the year's presidential election? a reporter asked. "It will only become an issue if the
policy has weaknesses worthy of criticism, if it is plagued with
inconsistency, improvisation, and uncertainty. That has been the
case in the past." Nixon couldn't resist a postscript. "There is no
substitute for victory."

Arriving in Asia, the Kennedy legacy in Vietnam remained
high on Nixon's agenda. In Pakistan, President Ayub Khan shared
his belief that the United States had been complicit in the killing
of President Diem. "I cannot say—perhaps you should never have

supported Diem in the first place. But you did support him for a long time, and everyone in Asia knew it. Whether they approved or disapproved, they knew it. And then, suddenly, you didn't support him anymore—and Diem was dead," Nixon would later quote his Pakistani host. The global message of the 1963 coup, he concluded, was that it was "dangerous to be a friend of the United States."

In Saigon, Nixon had dinner with Ambassador Lodge. Nixon recalled the briefing: "I know that a lot of people are impatient with the way things are going here, and I know that the military men don't like being held back. But there's a bigger and broader problem that can't be settled by fighting over it. The problem in South Vietnam is less military than economic. The Viet Cong draw their strength from hungry peasants, and if we want to wean them from Communism we shouldn't shoot at them—we should distribute food to them." Lodge argued against pursuing the Vietcong forces into Laos or Cambodia. He said U.S. troops should avoid fighting the Vietcong altogether except to retaliate when Americans were killed. Nixon decided that his former Cold War colleague had grown soft. "I could hardly believe that I was hearing this from one so versed as Henry Cabot Lodge in the tactics of international Communism."

THAT June, the Warren Commission, established by Lyndon Johnson to investigate the assassination of John F. Kennedy, heard Marina Nikolayevna Prusakova Oswald, Lee Harvey Oswald's wife, describe her husband's dangerous behavior in April 1963 after reading in the *Dallas Morning News* of Richard Nixon's call for a tougher policy against Castro's Cuba. When the commission queried Nixon about his later trip to Dallas in 1963, he wrote back that he had been there on November 20 and 21, thereby denying he left the Texas city on the morning of November 22. While most Americans can describe in detail where they were when they heard Kennedy had been shot, Richard Nixon, for whatever reason, would not admit to the commission that he was actually on his way back from the scene of the crime on November 22.

Nixon was still tantalized by the prospect of a presidential "draft" at the Republican convention that July. In San Francisco, however, he endorsed the candidacy of Arizona conservative Barry Goldwater, winning the gratitude of the party's emerging right wing. By agreeing to present the chosen nominee to the rambunctious convention, Nixon assumed the role of enduring party grandee, a leader standing in reserve for future fights. He clearly sensed the impending catastrophe that Goldwater's suicidal acceptance speech made inevitable. "Those who don't care for our cause, we don't expect to enter our ranks in any case," the 1964 presidential candidate declared. "Extremism in the defense of liberty is no vice; moderation in the pursuit of justice is no virtue." As the candidate's intemperate words echoed through the Cow Palace, Nixon quietly demonstrated both his wisdom and future ambitions. With aroused Goldwater delegates giving their man's defiance a standing ovation, the former vice president reached over to keep his wife in her seat.

IF Richard Nixon was looking toward the future, Lyndon Johnson was worrying hard about the present, especially the theatrics scheduled for the Democratic convention in Atlantic City. "He was afraid that because they had planned a tribute to John F. Kennedy and Bobby was to deliver it," his adviser Clark Clifford recalled, "it might very well stampede the convention and make Kennedy the vice presidential nominee." When Johnson tried persuading Kennedy to remove himself as a possible running mate, he refused. Out of desperation, the president issued a statement excluding from vice-presidential consideration all cabinet members and all who meet regularly with the cabinet, the latter phrase meant to include UN ambassador Adlai Stevenson. His prime target tried laughing it off, saying he was sorry that he had to take "so many nice fellows" down with him.

Johnson's fears were fully justified. A film eulogizing JFK was shown on the convention's last night. Narrated by Richard Burton, who had starred in the Broadway production of *Camelot*, it glowed with heartbreaking images of Jack and Jackie and Caroline, making the Kennedy presidency the stuff of myth, the New Frontier the court of King Arthur.

When the lights of the great convention hall came up, the slender figure of the late president's brother was there, standing atop the podium, alive! The waves of applause rolled on and on. " 'When he shall die, Take him and cut him out in little stars,' " the surviving brother quoted from Shakespeare's *Romeo and Juliet*. " 'And he will make the face of heaven so fine That all the world will be in love with night, And pay no worship to the garish sun.' "

Deprived of the chance to continue the dynasty, Bobby Kennedy began a desultory campaign for the U.S. Senate from New York, a state where he did not even have the right to vote. "Don't you know?" he told an aide, astounded by an emotional crowd in Buffalo. "That was for *him*, not for me." As Kennedy stumped around New York State, the gravel-voiced Paul Corbin saw that he was following the same route his brother had taken four years earlier. "Get out of this mysticism," Corbin growled. "Get out of your daze. Goddamn, Bob, be yourself. Get hold of yourself. You're *real*. Your brother's *dead*."

Richard Nixon, also campaigning in upstate New York that fall, darkly alluded to a "*cloud of corruption*" hanging over the Democratic administration. He predicted that Kennedy would be defeated in his Senate race. He won by 250,000 votes. With a strong new political base in the Empire State, the prospect of a Kennedy "restoration" seemed merely a matter of time. Richard Nixon, too, had kept his own presidential hopes alive, campaigning in thirty-six states for the doomed Republican ticket. A young Kansas congressman named Bob Dole would recall the former vice president peppering him with questions about his future. It would be the only presidential election year between 1952 and 1972 that Nixon would not be his party's candidate for national office.

CHAPTER NINETEEN

The New Nixon

BARRY Goldwater lost the 1964 presidential election to Lyndon Johnson by 26 million votes to 43 million votes—the worst Republican defeat of the century. The one leader not blamed for the debacle now prepared himself to answer his party's call.

Nixon's first step was to the right. He lashed out at the liberals surrounding John Kennedy, though not the slain hero himself, who had "enabled the United States to pull defeat out of the jaws of victory" during the 1962 Cuban Missile Crisis. Vietnam policy was another target of opportunity. "The United States must be prepared to meet the issue squarely and to commit whatever forces are necessary," he taunted Johnson. What he meant was more U.S. bombing. America could not afford to lose any more ground in Asia.

Nixon moved to the right on civil rights as well. "In this election year, Republicans will be urged by some to outpromise the Johnson administration on civil rights in the hope of political gains," he declared. "I am completely opposed to this kind of political demagoguery. Making promises that can't be kept—

raising hopes that can't be realized—are the cruelest hoaxes that can be perpetrated on a minority group that has suffered from such tactics for a hundred years." The man who once scared white southerners with his opposition to segregation was now, a year after passage of the 1964 Civil Rights Act, seeking to benefit from their backlash.

The headquarters of the Nixon political operation was his Lower Manhattan law office. "Between wars a campaign is more like an organism which can live for years in the national ganglion hidden from sight," John Ehrlichman described the scene at Nixon's law firm, "its vital signs discernible only to the most sensitive of political diagnosticians. On the twenty-fourth floor, amid the five floors leased to Nixon, Mudge, Rose, Guthrie and Alexander at 20 Broad Street, in a back corner close by the door to Richard Nixon's office, there incubated the incipient virus of a presidential campaign . . . slowly thawing from a cryogenic storage that had begun after Richard Nixon's defeat in the California gubernatorial election in 1962." At the start of 1965, the Nixon "virus" was still limited to some of his law partners, his secretary, Rose Mary Woods, and a "Miss Ryan," who came in to help out with the typing. Pat Nixon used her maiden name to remain as unobtrusive as she was helpful to her husband's cause.

As the years passed, Nixon began recruiting professionals to his embryonic comeback. A young, newly arrived Nixon, Mudge associate named John Sears saw two aspects of Nixon that were not evident in the well-known figure. One was a man without the mechanical quality of his public performances; the other, a politician very much haunted by his 1960 defeat. "Nixon always prided himself that he worked harder than anybody. Everything seemed to come easy to Jack. I think the Kennedys frightened Nixon."

IF Richard Nixon could not live with his defeat in 1960, the victorious Kennedys were determined to repeat it. To do it, they needed to finesse relations with President Johnson. Not yet weakened by Vietnam, he was the official champion of all that Jack Kennedy had begun and the most powerful man in the country besides. Suddenly, there loomed a malignant threat to the Kennedy-Johnson alliance: William Manchester's book on the assassination.

Four months before publication, *Time* reported that the book showed Johnson as an "unfeeling and boorish man." The men around Johnson, including Gov. John Connally, who had been wounded in the assassination, figured that Bobby Kennedy was behind the derogatory reference. In fact, the Kennedys were obsessed with getting the negative material excised, knowing people would assume that the late president's family had approved it. "I'll ruin you," Jacqueline Kennedy told Harper & Row editor Evan Thomas when they met at a cocktail party. Manchester suffered more brutal treatment, including a civil suit and surveillance by private detectives. He described it as the "Kennedy winter offensive of 1966–67." His chief assailant was the junior senator from New York, Robert Kennedy. "I spent three of the most uncomfortable hours of my life in his Washington office on the afternoon of August 12, watching, appalled, while he paced tiger-like between Evan Thomas, John Seigenthaler and me. He appeared to be wholly irrational. He accused me of raising my voice. He pretended to leave the room, hid in an alcove, and leapt out, pointing an accusing finger at me."

Kennedy suggested that Manchester "shred" the galleys of a *Look* magazine excerpt of the book so that they'd be unprintable. Again, the Kennedys were trying to trade money for reputation. He offered to pay Manchester not to publish. "How much do you want? Three hundred thousand? Four hundred thousand?"

When the author rejected the hush money, Kennedy tried getting editor Evan Thomas to kill the book. Manchester recalled Bobby Kennedy's rage: "Was it actually possible that my editor and I had sat grimly silent in a Manhattan hotel suite while a United States Senator, determined to alter the book, hammered on the door and repeatedly called my name? It was as though the First and Fourteenth Amendments had been struck from the U.S. Constitution," he would write in a long account of the episode.

What the Kennedys wanted deleted was any record of the friction existing between Bobby and Lyndon Johnson in those chaotic days following the tragedy in Dallas. A rift with LBJ could jeopardize the Kennedy succession. Eventually, the beleaguered author agreed to delete sixteen hundred words. It didn't appease the Johnson crowd. When the first installment appeared in *Look*, Connally called a press conference to blast the Manchester book as an "astonishing propaganda instrument cleverly woven to reflect favorably on those who gave it birth while rudely discrediting others."

By the summer of 1965, LBJ faced an even bigger menace than Jack Kennedy's little brother: Vietnam.

A lesson of the 1962 Cuban Missile Crisis was the prudence of a "measured response" to foreign policy conflicts. The United States should take only those steps that the adversary's conduct justifies. In the war with North Vietnam, the policy now translated to step-by-step escalation. Unwilling to fight a war of annihilation, such as the Allies prosecuted against Hitler and Tojo, the United States had joined in a war of attrition designed to keep Russia and China from entering the struggle. One man not satisfied with the strategy was Richard Nixon. He called Johnson's mention of "negotiations" a veiled move to capitulate that "would reward aggression." He was far tougher on Johnson's critics, accusing them of advocating "appeasement and retreat." "If the United States gives up Vietnam, the Pacific Ocean will become a Red Sea," Nixon wrote in the *Reader's Digest*. "The true enemy behind the Viet Cong and North Vietnam is China. If Vietnam is lost, Red China would gain vast new power. Indonesia, Thailand, Cambodia, and Laos would inevitably fall under Communist domination." He warned that the felled dominoes would position the Communist Chinese "only 14 miles from the Philippines and less than 100 miles from Australia."

In the fall, Nixon switched his sights to the Red threat at home. When Robert Kennedy spoke out and defended the right of a self-proclaimed "Marxist" and Vietcong enthusiast to teach at Rutgers, he was quickly challenged by the former vice president. The country was "at war," Nixon declared. The professor had no right to use his lectern to "give aid and comfort to the enemy."

Expecting Vietnam and inflation to hurt the Democrats in the 1966 elections, Nixon saw the combination spurring a sizable

Republican gain. NBC correspondent Robert MacNeil, meeting Nixon at his Fifth Avenue apartment, heard his host recite from memory the name of the Democratic incumbent, the Republican challenger, and the local campaign issues in the fifty congressional contests in which he was about to campaign. Nixon saw victory coming and banked on taking credit. "First '66!" he admonished Patrick Buchanan when his zealous new speechwriter had mentioned prospects for a White House run in 1964. Working with another speechwriter, the once-and-future candidate spent an inordinate amount of time trying to craft a contrapuntal line of the kind Ted Sorensen had scripted for John Kennedy. "For twenty minutes we worked on a single line," William Safire recalled.

Nixon saw the lack of victory in Vietnam as a major Democratic vulnerability. After visiting Saigon again in July 1966, he declared that there was "no possibility of negotiations" with North Vietnam and attacked President Johnson for an insufficient war effort. Two hundred and seventy thousand American troops, he said, were not enough.

In August, Nixon stirred the political pot again, predicting that President Johnson would drop Hubert Humphrey and make Robert Kennedy his running mate. It was a rerun of his mischievous November 21, 1963, forecast that Jack Kennedy would dump Johnson. "If Lyndon thinks he's in trouble," the troublemaker observed, "if Lyndon thinks he needs Bobby on the ticket to win, he'll sugarcoat him, swallow him, and regurgitate him later." Instead of a Kennedy dumping Lyndon Johnson, Johnson might be forced now to dump a loyal ally in order to accept a Kennedy.

Nixon's goal was to score attention from the press, chits from his fellow Republicans. He knew that all the press clips and party dinners would be redeemable two years later. Stephen Hess recalled Nixon's attitude toward this political scut work: "He was telling me about how he was a law student at Duke during the Depression and had a summer job. He had a professor who couldn't sell his textbook to a commercial publisher, so he decides he's going to mimeograph it and sell it to his students. Nixon gets the job of cranking the mimeograph machine . . . in the North Carolina summer in an airless room. And the reason he's telling me this story is that the end justifies the means. He needed to get his law degree, and he would do anything, including cranking the mimeograph machine in the North Carolina heat . . . all summer, to get the money to be a law student. That's the way he treated politics. It's what you've got to do."

On October 25, just days before the 1966 congressional elections, President Johnson met with South Vietnam president Thieu in Manila. They issued a joint communiqué on the war that now saw American troops in direct confrontation with the North Vietnamese regular army. A week later, Richard Nixon offered a point-by-point dissection. He was particularly critical of Johnson's reference to "mutual withdrawal" from South Vietnam by the two opposing armies. Nixon said that the South Vietnam Army could not defeat the Vietcong without American advisers, that Johnson's talk of a "mutual withdrawal" plan was really an offer to "surrender a decisive military advantage."

The president heard a report on Nixon's talk of his "surrender" on his way to a televised press conference. It was the Friday before the election, and he had mischief in mind. When asked about the former vice president's detailed criticism of his Vietnam policy, Johnson dismissed Nixon as a "chronic campaigner." "That ought to put him out front," Johnson said with a chuckle as the wire services began ticking away with news of the skirmish between the president of the United States and the man he had just anointed leader of the opposition.

Johnson had outsmarted himself. Believing that the press would run with his ridicule, to his horror he found them playing it as a David and Goliath situation, with LBJ in the role of ugly giant and Nixon wielding the slingshot. Two nights later, the Republicans bought Nixon thirty minutes of national television time to speak for the party. He used it to stick in the knife. He cited Johnson for "one of the most savage personal assaults ever leveled by a president of the United States against one of his political opponents." Then he twisted the blade. "I understand how a man can be very, very tired," he said of the Democratic president, "and how his temper then can be very short." In other words, it was time for the old president to retire, to turn the job over to someone a few years younger, someone a bit more seasoned in international matters.

On election night, just as Nixon had expected, his party won big, picking up 47 seats in the House of Representatives, 3 in the Senate, and 540 in state legislatures. Herb Klein, who received a call from his former boss that evening, said, "I never heard him sound happier."

As Nixon positioned himself for the prize that had been denied him in 1960, the legacy of the man who beat him was undergoing revision. In March 1967, columnist Drew Pearson revealed a CIA plan to assassinate Fidel Castro on Kennedy's watch. Lyndon Johnson, convinced that Castro had had a hand in President Kennedy's own assassination, ordered the intelligence agency to review any and all efforts to eliminate Castro. The final document, prepared by CIA inspector general S. I. Breckenridge, laid out the entire story of anti-Castro assassination plotting beginning under Eisenhower. His report detailed the attempted use of Sam Giancana and other Mafia figures, early attempts to humiliate Castro with drugs and bizarre beard-defoliating chemicals, Operation Mongoose, and the poison pills meant for the Cuban leader. Breckenridge placed the burden of the assassination efforts entirely on the shoulders of John and Robert Kennedy: "It became clear early in our investigation that the vigor with which schemes were pursued within the Agency to eliminate Castro personally varied with the intensity of the U.S. Government's efforts to overthrow the Castro regime." That intensity was greatest, the report stated, in the years 1961 through 1963. "We cannot over-emphasize the extent to which responsible Agency officers felt themselves subject to the Kennedy administration's severe pressures to do something about Castro and his regime."

It was now time for Richard Nixon to begin his extraordinary deviation from Cold War doctrine, much as Jack Kennedy had done with his Algeria speech a decade earlier. The '68 hopeful produced an essay in *Foreign Affairs* urging a diplomatic opening to Red China. Nixon suggested that the United States demonstrate to China "that its interest can be served only by accepting the basic rules of international civility." Such a policy, he reasoned, would lure "China back into the world community . . . as a great and progressing nation." The ardent Cold Warrior who had blasted Truman for the Communist takeover in 1949, who had hit Kennedy as too soft on Quemoy and Matsu and Johnson as weak-rooted on Vietnam, was now talking of normalizing relations with the Communist giant herself.

With the 1968 election approaching, Nixon was coming to terms with another danger: television. "The time has come for political campaigning, its techniques and strategies, to move out of the dark ages and into the brave new world of the omnipresent eye," aide Bob Haldeman wrote in a memo. Giving speeches all day, he argued, was no way to run for president. A candidate would "become punchy, mauled by his admirers, jeered and deflated by his opponent's supporters, misled by the super-stimulation of one frenzied rally after another."

Nixon received similar advice from a Philadelphia educator named William Gavin, who sent a quotation from Ortega y Gasset: "Those are the only genuine ideas; the ideas of the shipwrecked." Gavin urged Nixon, whom he had never met, to run; also to make bold use of television. "Instead of those wooden performances beloved by politicians, instead of a glamour-boy technique . . . be bold. Go on live and risk all. I know you can win if you see yourself for what you are: a man who has been beaten, humiliated, hated, but who still sees the truth."

The former vice-president could run a different kind of campaign, one that exploited television while protecting him from the uncertainties of the old-style campaign.

Three days after Christmas, Nixon left for Key Biscayne. Three weeks later, he returned home, having made what he told his daughter Julie was "the most important decision of his life." He would run for president again, not as the vice president defending the status quo but as a seasoned politician on the attack. And he would not have John F. Kennedy as his adversary. Nixon's aides began telling reporters the story of the little girl who, upon meeting Nixon on the campaign trail, remembered him as "President Kennedy's friend." Kennedy had called his campaign plane the *Caroline*; Nixon now named his the *Tricia*.

Chapter Twenty

1968

RICHARD Nixon began his second try for the presidency determined not to repeat past mistakes. To win, he needed to overcome the echoes of the past, both the crippling electoral setbacks of 1960 and 1962 that had tagged him a loser and his political identity as the villain of Camelot. Soon the campaign he had expected to wage against Lyndon Johnson would become, if only briefly, a reprise of his worst horror.

Nixon was obsessed, most of all, with avoiding another humiliation at the polls. To maximize the odds of victory, he set to work assembling a state-of-the-art campaign team, one that emphasized lightning-fast advance work, controlled and limited access to the candidate by the media, and zero interaction with opposing candidates. Richard Nixon's second effort would pay strict homage to what the Kennedy organization had accomplished in 1960, a day-to-day program to avert the fatigue and confusion of the last effort. He would win with new friends like law partner John Mitchell, who had offered refuge in the wilderness years, and a new cadre of no-excuses operatives led by H. R. Haldeman. Old allies like Bob Finch and Herb Klein, men who had lost Nixon's confidence

in the 1960 defeat and lacked the necessary, unswerving commitment to victory, would hold the secondary positions. Like Jack
Kennedy, Nixon had found the choice between old loyalist and
ruthless agent difficult but doable. Aide Jeb Magruder noted the
candidate's new preference for "tough, efficient managers like Bob
Haldeman and John Mitchell, men who loathed the media as
much as Nixon did and had as little to do with it as possible."

THE year 1968 was taking on a historic character well beyond
New Year's. The political season had commenced prematurely
with the October "March on the Pentagon" anti–Vietnam War
rally and the antiwar Democratic insurgency of Minnesota senator
Eugene McCarthy, who was challenging Johnson's renomination.
January brought the Buddhist New Year, *Tet*, and an all-out attack
on the cities of South Vietnam by 50,000 Vietcong and North
Vietnamese regulars. Thirty provincial capitals were all attacked
simultaneously, destroying the confidence of both the Saigon government and its U.S. allies. Suddenly, America lived with the
knowledge that the Vietnam War was not being won militarily.
Within weeks, Gen. William Westmoreland, the U.S. commander
in Vietnam, would decide that the 500,000 American troops in-
country were insufficient; he needed 200,000 more. Many Americans would view the additional troop request as a public admission
of defeat.

New York senator Robert Kennedy now offered a political verdict on the war. The Tet Offensive, he said, had smashed the
"illusion" that the Vietnam War could "be settled in our own way
and in our own time on our own terms." It had taught America
that a "total military victory is not within sight or around the
corner; that, in fact, it is probably beyond our grasp; and that the
effort to win such a victory will only result in the further slaughter
of thousands of innocent and helpless people." But he would go
no further, refusing the call of antiwar forces that he, too, challenge Johnson for the nomination. One fear drove him to consider such a divisive move. He declared the prospect of Richard
Nixon defeating LBJ in the November election, which polls now
showed as likely, "unacceptable."

On the eve of the March 12 New Hampshire primary, the "unacceptable" suddenly became probable. Michigan governor George Romney, undone by his claim to being "brainwashed" by upbeat Pentagon briefings on the war, quit his run for the Republican presidential nomination. Richard Nixon was now, as Kennedy feared, the voters' sole alternative to Lyndon Johnson.

But the primary itself changed everything. On the Democratic ballot, Johnson beat antiwar candidate Eugene McCarthy by an embarrassing margin of just 49 percent to 42 percent. Nixon swept the Republican primary. To Robert Kennedy, the results confirmed two realities: the weakness of Lyndon Johnson among Democrats and the acceptability of Richard Nixon among Republicans. Both became persuasive arguments for his own entry into the race. Four days later, in the same Senate caucus room where his brother had launched his candidacy, surrounded by the radiant Kennedy family, the former attorney general made his fateful bid for the long-awaited restoration, using precisely the same words as Jack: "Today I announce my candidacy for the presidency of the United States."

Across the country, in Portland, Oregon, Nixon watched the event from his suite in the Hotel Benson. After Kennedy had finished, he sat staring at the blank television screen. "We've just seen some terrible forces unleashed," Nixon said, breaking the silence. "Something bad is going to come of this. . . . God knows where this is going to lead."

John Ehrlichman would give voice years later to the mood that now gripped the Nixon camp: "The Kennedys are back!" Julie Nixon got word that many of her father's people were seized by political déjà vu. "Those who had lived through the election eight years before had memories too vivid to be able to look at the situation rationally." With one televised announcement, they found themselves back in another Kennedy race.

Bob Haldeman was less impressed. While Richard Nixon's "antennas were quivering all the time," Haldeman believed his man had been hardened by exile. He could see not just the love the Kennedys inspired but the fear. He knew that to millions of Americans the return of the Kennedy family to presidential politics meant not deliverance but trouble.

Robert Kennedy's abrupt entry into the 1968 race had an ironic ripple effect in Republican politics. New York governor Nelson Rockefeller had been threatening to make a late entry into the GOP presidential contest. To give Kennedy time to qualify for the Nebraska primary, state officials extended its filing deadline. This forced the hesitant Rockefeller to state his own intentions. Uncertain about the wisdom of challenging Nixon among rural Cornhuskers, the New York plutocrat pulled himself out of contention. The impulsive withdrawal opened an odd opportunity. The man leading the push for a Rockefeller candidacy was Maryland governor Spiro Agnew. Realizing that the New Yorker had pulled out without giving Agnew the courtesy of a heads up, Nixon aide John Sears suggested that his candidate take advantage of the situation. Over lunch with Nixon, Agnew speedily revealed his anger at the harsh treatment by the well-born Rockefeller. Nixon liked what he heard. Here was a new brother in the fraternity of resentment, a genuine *Orthogonian*. A quiet bond was forged.

ON St. Patrick's Day, Sen. Robert Kennedy marched exuberantly down Fifth Avenue. From an open window, Jacqueline Kennedy was photographed blowing him a kiss. The next day, he spoke to fourteen thousand students packed into a Kansas State University field house. His topic: Vietnam. "I am willing to bear my share of the responsibility before history and before my fellow citizens. But past error is no excuse for its own perpetuation." At the White House, President Johnson was getting some startling data from Larry O'Brien, the political strategist he had inherited from Bobby Kennedy's older brother: He was going to lose the Wisconsin primary. For Johnson, this settled the matter. He would not seek reelection and said so in a Sunday evening broadcast to the nation. One man could not believe what he was hearing, a politician yielding so valuable a prize so easily to such a bitter enemy. "I'd be surprised if President Johnson lets Bobby Kennedy have it on a platter," Richard Nixon observed. But a Nixon-Kennedy fight was now a live prospect. The Nixon and Kennedy campaign staffs, both headquartered at Portland's Benson Hotel for the upcoming

Oregon primary, were soon bumping into each other in the lobby, just as the Nixon and Kennedy staffs had spent the 1950s bumping into each other on the third floor of the Senate Office Building.

But Bobby Kennedy was evolving into a very different political personality from his debonair brother in 1964; he was transfiguring into a leader in his own right. Through his championing of the urban poor and rural farmworkers, he had become a one-man bridge between the warring elements of the Democratic party— angry blacks and Latinos on one side, fearful working-class whites on the other. He was part Irish cop, part civil rights advocate. "He was tough on law and order so that liberal programs and politics could work," aide John Seigenthaler explained. Kennedy's sympathy for the plight of the African American was learned, not inherited. Paul Corbin, a veteran of the 1960 primary battles, had grown exasperated with his wealthy young boss's cold professionalism on the civil rights issue. He asked Kennedy what he thought it might feel like to be a man driving through the South and having to go from gas station to gas station asking if his wife could "take a piss." His growing, impassioned empathy for black America in such human terms expanded the Kennedy appeal even as the Democratic party was coming apart.

Kennedy, who had voted for Eisenhower-Nixon over Stevenson-Kefauver in 1956, shared one critical sentiment with his older brother. Like Jack, Bobby Kennedy retained a tribal suspicion of the elite liberal establishment.

I just feel that those New York liberals are sick. They're not doing any work. They spend their time worrying about not being invited to the important parties, or seeing psychiatrists, or they are bored with all their affluence. I personally prefer many of the poor white people I've met here in Indiana. They are tough, and honest, and if you help them, they remember it, like the people who live in the poorer sections of West Virginia. They're not fickle. I think I just like the Poles in Gary better than those New York reformers, who are so filled up with hate and envy.

But it was his rapport with black America that brought the forty-two-year-old candidate fully into view, especially his conduct in the evening hours of April 4, the day Martin Luther King, Jr., was murdered in Memphis. With a rally planned for an inner-city neighborhood in Indianapolis, Kennedy went ahead with his schedule. It fell to him to tell the excited crowd what had just happened in Memphis. "What am I going to say?" he kept asking an aide as they drove into the Indianapolis ghetto.

He would find the words. "I have bad news for you, for all of our fellow citizens who love justice all over the world," he said from atop a flatbed truck, "and that is that Martin Luther King was shot and killed tonight." The crowd, initially, did not believe him. There was even some applause from those so buoyed by his presence and primed to applaud that they didn't hear, at first, the tragic call for atonement he was delivering. "We must make an effort, as Martin Luther King did, to understand with compassion and love. I had a member of my family killed, and he was killed by a white man. But we have to make an effort in the United States, we have to make an effort to understand." What followed were words that would never be confused with those of his elegant older brother. "What we need is not division. What we need is not hatred. What we need is not violence but love and wisdom and compassion toward one another and a feeling of justice toward those who still suffer within our country, whether they be black or they be white." Kennedy brought to the moment not just a shared cause but a shared victimhood. His reference to a "member of my family" being killed was his only public comment on what he would call as long as he lived "the events of late 1963." Through the ensuing weeks of riot, arson, and racial fury, he alone remained a figure of common hope.

Yet to millions of his countrymen Bobby Kennedy remained a political apparition of times past, especially when he began campaigning in his brother's old bomber jacket or when he put his hands in his suit-coat pockets or poked the air with his extended forefinger, declaiming in that same clipped Jack Kennedy cadence. To one of those millions he was both an avenging brother and a haunting flesh-and-blood reminder of his most horrible defeat.

Richard Nixon stayed up until 2:30 A.M. in his New York apartment the night of the California primary to watch Robert Kennedy claim victory at the Ambassador Hotel, the same Los

Angeles landmark where he had received the news of his own defeat eight years before. He believed Kennedy now had the momentum to carry him to the Democratic nomination and the all-out battle in November. "It looks like it's Bobby," he said before heading off to bed. Forty-five minutes later, a figure stood over him in the dark. "Mr. Nixon. Excuse me. Mr. Nixon." It was David Eisenhower, the grandson of the man who had taken him as his vice president, launching him into presidential politics, sixteen years before.

"What is it?" Nixon asked through his sleep.

"They've shot Kennedy. He's still alive, but he's unconscious. He was shot just after his victory speech."

Once again the gunfire felt closer than the public could imagine. Political soldiers in the two camps had shared the same hotels and campaign trail for years. "Here I was watching a friend, Frank Mankiewicz, nearly in tears as he courageously briefed the nation on a shooting in a hotel almost as familiar to me as my office," veteran Nixon press secretary Klein recalled. He remembered Nixon's practice of escaping crowds through the same kitchen.

The evocation of Dallas, just five years earlier, was ghastly. Lying on the Ambassador floor, Bobby Kennedy never looked more like his brother. Over the next days, the country would experience an eerie replay of five years before, another odd epoch of gloom in a cheery country's history. Candidate Nixon's immediate reaction was to declare a moratorium on campaigning. Underlying the courtesy was a new set of political calculations to be worked out amid the inevitable relief in not having to face Robert Kennedy.

At St. Patrick's Cathedral in New York, Ted Kennedy gave a powerful eulogy honoring his slain brother. "He saw suffering and tried to heal it; he saw war and tried to stop it." Now the spotlight was on him, Teddy, the handsome younger brother, and he never seemed so fine an emblem of his stricken family. Again, the torch had been passed.

NIXON now decided to do nothing that might interfere with what he saw as an inevitable swing toward the Republicans. He would appear on television, but only if no journalists were permitted to interfere with the script. Nor would he agree to any debates. "It's a shame a man has to use gimmicks like this to get elected," he confided to the young producer Roger Ailes.

"Television is not a gimmick," snapped the man who would become Nixon's television adviser.

"We're going to build this whole campaign around television," Nixon was heard telling his team. "You fellows just tell me what you want me to do and I'll do it."

Each day, with clockwork precision, a single campaign event would be scheduled early enough and near enough to an airport so that the film could be shipped to New York for inclusion in the evening news. Given no optional pictures to be aired that night, the networks fell into line, showing exactly what the Nixon people had programmed.

The goal was not just to get across the Nixon message but to protect him from the hapless stumbles of the 1960 race, when he had been driven to fatigue and mistakes and pummeled daily by a hostile press. Yet even as the Nixon operation presented its polished surface and clocklike rhythm, the restless candidate had a habit of breaking free. "I would call for him at his hotel room in a small midwestern city in the morning and find that he was missing," Bob Haldeman would recall. "Sometime in the early dawn he had gotten out of bed and slipped away, with a nervous Secret Service man tailing him. We'd search all over town until we found the candidate looking haggard and wan in a flea-bitten coffee shop."

But the retrofitted Nixon machine was doing the job. Like Kennedy eight years earlier, Nixon had his party's 1968 presidential nomination locked up long before the convention. Though California governor Ronald Reagan, the new star in the Republican heavens, hoped for a wide-open convention, Nixon had the situation firmly under control. "It's the fellow without the cards that does the strongest talking," said the veteran gambler who had won his first campaign grubstake playing poker. "I've got the cards." The nomination official, he appeared in the convention hall grinning and wigwagging the V for victory, the same two-handed gesture that once had made Kennedy cringe. Having named Agnew as his running mate, he accepted the Republican presidential nomination for the second time with a masterful address. With a husky voice, he spoke of a young boy growing up in Depression-hit California. "He hears the train go by at night, and he dreams of faraway places he would like to go. It seems an impossible dream." Recalling his youthful yearnings in a twenty-by-thirty-five-foot home amid the orange groves of Yorba Linda, his voice broke. "Tonight he stands before you nominated for president of the United States of America. You can see now why I believe so deeply in the American dream." It was the Orthogonian anthem. In 1960, he had been forced to play defense. Now he would help the squares once again dethrone the Franklins. Back at his hotel room, Nixon called speechwriter Bill Safire's attention to the moment in the address where he changed his voice, "that 'impossible dream' part."

Yet as Nixon held the convention enthralled with his Orthogonian anthem, the Muckers were also busy outside. A heavily pregnant woman, recruited by Democratic prankster Dick Tuck, stood with a large sign proclaiming "Nixon's the One!"

No Democratic prank could offset the nasty pyrotechnics surrounding their own convention that summer of 1968. Meeting in Chicago two weeks later, party officials soon lost control of the riotous situation in the streets beyond. "Chicago" would now evoke the image of angry antiwar students, brutal police, and delegates less than thrilled about nominating Vice President Hubert Humphrey, the man Jack Kennedy had clobbered in the 1960 primaries. Hoping to exploit the nasty situation, Nixon had dispatched to Chicago an eager trio of operatives: Bill Safire, Pat Buchanan, and Bill Timmons, who posted themselves at the Chicago Hilton, where Democrats had set up their headquarters. Their mission was to create a "truth squad," responding in kind to any shots against the Republican ticket. Watching the pandemonium break loose, however, Nixon hastily switched strategies. He directed his three men to stay clear of the line of fire; the Democrats were doing too good a job of destroying themselves.

Still, Chicago produced one grace note of danger for Richard

Nixon. With the convention about to open, Mayor Richard Daley still held hope of victory in November. He continued urging Ted Kennedy to run despite the reservations many fellow Democrats held about his age and the decency of running the grief-stricken brother of two assassination victims. Humphrey couldn't beat Nixon, the pugnacious mayor now told Kennedy over the phone. "But you're a winner. You can carry the convention; you can carry Illinois; you can carry the country," said the old-style boss whose "few good friends" had given Kennedy's older brother Illinois that unforgettable election night. Daley's appeal failed to change the younger man's mind. The convention would have to settle for yet another filmed tribute to another slain Kennedy, this one entitled "An Impossible Dream," narrated by Richard Burton, having performed the same task in 1964, now the official voice of Camelot.

Ted Kennedy had spent the six weeks after the assassination off Cape Cod in a rented yawl. When he came back to Washington, he could not bring himself to enter the Old Senate Office Building. "I just can't go in there and face them," he said. That same July day, John Connally, who had raised Jack Kennedy's Addison's disease at a Democratic convention eight years earlier, took a shot at the younger brother's maturity. He answered a reporter's questions by saying he wondered if Ted Kennedy even possessed the ability to serve as president of the country.

Chicago, the site of Nixon's debut on the national political scene in 1952, now became a source of his second chance. The Democratic convention of 1968, held amid the wildest antiwar demonstrations yet seen, became a symbol of the *Zeitgeist*. Recognizing the sense of widening chaos, enlarged still further by the independent presidential candidacy of Alabama's segregationist governor George Wallace, Nixon refused to let up, injecting his time-worn belief that a campaign can "peak" too early. Like Kennedy in 1960, he ran flat out from the beginning, believing he needed to seize the electoral windfall offered by the chaotic Democratic mayhem in Chicago. Also like Kennedy, he would end the campaign hanging on by his fingertips.

But if the Nixon presidential campaign of 1960 was fueled with more adrenaline than moxie, the 1968 model was the opposite.

Tightly choreographed rallies were geared to begin when the candidate arrived, never more than ten minutes late. The balloons tumbled down with similar synchronicity. "Smooth as a space satellite, precise as a computer, the 1968 Nixon-mobile whirs around the country like a politician's dream machine." His rival Hubert Humphrey was, in the same *Time* report, "as susceptible to programming as the Marx brothers." Facing hecklers at every stop demanding "Debate! Debate!" Nixon cannily avoided the trap. His allies on Capitol Hill killed a Democratic move suspending "equal time" rules to allow a television debate limited to the two major candidates. This gave Nixon his coveted escape route. When the eager Humphrey offered to pick up the tab for the debates, Nixon debunked such video sparring as "kid stuff." He would take considerable heat to avert another ambush like that which he suffered at Jack Kennedy's hands in the Great Debate.

In a September radio address, Nixon spelled out a personal notion of the presidency that echoed the New Frontier. "Let me be very clear about this: The next President must take an activist view of his office. He must articulate the nation's values, define its goals, and marshal its will." It was a speech Ted Sorensen himself might have drafted, saluting, as it did, the chief executive's need to stimulate intellectual debate in the country and to recruit a cabinet of brains and character to help him do it. Officials of a Nixon administration would "not have to check their consciences at the door."

One final hazard threatened the Republican march to power: peace. In mid-October, Nixon received a surprise call from Lyndon Johnson, who informed him that talks would soon begin on halting the U.S. bombing of North Vietnam. Nixon accused Johnson and the Democrats of being "squishy soft" on communism. But he was worried. Despite his 1960 losses to Jack Kennedy, his humiliating tenure in Lyndon Johnson's court, and his inveterate gabbiness, Hubert Humphrey was suddenly eating away at Nixon's lead. A deal that promised peace could put him over the top. The Thursday before the election, Johnson dropped the other shoe. He arranged a conference call to Nixon, Humphrey, and third-party candidate Wallace. He told the three men seeking his job that he had decided to cease bombing North Vietnam as a prelude to peace talks. Then came his veiled warning. "The fate of our country lies in your hands over the next few weeks. There would be serious trouble if anything anyone said were to interrupt or disrupt any progress we are trying to make to bring this war to a halt."

Nixon saw easily the electoral calamity the cagey Johnson was preparing for him. He later admitted his sentiments. "Had I done all this work and come all this way only to be undermined by the powers of an incumbent who had decided against seeking reelection?" Fortunately, he had allies of his own. Anna Chennault, widow of Flying Tigers hero Claire Chennault and a staunch Republican, agreed to relay Nixon's concerns about Johnson's preelection move to the South Vietnamese government. The "Who lost China?" crowd was back in business to elect Richard Nixon. When President Thieu declared that South Vietnam would boycott any talks involving the rebel Vietcong, Johnson instinctively knew he had been outflanked.

Nixon's enemies were desperate. Larry O'Brien, the old Kennedy hand now managing the Humphrey campaign, wanted to air television ads using the infamous "last press conference" that followed the 1962 California governor's race, to show an out-of-control Richard Nixon. The message would be that the Republican nominee was too unstable to trust with the U.S. military arsenal. Ultimately, the idea was discarded. Showing Nixon tearing into the press might score him some points.

Yet Nixon's big lead of the summer was shrinking under Humphrey's gung-ho assault. Fifty-eight thousand people packed the Houston Astrodome to cheer the fast-closing Democratic nominee. Gov. John Connally, angry at his party's leftward drift, was not among them.

But Texas wouldn't be enough. Saigon's election-eve rejection of the Johnson peace initiative had, according to Lou Harris's numbers, stopped the big swing to Humphrey. On election night, the results came in at 43.4 percent for Nixon, 42.7 percent for Humphrey, and 13 percent for Wallace. In the Electoral College, it was Nixon 301, Humphrey 191, and 46 for Wallace.

The day after achieving the longtime dream, a weary but elated Nixon sat alone in his Upper East Side hideaway listening to the

Richard Rodgers score for *Victory at Sea*, a television documentary on America's World War II success in the Pacific. "My thoughts meshed with the music," he would recall a decade later. Yet there was something unsettling in the voters' judgment even in victory. "I think in his own mind," Bob Haldeman would one day reflect, "he felt it was very strange that he could get elected."

CHAPTER
TWENTY-ONE

Haunting

ROM the moment Nixon was elected president, major forces were collaborating in his downfall, all sprung from the legacy of John F. Kennedy. They included the capital's bureaucratic, media, and social establishments, each spurning the Republican arrivistes with the same efficiency with which the human body rejects foreign tissue. Their hero and presidential role model was the slain hero who had graced the White House and the city. Though the New Frontier had ended quietly only six years before, it had managed to leave behind a raft of relics, the most prominent of which was John Kennedy's notion of a national leader. No man felt this more keenly than the rival who now sat in the Oval Office. "Nixon's standard as a modern President, conscious or not, was John F. Kennedy," speechwriter William Safire recalled. "Along with the envy for the way the Kennedys enthralled and bedazzled so much of the press went a genuine admiration for the way the Kennedys played the political game: with zest and calculation, with professionalism, with a high regard for personal loyalty and disregard of traditional obstacles. The Kennedys would come to play and play to win, and when you

•

beat a Kennedy you beat the best. The trouble was, nobody did."
The height of the Kennedy standard, raised still higher by the
deftly constructed myth of Camelot, became, in Safire's estimate,
a genuine threat to Nixon's reelection.

Another undermining factor was the conflict joined by Jack
Kennedy in Vietnam. By the start of Richard Nixon's presidency,
535,000 American troops were committed. "The war," with its
new and harrowing image of a South Vietnamese officer firing a
pistol at the head of a suspected Vietcong in the streets of Saigon,
would be the backdrop for the entire Nixon presidency.

Equally threatening to Nixon were those Kennedy people at
whose hands he had suffered in the past. In his darker moments
he would recall the harsh tricks he saw worked on him, from the
1960 vote counts in Chicago and Texas to the Kennedy-instigated
tax audits. He got a fresh reminder of Democratic hardball right
after the election. FBI director J. Edgar Hoover told him in his
Pierre Hotel transition headquarters how Johnson had tapped not
just Madame Chennault's phone and the South Vietnamese embassy's but also those on the Nixon and Humphrey campaign
planes. Nixon's knowledge of the LBJ wiretaps would provide a
dark standard of what presidents did in difficult circumstances.

Finally, there was the living, breathing presence of the last
surviving brother, Sen. Edward M. Kennedy. Nixon regarded his
1960 rival's brother as the prime danger to his hopes for a two-
term presidency. *Time* called him a "shining champion who had
not been bloodied at all in the conflict" of 1968 Democratic
politics and the party's "hope of future victory." The defeated
Hubert Humphrey offered to help Kennedy reclaim the family
prize. "Someday you will lead the nation, and I'm going to help
you get the chance to do it."

By the very force of his face, personality, and voice, Ted Kennedy
promised a return to the magic extinguished by the gunfire. Adding
to his myth as "Last Brother" was the cloying possibility that with
the help of Chicago's Richard Daley he could have taken the
1968 Democratic presidential nomination just for the asking.

Bolstering his prestige still further was Kennedy's surprise election to the Senate's number-two leadership position. On the eve
of the 1969 inauguration, the *Washington Star* ran a sly Pat Oli-

phant cartoon of Richard Nixon standing with his suitcases at the North Gate to the White House, pensively eyeing Ted Kennedy, also with luggage, just a few paces behind him. It was a punishing insight. Having lost contests in both 1960 and 1962 and having fumbled a monstrous lead in the final weeks of the 1968 election to win with only 43 percent of the vote, the new president had sufficient excuse to suspect his victory a fluke. If he dared forget the cruel lessons of the past, there stood Jack's ambitious younger brother to remind him. The month after Nixon's inauguration, the Gallup poll would show Ted Kennedy leading the Democratic pack for 1972.

From his Pierre Hotel transition headquarters, Nixon tried from the beginning to co-opt his enemies by bringing some of them into his camp. While he managed to recruit academic Daniel Patrick Moynihan, a Democrat with loyalties to the Kennedys, as his chief domestic-policy adviser, other overtures proved fruitless. One example was Washington senator Henry "Scoop" Jackson, a close Kennedy ally and 1960 campaign chairman, whom Nixon invited to be secretary of defense; the recruitment would have sealed the Vietnam War as a bipartisan problem, a parallel to what Jack Kennedy had done in making Henry Cabot Lodge his man in Saigon. Ted Kennedy quietly warned the hawkish Jackson that accepting Nixon's offer would finish him with the Democratic party.

Nixon kept trying. He asked Sargent Shriver to join the administration as his ambassador to the United Nations, adding that he was sure the Kennedy brother-in-law would enjoy working with William Rogers, the old Nixon friend about to become secretary of state. Listing the prominent clubs to which Rogers belonged, Nixon suggested that the well-born Shriver and the new chief diplomat, coming from the same social background, would work comfortably together. The Orthogonian was matchmaking among the Franklins.

Again, the Kennedy family resisted, but not before the former Peace Corps and War on Poverty director sought assurances from Nixon that the social programs created under the Democrats would be retained. Shriver realized too late that he had overstepped the bounds of a job seeker. Nixon, too, had spotted the inevitable conflict of interest. As a consolation, he allowed Shriver to remain in Paris as ambassador to France, a prized post he had been assigned under Lyndon Johnson. Even as Nixon attempted, vainly, to bring Kennedy people aboard, the media hit him for failing to match President-elect Kennedy's snappy pace of appointments when he formed his administration in the fall of 1960.

Like John F. Kennedy, Nixon was sworn into office on the Capitol's east front by Chief Justice Earl Warren, who had worsened relations still further with the president-elect by announcing his retirement the previous year, hoping to give Lyndon Johnson, not Richard Nixon, the chance to name his successor. Nixon's inaugural address paid tribute to a more persistent rivalry. "If every nation cannot be our friend, at least it does not have to be our enemy." The attempt to mimic the Kennedy speech of eight years earlier was unmistakable. Within two days of the inaugural, Ted Kennedy used a fund-raising dinner to remind Robert Kennedy's recent supporters that the dream of restoration remained. "The campaign of 1968 never really ended . . . because it remains with all of us. He often said, 'We have promises to keep' and these are the promises which will bring all of us together many times in the future."

THE triumphal parade down Pennsylvania Avenue to the White House on January 20, 1969, resembled an obscene pageant as the limousine bearing the Nixon family was pelted with sticks, stones, empty beer cans, and homemade smoke bombs. Lining one side of the avenue was an angry, chanting mob faced off against District of Columbia police and paratroopers from the Eighty-second Airborne Division, their arms linked to form a living barrier. The polarization in the streets of Washington was amply matched by the partisan lines drawn indoors. Speechwriter Patrick Buchanan later captured the sense of menace from those partisans within the inaugural bunker:

When he left as vice president in 1961, only 600 military advisers were stationed in Vietnam; by 1969, 535,000 troops were there, or on the way. Within months, the war—into which President Lyndon Johnson had for five years plunged the United States—would be called "Nixon's War." Liberal Democrats who had cheered on U.S. intervention now demanded to know why Nixon had not brought the boys home. Not only was Congress hostile, so, too, was a vast bureaucracy built in the New Deal and expanded in the Great Society. So, too, was the press, many members of which had never forgiven Nixon for his role in the red-baiting campaigns of the '50s. So, too, was a liberal establishment that had not only despised Nixon throughout his career but had seen itself repudiated by the great majority of Americans who had voted for Nixon or George Wallace.

The *Washington Post*'s Meg Greenfield gasped at the same wide divide from the other side. "There has been no more traumatic clash of cultures than that which marked the confrontation between the arriving Nixon administration and the awaiting resident press since Pizarro first dropped in on the Incas."

Nixon's new national security adviser, Harvard's Henry Kissinger, asked experts at the Rand Corporation, including Daniel Ellsberg, to write a set of Vietnam policy alternatives. He received back options from "military escalation aimed at negotiated victory" to "unilateral withdrawal of all U.S. forces," a policy path dismissed out of hand. "We could not simply walk away from an enterprise involving two administrations, five allied countries, and 31,000 dead as if we were switching a television channel," Kissinger insisted. Like Kennedy and Johnson, Nixon was now caught in a death grip by a war not one of the three politicians would have started had they known its cost. Rejecting both escalation and withdrawal, the new president would decide on a policy of "Vietnamization"—the same approach young Jack Kennedy had advised after his one-day visit to Hanoi eighteen years earlier. Following his dead rival's prescription, Nixon would raise "native armies" to fight the Communists.

The new president would offer more flamboyant tributes to the JFK legacy. Seeking the vanished glamour of Camelot, he had White House guards don uniforms more appropriate to a high school production of *The Student Prince*. The peaked hats, long, gold-braided white coats, and striped pants constituted one of several cloddish attempts to match the pageantry of the earlier presidency. Yet even as the Orthogonian earnestly sought to capture some of the Franklin's effortless appeal, he began also to strip the presidential mansion of all tangible relics of the Kennedy era itself. In her last day in the White House, Jack Kennedy's widow had ordered a small plaque placed in her bedroom. "In this room John Fitzgerald Kennedy lived with his wife Jacqueline . . ." Nixon had it removed. As a family gift to the White House the Kennedys had donated a Monet landscape to be hung in Jacqueline's beloved Green Room. That went, too. A garden named in her honor became the First Lady's Garden.

But the most dramatic alteration was Nixon's decision to do away with Jack Kennedy's favorite White House locale: the indoor swimming pool. Banished from sight was not just the pool itself but the grand, wall-long mural of sailboats anchored in a Virgin Islands harbor, a gift from Joseph Kennedy to grace his son's water hideaway. The metamorphosis carried irony. The space where Jack had enjoyed his presidency at eighty degrees water temperature, sometimes with even warmer company, had been transformed into a briefing room and work space for the White House press corps Richard Nixon would come to loathe.

Yet even as Nixon desecrated Kennedy's relics, he codified the Kennedy instinct for public relations. Two weeks after taking office, he ordered that a smartly produced copy of his inaugural speech be sent to every American embassy. "Kennedy had his sent by USIA in a classy slick production job with appropriate pictures," he wrote John Ehrlichman. The Nixon people should obviously do the same. Honoring the same principle, communications director Herb Klein learned how to get his boss to give shorter answers at televised press conferences: by telling him it was a practice "Kennedy" had mastered. And when Nixon saw a note of praise from the Israeli ambassador, he sent yet another memo to Ehrlichman: "You might pass this to some of the press. Why can't we get some of this kind of reaction out publicly? The Kennedys always did so." To keep score, Nixon instructed communications director Herb Klein to count the number of times Edward Kennedy was mentioned on the network television news.

Another homage to Kennedy could be seen in the way Nixon chose to organize his new administration. Like JFK, he centralized power in his White House staff, but with a fatal difference. Whereas Kennedy had adopted a "spokes of the wheel" approach, with himself as the axle, Nixon provided only a single narrow point of access. He allowed one man, Bob Haldeman, to bar his door to many. Old advisers like Herb Klein, who had once had easy access to Nixon, lost it. Cabinet members, presumably recruited for their political acumen, rarely got in to share it. But more than organizational skill was involved. The key to Haldeman's power, his deputy Jeb Magruder surmised, was that he "hated Nixon's political enemies as much as Nixon hated them."

A small overseas skirmish that occurred that first spring at the residence of the American ambassador to France, Sargent Shriver, served as a reminder that the Kennedys still topped the list. It happened when John Ehrlichman turned up at the U.S. ambassador's residence in Paris to advance his boss's first European tour, which was to include, as it had in JFK's time, a reception for President Charles de Gaulle. Seeing that the entire American residence was festooned with Kennedy family memorabilia—pictures of Jack and Jackie and Bobby and Ethel were everywhere— Ehrlichman flatly told the Shrivers that the mini-museum would have to be shut down before Nixon or de Gaulle stepped foot in the place. There were other ghosts abroad. When Nixon went over his draft arrival statement for London, he scratched out a paragraph referring to his earlier visit, while he was vice president, where he accompanied Queen Elizabeth to the American Chapel in St. Paul's Cathedral and "The Battle Hymn of the Republic" was played. "That's a Kennedy song," he said, aware that the echoes of Robert Kennedy's funeral train still rumbled through the American night. But he felt compelled to begin his toast at an Elysée Palace dinner given by de Gaulle with a wordy tribute to John F. Kennedy. "I realize that it was just a few years ago that you entertained another American president, a young man against whom I ran for office and one who came here and sat in the chair I now occupy. We were members of different parties. We disagreed on some issues. But we completely agreed on what was important.

We completely agreed, for example, in the importance of the French-American friendship. And we completely agreed in our dedication to the ideals, the ideals which our country stands for, the ideals that we share with you—ideals of freedom, of equality, of peace and justice for all nations." As Nixon continued his litany of Kennedy-Nixon agreements, Ehrlichman noticed an "emotional" Eunice Shriver, the late president's sister, pressing her fork hard into her plate.

ONE member of the family showed more overt contempt toward the new White House occupant. In March, Ted Kennedy and wife, Joan, attended the First Lady's yearly reception for members of Congress. Pat Nixon, like the other women attending, wore a floor-length gown. The president was in black tie. As Joan Kennedy passed through the receiving line, she caught every eye and camera. She had chosen a low-cut cocktail dress, shimmering with silver sequins and stopping a full half foot above her knees. "Wow!" a Nixon cabinet member exhaled.

In April, Ted Kennedy flashed a more lethal contempt for the new Nixon order. "This is the time to begin to get out of Southeast Asia, lock, stock, and barrel," he demanded. Next, Kennedy jumped on reports that the White House was wiretapping journalists it suspected of getting "leaks" about secret U.S. bombing in Cambodia. Kennedy's Judiciary Subcommittee demanded that the Justice Department come clean. Attorney General John Mitchell's people stonewalled the Kennedy request.

But events of the summer would bring the Kennedy family's high hopes for a "restoration" crashing to earth, even as the first men traveled to the moon and back. The first lunar landing of American astronauts in July 1969 was an accomplishment so mythical as to mark by itself John F. Kennedy's place in history. President Nixon invited Lyndon Johnson to join him at Cape Kennedy for the astronauts' liftoff. But his highest tribute was to the president who had spoken so grandly of Americans having "thrown our hat over the wall" of space. "His people gave him some great *word pictures*," the president told one of his speechwriters as he prepped for the occasion.

But no homage to JFK could protect Nixon from the charge of usurpation. The *Washington Post* objected with special sarcasm to his name on a marker to be planted by the astronauts on the moon's surface. How dare the space program be treated as some run-of-the-mill public works project! How dare Richard Nixon presume to take credit for a program "defined by President Kennedy. He was not, insofar as we understand the procedures last November, elected President of all mankind." The *New York Times* piled on. When NASA carried through on its idea of having the president speak to the astronauts by phone, it editorialized that the Republican president was "Nixoning the Moon."

THAT weekend in July changed everything. On Martha's Vineyard, in a car accident involving Ted Kennedy, a young woman, Mary Jo Kopechne, was killed. The news from the island off Cape Cod stirred instant reaction within the Nixon White House. "Wants to be sure he doesn't get away with it," Bob Haldeman jotted in his diary after briefing Nixon and his family on the crash at Chappaquiddick. "Real concern is realization of what they'd be doing if it were one of *our* people. Obviously he was drunk, escaped from car, let her drown. Shows fatal flaw in his character."

The next day, Nixon was in the midst of preparations for his historic telephone hookup with the *Apollo 11* astronauts. Speechwriter Bill Safire was present in case something went wrong and the president had to offer instead a grim farewell from earth. But despite the great occasion at hand, Nixon's real concerns were up in Massachusetts. "This is quite a day on another front, too!" he told Safire. "It'll be hard to hush this one up; too many reporters want to win a Pulitzer Prize." His aide disagreed. The episode at Chappaquiddick could very well be pushed to the back pages, given the historic events miles away. "No," Nixon said. "The fact that it happened this day would make it even more significant, especially the way they would be trying to make this a *Kennedy* day."

After the long *Air Force One* flight to Guam, site of the astronauts' splashdown, and meeting with the three men aboard the USS *Hornet*, Nixon remained obsessed with the Kennedys' plight. "I would get six or eight phone calls a day about Chappaquiddick," recalls John Ehrlichman, who had remained back at the White House. "Nixon saw it as a chance to drive a stake through their hearts."

To meet his boss's needs, Haldeman had an aide back at the White House sit at a telephone alongside the television, thereby allowing him to scribble notes of Kennedy's dramatic account for his questionable conduct before and after the accident. Listening intently, the president noted the "gaps and contradictions" in an appeal many would compare to the Checkers speech of a generation earlier. Nixon noted a crucial difference. "I could not help thinking if anyone other than a Kennedy had been involved and had given such a patently unacceptable explanation, the media and the public would not have permitted him to survive in public life." That list of "anyone else" began with the name Richard Milhous Nixon. Nixon's worst fear was that Ted Kennedy was going to get away with it, just as his brother had for so long escaped public knowledge of his relentless "girling." Like most Americans, including legions of those supporters of the Kennedy family in the past, he supposed that the real story of what happened that night on Chappaquiddick Island had been sanitized. Believing the Kennedy people would do everything they could to keep the truth permanently buried, Nixon ordered John Ehrlichman to get someone digging into the case.

Operating on presidential orders, Ehrlichman sent White House aide Jack Caulfield to Chappaquiddick. For two weeks, the former New York detective dug through the available evidence, asked damaging questions at press conferences, anything to keep the dirt flying. The Nixon team also worked Washington for clues, placing a wiretap in the Georgetown house where Mary Jo Kopechne had roomed with three other women. Nixon himself took a hand in the quest. Two weeks after the tragedy, the president equipped Ehrlichman with a fresh lead. "Talk to Henry Kissinger on a very confidential basis with regard to a talk he had with J. K. Galbraith as to what really happened in the EMK matter. It is a fascinating story. I'm sure HAK will tell you the story, and then you, of course, will know how to check it out to get it properly exploited."

Yet even as he worked to seal his feared rival's doom, Nixon made a show of trying to prove himself above that sort of behavior. When Kennedy arrived at the White House for the regular congressional leadership meeting, Nixon set aside ten minutes for a private bucking up.

Initially, neither press nor public needed any artificial stimulation regarding Chappaquiddick. A Bill Mauldin cartoon in the *Chicago Sun-Times* showed Ted Kennedy seeing Nixon and his dog Checkers looking back at him from a mirror. A Harris poll taken in October showed 55 percent of Americans agreeing that Kennedy "panicked in a crisis and should not be given high public trust, such as being president." Still, a third of those responding disagreed.

Nixon, dissatisfied with Kennedy's incomplete demise, was determined there would be no letup in the campaign. Convinced that Kennedy's loud criticism of his Vietnam policy was an attempt to deflect attention from Chappaquiddick, Nixon relished pointing out how the North Vietnamese were now quoting Kennedy's words "with devastating effect." He slyly suggested that Pat Buchanan send material to the nation's newspaper editors documenting Hanoi's boastful use of the Massachusetts senator's remarks, suggesting that the mailing be postmarked Boston. He also ordered his staff to procure hard intelligence on what Kennedy and other antiwar senators, such as South Dakota's George McGovern, were planning to say next. In September, Nixon put more pressure on Haldeman to produce results, adding to his team a White House newcomer who was an old hand at fighting the Kennedys. Charles Colson, the former top aide to Massachusetts Republican senator Leverett Saltonstall, was put in charge of what Nixon called the "Teddy Kennedy fight."

That same autumn, longtime Kennedy pollster Lou Harris received a surprising call from the White House. "Are you out to get me?" came the voice over the telephone.

"No, Mr. President," Harris responded. "You're the only president of the United States."

"You're sure you're not out to get me?" prodded Nixon, intently aware that the man he had on the line had worked not just for the Kennedys but also for Pat Brown in the 1962 gubernatorial campaign and whose last published poll during the 1968 campaign had called it for Humphrey by three points. Temporarily mollified, Nixon invited Harris in for a meeting.

When the pollster entered the Oval Office, he found Nixon with his chief of staff. "This is Bob Haldeman," the president told his visitor. "As you see, he doesn't have horns."

"Well, Mr. President," Harris shot back, "he doesn't have a halo over his head, either."

Nixon then showed his guest to one of two wing-backed chairs that were sitting side by side. "You sit there," the president said, indicating the seat to the right. "The last person who sat there, I want you to know, was an African tribal chief. He's dead now." This bizarre detail was a standard Nixon icebreaker. What struck Harris was the peculiar side-by-side arrangement of his and Nixon's chairs. They were the only two people left in the Oval Office and yet were positioned so as not to see each other. Here he was talking to the president of the United States *sideways!* Harris tried to remedy the odd arrangement by edging his chair, almost unconsciously, until it faced his host at a rough forty-five-degree angle. "See here," Nixon said, interrupting the conversation. "This is my office. Let's put these chairs back where they were."

If the seating arrangement was unexpected, Nixon's query of the long-term Kennedy pollster was even stranger still. "Do you think I can be a personality kid? My staff thinks I can."

"What do you mean?" Harris played for time.

"My staff thinks I can," Nixon plunged on. "*I* think I've got a lousy personality, and I'm not a personality kid."

Harris, eager to please, had brought with him every poll he'd ever taken on Nixon. Citing them, he said, "Mr. President, people don't *like* your personality." Nixon smiled. Harris sensed his host seemed relieved, even justified, to hear the hard verdict.

"That's good! That's absolutely right. I *knew* my staff was wrong!" He promptly invited Harris to stay and accompany him to the next event on his daily schedule, an address to a group of businessmen. This, he would soon prove to his guest, was a task at which he excelled.

Seeking to compensate Harris on the spot for his professional counsel, Nixon began digging through his drawer, finding souvenirs of all varieties, each bearing the presidential seal. "Here, this is for your wife or girlfriend," he said, handing his guest a woman's pin, "or whatever you've got." The awkward attempt at the locker-room machismo was another standard Nixonism. After rummaging through the cuff links, paperweights, and tie clasps, Nixon got down on his hands and knees to open his credenza, from which he pulled golf balls, *Richard Nixon* golf balls. "Here! You play golf?" asked Nixon. "I play tennis, Mr. President," responded Harris. At this, Nixon pushed a button, and a white-coated attendant appeared. "Get a bag for Mr. Harris," the president directed. When the sack arrived, Nixon loaded it with everything he had collected in his desperate quest. "Here," he implored Kennedy's pollster. "This is all I've got."

RICHARD Nixon's notion of becoming a "personality kid" would not die. "He was pushing it both ways," Haldeman recalled of his team's efforts to warm up his boss's public image. "One day they would say, 'You've got to be a lovable guy!' so he would try and figure out what that is. Then it would backfire, so he would say, 'See! It doesn't work!' " Haldeman deputy Jeb Magruder lived through it. "To some extent, as both Haldeman and the president realized, the problem was simply Nixon himself. He was not a lovable man, and no public relations program was going to make him so."

Nixon, however, still had an ace in the hole. Though popularity would have been a nice bonus, his strength lay with the brand of politics he had first employed that long-ago freshman year at Whittier. His first November in the White House, he went on television to defend not just his Vietnam policy but his kind of guy. Quoting John Kennedy's argument that an American withdrawal "would mean a collapse not only of South Vietnam but Southeast Asia," he issued a defiant call to arms. "I know it may not be fashionable to speak of patriotism or national destiny these days," he said to a country held in the grip of weekly casualty reports and recent witness to a mammoth antiwar rally. Twenty years after his infamous appeal to "cloth coat" Republicans, twenty-four years after being drafted by the Committee of 100 to fight the elite liberal Jerry Voorhis, Nixon was once again championing the Orthogonians he now rechristened "the great Silent Majority."

But still he craved something more: ammunition that would seal his 1968 victory and protect him, once and for all, from a restoration. What he needed, what he pestered his aides to get for him, was the goods on John F. Kennedy himself, on how he had botched and betrayed the Cuban exiles at the Bay of Pigs. For Nixon, this was the holy grail of *opposition research*. "He's continually cranking on about the Bay of Pigs, how the Kennedys got away with it," aide John Ehrlichman recalled. Defending the White House pursuit of Ted Kennedy's behavior at Chappaquiddick, H. R. Haldeman compared it to the far larger prize. "This was at least a chance to get something while it was still hot with some guys that ought to be able to find it out. We never did find out the stuff, the background on the Bay of Pigs."

CHAPTER
TWENTY-TWO

Escalation

A full year into his presidency, Richard Nixon continued to strive for legitimacy and for public affection. His backstage standard remained the man who had beaten him to the White House. Wondering aloud about White House relations with the media, he complained to Bob Haldeman that his people were emphasizing "what" the administration had done without spotlighting the leadership qualities of the president himself. Haldeman dutifully jotted down his boss's example of a predecessor who had succeeded by doing the opposite. "JFK did nothing but appeared great."

Nixon sensed now the revival of a live Kennedy menace. Lawrence O'Brien, the field director who had planted Jack Kennedy's political flag across the country in 1959 and 1960, was elected chairman of the Democratic National Committee. It was a sign to Nixon that Ted Kennedy would be calling the shots behind the scenes. He ordered Murray Chotiner, his street fighter from the Voorhis and Douglas campaigns, to neutralize O'Brien. A month later, Chotiner reported to Haldeman that he was checking into Larry O'Brien's affairs *systematically*. Nixon next ordered

Haldeman to put John Caulfield and fellow gumshoe Tony Ula-
sewicz to work digging up dirt on several liberal senators who
were challenging his Supreme Court nominations. The list started
with the well-known liberal from Massachusetts.

Nixon's fear of Kennedy, even in the months after Chappaquiddick, was well founded. Wielding his clout on the Senate Judiciary
Committee, Jack's younger brother kept up a rearguard action
against the Republican president's Supreme Court nominations.
Clement Haynesworth of Virginia was the first to fall. Determined
to name another southerner, Nixon and Attorney General John
Mitchell chose Harold Carswell. "Nixon-Mitchell have again
nominated a mediocre candidate with no indications of particular
intelligence, leadership, insight, or respect among his brethren,"
Kennedy's chief counsel James Flug briefed his boss. "In fact, his
official record is quite consistent with the notion that he is a
segregationist and white supremacist. I smell blood." Flug told
Kennedy that Carswell's nomination could be beaten if the civil
rights organizations could be brought into the fray. He listed a
number of senators who would go along with a dump-Carswell
effort, given the right amount of "brotherly pressure."

Kennedy went to work. On the first day of confirmation hearings, he asked Carswell for a list of clients he had represented in
private practice who later appeared before him in court. Accused
by a Republican senator of conducting a "fishing expedition," the
Massachusetts senator plunged even deeper into the fight. Carswell was defeated in the Senate, 51–40. Nixon, making the best
of the defeat, said the opposition would never confirm a southern
conservative to the Court.

IN April, the president announced a bold stroke by U.S. forces
in Vietnam. On national television he revealed that American
forces had invaded neighboring Cambodia, whose territory served
as both supply base and refuge for the attacking Vietcong and
North Vietnamese troops. The aerial pounding delivered by the
air force was matched by Nixon's defiant on-air rhetoric. "I would
rather be a one-term president and do what I believe was right
than to be a two-term president at the cost of seeing America

become a second-rate power," he declared self-righteously. America was no "pitiful, helpless giant," he declared, and neither was Richard Nixon.

The effect of this broadcast was to split an already divided country even further. On campuses, the heart of the American antiwar movement, Nixon's "incursion" into Cambodia had the impact of nitroglycerin. At Kent State University, Ohio National Guardsmen fired into a mass of demonstrators. Four students were killed. The news photo of a young woman kneeling over one of the fallen youths became a rallying cry against Nixon's "escalation" of the war. The war John Kennedy had begun was now Richard Nixon's, and those who served Kennedy the most ardently now unleashed the harshest criticism at their lost hero's 1960 rival. Democratic chief Larry O'Brien was especially vicious. Nixon would later say that the veteran Kennedy man had accused him of "virtually killing the four students" himself.

Yet even as he warred with the Camelot crowd, Nixon sought to capture a bit of its lost aura for himself. During a presidential stay in San Clemente, California, the press corps was alerted to a unique photo opportunity: Escorted by White House aides to a cliff near the Nixon home that commanded a panoramic view of the beach and the Pacific Ocean beyond, they looked down to see the solitary figure of President Richard Nixon walking along the water's edge. Nixon aides had placed him in the same wind-swept setting that had contributed to the Kennedys allure. One small detail had been overlooked. "He's wearing *shoes!*" the cry went up from the pack. In their promotion of the "personality kid," the White House ballyhoo boys had overlooked their client's penchant for black wing-tipped shoes. Even in the Technicolor setting, their boss bore no resemblance to the nautical Jack tacking his sailboat in Nantucket Sound or the barefoot Bobby running his dog along the same strand.

WITH the first half of his term coming to a close, Nixon lost the company of his Kennedy Democrat-in-residence, Daniel Patrick Moynihan, a social-policy expert with the wit to help Nixon negotiate among the shoals of establishment contempt. Moynihan's return to Harvard marked a symbolic end to Nixon's notion to become, in Moynihan's winsome phrase, "a Tory man with liberal policies." Nixon had created the Environmental Protection Agency, signed the Clean Air bill, instituted affirmative action in employment, and ended the dual school system in the South. Years after leaving Nixon's side, Moynihan would recall the shared sense of frustration: "After a while, you say, 'Why bother?'"

Moynihan's leave-taking signaled the ascendancy of Machiavellian politics over progressive policy. Heading back to Cambridge, he advised the cabinet, whom Nixon had assembled for the warm farewell, to "resist the temptation to respond in kind to the untruths and half-truths that begin to fill the air." But Herb Klein soon noted the difference in atmosphere. "The White House changed distinctly and became an organization where hardball replaced political philosophy as the major consideration."

With the 1970 elections for Congress approaching, Nixon shifted his attention to the urgent task of keeping the usual midterm losses to a minimum. Relying on an old standby, the politics of resentment, he strove to pit those "patriotic" Americans who backed his Asia policy against the despised cotillion of elite liberals and spoiled, ill-groomed students who opposed it. The elections would prove a rough repeat of the Whittier College fight for student-body president which pitted Dick Nixon, champion of the nerds, against his cooler Franklin counterpart. Nixon wanted to make that division, to use his favorite phrase, "perfectly clear." When antiwar demonstrators attempted to storm a Republican campaign rally in San Jose, he saw an opportunity for mischief. Delaying his departure so that the angry crowds could, in Bob Haldeman's phrase, "zero in," Nixon stood up, before ducking into his car, and gave the double V sign that he knew would drive the angry crowd to a frenzy. It worked. The belligerent mob obliged by pelting the presidential limousine with stones and other flying debris, creating just the television picture he wanted most.

But the plan backfired. His efforts to drive a wedge between the squares and the swells brought back the image of the early 1950s Red-baiter. A campaign speech broadcast on election eve showed the president less an above-the-battle peacemaker than a roughneck combatant amid troubling civil unrest. Soft-spoken senator Edmund Muskie, giving the television response for the Democrats, put Nixon's vitriol in stark relief. Speaking from the parlor of his rustic Maine home, he gave a partisan address crafted to seem otherwise. Nixon aide Jeb Magruder called the juxtaposition of the nonthreatening Muskie with the snarling president "like watching Grandma Moses debate the Boston Strangler."

M U S K I E ' S even-tempered performance on election eve, given credit for the Democrats' better-than-expected performance in the 1970 election, anointed him as the prime candidate to challenge Nixon in 1972. But the man in the White House was having none of it. Richard Nixon had his mind on another Democrat, Ted Kennedy, whose diatribes against the Nixon policy in Vietnam now contained extraordinary venom. "It is Asian, now, fighting Asian, and they do it for purposes more than their own. Vietnamization means war and more war." It was a searing indictment that the United States was arming Vietnamese to kill Vietnamese in order to advance Richard Nixon's geopolitical ambitions. Nixon himself ordered a stakeout of the senator. "Twenty-four-hour surveillance!" he demanded of Haldeman. "Catch him in the sack with one of his babes."

Charles Colson, deputized the year before to pursue the "Kennedy fight," threatened to punch the Massachusetts senator in the nose for his derision of Nixon's Vietnam policy. He managed to hit Kennedy in a softer spot. He succeeded in having a photograph taken of Teddy Kennedy leaving a Paris nightclub with a beautiful woman not his wife in the wee hours of the morning, before President Charles de Gaulle's funeral. Colson next arranged for the embarrassing photo to be published in the *National Enquirer*. The accompanying report observed that Kennedy's date was Italy's Princess Maria Pia de Savoy and that Kennedy had been jumping up and down froglike on the dance floor until only minutes before the funeral mass at Notre Dame. "The president *loved* that picture," Bob Haldeman recalled. "It stuck a knife into a Kennedy: one hundred points on the Oval Office chart."

Haldeman saw this coup cementing Colson's status in Nixon's

circle. The new recruit had won a battlefield promotion. "From now on, as far as the president was concerned," Haldeman would recall, "Colson was Mr. Can Do."

Colson was proud of his handiwork. "I sent somebody to Paris to get a picture, and Nixon loved it." Having endured Jack Kennedy's undetected escapades, Nixon wanted the younger brother to pay for every dance. Colson's success boosted his position dramatically. "He arrived in the White House with one secretary," Haldeman deputy Jeb Magruder would note. "By the time he left he had dozens of people reporting to him. The rest of us would joke about Colson's ever-expanding empire, 'The Department of Dirty Tricks.' "

Like his boss, Colson treated the threat of a Ted Kennedy candidacy in 1972 with deadly seriousness. "He was always in the political equation. There were times when we worried he would get in the race and resurrect the Kennedy charisma and we would be running against Jack Kennedy again." Colson's Parisian triumph won him a prized place at the table when Nixon summoned his advisers to Key Biscayne for a series of planning sessions after the 1970 elections. Just the mention of the name "Ted Kennedy" at such gatherings, Colson recalls, caused a stir. "You just sensed this was the flash point. Maybe we felt it ourselves. It was like we'd be running against the ghost of Jack Kennedy." To repel the specter, Colson pushed Nixon to woo Catholic voters who had voted for Kennedy in 1960 by appealing to their social conservatism and patriotic resentment toward well-off college kids burning flags and draft cards on the evening news.

In December, Nixon made a bold reach for another key piece of the coalition that elected JFK, killing his own dream, ten years earlier. He named John Connally his secretary of the treasury. Like him, the former Texas governor shared a long history with the Kennedys. As a campaign lieutenant of Lyndon Johnson's in 1960, he had accused JFK of having Addison's disease, a charge whose ferocity came from its being true. After serving Kennedy as secretary of the navy, he served as his host on the fateful presidential tour of Texas in November 1963. When the shots were fired at Dealey Plaza, the blood-soaked Connally believed that he, as well as Kennedy, had just seconds to live.

The intimations of shared mortality did not slow the political rift between Connally and the surviving Kennedys. From the outset, the Texan was a Johnson man sensitive to any slight from the wealthy, well-born clan that appeared to view Connally's mentor as an unpleasant interruption in the Kennedy reign. Starting in 1968, with his public derision of Ted Kennedy's worthiness to be president and, later, with his desultory backing of Hubert Humphrey, John Connally became an insurgent in his own party.

Picking the Texan for such a high-level post sealed, therefore, a natural pact of anti-Kennedy allies. It gave the conservative John Connally a respect and career path now closed to him in the party of his upbringing. It gave the loner Nixon a political kin able to rally resentful Democrats against the dominant liberals for whom Ted Kennedy shined, even after Chappaquiddick, as the brightest star.

Seven years after Dallas, Richard Nixon was surrounded by those whose personal loyalty to him and deep-felt antipathy toward the Kennedys was indivisible. Against the growing bitterness over Vietnam and with the economy growing weak, the men in the White House saw themselves in a deadly conflict for survival with those bent on their destruction. To meet this threat, Richard Nixon had fortified himself with a coterie of henchmen, including Charles Colson, prepared to train the full arsenal of the presidency, including all those dark weapons Kennedy and Johnson had used on him, against those who would seize what he had won at so high a price and after such a painful detour.

At year's end, Colson dug up some new opposition research: Howard Hughes was terminating old Kennedy hand Lawrence O'Brien as his Washington lobbyist. It was the kind of information on which Nixon thrived. He would soon demand more.

CHAPTER TWENTY-THREE

Interlude

ON January 1, 1971, as Nixon indulged in New Year's Day ramblings with chief of staff Bob Haldeman, he came to an old sore point: with the exception of their post–Bay of Pigs meeting, John F. Kennedy had never invited him to the White House. As the executive mansion's current occupant, he was ready to treat his rival's widow the way a former First Lady deserved, especially the wife of a fallen president. The official portraits of President and Mrs. Kennedy were about to be hung. Pat Nixon wrote Mrs. Kennedy asking her thoughts about an official ceremony. At first, Jacqueline was hesitant. "As you know, the thought of returning to the White House is difficult for me," she responded to Pat Nixon's inquiry. "I really do not have the courage to go through an official ceremony and bring the children back to the only home they both knew with their father under such traumatic conditions. With the press and everything, things I try to avoid in their young lives, I know the experience would be hard on them and not leave them with the memories of the White House I would like them to have." Pat Nixon then proposed that Mrs. Kennedy and her children might come to the White House for a private viewing.

Before the historic evening with the Kennedys, the president had other, dirtier business to complete. On January 14, the *Los Angeles Times* reported that a top aide to Hughes, the same Robert Maheu who had recruited mob assassins for the CIA campaign against Fidel Castro, was bringing a lawsuit against the tycoon. Nixon, who had paid politically for the $205,000 loan to his brother Don back in the 1950s and had just gotten a $100,000 campaign gift from Hughes, was now ready to attack. "It would seem that the time is approaching when Larry O'Brien is held accountable for his retainer with Hughes for 'services rendered' in the past," Nixon scribbled in a note to Haldeman as he traveled aboard *Air Force One* for a speech to the University of Nebraska. "Perhaps Colson should make a check on this."

On February 3, Jacqueline Kennedy, Caroline, thirteen, and John, Jr., ten, came to the White House for a secret dinner. President Nixon had sent a small presidential Jetstar to pick up the Kennedys in New York, and an intense effort was made to keep the nocturnal visit out of the media. The UPI's Helen Thomas, the only reporter to discover the identity of the president's mystery guests, succumbed to the promise of further information and agreed to delay her story.

Julie, Tricia, and Pat met the arrivals at the White House's second-floor elevator. From there the two families went down the broad stairs to the ground floor to view the ethereal portrait of Jacqueline Kennedy, then upstairs again to the painting of the late president, which bore a resemblance to a *Newsweek* photo of a stooped-over John F. Kennedy passing a few pensive last moments before his third debate with Richard Nixon.

The formal purpose of the evening behind them, the Nixon daughters led the smaller Kennedy children around the family quarters while Pat took Jacqueline on a separate tour of those public rooms that, a decade earlier, the former First Lady had worked to restore to their historic authenticity. At dinner, the guest of honor, whom Nixon described later as "very bright and talkative," reminded her host of the time she and Jack had met him by accident at a Chicago airport in 1959. "I always live in a dream world," Nixon recalled her saying as all of them negotiated their way through the dangerous terrain of memory. John Kennedy would recall betting his sister that she, not he, would spill something. He lost, his milk falling directly onto the presidential lap. Afterward, the president escorted his rival's children over to the West Wing to show them the Oval Office, where their father had worked and where John junior had once played under his father's desk. "It seemed to me a private moment," Julie recorded later. "Instinctively, we did not go inside but waited on the walkway outside the office."

Personal accounts of the evening are recorded in the letters that passed back and forth in the weeks ahead:

Dear Mr. President
Dear Mrs. Nixon

You were so kind to us yesterday.

Never have I seen such magnanimity and such tenderness.

Can you imagine the gift you gave us? To return to the White House privately with my little ones while they are still young enough to rediscover their childhood—with you both as guides— and with your daughters, such extraordinary young women.

What a tribute to have brought them up like that in the limelight. I pray I can do half the same with my Caroline. It was good to see her exposed to their example, and John to their charm.

You spoiled us beyond belief; the Jetstar, our tour, the superb dinner. Thank you, Mr. President, for opening one of your precious bottles of Bordeaux for us.

I have never seen the White House look so perfect. There is no hidden corner of it that is not beautiful now.

It was moving, when we left, to see that great House illuminated, with the fountains playing.

The way you have hung the portraits does them great honor— more than they deserve. They should not have been such trouble to you. You bent over backwards to be generous, and we are all deeply touched and grateful.

It made me happy to hear the children bursting with reminiscences all the way home.

Before John went to sleep, I could explain the photographs of Jack and him in his room, to him. "There you are with Daddy right where the President was describing the great seal; there, on the path where the President accompanied us to our car."

Your kindness made real memories of his shadowy ones.

Thank you with all my heart. A day I always dreaded turned out to be one of the most precious I have spent with my children.

May God bless all of you,

Most gratefully,

Jackie

Dear Mr. President
Dear Mrs. Nixon

I can never thank you more for showing us the White House.

I really liked everything about it. You were so nice to show us everything.

I don't think I could remember much about the White House but it was really nice seeing it all again.

When I sat on Lincoln's bed and wished for something, my wish really came true. I wished that I would have good luck at school. I loved all the pictures of the Indians and the ones of all the Presidents.

I also really liked the old pistols.

I really really loved the dogs. They were so funny. As soon as I came home my dogs kept on sniffing me. Maybe they remember the White House.

The food was the best I have ever had. The shrimp was by far the best I have ever tasted.

And the steak with the sauce was really good.

And I have never tasted anything as good as the souffle . . . was the best I ever tasted.

I really liked seeing the President's office and the cabinet room a lot. Thank you so much again.

Sincerely,

John Kennedy

Dear Mrs. Nixon,

Thank you so much for the incredible tour. You were so nice to do it and I just love everything about the house. All the rooms are so lovely and it was so sweet of you to take us around so specially.

I just love your dogs. King Timaho is beautiful and the others are so cute. The dinner was delicious. Your Swiss chef is the best thing that ever came out of Switzerland except maybe the chocolate. Your daughters were so nice to me, I had such a good time and it was so nice to see it all again. The President was so nice (*repeat—repeat*) to take so much time out of his schedule. Please thank him. The portraits were hung so nicely. You made them look so good. Everything was just perfect and everyone was so nice. Please thank them all for me, Allen, John, the one who met us at the door, and everyone else. But thank you and your family most of all. I will really never forget it.

Love Caroline

P.S. The plane is fantastic and the candy is wonderful. Sgt. Simmons is great and so is the pilot. All I seem to be saying is so nice, fantastic, thank you, but it is all I can say.

There came a handwritten note as well from President Kennedy's mother, Rose:

Dear Mrs. Nixon,

Jackie has just telephoned to me to tell me how happy she and the children were after their trip to Washington.

She related all the various details of her visit, and she was quite overwhelmed by your solicitude and your graciousness. I told her I wanted to write to you and thank you, too.

Your warm-hearted welcome to her and my grandchildren on a day which might have been most difficult for all of them, moved me deeply.

Your daughters completely captivated the children, and Jackie was glad the youngsters had an opportunity to see again the places in the White House which were familiar to them.

To have the President's visit at dinner was an unexpected pleasure and honor which they will always remember.

And so, dear Mrs. Nixon, you brought joy to many who are near and dear to me, and I want to thank you from my heart.

Very Sincerely,
Rose Kennedy

Several weeks later, Nixon wrote the two children back:

Dear Caroline—

I want you to know how much we appreciated your letter after our visit at The White House—We did not share the contents with anyone but our Swiss Chef was deeply touched when I told him that you had written so generously about his culinary creations.

I recall that you told us your favorite subject was history but that a poor teacher this year had somewhat dampened your interest. I know a teacher can make a great difference but I hope your enthusiasm for history continues.

History is the best foundation for almost any profession—but even more important you will find the really most fascinating reading as you grow older is in history and biography.

As far as the teacher is concerned I recall that some of the teachers I thought at the time were the worst (because they graded so hard) were actually the best in retrospect. I would guess you are an exceptionally good student and I hope the teacher doesn't discourage you!

Mrs. Nixon, Tricia and Julie join me in sending our best. You will always be welcome in this House.

Richard Nixon

Dear John—

We all greatly enjoyed your letter and we were particularly happy that your visit to the House where you lived as a very young boy left pleasant memories.

I will let you in on a little secret with regard to our dogs. *Usually* Mrs. Nixon—for obvious reasons—will not allow them to come to the second floor. So you can see that your visit was a special treat for them (and for me!—I don't worry so much about what happens to the furniture).

I was glad your wish which you made on the Lincoln bed came true—when you need another one like that—come back to see us. You will always be welcome in This House.

Sincerely
Richard Nixon

Targeting Teddy

VEN as he entertained his old rival's family at dinner, Richard Nixon was immersed in the battle that drove and nourished his soul. On a sunny afternoon in Key Biscayne he remained closeted inside discussing and rediscussing with Haldeman a new Harris poll that showed his personal approval rating steadily on the decline. Two days later, back in Washington, Nixon spent the whole day in his Executive Office hideaway fixating on a poll of American youth that showed him fourth among the "most admired men," behind John F. Kennedy, Martin Luther King, and Bobby Kennedy. The only consolation was that Edward Kennedy, the surviving brother, was not on the list.

Nixon now took the fateful step he hoped would secure his advantage in the long twilight struggle for "greatness." He ordered his chief of staff to install a White House taping system that would assure him, not his enemies, control of his presidential record. Worried that liberal, pro-Kennedy historians and scholars would skew the accounts of his accomplishments in order to deny him proper credit, he decided that the remedy lay in being prepared. With recordings of every syllable uttered either in the Oval

Office or in his Old Executive Office Building hideaway, Nixon would have the literal last word on the events of his administration.

The impetus, according to his chief of staff, was Lyndon Johnson. The former president made the compelling argument to Nixon that any chief executive needs a record of his meetings to defend his place in history. According to Haldeman, Nixon needed little prodding. "He was worried that in private, head-to-head meetings, he didn't want the burden on himself of having to be the only recorder of that meeting because there's a lot of work and he had to be thinking. He didn't want the other guy to have the sole record of the meeting, because the other guy could have been the guy on the other side."

Nixon had first tried other record-keeping techniques. At one point he had a staffer sit in the room and act as a "fly on the wall." He experimented with having aides debrief both him and his guest immediately following a presidential meeting or just a quick debriefing of the visitor on his way out. He rejected both methods. "Nixon didn't like someone sitting in, especially if they were taking notes, because that always bothers people because, you know, they keep looking over at the guy taking notes." One solution was to have Gen. Vernon Walters, a former Nixon military aide known for his uncannily sharp memory, sit in on meetings. The crusty Walters made clear to Nixon's chief of staff that generals commanded troops; they didn't sit in the corner memorizing Oval Office conversations.

Thus, a permanent eavesdropper came to the White House. Despite the eagerness with which Nixon embraced his new taping system, it was just the sort of technology he found unfriendly. Originally, the recording system was controlled by two buttons: one, marked "Butterfield," which turned the system on; the other, marked "Haldeman," which served as the off button. Uncomfortable fumbling with the buttons with people sitting right there watching him, Nixon switched later to a voice-activated system. When someone talked in the Oval Office or Nixon's Executive Office Building hideaway, the machine recorded it.

Having okayed the installation, Nixon never bothered to make use of it either to check or confirm with Haldeman an actual conversation—not until too late, when his words had become a matter of political life and death. "Do you want me to start getting someone to transcribe these things, because the tapes are piling up, and logistically it's going to be a real mess," Haldeman recalled asking. "Absolutely not" came Nixon's snap answer. "No one is going to hear these tapes but you and me."

But while the taping system was now in place to record Nixon's presidential glory, the actual seizing of such glory remained a vexing challenge. Haldeman observed the struggle from close range. "Nixon took pains with his public image," Haldeman recalled. "He dressed neatly and conservatively, handled himself calmly in public, made all of his ceremonial appearances in good style and humor—and yet, no matter what he did, he seemed to come across as flat, unattractive, unappealing. Jack Kennedy had only to stand up to project a charismatic image of 'class.' And, of course, to a lesser extent, this was also true of Kennedy's brothers."

Chuck Colson had emerged by early 1971 as Nixon's chief political confidant. "The Kennedy-Nixon comparison. It was always there. It was always the source of resentment: the eastern-Harvard-liberal establishment everybody would look up to. Nixon knew he was a whole lot brighter but never got respect from the people who always thought they would restore the Kennedy charisma."

His inability to create an aura around his presidency to captivate the hearts of Americans, as the memory of Camelot had done, continued to frustrate Nixon as he began the backstretch of his four-year term. It was more than a threat to his peace of mind. Ted Kennedy was reemerging as the chief obstacle between him and the validation of every American presidency—a second term. The surprise loss by Kennedy of his Senate leadership position to West Virginia's Robert Byrd did nothing to lessen Nixon's sense of foreboding and Kennedy's new confidence. In March, Teddy mocked the president's absence from the annual Gridiron Dinner, an evening of food, drink, and white-tie satire hosted by Washington's senior journalists, claiming the president had been unable to attend because he was down in Key Biscayne "at the local Bijou watching *Patton* for the forty-third time!" Critics had blamed George C. Scott's commanding screen portrait for Nixon's defiant move into Cambodia the year before.

Such jabs were being duly recorded by those around Nixon. Correspondent Dan Rather was meeting with Haldeman and Ehrlichman when a secretary rushed in with a wire story about Senator Kennedy. Haldeman, he learned, had issued standing orders that any Ted Kennedy item on the news wires be brought directly to him. The CBS reporter was unique in spotting the Kennedy obsession behind the White House plotting during these months.

In May, Kennedy pulled ahead of Democratic front-runner Sen. Edmund Muskie in the Gallup poll. Once more, the specter of a restoration loomed over the Nixon White House. Richard Nixon was increasingly seen by many as the illegitimate holder of the office that belonged, rightfully, to the dynasty that was waiting to reclaim it. Richard Nixon, viewed by many acolytes of "Camelot" as an illegitimate usurper, told Haldeman that the beloved Jack Kennedy was "colder, more ruthless" than him but came through as a "warm, human guy." To give voters a less worshipful look at Kennedy's younger brother, Nixon later told his chief of staff to put "permanent tails" on Teddy and other potential 1972 challengers.

That same month, Nixon ended his spring slump by defeating a move by Senate Democratic leader Mike Mansfield to cut the number of U.S. troops in Europe. He did so with the personal backing of Truman-era secretary of state Dean Acheson, a man he had once implied had been "taken in by the Communists."

But the stalemate in Southeast Asia was daily becoming a heavier burden. Ted Kennedy, brother and political heir of the man who first sent U.S. troops into South Vietnam, condemned Nixon not just for the war but for his handling of antiwar protests. "We were in their faces a lot," recalled James Flug, chief counsel of Kennedy's Judiciary Subcommittee. "We were directly on the case all the time and they knew it." When Attorney General John Mitchell ordered mass "field arrests" during a May demonstration at the Capitol, Senator Kennedy was quick to ridicule the action, directing his Judiciary Subcommittee staff to dig into the Nixon administration's tactics. "We must destroy the cancer that has been transforming the noble spirit of our nation in the eyes of our own citizens," he warned. Haldeman noted in his diary that Nixon raised the "Ted Kennedy question" again. Nixon said the White House needed to do some long-range planning regarding Kennedy, since "it may very well go his way" the next year. "There will be great pressures to forget Chappaquiddick, which is, of course, his most vulnerable point; that we can't let be forgotten."

In June, Nixon aide Dwight Chapin recruited a former ally in University of Southern California student politics, Donald Segretti, just ending his service as an army lawyer, to run the 1972 "dirty tricks" campaign. Segretti was told he would be a "Republican Dick Tuck," sowing seeds of discord and confusion in the enemy ranks, much as the mischievous pro-Kennedy partisan had done to Nixon over the years. Segretti was to create such fierce intramural hostility among the Democrats that they would be unable to coalesce as they had done to such frightening effect behind the campaign of Hubert Humphrey in the last weeks of the 1968 election. Segretti seized the work with gusto: "Love this Job," he jotted in the margin of one dispatch. He was, after all, doing work the president of the United States himself wanted done.

Before the month was out, there came another escalation in the domestic war. The day after Tricia Nixon wed Edward Cox in the Rose Garden, the *New York Times* carried a picture of the wedding on the left side of page 1; on the right side, where editors traditionally place the chief story of the day, was the first installment of the Pentagon Papers. The "Papers," leaked by former Kissinger associate Daniel Ellsberg, chronicled the history of U.S. involvement in Vietnam and offered to the Nixon camp hard documentary evidence that the Southeast Asian nightmare was the work of past presidents—Democratic presidents. "We should encourage, not discourage, the Hill from carrying on intensive hearings and well-publicized hearings over the Kennedy-Johnson papers and over how we got into Vietnam," a gleeful Chuck Colson urged Haldeman. But the conspiratorial aide could not resist converting a lucky break into an anti-Kennedy weapon. "We could, of course, plant and try to prove the thesis that Bobby Kennedy was behind the preparation of the papers," Colson enticed the Nixon team, "because he planned to use them to overthrow Lyndon Johnson."

Release of the Pentagon Papers whetted Nixon's appetite for

more anti-Kennedy disclosures. He ordered Henry Kissinger to get hold of "the Lodge Files" on the murder of South Vietnamese president Diem. But Kissinger was still focused on the impact the embarrassing release of top-secret documents could mean to his back-channel dealings with China. Rather than disseminate the Pentagon Papers message, that it was Democrats who plunged the country into the Vietnam quagmire, Kissinger pushed Nixon to destroy the messenger. Daniel Ellsberg was to be crushed. "If we can change the issue from one of release of the documents to one of the theft of the documents, we will have something going for us," Colson volunteered. Thus resulted the plan to sack the office of Daniel Ellsberg's psychiatrist in search of something to prove that the era's most celebrated whistle-blower was "sick."

Ellsberg was not the only target. "I don't give a damn how it is done," Nixon told Colson. "Do whatever has to be done to stop these leaks. I want results. I want it done, whatever the cost." The cost would be a White House operation dedicated to plugging security leaks. It would take its name from the word someone had humorously posted on the band's basement door in the Old Executive Office Building across from the White House.

The "Plumbers" were driven as much by political anger as the need to protect national secrets. Plied by Kissinger with tales of Ted Kennedy's aggressive love life, Nixon ordered Haldeman to get the senator in a "compromising situation." Colson now enlisted another fellow who didn't mind a little creative trouble: E. Howard Hunt. "The more I think about Howard Hunt's background, politics, disposition and experience, the more I think it would be worth your time to meet him," Colson wrote Ehrlichman. "I had forgotten when I talked to you that he was the CIA mastermind on the Bay of Pigs. He told me a long time ago that if the truth were ever known, Kennedy would be destroyed."

Like Colson, Hunt was a graduate of Brown University. Both men were active in the Washington alumni chapter. Colson was president of the local group; Hunt, vice president. Yet they shared something else besides an alma mater: a common enemy. Hunt was the embittered CIA agent "Eduardo" who had watched John Kennedy deny the Cuban exiles their promised "umbrella" of air cover over the Bay of Pigs. He was angry not just at the military defeat but at what he called the "lying and deception," the promise to provide cover to the landing brigade, followed by its denial in the midst of battle. "How ironic it seemed that Kennedy's successful campaign against Nixon had been largely waged—and won—on a promise to aid the Cuban exiles in their struggle against Communism," he had written. Hunt believed that Richard Nixon, who, as vice president, was the invasion's most aggressive booster, would not have failed in its execution. A less hesitant cold warrior, he would have stopped at nothing to ensure the success of the 1961 invasion.

Nixon hoped that his new recruit would help get out the true story of April 1961. Within a week of Hunt's hiring, he suggested that his aides get the former CIA agent's memoirs, nailing Kennedy for the Bay of Pigs, published in a prominent magazine. Getting Hunt's story out to the American public became, Colson would later testify, a "pet Nixon project."

But Hunt's first assignment was to knock the surviving Kennedy brother out of the 1972 race for president once and for all. To prepare for the task, the ex-agent checked out such books as *The Bridge at Chappaquiddick* from the Library of Congress, then headed to Hyannis to quiz hotel owners and others about the goings-on of the area's most famous summer residents.

It was amid this backroom plotting that Nixon announced to a stunned world his plan to hold a summit conference in Beijing with leaders of the People's Republic of China. The partisan warrior who had spent years shouting, "Who lost China?" and had scolded Jack Kennedy in the 1960 debates for refusing to fight for Quemoy and Matsu was himself opening the door to "Red China." It was a brilliant act of strategic surprise, leaving his enemies little recourse but to praise him. Ted Kennedy was particularly gracious. "Rarely, I think, has the action of any president so captured the imagination and support of the American people as President Nixon's magnificent gesture."

Yet while they made history and garnered new respect, the Nixon people fretted as the weekly newsmagazines continued to ask "Will He or Won't He?" teasing the Republicans with the possibility of a Kennedy candidacy. "Kennedy Non-Campaign," the *New York Times* wondered. "Some Read a No as a Yes." For the opposition, finding Kennedy "in the sack" became a White House cottage industry, especially after it was known that he was running two to one ahead of Muskie in California. His brother might have gotten away with it, but the younger man was to be given no such delicate treatment. To find evidence of girling, Nixon aide Jack Caulfield followed the Massachusetts senator to Hawaii, only to return home having found nothing "improper" to exploit. Caulfield would next rent a Manhattan apartment, furnishing it in a style one visitor called "Chicago whorehouse." The scheme was to have handsome young men lure some of Robert Kennedy's aides who had been at Chappaquiddick the night of the tragedy into the intended love nest in hopes of getting information on Ted Kennedy's behavior.

The pressure for dirt was relentless. "Does Caulfield have anything new on Kennedy?" Haldeman kept pressuring White House counsel John Dean. At the same time, facsimiles of Sen. Edmund Muskie's stationery were used to mail to members of Congress a Harris poll showing Chappaquiddick's drag on Sen. Edward Kennedy's presidential chances, thereby getting Kennedy angry at Muskie and Muskie angry at anyone who would think him guilty of such an obvious ploy. Donald Segretti suggested another Dick Tuck–like gimmick: creating a bogus "Massachusetts Safe Driving Committee" that could present its highest award to Kennedy.

Nixon's resentment toward the Kennedy family was never far from the surface. When the new John F. Kennedy Center for the Performing Arts prepared for a two-night opening extravaganza that September, Nixon derided the acclaim for the white marble building overlooking the Potomac River as "this orgasm over this utter architectural monstrosity." As the grand debut neared, he received an added reason not to go. Word reached him that composer Leonard Bernstein was preparing an antiwar theme for the Kennedy Center's opening. But a Haldeman-inspired plan to skip opening night and attend the second night, "letting the Kennedys take the glory," became inoperative when Rose Kennedy wrote how "disappointing" it would be for Nixon to skip the center's opening night. But when he read in his daily news summary that congressional Democrats were planning to request $1 million to spend on additional Kennedy Center furnishings, he scribbled his feelings in the margin. "No! Never!"

NIXON'S animus toward anything "Kennedy" was consistent with the changing political situation. In the fall of 1969, Ted Kennedy lay in the wreckage of Chappaquiddick. Two years later, he had come back from political death with as much gusto as Nixon himself had shown in the mid-1960s. The Gallup poll now showed the Massachusetts senator as Nixon's closest competitor in a head-to-head race. The antidote driving Ted Kennedy's electoral recovery between 1969 and 1971 and Nixon's in the years 1965–67 was precisely the same: Vietnam. Wanting to remove a president they identified with an unpopular conflict, people were perched to forgive the character flaws of a credible rival. What they could not forgive was the war.

To deflate Ted Kennedy's expanding popularity, Nixon decided that the moment was long overdue to tag his elder brother for the death of South Vietnamese president Ngo Dinh Diem, an episode Nixon would identify as the fateful step on the slippery slope to deeper U.S. involvement. When a reporter asked at a September press conference why the Nixon administration wasn't pushing hard for elections in Vietnam, Nixon turned historian: "I would remind all concerned that the way we got into Vietnam was through overthrowing Diem and the complicity in the murder of Diem." He had borrowed the word "complicity" from the Pentagon Papers.

Two days later, Nixon ordered Haldeman, Ehrlichman, Colson, and Attorney General John Mitchell to get the Diem files out to the public, just as the Pentagon Papers had been released. "We have to get someone to blast it out." He took the occasion to add several other exposés to his wish list. "We could also move to open the Bay of Pigs and the Cuban Missile Crisis," he told them. "I wanted ammunition against the anti-war critics," Nixon wrote later of his motive, "many of whom were the same men who, under Kennedy and Johnson, had led us into the Vietnam morass in the first place." His staff went into action. "The P ordered E to have the full Diem story on his desk by the end of next week," Haldeman noted in his diary, "also the Bay of Pigs."

Following up, John Ehrlichman had breakfast at CIA headquarters across the Potomac River in Langley, Virginia. "I went to Helms and said I had a list of files the president wants to see. I got it from Nixon. It had several items, but the biggest was the Bay of Pigs." The files Nixon asked Ehrlichman to retrieve included those on the assassinations of Diem and the Dominican Republic's Trujillo. Helms told Ehrlichman that he could only give such files to the president himself.

Nixon would not be deterred, inviting the CIA director to see him personally. With the reelection campaign looming, Nixon told Helms that he needed to be "fully advised in order to know what to duck" should the Diem killing or the Bay of Pigs arise as issues. "I want to protect the agency," the president told Helms, denying any intention to either hurt the agency or attack his predecessors. Helms then handed an envelope containing the requested files to Nixon, who placed them in a desk drawer. He would later complain that Helms had failed to give him the full story on the doomed invasion and Kennedy's role in it.

While the file Helms provided on the Bay of Pigs lacked the information Nixon most wanted, confirmation that President Kennedy had bungled and betrayed the mission, he still hoped to incriminate Kennedy in the Diem killing. Here again, the Nixon team would be stymied. "The closer one approached the assassination period," E. Howard Hunt would note, "the more frequently were cables missing from chronological order." Their suspicions of a cover-up turned out to be well founded. Years later, author Richard Reeves reported that President Kennedy had ordered many of the Washington-Saigon cables destroyed.

The lack of evidence did not stop Chuck Colson. Told by Hunt that none of the discovered cables tied Kennedy himself to the Diem killing, Colson had a suggestion: "Do you think you can improve on them?" Hunt, using a razor blade, a Xerox machine, and some creative surgery, then forged a cable from Kennedy denying asylum to President Diem and his influential brothers. The goal, Colson would later testify, was not merely to discredit JFK but to wound his brother as a presidential challenger, especially among the large bloc of Catholic voters Colson had targeted in 1972. "Complicity" in the grim Saigon affair of 1963 was not enough. He wanted to document that a Catholic president had conspired in the assassination of a Catholic leader of another country. He wanted voters thinking fondly of Ted Kennedy to see the blood of Diem and Nhu on his older brother's hands. The scheme failed only when *Life* insisted on photographing the doctored cable.

Even with Nixon's chances of reelection bolstered by his masterful turning of the tables on China policy, the dirty deeds continued to grow like fingernails on a corpse.

CHAPTER TWENTY-FIVE

Smoking Gun

LIKE Jack Kennedy before him, Richard Nixon pined for the political legitimacy that comes from winning a decisive reelection mandate. Though his grand dealings with China and the Soviet Union marked the handicraft of a great statesman, he never lost sight of the one man who could take it all away from him. Ever fearful of Teddy's gains, he was so reactive that if the Democrat stirred even for a second, the Republican president would twitch. When Kennedy declared he would have "crawled" to Hanoi to get prisoners of war released, the president showed up at a conference on POWs. When Kennedy's subcommittee held hearings on the plight of American Indians, the Nixon team proclaimed its own allegiance to the Native American cause. When the senator went to India and Pakistan to study the refugee problem, Secretary of State Rogers addressed the United Nations on the refugee problem. So predictable was the echo that Kennedy staffers figured there had to be a White House "Kennedy desk" where aides monitored the senator from Massachusetts the way the State Department keeps track of a tricky foreign country.

Every new indication of Kennedy's intentions served only to remind Nixon of past humiliations. Each criticism brought new evidence of a media double standard. When Hugh Sidey of *Time* went after the White House for monopolizing the news, Nixon angrily pointed out to Bob Haldeman that no similar complaints had been heard back in the early 1960s when President Kennedy held the spotlight and Nixon languished in the shadows. His indignation was recharged when the *New York Times* reported for the first time that Attorney General Robert Kennedy, that "ruthless little bastard" to Nixon, had a decade earlier ordered a backdoor Justice Department investigation of the $205,000 received by Nixon's brother from Howard Hughes.

But the same day's newspapers served up an even fresher exposé: Columnist Jack Anderson revealed that Nixon had recently received a $100,000 political contribution from the aerospace tycoon. Determined once and for all to force similar public scrutiny of the Kennedy camp, Nixon was now furious to get out the fact that the generous Hughes had other irons in the fire. "Nixon knew that O'Brien was on Howard Hughes's payroll, and Nixon had that Howard Hughes thing that had been pounded into him for years," Haldeman recalled. "It was 'How come they can nail me because Howard Hughes loans my brother money and they don't pay any attention that Howard Hughes is financing Larry O'Brien, who is the only effective spokesman the Democrats got.' He wanted to get him nailed."

O'Brien had come to assume a superhuman stature. "The presence of Lawrence O'Brien as chairman of the Democratic National Committee (DNC) unquestionably suggests that the Democratic nominee will have a strong, covert intelligence effort mounted against us in 1972," operative Jack Caulfield warned in an in-house memo. "Should this Kennedy mafia–dominated intelligence gun-for-hire be turned against us in '72, we would, indeed, have a dangerous and formidable foe." The president shared this estimate. "Larry O'Brien was one Democrat who was a grand master in the art of political gamesmanship. O'Brien had been tutored in the Kennedy political machine and further shaped by his years with Lyndon Johnson. He was a partisan in the most extreme and effective sense."

O'Brien would soon prove just how dangerous he was to Nixon. In February, a hot-on-the-trail Jack Anderson charged that the Republican president had stopped the Justice Department from appealing an antitrust action against the conglomerate ITT in exchange for a backdoor $400,000 contribution to the upcoming Republican National Convention. O'Brien jumped on the revelation, blasting Nixon with every media cannon in his armory. Beneath the partisan bombardment over ITT, Nixon issued his command to counterattack. Why was he taking heat from Democratic chairman O'Brien and the press over ITT when O'Brien himself was getting paid his salary as DNC chairman while simultaneously pulling down a retainer from Hughes? "O'Brien's not going to get away with it, Bob," Nixon told Haldeman, more eager than ever to get the details of O'Brien's Hughes connection into print. "We're going to get proof of his relationship with Hughes—and just what he's doing for the money." Yet Nixon was frustrated at his campaign's failure to find dirt on the Democrats, just as he was frustrated back before the 1960 election by the CIA's delay in invading Cuba. "When are they going to DO something over there?" he complained to Haldeman.

On the morning after Jack Anderson's column appeared on the Hughes gift, White House plumber G. Gordon Liddy presented Attorney General John Mitchell with a political espionage plan, code-named Gemstone. It was an ambitious scheme to gather opposition research and disrupt the Democratic operation through sabotage, the use of prostitutes for political blackmail, break-ins to obtain and photograph documents, and various forms of electronic surveillance and wiretapping. Mitchell's initial resistance was soon overwhelmed by the eagerness of campaign and White House lieutenants to meet Nixon's demand for dirt. "Why don't you guys get off the stick and get Liddy's budget approved?" Colson yelled over the phone to campaign deputy Jeb Magruder. "We need the information, particularly on O'Brien."

Colson was active on another front. Expecting Maine's Edmund Muskie to win the first-in-the-nation Democratic presidential primary in New Hampshire, he pulled a dirty trick: a mass mailing to New Hampshire voters urging that they write in the name of Ted Kennedy. The purpose was to get Muskie angry at Kennedy for trying to steal some of his margin over the long-shot antiwar candidate, South Dakota senator George McGovern. Magruder was resistant to the plot at first: "We liked the idea of sowing disunity among the Democrats, but we weren't convinced that one mailing would do very much. It seemed like a large outlay for a dubious result, so we stalled, hoping Colson would drop the plan." He soon had no choice but to go along, however. Colson, emerging from the Oval Office, was able to pull rank. "We've got to get that mailing going. I've just come from talking to the president, and he thinks it's crucial." As Haldeman observed, "In battle, Nixon always wanted 'to go for the jugular.' " That meant Teddy.

Even Nixon's historic visit to China that February could not assuage his anxieties. Chou En-lai hosted a state banquet at the Great Hall of the People. On their televisions, Americans saw their country's foremost Cold Warrior, the onetime Red-baiter, toasting a glass of strong mao-tai and quoting Chairman Mao. "Seize the day!" the American politician who had built his career asking "Who lost China?" kept repeating as he raised his glass to yet another official around the great table. "Seize the hour." Nixon was single-handedly taking China out of the global struggle between the United States and the USSR, making her more Cold War ally than enemy. He had done politically what no other president in the post–World War II era would have dared.

Yet it was a triumph that brought no relief. Even when George McGovern embarrassed Muskie by "winning" the New Hampshire primary, taking 37 percent to the front-runner's 46 percent, then went on to beat him in Wisconsin, the Nixon people kept on anticipating the Kennedy ambush. The single-minded Pat Buchanan noted that the antiwar McGovern's surprising success would only heighten pressure on Kennedy to run. A Jeff MacNelly cartoon in the *Richmond News-Leader* compared the fight for the 1972 Democratic nomination to an NCAA-basketball-championship draw, with each contest leading to the final playoff with Ted Kennedy.

Even the McGovern victory in the Wisconsin primary that April didn't diminish Kennedy's starring role in the worst-case Nixon scenario. "Somebody should be attacking Kennedy . . . personally," came a Nixon memo to Colson. He listened with interest to a Haldeman suggestion that Secret Service protection be offered to Teddy as a way of signaling what had to be his inevitable rival. "The P wanted to be sure to get people to follow-up on the line that K is now the obvious Democratic candidate," Haldeman penned in his diary. The strategy here was to make the expected late Kennedy entry into a fait accompli, thereby robbing it of excitement. Even when McGovern scored his biggest win so far in the 1972 primary season, sweeping Massachusetts, the incumbent still kept faith in Kennedy's running. "Noncandidacy would have been the best strategy for Kennedy in any event," Nixon said years later, defending his assessment, as if the fact of Kennedy not running were evidence that he would.

In Nixon's view the specter of Camelot loomed larger than ever. "Jackie Kennedy received bravos for years because she brought Pablo Casals to the White House to play his cello forty years after his prime," he complained to Haldeman. "When we look over the list of people that we have had to the White House, they make the Johnson years appear almost barbaric and the Kennedy years very thin indeed." He told Haldeman to get more "vicious" in pounding JFK's conduct of Vietnam policy. "The president asked me to remind you that he feels very strongly about someone taking Teddy on," Nixon secretary Rose Mary Woods wrote the chief of staff. "The country needs to be reminded how Richard Nixon, as a candidate for California governor, backed JFK in the Cuban Missile Crisis."

If Nixon was wrong about 1972, he was right about Ted Kennedy. His lack of an active candidacy did not mean the absence of an active hostility. From his seat on the Senate Judiciary Committee, Kennedy was coming at Nixon not as a nominee but as a prosecutor. Unwilling to let ITT drop, Kennedy's staff camped out at the senator's McLean, Virginia, home, staying till midnight, then returning early the next morning to brief the boss on any promising leads.

On April Fools' Day, the Nixon team began constructing a far more enticing scandal for the Kennedy team to investigate. On that day, G. Gordon Liddy received the go-ahead to bug the offices of Democratic National Chairman Lawrence O'Brien.

IN May, Richard Nixon became the first American president to visit Moscow. Yet even a historic meeting with Communist party chairman Leonid Brezhnev, capped by the joint signing of the Strategic Arms Limitation agreement, could not save Nixon from his disastrous campaign to gather dirt. As the U.S. president attended the Bolshoi's production of *Swan Lake*, G. Gordon Liddy shot out the streetlight in back of George McGovern's Washington headquarters, which was number two on the burglar team's list of targets. Three days later, with their candidate still in the Soviet Union, five men, all but one Cuban exiles loyal to E. Howard Hunt because of his anti-Castro zealotry during the Bay of Pigs, entered target number one: the office of Democratic party chairman Lawrence O'Brien at the Watergate complex, overlooking the Potomac River, alongside the new Kennedy Center.

The group took two full thirty-six-exposure rolls of film and numerous Polaroid shots. The attempt to bug the Democratic headquarters was not as successful. When the device placed on Larry O'Brien's phone somehow failed to work, the decision was made for the burglars to go back and repeat the job.

On June 17, ten days after George McGovern had locked up the Democratic presidential nomination with a victory over Hubert Humphrey in the California primary, E. Howard Hunt and Liddy launched the second illegal entry at the Watergate. Richard Nixon's command that his people hold Kennedy man Lawrence O'Brien "accountable" for his retainer from Howard Hughes was at last executed. So, too, was the president's feverish demand that his reelection intelligence operatives earn their pay in "opposition research," especially on the Kennedy crowd. Once again, the burglary team of the committee to reelect the president entered the Watergate looking for some campaign "meat." This time, James McCord and the four Cuban Americans were caught and arrested at two o'clock Saturday morning.

On Sunday morning, President Nixon, back at his Key Biscayne home after a weekend in the Bahamas, noticed an odd story on page 30 of the *New York Times.* "What's that crazy item about the DNC, Bob?" he asked Haldeman over the phone. "Track down Magruder and see what he knows about it." He would later claim to be unfazed by the report. "I had been in politics long enough and had seen everything from dirty tricks to vote fraud. I could not muster much moral outrage over a political bugging."

Nixon quickly moved to control the political damage by making the break-in look like the work of anti-Castro exiles worried about soft-line Democrats ready to cut a deal with the Communist leader. "This thing may be under control because of the Cubans who went in there," Nixon told Haldeman over the phone. "You know, those Cubans down there hate McGovern. Those people who got caught are going to need money. I've been thinking about how to do it. I'm going to have [Cuban American pal] Bebe [Rebozo] start a fund for them in Miami, call it an anti-Castro fund and publicize the hell out of the Cuban angle." The rationale would be that Hunt and the Cubans who broke into the Democratic headquarters suspected that the Democrats would get into power and betray them, as they had in denying them the promised "umbrella" of air protection in April 1961. "Tell Ehrlichman this whole group of Cubans is tied to the Bay of Pigs."

Lawrence O'Brien, the target of the Watergate caper, played the break-in story as a true partisan, saying that an attempt at interparty espionage "raised the ugliest questions about the integrity of the political process that I have encountered in a quarter century of political activity."

But it was Richard Nixon who converted what his press secretary Ron Ziegler called a "third-rate burglary" into a personal and partisan catastrophe. Fearful that a disclosure of campaign tricks would cost him a second term, he moved to conceal his people's involvement in the Watergate matter. A few minutes after 10:00 A.M. that Friday morning, Bob Haldeman suggested they get the FBI off the Watergate trail by telling them the break-in was a CIA-related operation. Nixon now gave orders that would fatally mar his career. He scripted for his chief of staff a rationale to use in explaining CIA involvement in the Watergate break-in based on the role of the Cubans and former agent E. Howard Hunt. "Hunt . . . That will uncover a lot of things. You open that scab, there's a hell of a lot of things, and we just feel that it would be very detrimental to have this thing go any further. This involves these Cubans, Hunt, and a lot of hanky-panky that we have nothing to do with ourselves."

Later in the long morning meeting, Nixon elaborated on how Haldeman should try and convince the FBI to pull back from Watergate. A firm believer that the CIA was hiding facts about the Bay of Pigs, Nixon decided to hide Watergate behind the same protective shell that had been guarding the legacy of President Kennedy from taint. Haldeman's presidential assignment was to meet with CIA director Richard Helms and deputy chief Vernon Walters, whom Haldeman had tried dragooning two years earlier as Nixon's human recording system, and have them tell the FBI to drop its investigation of the Watergate break-in on the grounds that the CIA was involved. "When you get in, say, 'Look, the problem is that this will open the whole, the whole Bay of Pigs thing and the president just feels that' . . . without going into the details—don't lie to them to the extent to say there is no involvement—but just say this is a comedy of errors, without getting into it. 'The president believes this is going to open the whole Bay of Pigs thing up again.' "

By employing what he saw as Kennedy hardball, Richard Nixon had sealed his fate. In trying to hide his reelection team's debacle behind the same elite shield that had guarded Jack Kennedy's, he had recorded an obstruction of justice. The man warned to avoid the assassin image in his 1960 encounter with Jack Kennedy was now the man who, in the soon-to-emerge lexicon of scandal, had fired the smoking gun.

He still saw the whole Watergate matter as par for the course. Later, as John Ehrlichman attempted to brief him on antibusing legislation, Nixon suddenly changed the subject. What was all the fuss about the Watergate bugging, he began wondering aloud. "We've reduced the number of wiretaps by fifty percent. *Robert Kennedy* tapped the most when he was attorney general."

* * *

WITHIN a week of the break-in, reporters Bob Woodward and Carl Bernstein of the *Washington Post* traced the lineage of Watergate from the burglars to E. Howard Hunt, Chuck Colson, and the Nixon White House. The two detected the political motive behind the plumbers' operation from the list of books Hunt had borrowed from the Library of Congress. "The White House is absolutely paranoid about Kennedy," a clerical aide told Bernstein. A public relations director of a Hyannis hotel told Woodward of Hunt's snooping the summer before. "Hunt wanted to know if I'd heard of any women-chasing by the Kennedy boys, if I'd heard any scandal-type material."

As the *Post* followed the myriad of trails from Watergate, the prime target of Hunt and his cohorts continued to tweak his predator. Ted Kennedy put out the misinformation that Nixon had been just as far ahead of his brother at this point in the 1960 campaign as he was now leading George McGovern.

In July, the Democrats met in Miami Beach to nominate George McGovern. Not until the last convention balloon was popped did Nixon finally stop anticipating the Kennedy coup he had so long imagined. When Hubert Humphrey sought to challenge the "unit rule," which gave the winner of the California primary, McGovern, the state's entire bloc of delegates, Nixon saw the fight as a backroom campaign to force a hung convention that would then turn to Ted Kennedy as the compromise candidate. "During most of my first term," Nixon would confirm years later, "I had assumed that my opponent in 1972 would be Kennedy, Muskie, or Humphrey. I thought that I could probably beat Muskie or Humphrey. A campaign against Teddy Kennedy would be much more difficult to predict because it would involve so many emotional elements."

Even after McGovern's nomination, Nixon's obsession fueled speculation. When the newly crowned Democratic presidential candidate prepared to name Missouri senator Thomas Eagleton his vice-presidential running mate, the White House saw it as a Kennedy-influenced choice. Watching Teddy arrive to present the victorious McGovern to the convention, Nixon kept his eye glued to the younger man. "Kennedy looked very good, though some thought he looked fat. He had a magnetic smile, a lot of style, and a brilliantly written speech."

Three weeks later, when press reports of past mental health problems forced Eagleton from the ticket, Nixon interpreted the sad turn of events as yet another ambush. "In the event he is able to replace him with Kennedy," he wrote in his diary, "this will make it a whole new ball game." Then, when Kennedy brother-in-law Sargent Shriver unexpectedly became McGovern's new running mate, Nixon unleashed his staff. "Destroy him," the president commanded Haldeman. "Kill him."

The president was now thinking about the Kennedy struggle to come. Recalling his own calculation in 1964, Nixon simply assumed that Ted Kennedy was now content to watch McGovern lose a landslide, just as Nixon had watched Goldwater, paving the way for his own electoral triumph in 1976. At a Texas barbecue, he told John Connally, the man he had named to head "Democrats for Nixon" and had privately dubbed as his successor, how important it was that after the Democrats got killed in 1972 the last brother not be the one to "pick up the pieces."

Nixon had the same intimations about the ongoing probe of Watergate, which the Democrats were trying without much success to make a campaign issue. "I guess the Kennedy crowd is just laying in the bushes waiting to make their move," he told Haldeman. On this point, his political antennae could not have been more accurate. Up at Ted Kennedy's Judiciary Subcommittee on Administrative Practices, maneuvers were under way to destroy him. When the White House had Republican leader Gerald Ford kill an investigation of Watergate by the House Banking Committee chairman, seventy-one-year-old Wright Patman, triggering what John Dean called a "sigh of relief" in the White House, the Kennedy staff knew it must fill the void. James Flug, chief counsel for the Kennedy subcommittee, with the help of the Library of Congress, had been keeping an extensive clipping file on Watergate since just after the break-in. Now Kennedy began urging Sen. Sam Ervin, chairman of the subcommittee with jurisdiction over such matters, to open an investigation. But Ervin suggested that Kennedy go ahead on his own, which he did after getting subpoena power from the full Judiciary Committee. "Teddy Kennedy decided that this was the sort of thing he should investigate *personally*," Richard Nixon would later observe in bitter hindsight.

In early October, the *Washington Post* fingered Nixon's appointments secretary, Dwight Chapin, as the White House "contact" for the dirty-tricks campaign being waged by Segretti and others. This revelation only added fuel to Nixon's already-long-burning resentment of what he considered a media double standard. He complained that when Dick Tuck worked his dirty tricks on the Republicans, journalists accepted such behavior as standard campaign high jinks. Kansas senator Robert Dole, Nixon's pick to chair the Republican National Committee, took the accusation public. Attacking the *Post* fifty times in a speech drafted by Nixon aide Pat Buchanan, he labeled editor Ben Bradlee "an old Kennedy coat holder," his newspaper a "partner" of the Democratic opposition.

Kennedy told his subcommittee to start digging. "I know the people around Nixon," he told the *Post's* Bernstein. "They're thugs." He also realized that to prove effective, the Congress's subpoena power needed to be exploited immediately; otherwise, documents might be destroyed and the chance of a serious investigation lost. Flug and committee investigator Carmine Bellino began scrutinizing the conduct of Nixon's reelection committee, with specific attention to Segretti's White House connections. Using telephone credit-card records, Kennedy's subcommittee sketched the stark outlines of Watergate from the burglars' numbers to the telltale "456" exchange of the White House. Its report would lay the foundation for Congress's investigation and prosecution of the case against Richard Nixon. Donald Segretti could sense the menace. "Kennedy is out for blood," he complained to reporter Bernstein. "Kennedy will tear me to shreds."

But Watergate could not compete with Vietnam as an election-eve story. On October 26, national security adviser Henry Kissinger called a press conference on Vietnam. "We believe that peace is at hand," he declared. The stumbling block was President Thieu, who could see no real difference between Kissinger's 1972 agreement and that which the North Vietnamese had demanded in May 1969. The U.S. Army would pull out of South Vietnam; the North Vietnamese Army would stay.

Yet the American people cheered the news. At long last, the United States was removing itself from the Vietnamese quagmire. On November 7, Richard Nixon received over 47 million votes, nearly 20 million more than the Democratic candidate. Sixty percent of the electorate had backed the Republican incumbent. No Republican had ever won the White House by so large a margin. No president had ever won more popular votes or carried so many states: forty-nine. Nixon could claim the additional satisfaction of beating an important member of the rival family, Sargent Shriver, who had referred to Nixon as a "psychiatric case" and other unkind expletives as the race reached its inevitable conclusion. Nixon had won every state except Massachusetts— Kennedy country.

That night, Nixon listened again to *Victory at Sea* in the White House residence, attended a victory rally at a Washington hotel, then sequestered himself from family, friends, old political allies, the world, retreating across the street from the White House to his hideaway in the Old Executive Office Building, the better to digest the last tidbits of electoral conquest. Old campaign hand Herb Klein was not alone in registering the strange hibernation as evidence his boss's resentments had returned. It was as if victory were not an occasion for reconciliation but an opportunity to revisit old wounds. Instead of celebrating in the bright light of fellowship, Nixon sat through the dark morning hours savoring with operatives Haldeman and Colson the state-by-state salute of his country that carried with it a decisive rebuke of his enemies.

The Saturday after the election, Nixon told Haldeman that he did not think "Teddy" would go after Watergate. You don't strike at the king, he postured, unless you can kill him. "He can't kill us; therefore, he won't strike."

Nixon was already making plans to consolidate his victory. To facilitate the purge of any lurking Kennedy holdovers still in the executive bureaucracy, he had Bob Haldeman demand the resignation of every member of the Nixon cabinet. Having seized all-out control of the government, the victorious Republican president's next objective was to construct a new political coalition of the conservatively inclined working class and all southerners enraged by the Democrats' tilt toward the left and their increasing control by cultural elites. And, finally, his political son, John Connally, would be anointed his champion to take on the battered forces of the Democratic party led by Ted Kennedy. Not only had he survived and come back from the humiliating defeat of 1960; Nixon now would create a new political order that would secure his victory for posterity.

However, as he ruminated on such satisfying dynastic visions, his enemies were gathering unnoticed at the moat. Obsessed with the presidential prize, the victor had allowed his partisan adversaries to secure even more tightly their power over Congress and with it what he knew from the Hiss case to be its all-potent power of subpoena. That and the eagerness to use it. Nixon's success in exploiting the generational and class rifts of the Vietnam debate had engendered, in the zealots among the Democratic forces, an even greater anti-Nixon rage. One of those partisans was Thomas P. "Tip" O'Neill, Jr., the man who had succeeded Jack Kennedy in Congress. When a plane carrying Louisiana's Hale Boggs was lost over a remote stretch of Alaska, O'Neill succeeded him as majority leader. The House was now led by the member from the most pro-Kennedy, anti-Nixon area in the country. O'Neill was an Irish-American Democrat who took tribal offense, moreover, at the strong-arm tactics of the Republican president's reelection team.

Chuck Colson's post-election attack on the *Washington Post* and its executive editor, Benjamin Bradlee, before a gathering of New England newspaper editors escalated another ancient war. "If Bradlee ever left the Georgetown cocktail circuit, where he and his pals dine on third-hand information and gossip and rumor, he might discover out here the real America." Bradlee got the message. "That's some pretty personal shit!" the editor told star Watergate sleuth Carl Bernstein. Already beating every other news organization on the Watergate story, the *Post* could hardly stop now. "I know it's there," Bradlee told his reporters. "I know it's there."

Nixon, brooding over his victory in the fastness of Camp David, the presidential retreat in the Catoctin Mountains of Maryland, could not see the enemy still advancing. Ted Kennedy's subcommittee was already sharpening its weapon for use by the Democratic-controlled Senate: a damning report that would trace the Watergate chain of command from the Committee to Re-Elect the President at 1701 Pennsylvania Avenue across the street and down the block to the president's own doorstep.

CHAPTER
TWENTY-SIX

Kennedy Versus Nixon—Again

TED Kennedy played a major, unseen role in the downfall of Richard Nixon. Part of this role was simply being who he was. From the moment he entered the White House, Nixon had faced the specter of a Kennedy restoration. After the two-year reprieve granted by Chappaquiddick, he watched the brother of Jack and Robert reemerge as the man posing the greatest danger to his reelection. Yet he knew that the Kennedy threat in 1972 arose not so much from the younger brother himself as from the glory he reflected from the past. "The Kennedy ghost haunting the Nixon White House was partly that of a person, a political contemporary, sometime Nixon friend, sometime rival, whose own path and Nixon's kept crossing and recrossing as each made his way to the top," wrote Nixon speechwriter and intimate Ray Price, who would be there at the end. More than that, it was a grand, lost spirit. "The ghost that dogged Nixon's footsteps, that disturbed his nights and plagued his days," Price recalled, "was less that of Kennedy himself than it was of Camelot." Thus, to besmirch the Camelot standard, the political grave of Diem had been exhumed. To thwart the dynastic succession, the sad scandal of Chappaquiddick had been revisited. To distract attention from the assortment of dirty tricks poised to bring him down, the Bay of Pigs had been invoked.

But Ted Kennedy's role in Richard Nixon's demise was not entirely passive, not by any means. Thanks to his position of respect on the Senate Judiciary Committee, Kennedy had the opportunity to be Nixon's most relentless prosecutor. It was a role that Jack Kennedy's brother seized with relish. Before election day in 1972 he was setting the charges that would explode the Nixon presidency. With allies Birch Bayh of Indiana and John Tunney of California, he pushed for full-dress Senate hearings on Watergate. In January 1973, the Democratic majority voted to create a select committee to probe the DNC break-in and other campaign activities against the Democrats during the 1972 presidential election. Kennedy's senior colleague on the Judiciary Committee, Sam Ervin of North Carolina, was named to chair the panel. The Massachusetts senator promoted Ervin's appointment believing that the genteel southern Democrat, schooled in the Constitution, would make the perfect prosecutor of the Republican president. It would allay the suspicion that the Watergate matter was being pushed hardest by Kennedy, which, in fact, it was.

Thanks to Senator Kennedy, the bipartisan panel had a head start. His Judiciary Subcommittee report, based on a seven-month investigation begun just after the June 1972 break-in and detailing the role of the White House and the Committee to Re-Elect the President in the "dirty tricks" campaign, as well as the Watergate break-in, became the Ervin committee's start-up manual.

While his enemies began their siege, the man behind the White House gates took his second oath to uphold the U.S. Constitution and ensure that its laws were faithfully executed. Having done so, he appropriated the cadence, if not the eloquence, of Jack Kennedy's most famous appeal. "Let each of us ask not just how can government help but how can I help?" But his huge electoral mandate, which he hoped would settle the rivalry, had set off a fierce new struggle. Nixon's announcement four days later of an accord with North Vietnam dictating the withdrawal of all American troops and the return of U.S. prisoners of war, which he christened "peace with honor," served to enrage his enemies further. When Judge John Sirica, a Republican, slapped the Watergate burglars with harsh sentences designed to make them talk, the forces poised against the president were eager to listen.

To Nixon, the mounting hostility spoke for a historic double standard. Unable to let pass an article in the *New York Times* criticizing his "Imperial Presidency," he ordered John Ehrlichman to take the piece apart, item by item, in order to demonstrate that JFK had impounded more congressional appropriations, *Kennedy* had done more wiretaps, *Kennedy* had conducted more illegal surveillance. When the Senate Judiciary Committee called White House counsel John Dean to testify, it confirmed Nixon's view of the Watergate probe as more a rearguard action than an all-out attack. "This is the last gasp of our hardest opponents," Nixon assured his nervous aide.

But as the Watergate story exploded in the morning headlines and on the evening news, Nixon seemed a prisoner to past intrigues, listening to Dean's sycophantic talk of catching Judiciary Committee member Kennedy in a "bear trap." Dean believed that the Judiciary Committee's digging into "dirty tricks" would showcase the Nixon team's own favorite dig: Chappaquiddick. Nixon told Dean that "hush money" for the Watergate burglars could be laundered through a "Cuban Committee." Nine months after the June 1972 break-in, he was still vainly attempting to tie the Watergate burglary to the Bay of Pigs, still trying to conceal Watergate in the shell of silence he saw protecting the true events of April 1961.

But the cover-up was unraveling. Two days after the president gave the orders to maintain the Cuban Committee as a laundry for hush money, Watergate burglar James McCord told Judge Sirica that he was under "political pressure to plead guilty and remain silent." The story was a bombshell, blasting aside nine months of intricate damage control. The president had said that the White House was not involved in Watergate. The top burglar was now saying differently. Desperate to save himself, Nixon announced the resignations of chief of staff Haldeman and domestic policy adviser Ehrlichman. He fired John Dean outright, leaving the clear suggestion that his counsel, who was cooperating with prosecutors, was the prime cover-up culprit. To set a higher tone for his administration, the president announced the nomination of Defense Secretary Elliot Richardson as attorney general.

Richardson, a patrician with an impeccable public record both in Massachusetts and Washington, understood the peril facing both president and country. Meeting with Nixon on a balmy spring day at Camp David, a day embittered by the senior staff dismissals, Richardson gamely sought to dispel Nixon's bunker mentality. "Mr. President, I believe your real problem is that you have somehow been unable to realize that you have *won*—not only won but been reelected by a tremendous margin," he told an embittered Nixon. "You are the president of *all* the people of the United States. There is no '*they*' out there—nobody trying to destroy you." But this well-meaning denial of any lurking danger was as poorly addressed as it was badly founded. Not only was the Orthogonian Nixon unlikely to accept the counsel of a Franklin, even one he employed, but events would soon prove that there were any number of people out to get Richard Nixon.

Heading the list, of course, was Ted Kennedy. Just as Nixon had once pushed for a special prosecutor in the second Hiss trial, Kennedy wanted one named now. More than that, he wanted the Watergate special prosecutor to have full authority. Until he was assured of this, he intended to use his clout on the Judiciary Committee to bar Elliot Richardson's confirmation. According to Kennedy counsel James Flug, there was no obfuscation. "When Richardson was nominated, Kennedy told him he could not be confirmed unless he had a special prosecutor mandate that was acceptable to us," Flug recalls. Also a special prosecutor who passed Kennedy's muster.

When Richardson, not yet confirmed, tried recruiting two possible candidates for special prosecutor, both rejected the offers. Kennedy was not yet satisfied with the special prosecutor's charter, and he was letting people know it. With Richardson's nomination in limbo, he had no choice but to call on the senator, who described the sort of special prosecutor that would be acceptable. One name Kennedy mentioned was that of Archibald Cox, the former Richardson law professor who had worked for both Jack and Bobby. Richardson named Cox the next day.

Kennedy was not finished. Getting the right special prosecutor was only the start. Now he wanted to guarantee that Cox would have a clear avenue of pursuit against Nixon. "The original terms of the special prosecutor's charter were my own," Richardson recalled. "Its final terms were worked out between Archibald Cox, members of the Senate Judiciary Committee, and myself." In other words, the terms had to be acceptable to Ted Kennedy. The Kennedy-approved charter would now grant "full authority" to the special prosecutor: Cox would have unlimited funds, unlimited time, unlimited authority to investigate, to grant immunity, to initiate prosecutions, to indict.

But the key point was Cox's own immunity from Nixon. "The Attorney General will not countermand or interfere with the Special Prosecutor's decisions or actions." The only person who could fire Cox was the man who had named him, Elliot Richardson. And he could only do that, by the terms of the Kennedy-approved charter, by accusing Cox of "extraordinary improprieties," a charge so unseemly that it would cost Richardson his own reputation. Thus, as the attorney general saw it, a "no-man's-land" had been created between the Watergate prosecutor and his ultimate target. That no-man's-land was in the person of Elliot Richardson. The new U.S. attorney general could not hinder Cox, nor could he fire him. The only way Richard Nixon could stop Cox was to fire Richardson, the very man whose dignity he had enlisted in the effort to salvage his administration's authority. To seal the deal, Richardson gave Kennedy a letter outlining the Watergate prosecutor's charter. After receiving the written guarantee, Kennedy and Judiciary Committee pal Tunney, an old University of Virginia law school mate, left for a jaunt to Europe.

Richard Nixon's presidency was now booby-trapped. To hinder the prosecution in any way would require that he fire Elliot Richardson, cutting the last thread of credibility holding him from the abyss. To allow Cox to exercise his unlimited authority, on the other hand, would take the Watergate probe on an even more perilous route.

While Richardson viewed Cox's political orientation as "unimportant," Nixon's more partisan loyalists were stunned by the selection of a special prosecutor who had run as a Muskie candi-

date for delegate to the 1972 Democratic National Convention
and served as solicitor general under the Kennedys. More ominous
was Cox's stint as chief of the speechwriting/research shop for
John F. Kennedy's presidential campaign, including preparation
for the Great Debate between his boss and the man he was about
to be sworn to investigate. Cox had watched the famous television encounter with Jacqueline Kennedy. "Cox will be a disaster,"
his ex-Harvard colleague Henry Kissinger predicted. "He has been
fanatically anti-Nixon all the years I've known him." To speechwriter Ray Price, Cox was the "high guru of the Cambridge chapter of the Kennedy government-in-waiting." The odd appointment spread gallows humor in the Nixon camp. At one late-night
White House meeting, a group of punchy aides tossed around
the imagined scene of Nixon confronting Richardson over his
hazardous appointment of Archibald Cox: "*Archie* Cox? I thought
you said you'd pick *Eddie* Cox." The reference was to the president's son-in-law, who had just graduated from law school.

Cox's swearing-in ceremony was no laughing matter. Among
the invited guests were Ethel Kennedy, widow of the man the
new prosecutor had once served, and Ted Kennedy, whose specter
had driven many of the dark deeds that the special prosecutor
would be pursuing. "If Richardson had searched specifically for
the man whom I would have least trusted to conduct so politically
sensitive an investigation in an unbiased way," Nixon wrote in
his memoirs, "he could hardly have done better than choose Archibald Cox." As Cox filled his staff with veterans of Bob Kennedy's Justice Department and of his 1968 presidential candidacy,
the worst fears were confirmed. Of the eleven senior counsels Cox
hired, seven had been associated with either Jack, Bobby, or
Teddy. The Watergate prosecution was going to be a Kennedy
operation.

In June, Nixon enjoyed the respite of a far more enjoyable
ceremony: the arrival in the United States of Soviet leader Leonid
Brezhnev. After meetings at the White House and Camp David,
the two men flew to Nixon's California home in San Clemente.
That night, after many drinks, the American host had to help his
Russian guest up the stairs to his daughter's room, where he had
been put up for the night. Twenty-three years after helping an

intoxicated Sen. Joe McCarthy, the country's most bellicose anti-Communist, home to bed, the U.S. president was doing the same for the world's reigning Communist leader.

In July, Nixon received the blow that would prove fatal to his presidency, and it was delivered by one of his own. Under questioning by the Senate Watergate Committee, Haldeman aide Alexander Butterfield divulged the existence of the audiotaping system that had been installed two years earlier. Richard Nixon would spend the rest of his days trying to keep the tapes from enemy ears.

Meanwhile, the daily focus on the moral failings of Richard Nixon eventually had the effect of dragging Teddy Kennedy back under the media's microscope. Endeavoring to assay the weight of Nixon's crimes, the country instinctively balanced in its other hand that of his chief rival's. In September, former Republican presidential candidate Barry Goldwater argued in a *New York Times* article that "the Democrats who want to make the most of their opportunities to capitalize on a 'Mr. Clean' image will find Teddy Kennedy a hard product to sell." At a terrible price to their patron, the Nixon operatives' effort to exhume the issue of Chappaquiddick had succeeded.

The same day as Goldwater's partisan conjecture, Ted Kennedy warned that if President Nixon dared to defy a Supreme Court order to turn over the tapes, "a responsible Congress would be left with no recourse but to exercise its power of *impeachment.*" *New York Times* columnist Tom Wicker called Kennedy's words "about as strong a statement on the substantive question of impeachment as any leading Democrat has been willing to make." The problem, he wrote, lay in Kennedy's own past. "The real crunch would come if Mr. Nixon, in fact, did defy a clear ruling of the Supreme Court, and the question implicit in Edward Kennedy's statement is how the country would react to the man of Chappaquiddick leading an impeachment battle against the man of Watergate."

In October, Egypt and Syria attacked Israel on Yom Kippur. As the war and the attendant danger of a U.S.-Soviet conflict monopolized the headlines, the Justice Department found Vice President Spiro Agnew indictable for taking kickbacks from Maryland contractors. His downfall threatened to speed the president's as well. The volatile, blunt-thinking former governor had served, in the parlance of Capitol Hill, as Richard Nixon's "impeachment insurance." To the president's foes, it was ghastly enough to have Nixon in the White House. Having Agnew—Nixon's *Nixon*—was beyond bearing.

Nixon's "insurance" was now being revoked. To save himself, Agnew asked Speaker Carl Albert to claim jurisdiction over his case in the House under the same constitutional procedure as that provided for the president. Agnew hoped this would preempt the Justice Department from indicting him, letting the case die in the Judiciary Committee. Listening to the vice president's complaint of political harassment by the U.S. Attorney in Maryland, the Democratic Speaker was inclined to accept. He and the House parliamentarian were drafting the appropriate resolution to protect the vice president when Majority Leader Tip O'Neill realized what was afoot and stopped the effort cold. Agnew had sought sanctuary at the wrong door, it turned out. O'Neill, not Albert, had the power of the Democratic rank and file behind him and knew it. Facing indictment, trial, and imprisonment, Agnew pled *nolo contendere* to a criminal tax charge and resigned.

Agnew's departure left Albert next in the presidential succession, just as his predecessor and he had been between the death of John F. Kennedy in November 1963 and the swearing in of Vice President Humphrey in January 1965. This time, Albert's tenure was far briefer. President Nixon became the first president to invoke the Twenty-fifth Amendment to the Constitution. Passed in the wake of the Kennedy assassination, it allows a president to fill a vice-presidential vacancy, subject to congressional approval. Within a week of Agnew's resignation, Nixon had named his old colleague Gerald Ford, House class of 1948, to succeed him. Before making the historic announcement, Nixon told the appointee his intention to back party convert John Connally for the Republican nomination in 1976. Under siege by the press, the Congress, and Archibald Cox, Nixon retained his grand hopes for the succession and the great bicentennial struggle with Ted Kennedy he figured would decide it.

Some of Nixon's adversaries entertained notions of a brisker change in power. With Albert now next in succession, several

Democratic zealots in the House flirted with a bold scenario: First, they would deny Gerald Ford confirmation; second, Congress would impeach and convict Nixon; third, Albert would take the presidential oath; fourth, the Congress would use the Twenty-fifth Amendment to pick as vice president a man the Democrats wanted to run the country; fifth, Albert would resign. Though only a few firebrands embraced this fanciful scheme, Nixon would point to a basic contingency plan for Albert's use in the event of a succession by New Frontiersman Ted Sorensen as sufficient evidence of a Kennedy-driven coup attempt.

Ted Kennedy, thinking more clearly, called for Gerald Ford's speedy confirmation. He wanted a Republican vice president in place before any dramatic steps were taken to oust Nixon. The Democrats could not afford having the American people suspect the whole Watergate probe had been aimed at recouping what the party had lost in the past two elections. But impeachment was clearly on the Democrats' minds. At a White House reception honoring Ford's ascension, Nixon cabinet member James Lynn mentioned to fellow guest Tip O'Neill the novelty of witnessing the oath taking of the first unelected vice president. The House Democratic leader could not resist retorting that another such transition was not far away.

O'Neill was not the only politician to spot the opportunity afforded by Agnew's departure. "Now that we have disposed of that matter," Richard Nixon told Attorney General Richardson, "we can go ahead and get rid of Cox."

The special prosecutor was not as easily banished as Spiro Agnew. Cox was protected by the deal Ted Kennedy had demanded of Elliot Richardson as the price of admission to the office once held by his brother. Nixon knew, too, that Archibald Cox was determined to get his hands on the White House tapes that would reveal the president plotting to use the Bay of Pigs as a cover for Watergate. If Cox agreed to ask for no additional tapes, Nixon now proposed he would provide written "summaries" of the subpoenaed recordings. Those summaries would be verified as accurate by Mississippi senator John Stennis. "Judge Stennis," as Nixon and his people came to call him in the next days of controversy, possessed appealing credentials for the job such as past judicial experience and a record of protecting presidential secrets, including the 1969 bombing of Cambodia. The seventy-two-year-old was also partially deaf.

The "Stennis compromise" was an offer Archibald Cox had no problem refusing. On Saturday, October 20, the special prosecutor called a one o'clock press conference at the National Press Club. There he issued his proclamation of war: He would demand tapes of any and every presidential conversation he decided was important. He would not relent. Asked about his job security, he said that Richard Nixon couldn't fire him; only Elliot Richardson could.

Now from the White House came Nixon's decision. At his command, chief of staff Alexander Haig called Richardson and said that the president wanted him to fire Cox. Asking for a meeting, Richardson reminded Nixon that he, the attorney general, could not carry out his orders because he had promised the Senate that he would "not countermand or interfere with the special prosecutor's decisions or actions." Richardson told Nixon that by asking him to dishonor his word, he gave him no choice but to resign.

Thus began the bloodbath. With Richardson's resignation in hand, Nixon told Haig to order Richardson's deputy, William Ruckelshaus, to fire Cox. When Ruckelshaus tried to resign, Nixon fired him. Nixon next asked the Justice Department's third-ranking official, Solicitor General Robert Bork, to fire Cox. Bork, a strict believer in constitutional authority, did as ordered. An attorney general had resigned. The deputy attorney general and the Watergate prosecutor had been fired. "The Saturday Night Massacre" was complete.

Now it was Ted Kennedy's turn. He called the firings "a reckless act of desperation by a President who is afraid of the Supreme Court, who has no respect for law and no regard for a man of conscience." Hearing these words above the din, Nixon recorded them that night in his diary.

Yet Kennedy's subsequent demand for an investigation of the massacre was steeped in irony. The events of Saturday, October 20, resulted as much from the Massachusetts senator's choreography as from any step improvised by Richard Nixon himself. Kennedy and his people knew the key players: Cox, Richardson, the president. Like a movie director, they could sketch each frame of the storyboard as the personalities of Nixon, Richardson, and Cox grappled. Cox would be relentless. Cox would protect his right to be relentless. To get Cox, Nixon would have to get Richardson first. That would mean destroying the one emblem of credibility the administration had left. It was a master's handiwork of law-making and patronage. Ted Kennedy had dictated the special prosecutor's charter and had lobbied for the appointment of Cox. As James Flug, chief counsel of Kennedy's subcommittee, concluded, "The Saturday Night Massacre was born in Kennedy's office."

By Tuesday, the national uproar over the massacre had forced a Nixon retreat. A new special prosecutor would be named, and there would be no further attempts to resist subpoenas to release White House tapes. Hearing of the reversal, Archibald Cox, now using a desk at the nonpartisan Library of Congress, went straight to Senator Kennedy's rooms in the Old Senate Office Building. "I don't have any office anymore," he explained to the press. That evening, he was a guest at the Kennedy riverside house in McLean, Virginia, invited there by Sen. Philip Hart, a Kennedy ally on the Judiciary Committee.

The new special prosecutor, Leon Jaworski, kept in place the entire staff of lawyers recruited by Archibald Cox, further hardened in their attitude toward the case's ultimate defendant. Informed over dinner one evening that President Nixon had requested money from Congress to pay for twelve additional White House lawyers, Jaworski told Kennedy aide Melody Miller, "He'll need every one of them!"

The massacre had thrown open the fortress door to Nixon's enemies. In the House of Representatives, twenty-one resolutions of impeachment were now filed in an anti-Nixon drive no longer limited to a few hotheads. As Nixon could see from the other end of Pennsylvania Avenue, the impeachment team now had a seasoned general manager. "I knew I was in trouble when I saw that Tip O'Neill was calling the shots up there. That man plays hardball. He doesn't know what a softball is."

Nixon had his opponent's measure. "Until now, I had stayed

behind the scenes," O'Neill recalled of the days after the massacre. But having risen to the leadership through friendships won and kept through endless nights of cardplaying and conversation, he could read the mood on the House floor better than anyone. The man who had coined the phrase "All Politics Is Local" knew, too, that he had bedrock support back home from the street-corner Irishmen as well as the Harvard Yard crowd for any move he might make against the Republican president. A popular Massachusetts bumper sticker recalled the commonwealth's holdout position in the 1972 election: "Don't blame us." Jack Kennedy's state had never liked or trusted Richard Nixon.

O'Neill began bullying New Jersey's Peter Rodino, the new chairman of the Judiciary Committee, to name a top-flight counsel to marshal the impeachment inquiry. "I had to light a fire under his seat," said O'Neill, recalling his many hectoring sessions alongside Rodino down in the front Democratic row in the House chamber. "Get the hell off my back!" Rodino finally barked at the persistent majority leader.

Five days before Christmas 1973, Rodino named John Doar, a registered Republican who had been a respected figure in Robert Kennedy's Justice Department, as his impeachment counsel. O'Neill kept up the heat on Nixon. When the beleaguered president began inviting members of Congress down to the White House for fence-mending visits, the Democratic leader accused him of "currying favor with his prospective grand jury."

The year 1973 ended with Nixon encircled by age-old adversaries: the special prosecutor's office, dominated by Bob Kennedy lawyers; the House of Representatives, led by the man who represented the martyred Jack Kennedy's district; the U.S. Senate, urged on by Ted Kennedy. Through the slits of the bunker, Nixon could see the hated *Washington Post*, whose editor Ben Bradlee Nixon's men had demonized as a "Kennedy" man. "Wherever Nixon turned he confronted Kennedy memories, old Kennedy loyalties hardened now into bitter anti-Nixon antagonisms," speechwriter Ray Price recalled, "old dreams conjured by courtiers and embellished by time, held up as standards against which presidents should be measured."

But the most deadly of all the weapons aimed at Richard M.

Nixon was the grim tones of the man himself, recorded on June 23, 1972—the "smoking gun" tape—when he tried hiding his misdeeds behind Jack Kennedy's greatest debacle. Each remaining month of the Nixon presidency would now spin and snap like the loose reel of a tape recorder.

CHAPTER
TWENTY-SEVEN

Death of a
Presidency

RICHARD Nixon spent the first two weeks of 1974 alone in California. The Watergate scandal had hit full force. The country's estimate of him, which had reached Jack Kennedy levels when the American prisoners of war came home from North Vietnam, had fallen thirty-nine points in the Gallup poll. It was the worst plunge in public approval the polling firm had ever recorded. "Opponents are savage destroyers, haters," Nixon penned in his diary. *Impeachment!* That quaint constitutional weapon wielded by Radical Republicans against Andrew Johnson after the Civil War suddenly led Congress's agenda.

The president, facing his career's end, was thinking about its beginning. "Don't assume that the time to run for an office is only when it is a sure thing," he exhorted a convention of Young Republicans. "Show me a candidate who is not a hungry candidate," he said, harking back to the night he and Pat had called the happiest of all. "Show me a candidate who isn't willing to take a risk and risk all, even risk losing, and I will show you a lousy candidate."

There followed an eerie coincidence of the kind that had

haunted Richard Nixon since he met John Kennedy that first day in Congress. It occurred on a suburban Virginia road just across the Potomac River from Washington. The next day's *Washington Post* had the first report:

A car driven by Murray Chotiner, long-time Nixon adviser, collided with a US government truck Wednesday morning and rolled into another car. It happened on Old Chain Bridge Road in McLean in front of the home of Sen. Edward M. Kennedy (D-MA) who called police.

The Nixons attended the funeral, paying homage to the man who had once told a young candidate that he needed some "meat" in his campaign, then went out and found it for him. It was Chotiner, too, who had ripped up Nixon's 1952 telegram quitting the Eisenhower ticket in those purgatorial hours after the Checkers speech but before the great war general declared Nixon his "boy."

Even as the president laid to rest the man who had tutored him in the art of *attack* politics, he found himself staring into his own political grave. In April, the House Judiciary Committee subpoenaed tapes of forty-three White House conversations. Desperate, Nixon appeared on prime-time television next to a stack of green binders containing the transcripts of the subpoenaed White House recordings. But his attempt to duplicate the success of Checkers was a flop. In his 1952 TV address, he had crushed a scandal by offering a full disclosure of his dealings. Now, twenty-two years later, he was resisting full disclosure, carrying on the cover-up. The transcripts he offered as a concession to his prosecutors only hurt Nixon's case by letting the public hear how a president, Quaker or not, talks when the network mikes aren't listening. "Expletive deleted" was now a household phrase.

The death knell continued. In May, Leon Jaworski sent word that the Watergate grand jury had named the president of the United States an "un-indicted co-conspirator" in the Watergate cover-up. For the first time, Nixon sat in his Executive Office hideaway and listened to the "smoking gun" tape from June 23, the conversation with Bob Haldeman in which he had ordered him to link the break-in of the Democratic National Committee headquarters to the debacle of the Bay of Pigs. Nixon knew that he could not let even his own lawyers hear him tell his chief of staff to have the CIA obstruct the FBI's probe of the Democratic National Committee break-in.

For the man in the White House bunker, it was now simply a matter of playing out his hand. In June, Nixon toured Egypt with President Anwar Sadat as millions lined the streets to mark the Arab country's shift from Soviet to American ally. Next came a meeting with Leonid Brezhnev in Moscow. Even in the Soviet capital he could not escape his pursuers. Ted Kennedy, building up his foreign policy credentials for a presidential run in 1976, had beaten him to a private session with the Communist leader. Attempting to make the best of the situation, Nixon told Brezhnev, with locker-room bravado, of the benefit of having both political parties exposed to the new American-Soviet détente. "Let's get them all a little pregnant."

Kennedy was experiencing a family matter of a far different sort. His eldest son, Teddy, Jr., had his right leg amputated due to cancer. The father was still accompanying the son for regular hospital treatments, with the outlook still precarious.

A man who, like Nixon, had always seemed diminished by his brother's idealized reputation now experienced his own fallout from Watergate. The revelations about the Nixon henchmen rooting around in the sands of Chappaquiddick had left their mark. So, too, had the national obsession with Nixon's misdeeds, which forced a new look at Kennedy's, if only as a counterbalance. In July, the *New York Times Magazine* published a long article on Chappaquiddick by investigative reporter Robert Sherrill. In a comprehensive review of the episode, which became a news story in itself, the author warned that his assault on Kennedy's explanation of the incident would not be the last. "If Kennedy, who is now obviously making tentative runs at the Democratic Presidential nomination for 1976, should officially announce his candidacy, then the post-Watergate press would be obliged to subject him to the same demands."

Out of camera eye, however, the senator from Massachusetts continued to work toward Nixon's downfall. As the Judiciary

Committee prepared to vote on impeachment, Nixon was counting on support from the panel's diehard southern Democrats. But when he called George Wallace to ask for help with Alabama congressman Walter Flowers, the governor politely but firmly put the president off. He had not examined the evidence sufficiently, Wallace told Nixon. Though he was praying for the president, he just didn't think it proper to telephone the congressman. Chief of staff Alexander Haig would be convinced that Wallace had been gotten to by none other than Ted Kennedy himself. "That's the presidency!" Nixon told his staff chief after receiving word that this last bastion had fallen.

In late July, the Supreme Court ruled, by unanimous vote, that Nixon must turn over the subpoenaed tapes, including the June 23 smoking gun. But without even waiting to hear them, the House Judiciary Committee voted the first article of impeachment. Facing the horrors of a trial in the U.S. Senate, Nixon decided to resign. As drivers honked horns on Pennsylvania Avenue and passersby yelled, "Jail to the Chief," speechwriter Ray Price chatted with his friend the president on what he wanted to tell the country. "We talked a bit about handling the point about his resignation's being the equivalent of impeachment. Nixon mentioned his taped instruction to staff chief Haldeman to use the 'Bay of Pigs' as a cover for Watergate. 'That six-minute conversation,' Nixon called it. 'It was a stupid damn thing—but wrong.' That was the heart of the crime."

Henry Kissinger tried to comfort Nixon in his last presidential hours. "History will treat you more kindly than your contemporaries," he prophesied.

"It depends on who writes the history," answered the man who feared from the moment he entered the White House that his enemies, those Kennedy-enchanted scholars, were already busy writing him off.

On the evening of August 8, Richard Nixon, the thirty-seventh president of the United States, went on national television to wrest some hint of grandeur from the ignoble verdict he was now forced to ratify. He quoted from Theodore Roosevelt's speech to the Sorbonne about the man in the arena "whose face is marred by dust and sweat and blood, who strives valiantly . . . and who at the worst, if he fails, at least fails while daring greatly." Yet even as he celebrated the struggle, the sixty-one-year-old president knew deep in his soul that he had forever squandered the prize.

THE last morning of his presidency, resigned to his fate and to the long, red-carpeted walk to the helicopter, Nixon offered a less guarded farewell. He tried, at first, to say, as JFK had, that life is unfair. He spoke of his father, who sold his lemon ranch not knowing there was oil beneath it. The son, too, was now forfeiting a property before tapping its wealth. "Nobody will ever write a book, probably, about my mother," he said, referring to the family-produced Rose Kennedy autobiography that had come out that spring. "Yes, she will have no books written about her, but she was a saint." Then he spoke about himself. "Always remember, others may hate you—but those who hate you don't win unless you hate them, and then you destroy yourself."

This is what had happened.

Epilogue

Twilight Struggle

T HE abrupt ending of Richard Nixon's presidency didn't stop the campaign he had initiated from reviving public indignation at the part Teddy Kennedy had played in the drowning death of Mary Jo Kopechne. Nixon was no longer in the White House, but neither would his enemy be. Barry Goldwater had gotten it right: His foes, after getting Nixon thrown out for his sins, suddenly found their own weighed heavier. "In going over the side, Richard Nixon may have taken Edward Kennedy down with him," decreed *New York Times* columnist William V. Shannon.

Still, for a while, Kennedy refused to acknowledge the fallout. Gerald Ford's pardon of his predecessor represented a "dual standard of justice," Teddy said, raising the very charge that so many made about the lenient treatment given him after Chappaquiddick. "Nobody drowned at Watergate," former congresswoman Clare Booth Luce smugly declared. Two weeks after the pardon, Senator Kennedy, burdened already by family concerns, announced that he would not seek the presidency in 1976. As before, Nixon remained skeptical, convinced that his nemesis was only indulging in subterfuge. From California, where he had gone into exile to recover and write his memoirs, word seeped out that he was predicting that Kennedy would not only run in 1976 but would win.

Teddy Kennedy's noncandidacy, however, would now prove more durable than it first appeared. Only forty-two and in good health, Edward M. Kennedy would never again find an open window of presidential opportunity. Though he tried once in 1980, an incumbent Democrat, Jimmy Carter, stood in his way. When veteran CBS correspondent Roger Mudd asked the senator on his family lawn in Hyannis Port why he wanted to be president, the candidate-to-be offered a meandering response that showed how much the Kennedy vision had faded into myth and memory.

> Well . . . I'm . . . were I to make the announcement and to run . . . the reasons that I would run is because I have a great belief in this country that is . . . there's more . . . more natural resources than any nation of the world; and the greatest political system in the world . . . the energies and resourcefulness of this nation . . . I think . . . should be focused on these problems in a way that brings a sense of restoration.

It took seventy-one words to reach the secret password, "restoration." But its power was dissipated. Twenty years after the Great Debate, a decade past the 1960s, six years after Richard Nixon's banishment from office, the youngest brother's strongest claim to the nation's highest office was a fading glimmer of what was. Even against a weakened opponent like Carter, the Kennedy magic could no longer work miracles.

Though he would become one of history's most productive senators, his White House run lacked a rationale. Not until the fight was lost did Kennedy find the words to excite the nostalgic legions. "For me a few hours ago, this campaign came to an end," he told teary-eyed delegates to the Democratic National Convention. "But for all those whose cares are our concern, the work goes on, the cause endures, the hope still lives, and the dream shall never die."

But if the brother was able to reprise Mozart's music only briefly, the Salieri of this saga could not get it out of his ears. In *The Real War*, published in 1981, Nixon struck yet again at the role Jack Kennedy had played in the death of South Vietnam president Diem. "The most charitable interpretation of the Kennedy Administration's part in this affair is that it greased the skids for Diem's downfall and did nothing to prevent his murder. It was a sordid episode in American foreign policy." And five years later, Nixon renewed the attack with *In the Arena*. America's role in Diem's death proved it was "dangerous to be a friend of the United States." It also made the Vietnam struggle an American war, he said. "When the Kennedy administration destabilized South Vietnam by conspiring in a coup to overthrow the government of South Vietnam, which led to the murder of President Ngo Dinh Diem, the resulting political and military chaos forced the Johnson administration to intervene massively to prevent defeat."

The Kennedy side also stayed alert to opportunity. When Robert Bork was nominated by Ronald Reagan for the Supreme Court in 1987, the man who had been willing to fire Archibald Cox now had to take the consequences. As hearings opened on the nomination, Edward Kennedy soberly listed his charges against the court nominee to the Senate Judiciary Committee, citing especially the former solicitor general's bias toward "presidential power." The allusion to the "Saturday Night Massacre" was unmistakable. With Kennedy fanning the flames, the Judiciary Committee decisively buried the nomination.

With the end of the cold war, marked by the failure of the 1991 Moscow coup, the former president began a strange rapprochement with the ghost of the rival he had bested only by surviving. In a 1992 speech to a Washington crowd packed with old advisers and foreign policy hands, he recalled the historic votes he and Kennedy both had cast for the Greek-Turkish aid bill back in 1947. "It was a very tough vote for two very young and both, as history later indicated, rather ambitious young congressmen." He proudly described that initial stand as one that "not only contained communism but bought the time that was essential for communism to fail."

Nixon was trying to salve the bitterness of his personal struggle by sharing the victory over the common enemy. One rival had dared an ambivalent world to "come to Berlin" and see the difference between the two systems. The other had retorted to Khrushchev's boast that America's "grandchildren will live under communism" with the promise that the Soviet leader's would live "in freedom." In paying tribute to the votes Kennedy and he had cast for the Truman Doctrine, Nixon was trying to rekindle the common purpose and nobility of the global struggle those two young congressmen had seen coming on that long-ago midnight train back from that first debate in Pennsylvania.

In 1992, a young Democratic presidential candidate, Bill Clinton, used as his emblem a 1963 film that showed a moment when he had shaken John F. Kennedy's hand at a White House ceremony for high school students. Less emblematic but more poignant was advice the new Clinton team received from H. R. Haldeman at the funeral of Pat Nixon in 1993. "Tell them not to make the mistakes that we did," the Watergate-era staff chief told a close friend of the newly inaugurated president. Clinton would become the first president to welcome Richard Nixon back to the White House as an adviser.

In one of his last public utterances, Richard Nixon wrote an introduction to a volume of Winston Churchill quotes that he recommended to "aspiring world leaders." It was meant without irony, as if there really were such young men abroad in the land as he and Jack Kennedy.

When John Kennedy's son and namesake passed the New York bar exam, Nixon sent him a message of kind congratulation. "I have endured a few crises in my lifetime," he noted dryly. "I'm sure your father would be very proud of you." And when a close Nixon staffer made a derisive crack about a speech John F. Kennedy, Jr., had delivered, it got him a firm rebuke from a seventy-five-year-old Nixon.

"Don't say that. He's a fine young man." Then, after a pause to reflect, he added a thought. "He shouldn't go into politics."

After suffering a stroke in April 1994, Nixon spent his last days in the same New York hospital where Jacqueline Kennedy lay, undergoing treatment for lymphoma. When he died on April 22, the country showed an appreciation that the deceased could not have expected. "Despite the intensity of the campaign and the narrow outcome," said Ted Kennedy, paying the family's first tribute to Nixon's crucial magnanimity, "he accepted the results with grace and without rancor." Alexander Haig, who had stayed close to Nixon until the end, saved for later the man's own recollection of the legacy of 1960. "He believed until the day he died that Kennedy had stolen the election."

At his death, Nixon made the cover of *Time* for the fifty-sixth time, a record. "By sheer endurance," its editors observed, "he was the most important figure of the post-War era." President Clinton spoke at the grave site at Nixon's boyhood home in Yorba Linda where he had heard that long-ago train whistle in the night. Yet within the month, the Nixon funeral dirge was overtaken by the classic, spritely tones of Mozart. When his rival's widow succumbed to her illness just weeks later, there was a stirring in the national air, a momentary glimpse back to the magic of Camelot.

Today, the Kennedy Center and the Watergate sit beside each other along the Potomac—like unmatched bookends.

AFTERWORD

The
White House Tapes

IN February 1971, Richard Nixon installed a secret recording system in the White House. The tapes, two hundred hours of which were released to the public in November 1996, offer spectacular glimpses into the Kennedy-Nixon rivalry.

By May 1971, Senator Edward M. Kennedy had emerged from political purgatory. With voter memories of Chappaquiddick fading, he was a credible if troubling prospect for the 1972 Democratic presidential nomination. The specter of a Kennedy "restoration" had risen from the dead, and clearly this disturbed Richard Nixon.

On May 5, White House chief of staff H. R. Haldeman tried boosting Nixon's morale. Nixon would enter the 1972 reelection campaign, Haldeman comforted him, armed with a daunting new weapon: billions in federal dollars that could be directed wherever they would do the most good politically. "All of us have talked about . . . if we only had the Kennedys' money, how much fun a campaign would be. We *do* have the Kennedys' money. We have two hundred billion dollars!"

Nixon reminded Haldeman on May 13 how the Kennedys had

used their official power against *him* following JFK's 1960 victory. The president was particularly bitter about what he saw as the Kennedys' use of the IRS to dig into his affairs. "Bob, do you remember when the Kennedys ordered them to go after me and that goddamned house I bought? Huh?" Nixon demanded, referring to a "restrictive covenant" he had signed when purchasing his Washington, D.C., home in 1951. The covenant, which barred resale of the property to blacks or Jews, had caused Nixon some nasty publicity in his 1962 gubernatorial campaign.

The White House tape of May 27 finds Nixon still fixated on the Kennedys and what he viewed as their successful campaign espionage back in 1961. What ripped open the old wound was a report from domestic-policy aide John Ehrlichman that the IRS was demanding tax records from the local Republican party organization in South Carolina.

> NIXON: Did you ever find out? . . . Who ordered the audit of my income taxes in '61? Why don't you find out, John? Find out who was there, who ordered it. It was not routine.

Nixon also wanted evidence that Attorney General Robert Kennedy had ordered FBI chief J. Edgar Hoover to bug his phones.

> NIXON: Do you think we could get from Hoover whether he ever was ordered to put a wiretap . . . ?
> EHRLICHMAN: There's no record of it ever being ordered. He said he would never countenance such a thing and didn't. There is no record of it. I would expect there would not be.
> NIXON: Knowing Bobby Kennedy, I saw that great number of taps when he was in and that's a time of much less national-security problems than now, so why the hell did he do it? *You know goddamned well what he was doing. He was tapping his political enemies.*

The following morning, Nixon instructed Haldeman on the imperative to "go after" one's political enemies. "That's why I want more use of wiretapping. Are we dealing adequately with their candidates, tailing them and so forth?"

HALDEMAN: We're on and off.

NIXON: Well, it shouldn't be on and off. I mean, that's something we can afford. That's better than hiring eighteen more researchers, you know, little boys to go over there and try and figure out what the PR line should be. We can figure that one out. We can't get any information. Why don't you do that? Why don't you put your money on that?

Nixon turns to Ted Kennedy, who now leads the Gallup poll as the most popular Democratic candidate to challenge Nixon's reelection:

NIXON: I don't know whether he's a candidate or ... maybe there's better targets.

HALDEMAN: We've got spot coverage on Teddy, just because we wanted to know what he's doing. We have access on all of them through this guy who moves in and out.

NIXON: Oh, yeah.

HALDEMAN: And we have a pretty good fix on what they're all doing.

But Nixon was not impressed with Haldeman's gumshoe operation. He alerted his chief of staff once again to the key role political espionage had played in his most humiliating defeat, the 1962 campaign for California governor. In that race, Nixon reminded Haldeman, his political enemies had raised political snooping to an art form, exposing details of both his brother Donald's $205,000 loan from Howard Hughes and the embarrassing covenant he had signed on his new Washington, D.C., home.

NIXON: Look! In '62! Best test we ever had. How'd I lose? They had access to every goddamned thing you could imagine. Don! My house! They had every goddamned thing you could imagine. Now that was a clever deal, see? Keep after 'em!

Nixon now worried that an extensive snooping campaign could be traced back to him. He didn't want his political aide Charles Colson to have anything to do with it, and agreed to Haldeman's proposal that the operation be handled through a pair of former New York detectives, one of whom, Jack Caulfield, had been on the Nixon payroll for years.

> NIXON: Who have you got you could put in charge? Not Colson, you understand. Can't do that out of the White House.
> HALDEMAN: We've got a guy we've got outside. I think that's the way to do it.
> NIXON: You have a guy?
> HALDEMAN: Through Colson, I mean, through—
> NIXON: The cop.
> HALDEMAN: Caulfield.
> NIXON: I don't know. Maybe it's the wrong thing to do, but I have a feeling if you're gonna start, you got to start now.
> HALDEMAN: Probably so, before they . . . I think mainly just to . . .
> NIXON: Keep them. They're gonna beat up, you know.
> HALDEMAN: You figure just the three of them?
> NIXON: Oh, yes.
> HALDEMAN: Teddy, Muskie, and McG . . . ?
> NIXON: I don't mean to . . . Maybe we can get a scandal on any, any one of the leading Democrats.
> HALDEMAN: In the general range of Democrats.
> NIXON: Now you're talking.
> HALDEMAN: Just looking for scandal or impropriety or anything.

The following month, the *New York Times* published the Pentagon Papers. Enraged at what he saw as an historic violation of national security, Nixon ordered Bob Haldeman on June 30 to burglarize the Brookings Institution, a liberal Washington think tank he believed was housing other sensitive Vietnam War records.

> NIXON: The way I want that handled, Bob, is . . . just to break in. Break in and take it out! You understand!
> HALDEMAN: But who do we have to do it?
> NIXON: Well, don't discuss it here. You talk to . . . You're to break into the place, rifle the files, and bring me—

HALDEMAN: I don't have any problem breaking in. This isn't a domestic. This isn't a foreign, approved security . . .

NIXON: Just go in and take it. Go in around eight or nine o'clock and clean it up.

Nixon shifted strategy on July 6. Instead of protecting government secrets, he wanted his staff to release as many old government documents as they could placing blame for the Vietnam War on his Democratic predecessors.

NIXON: We've got to keep Vietnam as an issue. We've got to pin the whole Johnson-Kennedy . . . on these factors. We have to start getting out stuff. It ruins 'em.

HALDEMAN: We've got to get the papers out before our second term is over.

NIXON: You see why.

HALDEMAN: It'll all disappear.

NIXON: What the hell do you think they'd be doing to us?

On July 27, Nixon told Haldeman that he wanted to see the Kennedy and Johnson documents "personally." He was interested most in those related to Kennedy's role in the Bay of Pigs and the Johnson-ordered "bombing pause" on the eve of the 1968 presidential election. "I want to get those documents. I'm supposed to have access to them. I want to see it in my files."

Nevertheless, the White House was still facing resistance on September 8 from CIA director Richard Helms, especially in extracting agency files on what had become Nixon's pet project, the Bay of Pigs.

EHRLICHMAN: We're running into a little problem. I'm talking to Helms about getting some documents the CIA has about the Bay of Pigs, things like that, which they would rather not see out. It's a challenge. It's going to be hard.

NIXON: They are very sensitive about that.

ERHLICHMAN: Helms especially. Allen Dulles was the head but Helms was the operating. So Helms knows everything about it.

Nixon was now fighting a two-front war, against the legacy of Jack Kennedy and the prospect of a tough reelection fight, perhaps against another Kennedy, in 1972. On the same day he conspired with Ehrlichman to obtain the Bay of Pigs files, he also told Ehrlichman to target top Democratic contributors for tax audits.

NIXON: John, we have the power. Are we using it now to investigate contributors to Hubert Humphrey, contributors to Muskie? Are we looking into Muskie's returns? Does he have any? Hubert's? Hubert's been in a lot of deals. Teddy? Who knows about the Kennedys? Shouldn't they be investigated?

EHRLICHMAN: IRS-wise, I don't know the answer. Teddy we are covering personally. When he moves on holidays. When he stopped in Hawaii on the way back from Pakistan.

NIXON: Did he do anything?

EHRLICHMAN: He was very clean. Very clean. He's very careful now. He was staying at some guy's villa and [we] had a guy on him. He was just as nice as he could be the whole time.

NIXON: The thing to do is to watch him because what happens to fellows like that, who have that kind of problem, is that they go for quite a while and—

EHRLICHMAN: That's what I'm hoping. This time, between now and convention time, may be the time period.

NIXON: You mean he'd be under great pressure?

EHRLICHMAN: The added pressure. He would also be out of the limelight. Now he was in Hawaii very much incognito, and played tennis, fooled around, visited with people, and socialized and stuff. So you would expect at a time like that that you would catch him.

Erhlichman mentioned his recent visit to Martha's Vineyard and Cape Cod. This raised the issue of Chappaquiddick.

NIXON: He will never live that down. I don't think he will. No, not that one.

EHRLICHMAN: I think it'll be around his neck forever.

NIXON: It's not like a divorce [where] most people will forget it.

EHRLICHMAN: This has a geographic identity. They tell me that business on the ferry has tripled since the accident. It's getting into the folklore.

On October 14, Nixon's men can be heard giggling over a plan to mass-produce posters showing Ted Kennedy's face over the caption: "WOULD YOU RIDE IN A CAR WITH THIS MAN?" Colson pointed to the irony. "You know how they hurt you, tried to hurt you with, 'Would you buy a used car from this man?' Well, would you ride in a car . . . ?"

Two weeks later, Nixon was delighted when on October 30 a British newspaper published an embarrassing cartoon of Kennedy. He told Colson to mail it to "every member of the Senate." A few days later, he escalated the plan. "I think that should have a circulation of about a *quarter million,*" he ordered Colson. He wanted the anti-Kennedy cartoon mailed from a New York address where it could not be traced to the White House "to every member of Congress, senator, governor . . . Democrat or Republican . . . editors . . . society pages."

When Nixon asked Colson on November 10 to tell him "what's new on the political front," the senator from Massachusetts was again Topic A. "I think the Kennedy thing has me fascinated the most, the way in which he's trying in every way to step to the front." Colson described a conversation with Teamster boss Frank Fitzsimmons in which the labor leader promised to share "all he knows about Kennedy" if the Nixon people would send an investigator out to Las Vegas to collect the material. "Put the investigator out there," Nixon ordered Colson.

On June 17, 1972, Colson's "plumbers" executed their historic break-in of the Democratic National Committee headquarters at the Watergate office-and-apartment complex. On July 1, Nixon suggested that Colson organize a parallel break-in of the Republican National Committee headquarters, thereby creating the public impression of a partisan tit for tat. This, he said, would put Senator Robert Dole, the Republican party chairman, in an ideal position to sue the Democrats just as Democratic chairman Lawrence O'Brien was suing the Republicans.

NIXON: What would you think if that happened?

COLSON: I think it would be very helpful if they came in one morning and found files strewn all over the place.

NIXON: And some missing. I mean something could be very open, I mean demolished. Three or four thousand dollars' worth of damage.

COLSON: That would have a very good effect.

NIXON: Right there in their convention.

COLSON: During theirs? During ours.

NIXON: Theirs. Next week.

COLSON: And then Dole is in a perfect position to say . . .

NIXON: Sue . . . sue the Committee. I'd sue 'em. But what I meant is . . . it should be . . . where it's really torn up.

Later that same day, Nixon told Colson his reasons for wanting to get the Watergate story behind them. "I don't want the impression of this Big Brother in the White House, the president ordering, you know, bugging and snooping and the rest. *Goddamned Kennedy did it all the time.* Bobby Kennedy did a record number."

On September 7, Nixon approved an additional snooping campaign against Ted Kennedy, who was about to commence nationwide campaigning for the Democratic ticket. Worried that Kennedy would emerge from the 1972 election as his party's savior, Nixon ordered that agents who would report back on any misconduct be assigned to Kennedy's bodyguard. "Plant one, plant two guys on him. This could be very useful. We just might be lucky and catch this son of a bitch. Ruin him in '76. He doesn't know what he's really getting into. We're going to cover him, and we're not going to take 'no' for an answer. He can't say 'no' to the Secret Service."

The next day, Nixon talked with Ehrlichman about the political fallout from Watergate. "I'd a helluva lot rather have them talking about this than the fact we're the party of the rich and that prices are high. This story is not helpful but, *to the average guy, whether the Republicans bugged the Democrats doesn't mean a goddamned thing.* It means something to intellectuals. It means something to people who are concerned about repression and credibility and all that bullshit. But the average guy is chewing his pretzel. He's interested in jobs. He's interested in war and peace and defense and patriotism and that's about it . . . a little bit on the social issues."

But Democratic efforts to exploit Watergate, including those by Senator Kennedy's Judiciary subcommittee, had Nixon's men worried. "They're going to try to haul the thing up publicly,"

Haldeman reported on September 11. Nixon also worried that, thanks to the upcoming elections, the majority Democrats would retain the power to subpoena witnesses and demand government documents. "You see these committees. It shows you how important it is to win the Congress. You win Congress, you take control of the committees."

On January 3, 1973, swearing-in day on Capitol Hill, Haldeman wondered aloud how far the Democrats would go in probing Watergate: "There's supposedly some question of what the Congress is going to do still. Indications are that the Kennedy staff have faded away in their activity. It may just all go away, you know."

But Haldeman's boss was wondering how the whole calamity could have happened in the first place. "I can see Mitchell. I can't see Colson getting to the Democratic . . . What the Christ was he looking for?"

HALDEMAN: They were looking for stuff on two things: one on financial stuff and the other on what they thought they [the Democrats] were going to do in Miami [site of the Republican convention] to screw up, which apparently was a Democratic plot, and they thought they had it uncovered. Colson was salivating with glee at what they might be able to do with it.

NIXON: You mean Colson was *aware* of the Watergate bugging? That's hard for me to believe.

HALDEMAN: Not only was he aware of it, he was pushing very hard for results from it and very specifically that.

NIXON: Who was he pushing?

HALDEMAN: Magruder and Liddy.

NIXON: Colson was pushing Magruder? Was that what it was? And Liddy?

HALDEMAN: It gets down to undeniable specifics—times of meeting, with times and places and that sort of thing. And the other one, of course, on Teddy.

NIXON: The question was whether he was pushing to get information or pushing to get information from *bugging.*

HALDEMAN: This here is very specific. He was on that particular—

NIXON: Venture.

HALDEMAN: —and the other one, I guess, on Teddy.

NIXON: You mean the tail on him and that sort of thing?

HALDEMAN: Apparently they tried—I don't know the details. They tried or did bug him, too, in his operation or something. But the tail was something else.

NIXON: I see.

Notes

Students
Page
23 As a seventeen-year-old senior: the account of the "Muckers" club is drawn primarily from Nigel Hamilton, *JFK Reckless Youth* (New York: Random House, 1992), pp. 122–32.

24 From his first run for Congress: the case that Jack Kennedy was primarily loyal to the "Kennedy party" is made by Thomas P. O'Neill, Jr., *Man of the House* (New York: Random House, 1987), p. 76.

24 Arriving at California's Whittier College: the account of the "Orthogonians" is drawn primarily from Stephen E. Ambrose, *Nixon: The Education of a Politician 1913–1962* (New York: Simon & Schuster, 1987), pp. 59–64.

24 "tuxedo boys": Robert Farnham Oral History, California State University, Fullerton, p. 18.

Chapter 1: World War II Was Their Greatest Campaign Manager

27 "Operation Titanic": account of Kennedy covering San Francisco conference drawn primarily from Hamilton, *JFK Reckless Youth*, p. 694.

28 "I give him about two more minutes": Paul B. Fay, Jr., int.

28 "That's pretty much the way it was": Charles Spalding int.

28 "Americans can now see": Hearst Newspapers, May 4, 1945.

28 The Hearst reporter: Herbert S. Parmet, *Jack: The Struggles of John F. Kennedy* (New York: Dial Press, 1980), p. 131.

29 "He had this attractive gal": Fay int.

29 his father had persuaded: Joseph Kennedy used former Boston police chief Joseph Timulty as his go-between, Hamilton, *JFK Reckless Youth*, p. 674.

29 The archdiocese of Boston got a check for $600,000: Doris Kearns Goodwin, *The Fitzgeralds and the Kennedys* (New York: Simon & Schuster, 1987), p. 720.

29 The $10,000 gift to the Guild of Appolonia: Hamilton, *JFK Reckless Youth*, p. 686.

30 Sgt. Billy Sutton was the first aboard: Billy Sutton int.; account of '46 Kennedy campaign primarily drawn from Parmet, *Jack*, and Hamilton, *JFK Reckless Youth*.

30 He had missed the deadline for filing his petitions: account of Kennedy's after-hours entry of statehouse in Paul B. Fay, Jr., *The Pleasure of His Company* (New York: Harper & Row, 1966), p. 147.

30 Instead of becoming angry at Russo: former police chief Timulty approached the second Russo with the offer. *Boston Magazine*, June 1993.

31 "Joe Kennedy called my dad": Robert Neville int.

31 For the last sixty days: O'Neill, *Man of the House*, p. 76.

31 "The Kennedy strategy was to buy you out or blast you out": Hamilton, *JFK Reckless Youth*, p. 755.

31 A fellow worked for the party: history of "snow button," Thomas P. O'Neill, Jr., int.

31 "I couldn't believe this skinny, pasty-faced kid": O'Neill, *Man of the House*, p. 73.

31 "He wasn't looking healthy then": Sutton int.

31 "a skeleton": Mark Dalton int.

32 "If you agreed to invite a few friends": O'Neill, *Man of the House*, p. 77.

32 "Kennedy buttons": Thomas Reeves, *A Question of Character* (New York: Free Press, 1991), pp. 81–82.

32 "I do seem to be the only one here": Peter Collier and David Horowitz, *The Kennedys—An American Drama* (New York: Summit Books, 1984), p. 153.

33 "I would like to drink a toast to the brother who isn't here": Dalton int.

33 a pickpocket had gotten to his wallet: Jonathan Aitken, *Nixon: A Life* (London: Weidenfeld and Nicolson, 1993), p. 112.

34 "an aggressive, vigorous campaign": Stephen E. Ambrose, *Nixon*, p. 118; Ambrose book served as primary source on Nixon '46 race.

35 Too excited to go back to sleep: Julie Nixon Eisenhower, *Pat Nixon, The Untold Story* (New York: Zebra Books, 1986), p. 122.

35 "I say to you in all sincerity": Garry Wills, *Nixon Agonistes* (New York: New American Library, 1969), p. 82.

36 "Now that the Political Action Committee": Ambrose, *Nixon*, p. 129.

37 "I believe the Communists are in substantial control of CIO": Roger Morris, *Richard Milhous Nixon: The Rise of an American Politician* (New York: Henry Holt & Company, 1990), p. 293. Account of "PAC" issue in '46 campaign drawn primarily from Morris.

39 "This is a friend of yours": Morris, *Richard Milhous Nixon*, p. 332.

40 "Mr. Roosevelt has contributed to the end of capitalism": John F. Kennedy, *Prelude to Leadership: The European Diary of John F. Kennedy —Summer, 1945* (Washington, D.C.: Regnery Publishing, 1995), p. 10.

40 "I told them": Hamilton, *JFK Reckless Youth*, pp. 787–88.

41 "Son of Kennedy Congress Winner": *Los Angeles Times*, November 6, 1946.

CHAPTER 2: STRANGERS ON A TRAIN

43 He and Pat drove cross-country: Morris, *Richard Milhous Nixon*, p. 339.

43 a U.S. border guard insisted: Eisenhower, *Pat Nixon*, p. 133.

43 "same lost feeling": Ambrose, *Nixon*, p. 143.

44 Billy Sutton: Billy Sutton, Oral History, John F. Kennedy Library; account of Kennedy's behavior the morning of swearing in comes from Sutton.

45 "there was this fellow over in the corner": Sutton int.; account of first Kennedy-Nixon meeting comes from Sutton.

45 "By one of those curious coincidences of history": Richard M. Nixon, *RN—The Memories of Richard Nixon* (New York: Simon & Schuster, 1978), p. 42.

47 Back in Washington: Ambrose, *Nixon*, pp. 146–47.

48 One was the young State Department whiz kid: Allen Weinstein, *Perjury—The Hiss-Chambers Case* (New York: Alfred A. Knopf, 1978), pp. 7–8.

48 The day after Truman spoke: Parmet, *Jack*, pp. 176–78.

49 "I was elected to smash the labor bosses": Morris, *Richard Milhous Nixon*, p. 343.

50 "fighting conservative": Hamilton, *JFK Reckless Youth*, p. 773.

50 "John wanted to know": Dalton int.

50 "Listen to this fellow": Dalton int.

51 "The public was satisfied with labor laws": *McKeesport Daily News*, April 25, 1947.

51 the jeers from the labor seats grew so bellicose: *McKeesport Daily News*, April 17, 1947.

51 "The way some of those provisions read": *McKeesport Daily News*, April 25, 1947.

52 "Kennedy was smooth and genteel": *McKeesport Daily News*, July 21, 1960.

52 Nixon was "going to go places": *McKeesport Daily News*, July 21, 1960.

52 "It was hard to tell who had come from the wealthy family": *McKeesport Daily News*, July 21, 1960.

52 "young fellows whom you could like": *McKeesport Daily News*, July 21, 1960.

52 "genuine friendliness": Eric F. Goldman, *Saturday Review*, October 16, 1976, pp. 12–13.

52 Bernard Baruch had just christened the "cold war": William Manchester, *The Glory and the Dream: A Narrative History of America, 1932–1972* (Boston: Little, Brown, 1973), p. 436.

52 Jack Kennedy went Red hunting: account comes from Parmet, *Jack*, pp. 178–82.
54 "I think his whole life ambition in foreign policy started": Herb Klein int.
55 his Massachusetts friend: Aitken, *Nixon*, p. 136.

CHAPTER 3: WHILE KENNEDY SLEPT
56 "one of a row of identical duplexes": Eisenhower, *Pat Nixon*, p. 134.
56 "Thinking about girls is what kept Jack alive": Sutton int.
57 "Emaciated": George Smathers int.
57 "You'll just have to work a little harder": Parmet, *Jack*, p. 166.
58 "I'm coming to your district": Smathers int.
58 "Nixon was always supplying us with the red meat": George Reedy int.
59 "Mr. Nixon was always a restless soul": Bill Arnold, *Back When It All Began: The Early Nixon Years* (New York: Vantage Press, 1975), p. 21.
60 On August 3, 1948: account of Hiss case drawn from Ambrose, *Nixon*, pp. 169–72, and Allen Weinstein, *Perjury*, pp. 5–7.
61 "I understand yours was Whittier": Aitken, *Nixon*, p. 165.
61 "Nixon had a transcript of the Hiss testimony": Reedy int.
62 "If the American people understood the real character of Alger Hiss": Whittaker Chambers, *Witness*, as quoted in *Time*, August 25, 1952.
64 "None of us wanted him to be guilty": Reedy int.
64 "I'm going to debate Norman Thomas": Dalton int.
65 "I'm going to dig into this thing": Timothy J. "Ted" Reardon int.

CHAPTER 4: THE CASTLE OR THE OUTHOUSE!
66 Quietly, he sought the advance backing of the *Los Angeles Times*: Ambrose, *Nixon*, p. 199.
66 the California congressman called for the appointment of a "special prosecutor": Ambrose, *Nixon*, p. 201.
67 "The responsibility for the failure of our foreign policy": *Congressional Record*, January 29, 1949.
67 secret lover of that rising Texas star Sen. Lyndon Johnson: Joseph A. Califano, Jr., *The Triumph and Tragedy of Lyndon Johnson* (New York: Simon & Schuster, 1991), p. 337.
69 "cheap gimmick": Ambrose, *Nixon*, p. 209.
69 "Tell Nicky to get on this thing!": Earl Mazo, *Nixon, A Political and Personal Portrait* (New York: Harper & Brothers, 1959), p. 74.
70 "Do me a favor": Smathers int.
70 "I will never forget the feeling of revulsion": Claude Pepper int.
70 One day that summer: Arnold, *Back When It All Began*, p. 14. O'Neill, *Man of the House*, p. 81. A March 3, 1960, note from Rose Mary Woods to Vice President Nixon confirms Kennedy's visit and campaign contribution, also Nixon's "flabbergasted" reaction.

71 In an internal White House directive: report by Secretaries of State and Defense—April 12, 1950.

71 Nixon's own campaign: Ron Walker int.

72 A student at the University of California at Santa Barbara named Richard Tuck: *Los Angeles Times,* January 31, 1990.

73 "Why, I'll castrate her": Arnold, *Back When It All Began,* p. 13.

73 Just before the election: account of Nixon-Warren episode drawn from Ambrose, *Nixon,* p. 219.

74 One Democrat remained in Dick Nixon's corner: John P. Mallan, "Massachusetts: Liberal and Corrupt," *New Republic,* October 13, 1952, pp. 10–11.

74 Kennedy repeated the judgment: Fay int.

74 To give California's: Ambrose, *Nixon,* pp. 237–38; Nixon's own dramatic account of episode can be found in Robert Sam Anson, *Exile: The Unquiet Oblivion of Richard M. Nixon* (New York: Simon & Schuster, 1984), p. 219.

75 The Wisconsin senator "may have something": Mallan, *New Republic,* October 13, 1952, pp. 10–11.

75 In February 1952: Parmet, *Jack,* p. 245.

75 "The political point of the Kennedy speech": *Haverhill* (Mass.) *Gazette,* August 21, 1950.

76 "I'm going to run!": Smathers int.

76 "I'm not going to stay in the House": Lawrence O'Brien, *No Final Victories* (New York: Doubleday, 1974), p. 17.

76 "For the Kennedys, it's either the castle": Jack Newfield, *Robert Kennedy* (New York: E. P. Dutton & Co., 1969), p. 42.

77 Henry Cabot Lodge: account of Lodge's masterful engineering of the Eisenhower presidential campaign drawn from Herbert Parmet, *Eisenhower and the American Crusade* (New York: Macmillan, 1972), pp. 46–56.

79 Back in Washington: Kennedy letter obtained from Richard M. Nixon Library and Birthplace.

79 Three hundred Capitol Hill news correspondents: United Press story ran in *Boston Globe,* June 2, 1952.

79 He first heard the news: *Boston Globe,* July 2, 1952.

CHAPTER 5: CLOTH COATS AND LACE CURTAINS

82 "I am in your corner 100 percent": James Cannon, *Time and Change* (New York: HarperCollins, 1994), p. 61.

82 "There comes a time": Tom Wicker, *One of Us,* p. 93.

83 "Dick was sitting": Wicker, *One of Us,* p. 89.

83 But the final blow was still to come: account of "Checkers" drawn primarily from Ambrose, *Nixon,* pp. 276–92.

84 For several minutes: Hillings int.

85 Riding back to the hotel: Patrick J. Hillings, *Pat Hillings*, published by Howard D. Dean, 1993, p. 61.
86 In the same weeks: Dalton int.
87 "In all my years of public life": O'Neill, *Man of the House*, p. 87.
87 His father had to "buy a fuckin' newspaper": Parmet, *Jack*, p. 511.
87 The one man: William F. Buckley, Jr., *Boston Sunday Globe*, September 30, 1962.
88 The Kennedy campaign: Parmet, *Jack*, p. 250.
88 Their son's sex appeal was such a tremendous asset: Robert Griffin int.
88 But Tip O'Neill recalled: O'Neill, *Man of the House*, p. 88.
88 If Dick Nixon: Eisenhower, *Pat Nixon*, p. 188.

CHAPTER 6: HALL MATES
90 "It was a busy corridor": Evelyn Lincoln, notes written for author, July 20, 1993.
91 "We had a very nice relationship": Evelyn Lincoln int.
91 "I have known Senator Kennedy for a number of years as a personal friend": letter courtesy of Richard M. Nixon Library and Birthplace.
92 "Jack had the ability": Reardon int.
92 "If you work for a politician": O'Brien, *No Final Victories*, p. 39.
93 "I gave everything a good deal of thought": Fay, *The Pleasure of His Company*, p. 160.
93 He managed to keep secret his engagement: Kenneth P. O'Donnell and Dave F. Powers, *"Johnny, We Hardly Knew Ye"* (Boston: Little, Brown, 1970), p. 95.
93 "That would be a helluva place": quoted in Thomas C. Reeves, *A Question of Character*, p. 114.
94 "If we do not stand firm": quoted in Parmet, *Jack*, p. 276.
94 Ho Chi Minh: Aitken, *Nixon*, p. 227.
95 He backed a secret plan: Wicker, *One of Us*, p. 146.
95 "We simply cannot afford further losses in Asia": *Des Moines Register*, April 22, 1954.
95 "To pour money, material and men into the jungles": quoted in Cross, *JFK—A Hidden Life* (Boston: Charles E. Tuttle, 1992), p. 68.
95 "What Indo-China proves": *U.S. News & World Report*, 1954.
95 "Vietnam represents the cornerstone": Richard Reeves, *President Kennedy—Profile of Power* (New York: Simon & Schuster, 1993), p. 254.
95 He became a founding member of the Friends of Vietnam: Reeves, *President Kennedy*, p. 254.
96 "I resented being constantly vilified": quoted in Aitken, *Nixon*, p. 233.
96 Tormented, he had already made several trips: Aitken, *Nixon*, p. 196.
98 "We used to ride home together": Reardon int.
98 "He was always talking about dying": Smathers int.
98 "At least half": John H. Davis, *The Kennedys—Dynasty or Disaster* (New York: McGraw-Hill, 1984), p. 137.

98 "Please call the vice president's office": Evelyn Lincoln notes.

99 "The doctors did not expect": Lincoln notes.

99 "That poor young man": Aitken, *Nixon*, p. 137; conversation with Rex Scouten.

99 "The doctors don't understand": Lincoln notes.

99 "I'm the new night nurse": C. David Heymann, *A Woman Named Jackie* (New York: Lyle Stuart, Carol Communications, 1989), p. 171.

99 "You know when I get downstairs": Parmet, *Jack*, p. 310.

100 "They're not queer at State": Collier and Horowitz, *The Kennedys*, p. 264.

100 "I'd be very happy to tell them": Parmet, *Jack*, p. 171.

100 "One thing about Nixon, God bless him": Reardon int.

100 To take the pressure off Kennedy: Sorensen int.

100 "Dear Mr. Vice President": letters courtesy of Richard M. Nixon Library and Birthplace.

101 "It made Jack feel very good": Reardon int.

102 When a Senate page: Martin Dowd int.

102 Greeting the Massachusetts senator: Parmet, *Jack*, p. 315; Reardon int.

CHAPTER 7: PROFILES IN AMBITION

103 In June 1954: Richard Nixon, *Leaders* (New York: Warner Books, 1982), pp. 7–9.

103 "I think he thought": Heymann, *A Woman Named Jackie*, p. 178.

104 Privately, he kept turning the screws: Ambrose, *Nixon*, p. 388.

105 Robert Kennedy, now chief counsel: Collier and Horowitz, *The Kennedys*, p. 218.

105 Called to testify: Herbert Parmet, *Richard Nixon and His America* (Boston: Little, Brown, 1990), p. 271.

105 However, committee chairman John McClellan: Collier and Horowitz, *The Kennedys*, p. 218.

105 Former House colleague Gerald Ford: Gerald Ford int.

106 "Where else, in a non-totalitarian country, but in the political profession": John F. Kennedy, *Profiles in Courage* (New York: Harper & Brothers, 1956), p. 7.

106 "We've got the Pulitzer": Evan Thomas, Jr., int.

106 "Dear Jack": letter courtesy of Richard M. Nixon Library and Birthplace.

107 William "Onions" Burke: account of the "Onions" Burke episode drawn from Parmet, *Jack*, pp. 347–51, 354.

107 "Anybody who's for Stevenson": quoted in O'Donnell and Powers, *"Johnny, We Hardly Knew Ye,"* p. 109.

108 Ted Sorensen prepared: Parmet, *Jack*, p. 359.

109 "two tough candidates": quoted in Parmet, *Jack*, p. 372.

110 "George, old pal": Smathers int.

111 "The senator was convinced": O'Donnell and Powers, *"Johnny, We Hardly Knew Ye,"* p. 123.

111 "If we have to have a Catholic": quoted in Parmet, *Jack*, p. 362.

111 One moment: *Time*, August 27, 1956.

111 "I've learned": O'Donnell and Powers, *"Johnny, We Hardly Knew Ye,"* p. 126.

112 "Our nation stands": *New York Times*, November 6, 1956.

CHAPTER 8: TWO MEN ON THIRD

114 "Give me some reasons": Robert Choate letter courtesy of Princeton University Library.

115 "I am quite confident": Robert Choate letter courtesy of Princeton University Library.

115 Rose Kennedy: Lawrence Leamer, *The Kennedy Women* (New York: Villard Books, 1994), p. 467.

115 "Sue the bastards!": Clark Clifford int.

116 "He had the publicity": Hubert Humphrey, John F. Kennedy Library oral history.

117 "Kennedy has been regarded": *Winchester Evening Star*, February 15, 1957.

117 "Once he started in 1956": Smathers int.

119 "He never said a word of importance": Robert Dallek, *Lone Star Rising: Lyndon Johnson and His Times* (New York: Oxford University Press, 1991), p. 555.

119 "I might have used a Latin phrase": Charles Colson int.

120 "I always had a feeling": Charles Bartlett int.

121 "a vote against the right to vote": Taylor Branch, *Parting the Waters* (New York: Simon & Schuster, 1988), p. 221.

121 "Their doors were opposite each other": Bob Thompson int.

122 "Parents are always special people": letter courtesy of Richard M. Nixon Library and Birthplace.

122 "Welcome to the Father-Daughter club": telegram courtesy of Richard M. Nixon Library and Birthplace.

122 Using Smathers: Ambrose, *Nixon*, p. 494.

122 Despite a growing possibility: Dave Powers int.

123 "that didn't mean": Lincoln int.

123 One fall day: Joan Gardner int.

123 Kennedy told: *New York Times Magazine*, July 1958.

123 "Nixon is a nice fellow in private": Ralph Martin, *A Hero for Our Time* (New York: Macmillan, 1983), p. 221.

124 "When Mr. Eisenhower talks": Associated Press, October 15, 1959.

126 "strongest possible": *Time*, July 18, 1960, p. 10.

127 Tip O'Neill would recall: Paul Clancy and Shirley Elder, *Tip: A Biography of Thomas P. O'Neill, Speaker of the House* (New York: Macmillan, 1980), p. 139; conversations with O'Neill.

128 A *Washington Post* editorial cartoon: *New York World Telegram & Sun*, August 15, 1959.

128 "Before the 1960 Kennedy-Nixon debates": Benjamin C. Bradlee, *Conversations with Kennedy* (New York: W. W. Norton, 1975), p. 32.

128 Longtime journalist: Bartlett int.

128 "You think I'm out here": Thomas Reeves, A *Question of Character*, p. 159.

129 "You could go to the A & P store": Hubert Humphrey, JFK Library oral history.

129 "I believe to this day": Louis Harris int.

131 Franklin Roosevelt, Jr.: Robin Cross, *JFK: A Hidden Life*, (Boston: Little, Brown, 1992), p. 90.

131 "They went through West Virginia": Charles McWhorter int.

131 After trying another theater: Bradlee, *Conversations with Kennedy*, p. 17.

CHAPTER 9: KENNEDY VERSUS NIXON

133 Pat Hillings: Hillings int.

133 "It was the goddamndest thing": Cross, *JFK*, p. 78.

136 "Our next president": quoted from Freedom of Information, Senate Commerce Committee, Government Printing Office. All Nixon campaign speeches taken from this source.

137 Appearing on the *Jack Paar Show*: Freedom of Information, Senate Commerce Committee, Government Printing Office. All Kennedy and Nixon campaign statements, as well as their debates, taken from this source.

138 "The case that there": Eric Sevareid, *Boston Globe*.

138 "If I have to": O'Donnell and Powers, *"Johnny, We Hardly Knew Ye,"* p. 201.

138 Manhattan fashion: Robert Lacey, *Grace* (New York: G. P. Putnam's Sons, 1994), p. 204.

138 he had been coached: Reeves, *President Kennedy*, p. 41.

138 One campaign worker: Fred Dutton int.

139 Billy Sutton: Sutton int.

139 "I wonder where Dick Nixon is": Powers int.

139 Western Union Telegram: telegram courtesy of Richard Nixon Library and Birthplace.

140 To: The Hon John F Kennedy: courtesy of Richard Nixon Library and Birthplace.

140 Lou Harris: Harris int.

142 Robert S. Strauss: Robert Strauss int.

143 "He's eating them blood-raw!": O'Donnell and Powers, *"Johnny We Hardly Knew Ye,"* p. 210.

CHAPTER 10: THE GREAT DEBATE
145 Kennedy was already moving: Don Hewitt int.
145 Lou Harris: Harris int.
145 headed by Prof. Archibald Cox: Richard N. Goodwin, *Remembering America* (Boston: Little, Brown, 1988), p. 113.
146 "I will never forget": Harris int.
146 "he came out": Harris int.
146 "He was upset": Robert Finch int.
147 "We kept pushing": Finch int.
147 "Erase the *assassin* image!": Theodore White, *The Making of the President—1960* (New York: Atheneum, 1961), p. 285.
148 "He was in the right seat": Herb Klein int.
148 "He and I": Hewitt int.
148 "He looked like a young Adonis": Hewitt int.
149 "Do you want some makeup?": Hewitt int.
149 he discarded his long reliance: Ambrose, *Nixon*, p. 430.
149 Herb Klein: Klein int.
149 Lawrence O'Brien: O'Brien, *No Final Victories*, p. 93.
150 "I couldn't believe": Finch int.
153 Lyndon Johnson: Reeves, *A Question of Character*, p. 195.
155 "Right after": Harris int.
155 "That son": Fawn Brodie, *Richard Nixon* (Cambridge, Mass.: Harvard University Press, 1983), p. 427.
155 an apparent Nixon booster: *Los Angeles Times*, January 30, 1990.
156 For the rest of his life: Klein int.

CHAPTER 11: BEARING ANY BURDEN
159 Newsman John Harter: John Harter int.
164 Nixon sent a memo: Ambrose, *Nixon*, p. 550.
164 Bissell struck up a relationship: Harris int.
165 "Of course": Goodwin, *Remembering America*, p. 75.
165 "Are they falling dead": Ambrose, *Nixon*, p. 550.
165 Lou Harris was pushing: Harris int.
167 the vice president exploded: Ambrose, *Nixon*, p. 502.
167 Gov. John Patterson: Gerald S. and Deborah Strober, *Let Us Begin: An Oral History of the Kennedy Presidency* (New York: HarperCollins, 1993), p. 326.

CHAPTER 12: THE VERDICT
171 Mrs. King: Harris Wofford, *Of Kennedys and Kings* (Pittsburgh: University of Pittsburgh Press, 1980), p. 16.
172 Nixon now feared: Klein int.
172 Jackie Robinson tried: Wicker, *One of Us*, p. 238.
172 "I had expected": Wofford, *Of Kennedys and Kings*, p. 23.
173 they found a pair: Wofford, *Of Kennedys and Kings*, p. 24.

173 "I earnestly and sincerely feel": Wofford, *Of Kennedys and Kings*, p. 24.

173 "I'm going to do": Wicker, *One of Us*, p. 242.

174 "Goddammit": Wicker, *One of Us*, p. 242.

174 "he had stood": Hillings int.

175 "Now I've heard complaints": quoted in Wicker, *One of Us*, p. 244.

175 "Unlike a lot of Republicans": O'Donnell and Powers, *"Johnny, We Hardly Knew Ye,"* p. 216.

175 "Last week Dick Nixon": Fay, *The Pleasure of His Company*, p. 60.

177 "I knew Kennedy too well": Eisenhower, *Pat Nixon*, p. 290.

177 "He's a filthy": Goodwin, *Remembering America*, p. 105.

178 One Nixon aide: Bryce Harlow quoted in Wicker, *One of Us*, p. 248.

178 After a weak attempt: Ambrose, *Nixon*, p. 601.

178 "help of a few close friends": Bradlee, *Conversations with Kennedy*, p. 33.

178 One Chicago voter: Earl Mazo, *New York Herald Tribune*, December 5, 1960.

179 "Why don't you": O'Brien, *No Final Victories*, p. 96.

179 "I want to repeat": telegram courtesy of Richard M. Nixon Library and Birthplace.

179 "Your sincere good wishes": telegram courtesy of Richard M. Nixon Library and Birthplace.

179 "He went out": Reeves, *A Question of Character*, p. 214.

CHAPTER 13: IF

181 They had enough reports: Finch int.

182 "We had enough evidence": Finch int.

182 urged the *Herald Tribune*'s: Earl Mazo int.

182 "I had been through": Nixon, *RN*, p. 225.

183 "Nixon was": Klein int.

184 "Hello, Chief!": account drawn from Richard M. Nixon, *Six Crises* (New York: Simon & Schuster, 1962), p. 404.

184 "It was the difference": Klein int.

184 "He was very, very chatty": Klein int.

185 "if it won't interfere": Nixon, *Six Crises*, p. 405.

185 "Well, it's hard": Nixon, *Six Crises*, p. 407.

186 "My only regret": form letter courtesy of Richard M. Nixon Library and Birthplace.

187 "Jack, if": Reeves, *President Kennedy*, p. 25.

187 "Kennedy has done": *Time*, November 16, 1960.

188 "This is the first": *Time*, January 13, 1961.

189 Eisenhower regarded: Clark Clifford int.

191 "No one noticed": Nixon, *RN*, p. 227.

CHAPTER 14: BAY OF PIGS

192 Though he joked: Martin, *A Hero for Our Time*, p. 389.

192 "Wait till I'm ready": George Tames int.

193 Robert Kennedy: *New York Times*, January 24, 1972.
193 At one point: Philip Kaiser, *Journeying Far and Wide: A Political and Diplomatic Mission* (New York: Macmillan Books, 1992), p. 186.
193 "Defeat Communist insurgency": Reeves, *President Kennedy*, p. 50.
194 Hoping to reverse: Reeves, *President Kennedy*, p. 51.
194 RNC hired: Stephen Hess int.
195 "I traveled": Robert Finch int.
195 "The State Department": Collier and Horowitz, *The Kennedys*, p. 264.
195 CIA efforts: Evan Thomas, *The Very Best Men: Four Who Dared the Early Years of the CIA* (New York: Simon & Schuster, 1995), pp. 226–29.
196 "It was on": E. Howard Hunt, *Undercover—Memoirs of a Secret Agent* (New York: G. P. Putnam's Sons, 1974), p. 130.
197 With fifteen hundred exiles: Reeves, *President Kennedy*, p. 91.
197 "All my life": Theodore Sorensen, *Kennedy* (New York: Harper & Row, 1965), p. 309.
197 He'd been "given to believe": Thomas, *The Very Best Men*, p. 396.
198 "I certainly would": Nixon, *RN*, p. 233.
198 "JFK called": Nixon, *RN*, p. 233.
198 "I was assured": account of meeting drawn from Nixon, *RN*, p. 234.
199 Flattered by Kennedy's rare: Wills, *Nixon Agonistes*, p. 40.
200 "Bobby is a wild man": Reeves, *President Kennedy*, p. 265.
200 "Get off your": Reeves, *President Kennedy*, p. 263.
202 "Pat, what": Hillings, *Pat Hillings*, pp. 89–90.
203 Ted Sorensen: Sorensen int.
204 "Why is he running?": O'Donnell and Powers, *"Johnny, We Hardly Knew Ye,"* p. 345.
204 "The important thing": Hess int.
204 "Nixon": Hillings int.
205 "My own political": Nixon, *RN*, p. 239.
205 "Despite all the talk": *Time*, October 6, 1961.
205 "There would be the all-out": Finch int.
206 "What do you feel": Bartlett int.

Chapter 15: Coup de Grâce
208 "Just the 1960 campaign stuff": Bradlee, *Conversations with Kennedy*, p. 75.
209 "Mr. Blough": Fay int.
209 "You find out": Fay int.
209 "I told him that": Bradlee, *Conversations with Kennedy*, p. 111.
209 "It looks like": Bradlee, *Conversations with Kennedy*, p. 76.
209 "We looked over": Robert F. Kennedy, JFK Library oral history.
211 Aide Stephen Hess: Hess int.
213 The goal: Dutton int.

215 "If Kennedy": quoted in O'Donnell and Powers, *"Johnny, We Hardly Knew Ye,"* p. 284.

215 "We're in LA": *Los Angeles Times*, January 31, 1990.

216 Once, when candidate Nixon: *Los Angeles Times*, January 31, 1990.

216 "Yes": Hess int.

217 "To hell with": Hillings, *Pat Hillings*, p. 94.

217 "One last thing": Jules Witcover, *The Resurrection of Richard Nixon* (New York: G. P. Putnam & Sons, 1970), p. 19.

218 Back at home: Eisenhower, *Pat Nixon*, p. 318.

218 He called the program: Bradlee, *Conversations with Kennedy*, p. 121.

CHAPTER 16: DIEM

220 "If I have": Hess int.

222 On the morning of April 21: On June 11, 1964, Marina Oswald gave this account of her husband's behavior on April 21, 1963. *Hearings Before the President's Commission on the Assassination of President Kennedy*, vol. 5, p. 389. The episode is recounted in Priscilla Johnson McMillan, *Marina and Lee* (New York: Harper and Row, 1977), p. 368. The Warren Commission report (pp. 188–89) dismissed Mrs. Oswald's account as having "no probative value" after reviewing editions of the *Dallas Morning News* from January 1 through May 15, 1963, and finding no reference to a Nixon trip to Dallas. The commission failed to notice the dramatic headline of April 21, "Nixon Calls for Decision to Force Reds Out of Cuba," which corroborates Mrs. Oswald's account both in timing and circumstance.

224 "Too many people": Stephen E. Ambrose, *Nixon, The Triumph of a Politician 1962–1972* (New York: Simon & Schuster, 1989), p. 23.

225 Later that month: Bradlee, *Conversations with Kennedy*, p. 95.

226 Stephen Hess: Hess int.

226 Nixon planned to write a book: Hess int.

228 The Lodge appointment: account of Diem overthrow drawn from Reeves, *President Kennedy*, p. 465.

228 Averell Harriman: Reeves, *President Kennedy*, p. 561.

229 "It shocks and saddens me": Robert McNamara, *In Retrospect—The Tragedy and Lessons of Vietnam* (New York: Random House, 1995), p. 55.

229 "My God!": Reeves, *President Kennedy*, p. 565.

230 "We don't have a prayer": Reeves, *President Kennedy*, p. 464.

231 "What would we have done": Neil Sheehan, *Bright Shining Lie* (New York: Vintage Books, 1988), p. 371.

231 When a younger: Sheehan, *Bright Shining Lie*, p. 371.

232 Kennedy rushing from the room: Reeves, *President Kennedy*, p. 649.

232 "I like him, too": Reeves, *President Kennedy*, p. 465.

233 "Richard Nixon suddenly seems": *Time*, November 22, 1963.

CHAPTER 17: DALLAS

236 "Nixon Predicts": *Dallas Morning News*, November 22, 1963.

236 "Damn it": Smathers int.

236 Back at the White House: conversations with Thomas P. O'Neill, Jr.

236 Charles Bartlett: Bartlett int.

238 "Nixon opens": Hess int.

239 that afternoon: Hess int.

239 "Dear Jackie": letter courtesy of Richard M. Nixon Library and Birthplace.

CHAPTER 18: ETERNAL FLAME

241 Don Hewitt: Hewitt int.

241 "Dear Mr. Vice President": letter courtesy of Richard M. Nixon Library and Birthplace.

243 Jacqueline Kennedy's instrument: White, *In Search of History*, pp. 672–81.

245 "You always": PBS broadcast, *The Kennedys*, September 1992.

245 "He wanted to be there": PBS broadcast, *The Kennedys*, September 1992.

246 "There is no substitute": *New York Times*, April 2, 1964.

246 In Pakistan: Nixon, *In the Arena* (New York: Simon & Schuster, 1990), p. 71.

247 "I know that": Nixon, *RN*, p. 257.

247 When the commission: Nixon letter to commission of August 4, 1964, courtesy of Richard M. Nixon Library and Birthplace.

248 With aroused Goldwater: Eisenhower, *Pat Nixon*, p. 329.

249 "Get out of this mysticism": Schlesinger, *Robert Kennedy and His Times*.

249 A young Kansas congressman: Jake H. Thompson, *Bob Dole: The Republicans' Man for All Seasons* (New York: Donald I. Fine, 1994), p. 53.

CHAPTER 19: THE NEW NIXON

251 "Between wars": John Ehrlichman, *The China Card* (New York: Bantam Books, 1987), p. 23.

252 "I'll ruin you!": Evan Thomas, Jr., int.

252 Manchester suffered: account drawn from William Manchester article in *Look*, August 4, 1967.

254 Robert MacNeil: conversation with Robert MacNeil.

254 "First '66": conversation with Patrick J. Buchanan.

254 Johnson would drop: Ambrose, *Nixon (1962–1972)*, p. 90.

254 "He was telling": Hess int.

255 "I understand how": Ambrose, *Nixon (1962–1972)*, p. 99.

256 "It became clear": Report of the Inspector General, Central Intelligence Agency, 23 May 1967.

256 His rival now produced: *Foreign Affairs,* 1967.

257 Nixon received similar advice: letter obtained from William Gavin, who later served as a speechwriter for President Nixon.

CHAPTER 20: 1968

260 "We've just seen some terrible": Ehrlichman int.

260 "Those who had": Eisenhower, *Pat Nixon,* p. 355.

261 Realizing that the New Yorker: Sears int.

262 "I just feel": Newfield, *Robert Kennedy,* p. 258.

268 "Let me be very clear": *Time,* September 27, 1968.

269 Larry O'Brien: O'Brien, *No Final Victories,* p. 380.

CHAPTER 21: HAUNTING

271 "Nixon standard": William Safire, *Before the Fall* (New York: Doubleday, 1975), p. 152.

272 FBI director: Ambrose, *Nixon (1962–1972),* p. 235.

272 On the eve: *Washington Star,* January 20, 1969.

273 Ted Kennedy quietly warned: Herbert G. Klein, *Making It Perfectly Clear* (Garden City, N.Y.: Doubleday, 1980), p. 299.

273 He asked Sargent Shriver: Sargent Shriver int.

274 the media hit him: Klein, *Making It Perfectly Clear,* p. 298.

274 "The campaign of 1968": Lester David, *Good Ted Bad Ted* (New York: Birch Lane Press, 1993), p. 161.

275 "There has been no more traumatic": Ray Price, *With Nixon* (New York: Viking, 1977), p. 64.

275 "We could not simply": Walter Isaacson, *Kissinger* (New York: Simon & Schuster, 1992), p. 165.

276 "Kennedy had his sent": Ambrose, *Nixon,* p. 250.

276 "You might pass": Ambrose, *Nixon, (1962–1972)* p. 250.

277 The key to Haldeman's power: Jeb Magruder, *An American Life—One Man's Road to Watergate* (New York: Atheneum, 1974), p. 64.

277 A small overseas skirmish: John Ehrlichman int.

277 "That's a Kennedy song": Safire, *Before the Fall,* p. 153.

278 Ehrlichman noticed: Ehrlichman int.

278 "Wow!": David, *Good Ted Bad Ted,* p. 94.

278 Next, Kennedy jumped: Harris book; James Flug int.

278 "His people gave him some great *word pictures*": Safire, *Before the Fall,* p. 154.

279 How dare Richard Nixon: *Washington Post,* July 19, 1969.

279 The *New York Times* piled on: *New York Times,* July 20, 1969.

279 "Wants to be sure": H. R. Haldeman, *Haldeman Diaries* (New York: G. P. Putnam's Sons, 1994), p. 72.

279 "This is quite a day": Safire, *Before the Fall,* p. 152.

280 "I would get": Ehrlichman int.

280 "Nixon saw it as": Ehrlichman int.
280 To meet his boss's needs: Haldeman int.
280 Operating on presidential orders: Lukas, *Nightmare*, p. 16.
280 The Nixon team: *New York Times*, July 7, 1973.
280 Two weeks after: John Ehrlichman, *Witness to Power* (New York: Simon & Schuster, 1982), p. 292.
281 Nixon relished pointing out: Bruce Oudes, ed., *From: The President* (New York: Harper & Row, 1989), p. 44.
281 He also ordered his staff: Oudes, *From: The President*, p. 45.
281 That same autumn: Louis Harris int.; Haldeman int.
283 "He was pushing it both ways": Haldeman int.
284 "He's continually cranking": Ehrlichman int.; Haldeman int.; conversation with Patrick J. Buchanan.

CHAPTER 22: ESCALATION
285 Wondering aloud: Haldeman, *Diaries*, p. 123.
285 Lawrence O'Brien: Haldeman, *Diaries*, p. 134.
285 Nixon next ordered: Haldeman, *Diaries*, p. 148.
288 "After a while": Daniel Patrick Moynihan int.
288 When antiwar demonstrators: Haldeman, *Diaries*, p. 205.
289 Nixon aide Jeb Magruder: Magruder, *One Man's Road to Watergate*, p. 143.
289 Charles Colson: Lukas, *Nightmare*, p. 82.
289 He succeeded in having: Haldeman, *Diaries*, p. 215.
289 "The president *loved* that picture": Haldeman int.
290 "I sent somebody": Colson int.
290 "He arrived in the White House": Magruder, *One Man's Road to Watergate*, p. 71.
290 "He was always": Colson int.
290 "You just sensed": Colson int.
290 At year's end: Ambrose, *Nixon (1962–1972)*, p. 421.

CHAPTER 23: INTERLUDE
292 On January 1, 1971: Haldeman, *Diaries*, p. 229.
292 "As you know": Eisenhower, *Pat Nixon*, p. 468.
293 On February 3: account of Kennedys' White House visit taken from Eisenhower, *Pat Nixon*, pp. 468–70.
294 Personal accounts: letters courtesy of Richard M. Nixon Library and Birthplace.

CHAPTER 24: TARGETING TEDDY
298 On a sunny afternoon: Haldeman, *Diaries*, p. 248.
298 Two days later: Haldeman, *Diaries*, p. 249.

300 "Nixon took pains": H. R. Haldeman, *Ends of Power* (New York: Dell Publishing, 1978), p. 105.
300 "The Kennedy-Nixon comparison": Colson int.
300 The surprise loss: Haldeman, *Diaries*, p. 237.
301 Haldeman, he learned: Dan Rather, *The Camera Never Blinks* (New York: Ballantine, 1977), p. 249.
301 "We were in their faces": Flug int.
301 "We must destroy": David, *Good Ted Bad Ted*, p. 122.
302 In June: Lukas, *Nightmare*, p. 53.
302 "We should encourage": quoted in Oudes, *From: The President*, p. 284.
303 He ordered Henry Kissinger: Haldeman, *Diaries*, p. 302.
303 Kissinger pushed Nixon: Haldeman, *Ends of Power*, p. 110.
303 "If we can change": quoted in Oudes, *From: The President*, p. 283.
303 "I don't give a damn": Haldeman, *Ends of Power*, p. 112.
303 "The more I think about": Lukas, *Nightmare*, p. 82.
303 "Eduardo": Hunt, *Undercover*, p. 141.
304 To prepare for the task: Lukas, *Nightmare*, p. 81.
305 Segretti suggested: Lukas, *Nightmare*, p. 154.
305 Nixon derided the white marble building: quoted from Ambrose, *Nixon (1962–1972)*, p. 417.
305 Word reached him: Oudes, *From: The President*, p. 298.
305 Haldeman-inspired plan: Haldeman, *Diaries*, p. 338.
305 Rose Kennedy wrote: Oudes, *From: The President*, p. 312.
306 "No! Never!": quoted from Ambrose, *Nixon (1962–1972)*, p. 417.
306 Two days later: Haldeman, *Diaries*, p. 356.
306 "I wanted ammunition": Nixon, *RN*, p. 513.
306 "The P ordered": Haldeman, *Diaries*, p. 356.
307 "I went to Helms": Ehrlichman int.
307 "I want to protect the agency": Richard Helms int.
307 He would later complain: Ehrlichman int.; Haldeman int.
307 Years later: Reeves, *President Kennedy*, p. 577.

CHAPTER 25: SMOKING GUN
310 When Hugh Sidey: Haldeman, *Diaries*, p. 401.
310 His indignation: *New York Times*, January 24, 1972.
310 "Nixon knew": Haldeman int.
310 "Should this Kennedy mafia–dominated": Lukas, *Nightmare*, p. 181.
311 "O'Brien's not going": Haldeman, *Ends of Power*, p. 11.
311 "When are they going": Haldeman, *Ends of Power*, p. 155.
311 "Why don't you guys": Magruder, *One Man's Road to Watergate*, p. 197.
311 he pulled a dirty trick: Magruder, *One Man's Road to Watergate*, p. 203.
312 The single-minded: Oudes, *From: The President*, p. 402.
313 He listened with interest: Haldeman, *Diaries*, p. 435.
315 Lawrence O'Brien: O'Brien, *No Final Victories*, p. 298.

317 Within a week: Bob Woodward and Carl Bernstein, *All the President's Men* (New York: Simon & Schuster, 1974), pp. 31–32.
317 A public relations director: Woodward and Bernstein, *All the President's Men*, p. 253.
318 "Destroy him": Ambrose, *Nixon (1962–1972)*, p. 583.
318 the Kennedy staff: Flug int.
319 "I know the people around Nixon": Woodward and Bernstein, *All the President's Men*, p. 274.
319 He also realized: Flug int.
319 "Kennedy is out for blood": Woodward and Bernstein, *All the President's Men*, p. 202.
320 That night: Haldeman, *Diaries*, p. 531.
321 And, finally: Haldeman, *Diaries*, p. 536.
321 "If Bradlee ever": Woodward and Bernstein, *All the President's Men*, p. 205.
321 "That's some pretty personal": Woodward and Bernstein, *All the President's Men*, p. 205.
321 "I know it's there": Woodward and Bernstein, *All the President's Men*, p. 205.

CHAPTER 26: KENNEDY VERSUS NIXON—AGAIN
323 "The Kennedy ghost": Price, *With Nixon*, p. 62.
324 Thanks to Senator Kennedy: Flug int.
325 Unable to let pass: Stephen E. Ambrose, *Nixon: Ruin and Recovery, 1973–1990* (New York: Simon & Schuster, 1991), p. 60.
325 "bear trap": Ambrose, *Nixon (1973–1990)*, p. 76.
325 Nixon told Dean: Ambrose, *Nixon (1973–1990)*, p. 85.
326 Until he was assured: Flug int.
326 One name Kennedy mentioned: Robert Healy, *Boston Globe*, May 27, 1973.
327 "The original terms": Elliot Richardson, *The Creative Balance* (New York: Holt, Rinehart & Winston, 1976), p. 37.
327 no-man's-land: Richardson, *The Creative Balance*, p. 37.
327 While Richardson viewed: Richardson, *The Creative Balance*, p. 37.
328 "Cox will be a disaster": Nixon, *RN*, p. 910.
328 To speechwriter Ray Price: Price, *With Nixon*, p. 236.
328 "*Archie Cox?*": Price, *With Nixon*, p. 236.
328 "If Richardson": Nixon, *RN*, p. 910.
328 after many drinks: Anatoli Dobrynin, *In Confidence* (New York: Times Books, 1995), p. 182.
330 He and the House parliamentarian: conversation with Thomas P. O'Neill, Jr.
330 Before making: James Reston, Jr., *Lone Star: The Life Story of John Connally* (New York: Harper & Row, 1989) p. 460.

330 With Albert now next: Joe Foote int.
332 He called the firings: Ambrose, *Nixon (1973–1990)*, p. 250.
333 As James Flug: Flug int.
333 "I don't have any office": David Nyan, *Boston Globe*, October 24, 1973.
334 "I had to light a fire": O'Neill, *Man of the House*, p. 251.
334 When the beleaguered: Ambrose, *Nixon (1973–1990)*, p. 268.
334 "Wherever Nixon turned": Price, *With Nixon*, p. 62.

CHAPTER 27: DEATH OF A PRESIDENCY
336 "Opponents are savage": Nixon, *RN*, p. 971.
337 "A car driven by": *Washington Post*, January 27, 1974.
338 "Let's get them all": Ambrose, *Nixon (1973–1990)*, p. 370.
338 In July: *New York Times Magazine*, July 14, 1974.
339 Alexander Haig: Haig int.
339 "We talked a bit": Price, *With Nixon*, p. 340.
339 "History will treat": Isaacson, *Kissinger*, p. 597.
339 "It depends": Isaacson, *Kissinger*, p. 597.

EPILOGUE: TWILIGHT
341 "In going over the side": William V. Shannon column, *New York Times*, August 18, 1974.
341 "dual standard of justice": quoted in *New York Times*, Sepember. 16, 1974.
341 "Nobody drowned at Watergate": Clare Booth Luce, *New York Times*, August 1974.
342 he was predicting: Rowland Evans–Robert Novak column quoted in *Christian Science Monitor*, November 4, 1974.
343 "The most charitable": Richard M. Nixon, *The Real War* (New York: Simon & Schuster, 1990), p. 113.
343 America's role: Nixon, *In the Arena*, pp. 91, 341.
343 "presidential power": David, *Good Ted Bad Ted*, p. 211.
344 "Tell them not to make the mistakes we did": Vernon Jordan int.
344 "I have endured a few crises in my lifetime": letter courtesy of Richard M. Nixon Library and Birthplace.
344 "Don't say that": conversation with John Taylor.
344 "Despite the intensity": *Washington Post*, April 23, 1994.
345 "He believed": Haig int.
345 Nixon made the cover of *Time*: *Time*, May 2, 1994.

INDEX

Rayburn, Sam, 44, 111, 126, 143
Reader's Digest, 32, 87, 199, 226, 253
Reagan, Ronald, 265, 343
Real War, The (Nixon), 343
Reardon, Timothy "Ted," 10, 58, 65, 77, 92, 98, 100, 101, 146, 155
Rebozo, Bebe, 183, 315
Reedy, George, 49, 58–59, 61, 64, 245
Reeves, Richard, 307
Republic Steel, 209
Republican party, 17–19, 49, 75, 88, 94, 184, 186, 188, 189, 194, 199, 203, 271, 283, 286, 319, 336; in California, 34, 37, 38, 42, 73, 210; foreign policy of, 95; in House, 45–47, 71; ITT and, 311; labor unions and, 50; in Massachusetts, 87, 99, 281; McCarthy's attacks on, 96; in 1946 election, 40; in 1948 election, 60, 62; in 1952 election, 25, 78, 82–84, 86, 89; in 1956 election, 104–5, 108, 109, 112, 113; in 1958 election, 122; in 1960 election, 16, 77, 91, 119, 121, 123, 124, 135–38, 141, 154, 160, 161, 163–65, 172–76; in 1964 election, 195, 233, 249, 250; in 1966 election, 254; in 1968 election, 260, 261, 264–66, 268, 269; in 1970 election, 288; in 1972 election, 304, 320; in 1976 election, 330; in Senate, 100; and Vietnam, 228, 232; and Watergate, 325
Reston, James, 167–68, 220, 233
Richardson, Elliot, 326–28, 331–33
Richmond News-Leader, 312
Robinson, Jackie, 172
Rockefeller, Nelson, 27, 233, 242, 246, 261
Rodgers, Richard, 270
Rodino, Peter, 334
Rogers, Ted, 149
Rogers, William, 62, 84, 96, 131, 147, 273, 309
Romney, George, 260
Roosevelt, Eleanor, 108–9, 120, 134, 218

Roosevelt, Franklin D., 23, 25, 28, 40, 41, 46, 48, 53, 60, 67, 108, 135, 158
Roosevelt, Franklin D., Jr., 131, 243
Roosevelt, James, 73
Roosevelt, Theodore, 339–40
Roselli, Johnny, 195–96
Rosenberg, Ethel, 71
Rosenberg, Julius, 71
Rostow, Walt Whitman, 119
Rubinstein, Arthur, 27
Ruckelshaus, William, 332
Rusk, Dean, 229
Russo, Joseph, 30–31
Rutgers University, 253

Sadat, Anwar, 338
Safire, William, 254, 266, 271–72, 279
St. John, George, 23
Salinger, Pierre, 134, 184, 199–201, 244
Saltonstall, Leverett, 120, 127, 281
Samuelson, Paul, 119
Saturday Evening Post, 93, 100, 226
Saturday Night Massacre, 332–34, 343
Schlesinger, Arthur, Jr., 119
Scott, George C., 300
Scott, Randolph, 220–21
Scouten, Rex, 99
Sears, John, 251, 261
Securities and Exchange Commission, 23
Segretti, Donald, 302, 305, 319
Seigenthaler, John, 252, 262
Senate, U.S., 62, 69–74, 98–100, 102, 106, 116–21, 136, 146, 152, 188, 213, 256, 301, 322, 339; Foreign Relations Committee, 124, 162; Government Operations Committee, 105; Judiciary Committee, 278, 286, 301, 313, 318, 324, 326, 327, 333, 334, 343; Watergate Committee, 329, 332
Sevareid, Eric, 138
Shannon, William V., 341
Shaw, Artie, 27
Shell, Joseph, 210

PICTURE CREDITS

1 Whittier College
2 John F. Kennedy Library
3 Joel Yale, *Life* Magazine © Time Inc.
4 George Lacks, *Life* Magazine © Time Inc.
5 Richard Nixon Library
6 John F. Kennedy Library
7 Courtesy of Richard Nixon Library
8 The Bettmann Archive
9 Eisenhower Library
10 John F. Kennedy Library
11 John F. Kennedy Library
12 The FORBES Magazine Collection, New York
13 The Bettmann Archive
14 © 1960 Newsweek, Inc. All rights reserved. Reprinted by permission.
15 Walter Bennett/Time Magazine
16 Richard Nixon Library
17 John F. Kennedy Library
18 Associated Press
19 © Pat Oliphant—courtesy Susan Conway Gallery, Washington D.C. Originally published by Los Angeles Times Syndicate, January 1969.
20 White House photo
21 Kathleen Matthews

About the Author

Christopher Matthews, host of CNBC's *Hardball*, is Washington bureau chief for the *San Francisco Examiner* and a nationally syndicated columnist. A graduate of Holy Cross, he served with the U.S. Peace Corps in Swaziland, was a presidential speechwriter for Jimmy Carter, and was a top aide to Speaker of the House Thomas P. "Tip" O'Neill, Jr. Matthews wrote the bestselling *Hardball: How Politics Is Played, Told by One Who Knows the Game*.